Economies of Scale in Manufacturing Industry

by C.F. Pratten

CAMBRIDGE

AT THE UNIVERSITY PRESS

1971

Published by
the Syndics of the Cambridge University Press
Bentley House, 200 Euston Road, London N.W.1 2DB
American Branch: 32 East 57th Street, New York, N.Y. 10022

© Department of Applied Economics, University of Cambridge 1971

Library of Congress Catalogue Card Number: 77–161282

ISBN: 0 521 09669 3

Set in cold type by E.W.C. Wilkins & Associates Ltd,
and printed in Great Britain by Alden & Mowbray Ltd,
at the Alden Press, Oxford

Contents

Tables

APPENDICES

Diagrams

Preface

I should like to thank the many people whose help has made this book possible. Measurement of the economies of scale requires detailed knowledge of industries, and the collection of a great deal of data from firms. Fortunately, many companies were willing to provide information for our study, and I am particularly grateful for all the help provided by the executives of these companies.

On the academic side I should like to acknowledge my debt to Aubrey Silberston who initiated the study and directed the research. Throughout the study he provided a great deal of valuable advice, comment and encouragement. Professor Reddaway suggested clues to the best way of making progress at critical points during the research, and Professor E.A.G. Robinson made many helpful comments on earlier drafts. I am grateful to Dr John Hatch, Tony Cockerill and Brian Chiplin for allowing me to use some of the results of their research, and to Mr Owen Hooker for obtaining much of the information used in preparing chapter 22.

Finally I should like to thank the staff of the Department for their help in preparing the book, and in particular Mrs Silk and her colleagues for typing numerous drafts.

Introduction

Ever since Adam Smith's description of the importance of the division of labour, economists have discussed the forces determining the economies of scale and the optimum size of business units. But, though the sources of economies of scale were a subject for detailed analysis in the literature, few estimates of their magnitude were published prior to 1940. During the 1920's this failure was recognised in the controversy about 'the empty boxes of economic theory' which was concerned with the inability of economists to classify industries into those with increasing, constant and decreasing costs. In recent years economists have given more attention to measuring economies of scale, and much quantitative information is now available.

Quantitative estimates of the economies of scale are required for several purposes. Economies of scale are one of the forces contributing to the growth of the economy, and estimates of these forces are required to find out more about the sources of growth. Businessmen require a knowledge of the economies of scale as this is one of the factors which determines the optimum method of organising production. Similarly developing countries should consider the economies of scale when deciding which industries should be set up, and how they should be organized. Research to determine the economies of scale is required to provide information which will throw some light on the results of government economic policies which, intentionally or incidentally, affect the scale of production. Examples of such government intervention are the regulations governing monopolies, government pressure on firms to merge, tax concessions to small firms, and incentives to firms to set up new factories in development areas. One of the arguments used to support policies designed to reduce tariff barriers and for joining the E.E.C. is that the expanded markets so provided will reduce unit production costs because of the economies of scale.

The main source of information for the study was information we obtained from companies. A standard questionnaire could not be used for the purpose of obtaining data because the sources of economies of scale vary so much between industries, and so we prepared a set of questions for each interview with the officials of companies. The industry studies which are based on the answers to these questions are described in Book 2.

Before describing the industry studies in Book 2, we discuss the meaning and problems of measuring the economies of scale and growth, and the methods used for this research, in Book 1. We decided to present our results industry by industry, but we have included a summary of the industry studies in Book 3. This book also includes a review of those effects of scale which are common to many industries, and are not readily measurable

1

by the methods we have used. A danger inherent in our presentation is that there might be a good deal of duplication, and, in order to minimize this, we have concentrated on the main sources of economies of scale for each industry in the industry studies.

Other writers have attempted to draw conclusions about economies of scale from analyses of data from company accounts and Censuses of Production. We consider that these data are not a satisfactory source for making estimates of economies of scale, but we have analysed the data available, and the results of these analyses are described in Appendices C and D.

A progress report on the research was published as an Occasional Paper, 'The Economies of Large-Scale Production in British Industry - An Introductory Study', Cambridge University Press, 1965. This paper was written with Mr. R.M. Dean and Aubrey Silberston. Book 1 of this study covers the same topics as chapter one of the earlier Occasional Paper, and Book 3 the same topics as chaper 6.

Book 1. The Meaning and Measurement of Economies of Scale

1. The Meaning and Sources of Economies of Scale

I. Definition of economies of scale

So much is now being written about the economies of scale that it is worth spending some time discussing exactly what the concept means. This is something that we need to do as a prelude to the empirical studies contained in this book, but this task is made doubly necessary by the very loose way in which the concept is now used.

Very crudely economies of scale are reductions in average costs attributable to increases in scale. They can be defined, most readily, in relation to *plants*.[1] If it were possible to make experiments to determine the economies of scale associated with the size of plants in an industry, producing one product by one process, plants would be designed and set up to produce the single standard product at varying levels of output, and comparisons could be made between the unit costs of production for these plants. Each plant would be designed to produce a certain output at the lowest possible cost, and all other conditions except the level of output and the consequences flowing from this condition would be held constant.[2] From the operating data for such plants it would be possible to estimate the short run cost curves for each plant and the long run average cost curve for new plants in the industry. The 'short-run' cost curves trace out the relationship between average costs of production and the extent to which plants are

(1) The term 'units of plant' as used in this study refers to individual items of plant such as kilns, furnaces and tanks. The term 'plant' refers to a unit of plant, or a group of such units on one site, which are commonly regarded as part of the same works, because similar operations, or a sequence of operations are performed in them, e.g. a steelworks, a refinery or a brickworks.

(2) This would not mean that each plant would necessarily operate at the level of production which minimized its unit costs. Over a range of output for which unit costs of production continuously decline with increases in the capacity of plants, each output would be produced most efficiently by plants operating below the level of capacity at which their unit costs of production would be a minimum. Each plant would be operated at the point where short run average cost curve and the long run average cost curve were tangential. However in many industries short run average costs rise quite sharply as the level of capacity utilization falls below the optimum level and, as this rise in unit costs is sharp compared to the increase in the long run average costs for similar reductions in capacity, the extent to which plants would operate below the short run optimum referred to above would be slight.

utilized. The 'long-run' curve is the 'envelope' of the short-run curves.[1] The long-run average cost curve shows the lowest possible cost of producing at any scale of output after all possible adaptation to that scale has taken place.

Scale curve

The *long-run* average cost curve does not show what happens to costs as the scale of production is increased over time. It answers the question — what would the effect of scale be on the average costs of production of a series of alternative plants built at a point in time, each perfectly adapted to the required scale and operated at that scale. For this reason it is misleading to talk of a *long-run* cost curve, although this is of course the accepted term. It would be more appropriate to talk of a *scale curve*. The relationship between short run average cost curves and scale curves is illustrated in diagram 1.1.

Diagram 1.1. A scale curve

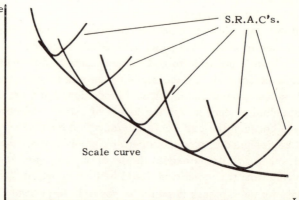

Techniques

This approach carries important implications regarding technical progress. At a particular moment of time, there is a certain body of technical knowledge. Let us assume that it is widely available. Then, when we consider the different points on our scale curve, we do so in the light of our present technical knowledge. If we consider a plant to be built to produce a large output, as compared with one to produce a small output, the large plant is likely to be a rather different sort of plant. It may, for example, contain specialised machinery not appropriate to the small plant. But this specialised machinery would not have been invented especially for that plant. We know perfectly well, when we decide to build the large plant, that this is the appropriate machinery to install. We would not install it in the small plant because it would not be economical to do so at a small scale of pro-

(1) The long-run average cost curve was first discussed by Jacob Viner in Zeitschrift fur Nationalokonome, Vol. III 1931-1, pp.23-46 and reprinted in 'The Long View and the Short - Studies in Economic Theory and Policy' by Jacob Viner. Glencoe, Illinois, 1958.

duction. This comes to the same thing as saying that the whole scale curve is drawn on the basis of *given* technical knowledge.

In practice technical progress occurs continuously, and each vintage of plant will have a distinct scale curve. Given constant factor prices the scale curve for each vintage of plant would be expected to be lower than the previous one. (Diagram 1.2.)

Diagram 1.2. Scale curves for successive vintages of plants

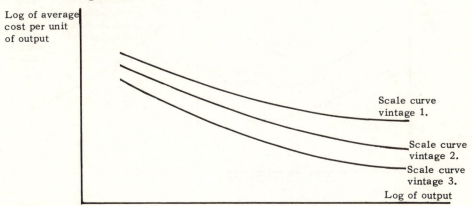

The notion of given technical knowledge is a difficult one to sustain in practice. If we consider building a larger plant than anyone has built before, we are likely to be faced with new problems. We may need to devote resources to research and development in order to solve these problems. We may succeed in making technical advances, but if we do so, our assumption of given technical knowledge will be invalidated. In practice we may not be able to draw the right-hand section of the scale curve, i.e. the section relating to larger scales of production than those currently employed or planned,[1] at all precisely. This is because for some industries we cannot be sure what techniques would be used in a larger plant until one is planned in detail. We should expect the margin of error for our estimates to increase the further the scales, for which estimates are made, are beyond existing experience. But there are qualifications to these arguments. Engineers have a good deal of experience of 'scaling up' plants and should be able to forecast the effects of further scaling up on costs. Also in some industries including machine tools, electric motors and chemicals, products are made in widely differing quantities, and it is therefore possible to assess the effects of greatly increasing the output of most products without exceeding the experience of U.K. manufacturers.

Plant scale curves are often kinked about or a little above the maximum capacity for which experience has been obtained. For the production of a product for which there are technical constraints on further increases in the size of plants, the scale curve may rise sharply for larger plants, and it may be more economic to duplicate plants than to build a larger plant.

Even when there are no technical constraints on building larger plants, there are likely to be initial design costs for building larger plants than

(1) For this purpose we are not necessarily limited to U.K. experience.

5

those built in the past. If these special design costs are substantial they may give a kink to the scale curve. Through time the kink in a scale curve is likely to be pushed to higher levels of capacity. Possible kinked scale curves are illustrated in diagram 1.3.

Diagram 1.3. Kinked scale curves

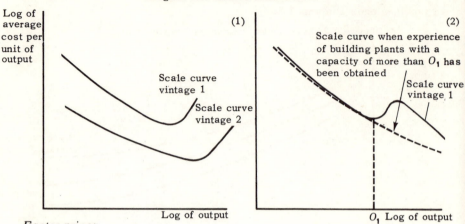

Factor prices

Another important assumption which we make is that relative factor prices are not affected by scale. We assume that no matter how many men we wish to employ as scale increases, or however much space we require on which to build our plant, the wages of a given type of labour and the price per acre of land remain constant in money terms i.e. we assume that the supply of factors of production is infinitely elastic. In practice it may be necessary to pay higher wages as scale increases, because a firm has to attract labour from a wider area than previously, and land prices may be affected by the amount of space required, but in drawing up our scale curve, we ignore such possibilities. One practical reason for making this type of assumption is that the relationship between factor costs and scale is subject to local conditions and is related to the particular site selected.

There is a more important proviso relating to factor prices. The determination of the lowest possible average costs of production at any given scale is not simply a technical matter: it also depends on relative factor prices. Changes in relative factor prices over time and differences between countries may affect the shape of scale curves. Thus, for example, the scale curve for Britain's Industry X is not necessarily applicable to India's Industry X.

Many of the purchases made by firms are for goods and services made by other firms. The scale of the plants we are considering may affect the costs of producing the goods and services used at a plant, and the prices paid may reflect the real *external* economies (or diseconomies) very imperfectly. [1]
For some purposes we need to know the effects of scale on prices actually paid — the pecuniary economies: for example, to enable us to assess the

(1) Whether economies are internal or external depends on where the dividing line between plants (or firms) is drawn. Economies which are external to one plant may be internal for a plant with a greater degree of vertical integration.

scale effects for competition between firms of differing size. But we also require a knowledge of the real external economies so that we can consider the effects of scale on resource allocation.

Economies of scale

We are now in a position to define the economies of scale for plants. These occur when the scale curve falls downward to the right, i.e. where unit costs of production decline as the size of a plant is increased. In this case there would be *economies of large scale production* or, more briefly, *economies of scale*. Whether the scale curve for a type of plant does indeed slope downwards to the right is a question of fact. It might slope upwards to the right, in which case there are *dis*economies of scale. Alternatively, it may slope down over a certain range of scale and then slope up beyond that range. This last type of scale curve is one which is much discussed in the literature – it is the familiar 'U-shaped' long-run average cost curve. With this type of scale curve there is only one scale of output at which average costs are at a minimum – both before and after this scale, average costs are higher. This minimum point is known as the point of *optimum scale* and is of considerable significance for discussions of long-run equilibrium under conditions of perfect competition. If there are economies of scale up to a certain scale of output, but beyond that scale average costs neither rise nor fall as scale is increased, the curve is said to be 'L' shaped, and the point at which average costs cease to fall is known as the point of *minimum optimum scale*, or as we prefer to term it, the point of *minimum efficient scale*.

It may not in practice be possible to make an immediate assessment of the costs of plants of varying capacity because of the 'learning effect'. It takes some *time* for plants to be worked up to full efficiency, because personnel need to obtain experience of operating plant and take some time to acquire skills. There is therefore a 'family of scale curves' for a new plant relating to successive points in time. To avoid this problem a 'representative scale curve' could be prepared at one point in time, for example when the plants have been 'run in'. But it is conceivable that the learning effect and the prospects of development may be greater for some sizes of plant than for others, and any comparisons of unit costs for plants of varying size might therefore depend upon the point in time when measurements of costs were made. In particular we should expect the delay in achieving full efficiency to be greater for new sizes of plant. The time dimension of output and the learning effect are more important if a range of products is made, and particularly if the range changes over time.

II. The dimensions of scale

There are other dimensions of scale besides the output capacity of plants to which economies may relate. Even in the case of plants to produce a homogeneous product, some assumptions would have to be made about the duration of production; for example, it might be assumed that production

7

would continue for, say, 20 years. The expected duration of production may affect the techniques of production employed, the durability of the capital goods chosen and the combination of capital and other factors. Also, in practice, there are very few plants at which only one product is produced, and many firms operate a number of plants and produce a range of products which changes through time. There are thus many *dimensions* of scale. These dimensions of scale involve horizontal scale — for example, the size of units of plant at one point in time — vertical scale — the degree to which different stages of production are physically integrated or performed at one plant or controlled by one firm — and the duration of production or *time*. We have to consider output through time because some important costs are related to this. For example initial costs for products are related to the total output of the product through time (see below).

The main dimensions of scale are:

(a) *Dimensions affecting the efficiency of production*

1. The total output of particular products through time.

2. The duration of production runs — the period during which a distinct product is made or processed before switching to the processing of another product.

3. The rate of production of particular products per unit of time. (The size of batches is determined by the duration of production runs and the rate of production).

4. The extent of standardization.

5. The capacity of units of plant, machines and production lines within plants.

6. The total capacity of individual plants.

7. The overall size of a complex of plants at one site.

8. The extent of vertical integration — the range of operations and stages of production performed at plants and by firms.

(b) *Dimensions affecting selling and distribution costs*

9. Sales to each customer.

10. The geographic concentration of customers.

11. The size of consignments to customers.

(c) *Overall dimensions of scale*

12. The size of firms.

13. The scale of an industry.

14. The scale of a national economy.

(Many of the headings themselves involve a number of dimensions of scale).

Scale economies are reductions in costs attributable to different positions along dimensions of scale. In the same way that there are scale economies attributable to the size of plant, scale economies may relate to the size of batches, the size of firm or industry, etc.

In practice, most of the estimates of economies of scale which we have assembled relate to the output of products and the capacity of plants or firms to produce products. We have concentrated on the technical economies of scale, or production costs and scale, but we have presented some quantitative evidence about the relationship between scale and management, marketing and research expenditure where this was available.

III. Growth

So far we have considered differences in costs attributable to positions on the dimensions of scale after perfect adaptation to scale has occurred. In practice firms and plants are not perfectly adapted to the scales at which they operate, they adapt over time to their expected scale, and expansion or contraction affect the unit costs of firms. It is not only the movement along dimensions of scale which affect costs, but also the rate of change or *growth*. The effects of growth on costs can be most readily assessed by considering two firms with the same initial characteristics but which are growing at different rates.[1] If there are economies of growth, the faster growing firm will achieve lower average costs. Often attention is focussed on one element of costs — labour costs — when considering the effects of growth. The sources of economies of growth have been discussed in the literature [2] and are discussed later.

IV. Technical progress

Now that the full diversity of dimensions of scale has been introduced we must reconsider technical progress. It is no longer always possible, in practice, to isolate the economies of scale and economies attributable to technical progress.

(a) Development and other initial costs which may, or may not, involve technical progress relate to the output of products. These costs are an important component of costs, and spreading such costs is often an important source of economies for a large output of a product. In practice, it is not always possible to distinguish development costs which produce, or require,

(1) Some economies of growth occur irrespective of the rate of growth. For example if a firm has spare management capacity or other overheads which can support a larger output, some economies may be obtained whatever rate of expansion is achieved, the rate of growth will determine the time lag before the economies are fully reaped. On the other hand some economies, e.g. from the construction of large plants, may be obtained, only if a rapid rate of growth is achieved.

(2) Edith Penrose, 'The Theory of the Growth of the Firm', OXFORD, 1959.

new knowledge or techniques, and those which do not.

(b) Learning, which may be included as a component of technical progress, relates to movements along some of the dimensions of scale. It is a source of economies attributable to the rate of production and the duration of production runs. In theory the effects of learning might be divided between the invention and introduction of new techniques — technical progress — during a production run, and the other cost-reducing effects of sustained production of a good. Possible examples of the latter effects are reduced average unit costs for organizing production and for setting up machinery for long runs, greater manual dexterity brought about by experience of production, and machining successive components to fit more exactly as experience of assembly is obtained. Both types of learning effects may be applicable to other products made at the same time and/or later generations of products, but some learning effects are specific to products. In practice, it is not always possible to distinguish the two types of learning.

(c) Firms have to adapt to changes in the techniques of production through time, and it is sometimes claimed that large firms have advantages for achieving and introducing technical progress.

The estimates of the effects of scale given in the industry studies, include the economies of spreading development and initial costs, and for outputs of products and production runs, the effects of learning. Some of our estimates therefore include an element of technical progress. We have also discussed the relationship between scale and technical progress in some of the industry studies.

Change through time

Technical progress is one source of change to which businessmen have to react. There are of course many other sources of change. Changes in tastes, incomes, monetary and fiscal policy, exchange rates etc. affect businesses, and a very important determinant of the success of a business is its ability to react to change. Also firms can themselves influence changes through time by the invention of new products, advertising, putting pressure on governments to take actions favourable to their interests, etc. It is therefore vitally important to consider the relationship between scale and change, otherwise we should be considering the effects of scale in a 'Canute economy', a fruitless exercise. Indeed to consider the full effects of scale it is also necessary to consider the effect of scale on the range of products made by firms and their revenue; it is not possible to limit the study to costs alone. However we have concentrated on the relationship between scale and costs, and in this sense our study is a partial one.

V. The sources of the economies of scale

It is not proposed to describe the forces determining the economies of scale in detail in this chapter because many of the sources of economies are discussed at length in later chapters. Nevertheless it is necessary to outline the sources of the economies of scale at this stage.

The forces making for economies of scale are listed separately although they are interrelated.

(a) Indivisibilities

There are many costs which are at least *partly* independent of scale over certain ranges of output i.e. costs which are wholly or partly indivisible with respect to output. The following are examples:

Type of cost:	Partly or wholly indivisible with respect to:
Initial development and design costs.	The output of a product.
First copy costs of books, newspapers etc.	The number of copies produced.
Inventing new techniques.	The output produced by using the techniques.
Obtaining tenders and studying sources of supply.	The size of orders placed.
Items of capital equipment e.g. gauges in units of chemical plant, presses used for stamping metal parts and cranes.	The total output for which equipment is required.
Office records for a batch of a product.	The size of the batch.
The senior management personnel at a plant.	The output of the plant.
Calls by salesmen on customers.	The number of lines carried by salesmen.
Preparation of advertisements.	The area of the country in which the advertisements are shown.
Issuing a prospectus in connection with raising capital by an issue of shares or debentures.	The size of the issue.

As the relevant dimensions of scale are increased, indivisible costs can be spread over a larger throughput and the cost per unit is therefore reduced.[1]

(1) In practice firms employ a range of factors of production and these factors of production have different minimum capacities. Above some lower limit it may be possible to obtain factors of production with any required capacity, but for the purpose of this footnote it is assumed that each factor of production can only be obtained in quantities which are multiples of the minimum capacity. A firm requires an output equal to the lowest common multiple of the capacities of the factors of production to be able to fully employ these factors of production. Also there will be levels of capacity above the LCM where factors of production cannot be fully employed (i.e. levels of capacity which are not common multiples of the capacity of the factors of production) and so costs will be higher at these levels of output other things being equal. Thus indivisibilities can be a source of diseconomies of scale over certain ranges of scale.

(b) *The economies of increased dimensions* [1]

For many types of capital equipment both initial and operating costs increase less rapidly than capacity. A typical example of such economies occurs in the construction of tanks, pressure vessels and road and sea tankers which are commonly used in the chemical and oil industries. If the thickness of the walls of a tank are not affected by its size, then the cost of increasing capacity increases approximately in proportion to the surface area, while the capacity of the tank rises in proportion to its cubic capacity. Another reason for large units being relatively less costly is that there are proportionately fewer parts to make and fabricate. Operating costs may also be affected by the size of units. In the processing industries the total direct labour costs of operating units of equipment are not much affected by their size, and maintenance costs are usually assumed to be proportional to the capital costs of equipment.

One possible source of diseconomies for using larger units of capital equipment is that they may take longer to design, build and run in, particularly if the size is outside the manufacturer's existing experience. If large plants take longer to construct this will increase the cost of equipment because of the cost of capital tied up while the plant is built and run in.

(c) *The economies of specialisation*

The larger the output of a product, plant or firm, the greater will be the opportunities for, and advantages of, specialisation of both the labour force and the capital equipment. Increased output may enable a firm to employ staff with special skills, or staff with more highly developed skills. Also it may be economic for firms with a large throughput to use special purpose machinery.

Increased output will provide greater opportunities for specialisation, not only within a plant, but also for suppliers of materials and services bought out.

(d) *The economies of massed resources* [2]

The operation of the law of large numbers may result in economies of massed resources. For example, a firm using several identical machines

(1) The economies of increased dimensions and the economies of specialisation which are considered in the following sub-section, may be considered as examples of indivisibilities. If labour and capital equipment were divisible in the same way, as say, a bucket of sand, then there would be no economies from these sources. Many types of equipment and labour are divisible in the sense that it is possible to build units with smaller capacity and employ less expensive labour, or to employ staff on a part-time basis, but the cost per unit of capacity may be higher because of the economies of increased dimensions and of specialisation, i.e. if the factors are purchased in small quantities, they may be less efficient. This distinction was made by E.H. Chamberlin in 'Proportionality, Divisibility and Economies of Scale'. Q. Jnl of Econ., 1948.

(2) If all factors of production and all products were infinitely divisible, there would be no economies of massed resources i.e. the economies of massed resources may also be regarded as a type of economy caused by indivisibilities.

will have to stock proportionately fewer spare parts than a firm with only one, because the firm with several machines can assume that its machines are unlikely to develop the same faults at the same time. There may be similar economies for stocks of raw materials, and intermediate and final products, part of which may be held to meet interruptions to the supply of raw materials, a temporary breakdown of intermediate plants, and the uncertain flow of orders from customers. Similar economies for certain types of labour and monetary resources may be achieved by a large firm.

A large company's ability to spread risk may enable it to take greater risks. Large concerns have a greater opportunity for experimenting with new methods and introducing new products without jeopardising the future of the business if particular new methods or products are unsuccessful. Similarly if a firm operates in a number of national markets it can experiment with different policies in individual markets.

(e) Superior techniques or organisation of production

Increased scale may make it possible to use more efficient techniques or methods of organising production; for example, as scale is increased automatic machinery may be used instead of manually operated machinery, or it may be possible to substitute methods of flow production for batch production. Some techniques may require proportionately more indivisible factors of production, factors to which economies of increased dimensions apply or specialized factors of production. If high rates of output enable a firm to substitute flow for batch production, this usually results in a faster rate of production i.e. the time taken between work commencing on a product and its completion is reduced, and this should reduce unit costs for stocks and work in progress.

(f) The learning effect

This source of economies has been described above.

(g) Economies through control of markets

A vertically integrated concern may be able to achieve economies by evening out the flow of output. If the operation of two consecutive processes required to produce a product are under independent ownership, a conflict of interest may arise and result in fluctuating output. For example an independent retailer when reducing his stocks will not take into account the losses to be incurred by a manufacturer due to lost production. The price system, operating through reductions in prices by manufacturers at times of slack capacity, may not counter this tendency because retailers may assume that the slackness of demand on manufacturers will continue for some time, and that prices will fall still further, and so price cuts may not stimulate orders. (In practice in some industries there is little or no price flexibility).

Control of a market by a manufacturer may reduce the uncertainty he faces – he will know that customers cannot switch their custom to competitors – and so enable him to invest more heavily in capital intensive methods of production, or offer longer delivery times when order books are full to even out production through time. The possible economies a firm can achieve through the control of its markets which have been outlined so far are advantages attributable to a monopoly situation — the supplier controls the customer. Also they only occur because there are changes through time in market conditions.

Apart from the scale economies[1] which may be achieved by vertical expansion there are also other economies — such as reductions in buying and selling costs, reduced need for checking the quality of consignments and control of the timing of deliveries and quality — which are attributable to the control of suppliers.

VI. The sources of diseconomies of scale

Increases in unit costs may occur as scale increases for two groups of reasons.

(a) The supply of a factor of production is fixed or the cost of a factor increases as demand for the factor rises. (Examples of factor limitations are:

(i) the labour supply in an area available to a firm

(ii) the space available at one site for a factory

(iii) the supply of water which can be taken from a river for purposes of cooling a plant

(iv) the supply of a material produced as a by-product of another process

(v) the size of ship which can dock at a port).

(b) The efficiency in use of a factor of production declines as the quantity of the factor of production used by a firm increases.

The first source of increases in costs is not a source of diseconomies of scale as we have defined them. As stated earlier, for the purpose of measuring the economies of scale, it is assumed that there is a perfectly elastic supply of factors of production available to firms — the quantity of factors they buy does not affect the price. In practice factor costs may rise with increasing scale.

(a) Technical forces

There are some technical forces which cause diseconomies of scale. As the capacity of individual units of plant is increased, increased stresses and strains[2] and friction may result, and to combat these, wider gauge walls

---

(1) An example of a scale economy of this type would be the spreading of the costs of senior management over a larger output (measured in terms of value added).

(2) An example of stresses and strains increasing more than proportionately over a range of output is provided by turbines. If very large turbines are built the ends of the blades travel at a speed near to that of sound. At this speed the strains and stresses increase more than proportionately with the capacity of the turbines.

14

etc., may have to be used, different, and more expensive materials employed, cooling systems, or improved cooling systems be introduced, or more elaborate foundations may have to be built. It is usually technically possible to overcome the problems caused by increasing stresses and strains etc., in large plants, but in certain cases, and over certain ranges of capacity, the costs of overcoming them increase faster than increase in scale. There are in practice two types of costs required to overcome these problems — it may be necessary to use more expensive (and stronger) materials etc., and/or there may be initial costs required to invent new techniques to overcome the technical limitations when the first of a larger scale of plant is built. A way of avoiding any net diseconomies because of increased stresses and strains in many cases is to duplicate units of plant. Thus stresses etc. are a limitation on the sources of economies of scale rather than a source of diseconomies.

(b) Management

The relationship between scale and the cost and effectiveness of management is discussed in the industry studies and the subject is introduced very briefly at this point in order to minimize the extent of duplication. It has been argued that the costs of management may increase more than proportionately with scale or the effectiveness of management may decline as scale is increased. If so this could set a limit to the optimum scale for plants or firms.[1] Given a changing environment, and evolving firms, as scale increases, the costs of coordinating and organising production may rise more than proportionately. The effectiveness of management may decline as the chain of management is extended because of delays in taking decisions brought about by the length of the management chain and/or the tendency for those ultimately taking decisions to get out of touch with events affecting the decisions. Scale may also affect the motivation of managers. Whether or not the management and ownership of a large firm are separated, the determination to maximise profits at the expense of other objectives may decline as scale is increased. In some cases the management of large firms may be able to shelter behind the technical economies of scale achieved by their firms. Small firms may face the choice between economising and achieving a higher level of efficiency, or being forced out of business, and this may spur the managers to achieve relatively greater efficiency.[2]

On the other hand a large firm can employ more specialists, and increasing scale may result in a less than proportionate demand for decision taking and management expertise. For example the problems of managing some

(1) If the effectiveness of management falls as scale is increased, the costs of production are increased, but not necessarily the cost of management itself.

(2) Small firms may operate nearer to the bounds of their production possibility surface (p.p.s.). For a discussion of X- efficiency (the degree to which firms operate within the bounds of their p.p.s.) see Harvey Leibenstein, Am. Econ. Rev. LVI (June, 1966) and Q. Jnl. of Econ. (Nov. 1969).

types of large plant may not increase proportionately because of the economies of scale for direct labour costs.

(c) Labour relations

As scale is increased people may simply work less well. The possibility that the performance of employees declines with scale could apply to more than one dimension of scale. As the length of production runs increases this may result in specialized and/or repetitive work, as the size of factories is increased it may be difficult to retain a 'family spirit', and similarly in a large firm labour relations may be inherently worse. The larger the factory or firm the greater the hierarchical chain must be — employees tend to be further away from the 'boss', and he is less likely to understand them. Also it may be easier for the employees of a large firm, or at a large factory, to oppose the management and to organise restrictive practices. This could be because the management of a small firm can spot sooner, and remove, employees who might create dissension, or because in a large organization it is easier to whip up feelings in the same way that it is easier to whip up mass hysteria at a football match watched by a great many spectators, compared to a match watched by very few spectators, or simply because a large organisation breeds more dissatisfaction.

The relationship between labour relations and scale is an important aspect of the subject which we have not attempted to study in depth.

(d) Selling and distribution

Selling and distribution costs are also possible sources of increased costs at higher scales of output. For example, if, as the scale of a plant is increased, the geographic spread of markets, and so the average length of haul, is increased, the average unit costs of transport will rise. If the additional sales are obtained from a new, less concentrated, market, the costs per unit of representation may also be increased. On the other hand if the additional sales are made to existing customers and the size of consignments are increased, both selling and delivery costs per unit may be reduced. Whether there are increased costs at higher scales of output depends on which marketing dimensions of scale are increased.

VII. The economies of rapid growth

There are a number of forces (apart from the more rapid utilization of spare capacity) which may enable a firm which increases its output rapidly to achieve lower costs than a firm which expands less rapidly.

(1) There may be disequilibrium between the capacity for different operations — existing resources may not be in perfect balance — and by bottleneck breaking it may be possible to achieve some increase in overall capacity without a proportionate increase in costs. The disequilibrium may occur because of indivisibilities, errors when the original plant was built or extended, differential rates of learning or technical progress for different operations, the freeing of resources, particularly management resources,

engaged in previous expansion, etc. The rate of growth of output will determine the extent to which a firm takes up these economies in a given period.

(2) There may be scope for taking advantage of the economies of scale, by, for example, spreading first copy costs over a larger output, by building larger units of plant, and by extending existing plants. The rate of growth is a factor determining the extent to which the economies for spreading initial costs are achieved and the size of new plants and extensions to existing plants.

(3) New techniques which were not available, or were not used, when existing plants were built may be incorporated in new capacity: growth may enable a firm to take advantage of technical progress. Also the rate of growth of a firm may affect, or depend upon, technical progress. For example a firm which is expanding rapidly may have more incentive to invest in developing new techniques of production which it can incorporate in its new capacity.

The following are the main sources of increased unit costs or diseconomies of rapid growth.

(1) Existing capacity will have been built when *price* levels were lower, and, other things being equal, in *book value terms*, but not in real terms, capital costs will be lower than for new plants. Also in practice much of the capital equipment employed in old plants has been written off against previous profits and capital costs may be small. The rate of growth will determine the proportion of 'high cost' new plant operated by a firm.

(2) The costs of some factors may increase if scale is increased. Examples of limitations on the supply of factors were given on page 14.

(3) Growth may result in firms reaching levels of output where technical diseconomies of scale operate.

(4) Marketing and distribution costs per unit of output may have to be increased to dispose of a larger output.

(5) Rapid growth may influence the cost and effectiveness of management and labour relations favourably or otherwise. For example rapid rates of growth may enable a firm to maintain a balanced, or an average younger labour force, alternatively it may result in the dilution of a skilled and loyal labour force.

VIII. Other advantages and disadvantages of large size

This study is primarily concerned with the real economies of scale, the reduction in real resources consumed per unit of output at higher scales of output. Apart from providing these economies, large scale may result in other advantages and disadvantages both for firms and for the economy as a whole.

First there are the well known advantages of monopoly. A firm large enough to control the market for its product may be able to charge higher prices than a number of small firms competing for a similar market, especially if demand is not increasing. Similarly a firm buying large quantities may be able to obtain supplies at lower prices and, though these prices may reflect lower real costs of production and transport for firms supplying the products, a large scale buyer may get special discounts over and above the savings in costs.

As far as possible the advantages of monopoly in product markets have been ignored in this study.

Large companies may be able to exert more influence on the public authorities than small firms, even if the small firms are supported by a trade association. This pressure may be used to obtain legislation or action by the government favourable to the companies' interests. In some cases this legislation may reduce costs — for example, when the government agrees to provide improved transport facilities for an isolated plant. But it may be a matter of increasing sales rather than reducing costs. For example, the government may give a company preferential treatment when buying military equipment, so as to maintain employment in a particular region. The power of a large firm to influence government decisions may, or may not, be regarded as an economy of scale. It may reflect the ability of a large company to meet the costs of presenting its case to government officials or to spread these costs over a larger output. On the other hand, it may reflect the willingness of politicians and civil servants to ignore the wishes of small groups, but to respond to the wishes of much larger groups. In the latter case it is not possible to regard the benefits of large size as an economy of scale, though it is an effect of scale. Another example of the power of a large firm, whether or not it specializes in producing a small range of products, is that it may be able to use its financial power to reduce competition by accepting losses, and this power may make other firms reluctant to enter an industry to compete with it.

It may be noted that, though the achievement of real economies of scale will generally be in the national interest, the enjoyment of the monopolistic advantages of scale, and the exercise of power by large companies may be against the national interest.

Apart from the economies and advantages of large scale which may be obtained by individual firms, there are some advantages and disadvantages for the economy as a whole which may not be reflected in economies for individual firms. For example, scale may increase, or reduce, investment, exports, growth, etc.

IX. Efficiency

This discussion of the sources of economies and diseconomies of scale and growth would be incomplete without a brief reference to the other forces affecting the success of a business. Most important is the ability of management to ensure efficient operation and to move with the times. More specifically in many industries the ability of management to control the quality of products and rejection rates, to organise production efficiently within the limits set by the size of plant and firm, to develop and introduce new or improved products, to search for profitable investment opportunities,

18

to maintain a high level of capacity utilisation, etc. are very important to the success of a business. Firms which are so large that they control their markets may use their monopoly position to go peacefully to sleep, and efficient firms of less than optimum size may be absolutely more efficient than sleepy firms of a technically optimum size. However, though there may be evidence of a substantial variation in output for similar inputs of capital and labour and for similar techniques,[1] there is at present no firm evidence that the quality of management, or degree of 'X' efficiency, is related to scale, or to the degree of competition in a market.

We accept that scale is only one of the forces determining the efficiency with which resources are used, but we show that the economies of scale are substantial in many industries, and for these industries it would be difficult for these economies to be swamped by other factors.

---

(1) This evidence is quoted by R.M. Cyert and K.D. George in 'Competition, Growth and Efficiency', Econ. Jnl. March, 1969. It may be noted that some part of the measured differences in 'X' efficiency referred to by these authors is probably attributable to scale economies where scale includes all the dimensions of scale. For example some small firms achieve a high level of 'X' efficiency by concentrating on a narrow range of products.

2. The Measurement of Economies of Scale

I. The method used for obtaining estimates of economies of scale

For the studies of individual industries described in Book 2, the methods of production have been broken down into individual processes and operations, and the technical basis for economies of scale has been investigated. Usually it is not possible to describe processes in terms of engineering production functions which are based on scientific laws or experimental data, and so we have had to base our estimates of the economies of scale for machines, process units, and operations, on engineers', cost accountants' and managers' estimates of costs. Their estimates were based on operating experience for plants of varying size, the experience of expanding plant capacity and general experience of their industry. Estimates of the components of costs, capital and operating costs for individual items of equipment of varying size, costs for processes and/or for groups of processes, first copy or initial costs for products etc. were assembled for each industry, and were used to estimate the relationships between unit costs and the various dimensions of scale.

For some industries this process was short circuited by making use of published and unpublished estimates of the economies of scale already prepared by other people using similar methods. One reason for using these estimates was that the preparation of detailed estimates of costs for plants of varying size for such industries as oil refining and steel production, requires especially detailed knowledge of the technology, and an assurance that hypothetical plants of alternative sizes really represent the best results that could be achieved at each size in the given state of technical knowledge. For this we must rely on the knowledge and skill of the expert.

The weakness of 'engineering' estimates of the type described are that they are subject to a margin of error and that they lack rigour. Their accuracy is particularly suspect when dealing with some of the non-technical forces determining the effects of scale, for example when estimating the relationship between size and the quality of management, and the effect of scale on the development of new techniques and products.

The main advantage of the engineering approach is that it enables us to hold other conditions, such as the state of the arts, the quality of factors of production, their relative prices, and some dimensions of scale, constant when making estimates of the economies of scale. In spite of the limitations of the engineering approach it has been used for this research because we considered it to be the most satisfactory method of making estimates of the economies of scale for the industries studied. A leading American expert in this field, Professor J.S. Bain,[1] relied on similar methods to estimate the economies of scale for twenty industries in the U.S.A.

II. The measurement of costs

Estimates of economies of scale are based on cost data for batches, plants etc. In this section we examine some of the more important problems involved in measuring costs.

Costs are made up of the costs of materials and services bought out, wages and salaries, and charges in respect of capital employed. The valuation of materials, services and components bought out, labour, new capital goods, and working capital, is generally straightforward as prices paid or market prices can be used, but the estimation of capital charges for new or existing plant is more complex, and we discuss the calculation of these charges next.

Capital charges

Depreciation, the charge by which the cost of fixed assets is spread over their useful lives, is made up of two components, physical wear and tear, and obsolescence, which is determined by improvements to new capital equipment, the introduction of new techniques and products,[2] and changes in demand for products. The total charge for depreciation during the life of an asset is the cost of the asset less any final resale or scrap value (ignoring price changes during the life of the asset) but there are theoretical and practical problems concerning the allocation of the charge for depreciation and interest on capital over the life of an asset.

Assuming that the general level of prices is constant, one method of allocating capital charges is in proportion to the expected future gross earnings,[3] i.e. where C is the total of the capital charges, C_t the capital charges for accounting period t, E the expected total gross earnings, and E_t the expected gross earnings in period t, then $C_t = E_t / E \times C$. For making these calculations, future gross earnings would be estimated after allowing for the effects of the age of assets on costs of maintenance, and for expectations about changes in technology and demand. (When estimating gross earnings, changes in relative market prices of factors of production over time, brought about by changes in technology and demand, would also be taken into account).

One assumption which can be made about future gross earnings from assets is that they remain constant in each accounting period covering the expected life of an asset. If this assumption is made, the charge for

(1) J.S. Bain, 'Barriers to New Competition'. Cambridge, Mass. 1956.

(2) If estimates of depreciation include an allowance for obsolescence, they do, of course, make some allowance for technical progress.

(3) The expected gross earnings of a new asset are the future revenue expected from the use of the asset, less material and selling costs, and the costs of operating the asset, but before the deduction of depreciation and interest on capital.

depreciation and interest on capital can be spread over the life of each asset in equal instalments.

So far we have discussed the calculation of depreciation for newly acquired assets and, as many of our estimates of economies of scale are for new plants, this is relevant to the study. But for some industries we have obtained estimates of costs for different scales of output, based on cost information for firms using plant built up over time, i.e., the plant they use is drawn from a number of vintages.

There are many theoretical and practical problems involved in the valuation of the fixed capital of a plant built up over a period of time. One method of calculating the capital charges for our purpose would be to take the original cost of each asset and base the capital charges on this cost. Any change in the level of prices since the asset was acquired, could then be allowed for by increasing the annual capital charges based on the initial cost of the asset, in proportion to the change in an index of prices for new plant between the date of acquisition of the asset and the accounting period considered. Alternatively the current replacement cost of each asset could be estimated and the capital charges could be based on these values.

In practice companies' estimates of costs, including their estimates of depreciation, have been used to calculate the economies of scale. For estimating depreciation accountants generally estimate the lives of assets on a conservative basis and write off fixed assets by constant annual depreciation charges — the straight line method of calculating depreciation.

The decision to accept businessmen's estimates of costs was a matter of expediency. The estimates of depreciation are the most likely source of error in these estimates, but businessmen have the knowledge necessary to estimate the lives of assets and to select a realistic method of charging depreciation. Also it would have been very difficult to have obtained the information required — the expected lives of assets, scrap values, etc. — to make separate estimates.

The decision to use businessmen's estimates of depreciation would be unfortunate if the estimates were likely to be misleading. Fortunately, however, any errors are not likely to be very important when computing costs for plants of varying size in some industries because the charge for depreciation forms a small proportion of total costs in these industries. [1] Also, and this is more important, the absolute level of depreciation may be inaccurate, but it is less likely that there will be *bias* in the estimates for plants of varying size, and so the estimates of economies of scale may not be greatly affected by any errors, though in industries in which large plants or firms use capital intensive techniques, there will be some bias. In order

(1) There is a qualification to this argument. For many *plants*, raw material costs form a high proportion of costs, and the capital charges are a much smaller proportion of total costs, but many *products* are made by a series of processes in different plants, often in different industries, and, if the costs for these processes are consolidated, the charge for depreciation is a more important component of total costs, i.e. depreciation forms a higher proportion of value added.

to be sure that our estimates of depreciation were not resulting in misleading estimates of the economies of scale, we considered the effects of changing the charges for depreciation. We describe our conclusions in Appendix B.

For the industry studies, the rates of interest selected by businessmen have also been used where these were available. But in many cases estimates of economies of scale were obtained which did not allow for a return on capital, and in these cases a rate of 10% on average fixed and working capital has been used. The rates of interest selected by businessmen might allow for differences in the riskiness of investment in different industries, but there are also other forces, such as the cost of finance, and arbitrary accounting rules, determining the rates of interest selected by different firms.

A rate of interest of 10% could be justified because interest rates on government securities are about this level or by the ability of large public companies, in the absence of exceptional circumstances, to raise debenture finance and loans from banks at rates of interest of about 10% p.a., or less, for new projects at the time the estimates made for this study were prepared. Also the government has suggested that the nationalized industries use a rate of 10% as a test rate of discount for investment calculations.[1] Alternatively, the yield on investment in equity shares of other companies could be used as a guide to the opportunity cost of capital. During the period since 1950, the pretax yield, including capital appreciation, on this type of investment has been higher than the yield on government securities over the same period. Another alternative would be to use a rate of about 15%, the rate many businessmen look for on new investment. Again we have considered the effects of varying the rate of interest selected in Appendix B.

In many of the industry studies the assumption that future earnings will be spread evenly over the lives of assets is implied. Depreciation has been calculated by the 'straight line method' and a charge for interest on the average fixed capital employed during the life of the asset has been included as a cost.[2]

---

(1) Nationalised Industries, 'A Review of Economic and Financial Objectives', H.M.S.O. 1967. The test rate was raised from 8% to 10% in 1969.

(2) In making estimates of costs of production for new plants, businessmen sometimes include a cost for interest on the initial investment and not the average capital employed. Capital charges calculated in this way are excessive because the capital employed declines over the life of an asset as depreciation accumulates.

The distribution of expected gross earnings may not, in practice, conform to the pattern described, for example, for many investments gross earnings are higher during the early years of operation of an asset, or they rise during the early years and then decline.

Initial costs

Ideally, the design, development and first copy costs for products with a substantial life should be treated in the same way as capital costs.[1] [2] In the case of initial costs, a practical difficulty for making ex-ante estimates of costs per unit is that the total output of products is not known in advance. This is one reason why firms in practice usually write off many initial costs when these costs are incurred. Firms also adopt this procedure because of traditional accounting procedures which were developed when initial costs were of much less importance. In general we have not capitalized initial costs or allowed for interest on these costs, but in trades where initial costs are important we have shown them separately.

It is often difficult to trace the development and other initial costs (including marketing costs) for new products. An alternative procedure which we have used to indicate their relative importance is to consider current expenditure on initial costs in relation to total costs, but there are qualifications to this approach because the rate of expenditure on initial costs is related to future output more directly than current output. Nevertheless the comparisons do provide a general indication of the relative importance of these costs.

III. Estimates of present value

Instead of comparing unit costs for plants of varying size, a different approach to measuring the economies of scale would be to compare the present value of plants, firms, etc. For this purpose, the net cash flow for plants of varying scale, as measured by output capacity, could be discounted at the opportunity costs of capital. In order to isolate scale effects on costs, revenue per unit of output would be assumed to be unaffected by scale. The present value of plants to produce each level of output would be the discounted net cash flow, and, if the present value increased more than proportionately with scale, then net economies of scale would exist. If the present value increased less than proportionately, there would be diseconomies of scale. This method would avoid the need to spread capital charges over the lives of assets.

When estimating the present value of plants account could be taken of differences in the time it takes to build plants of varying size and the receipt of tax allowances and investment grants. The effects of these factors on costs, can, of course, be allowed for when estimating unit costs in the conventional manner, but the present value method is more flexible. If small plants can be constructed in less time than large plants, this may affect revenue as well as costs, and could be allowed for when calculating the

(1) The life of some products, e.g. newspapers, is so short that initial costs do not have to be capitalized.

(2) Some selling and promotion costs are very similar to initial development costs, expenditure especially for the promotion of new products, is often expected to affect sales in subsequent accounting periods.

24

discounted cash flow of plants of differing size. Also, the effects of varying assumptions about changes in relative cost of factors of production through time, and of varying the degree of flexibility of a plant etc. could be assessed.

The estimates of economies of scale given in this study are in terms of the unit costs of production, and the economies of scale are compared to total unit costs of production to illustrate their magnitude in relation to the total factors used. The present value method would facilitate the inclusion of more of the effects of scale, but these effects are of secondary importance in many industries and, as many of the estimates of the economies of scale which have been obtained are very crude, the use of a more sophisticated method than a comparison of unit costs would not add to their value. Also, calculation of present values would be a roundabout way of calculating the effect on costs of changes in such dimensions of scale as the length of production runs and the extent of standardisation. We therefore decided to work in terms of unit costs.

IV. Vintages of plant

One problem we had to consider when collecting and preparing 'engineering estimates' of the economies of scale was the vintage of plants we were dealing with. For some industries such as chemicals, oil refining, and man-made fibres, we obtained estimates of costs for new plants of varying size. But for some other industries, such as the electrical industry and marine diesels, it was not possible to obtain estimates of costs for completely new factories or production lines because U.K. firms in these industries more often build up capacity by adding new machines and extending their fac-tories, rather than building completely new plants. We had to accept which-ever type of estimate could be provided, but we make clear in the text whether the estimates are for new or existing plants. For estimates of costs for different scales based on costs for existing plants, it was assumed that all the plants were built up over the same period, in effect that they had similar proportions of assets of each vintage, and the same basis for cal-culating capital costs was used for plants of each size.

The distinction between estimates of economies of scale for new and for earlier vintages of plants is important because we should generally (but not always) expect the economies of scale to be greater for new plants because they incorporate the latest techniques and are often more capital intensive. (We deal with these points in more detail in Chapter 34). The economies of scale for the latest vintage of plants have a special importance because it is through the construction of new plants that the scale of production is often changed. On the other hand for establishing the effect of scale for the competitive position of firms, comparing estimated costs for firms with plants built over a period of time is more realistic in industries where firms in fact build up the capacity of their plants over time.

V. Definition of minimum efficient scale

In many industries there is no clear point at which costs cease to fall or where there is sharp change in the rate of fall. It is therefore necessary to select an arbitrary point after which the decline in costs is relatively insignificant. For the purpose of this study we have used the following definition of the minimum efficient scale (m.e.s.). Within the range of scale for which we have estimates, the m.e.s. is the minimum scale above which *any* possible subsequent doubling in scale would reduce *total* average unit costs by less than 5% *and* above which *any* possible subsequent doubling in scale would reduce value added per unit (total costs less the cost of bought out materials, services, and components) by less than 10%.[1] Where there are economies of scale for value added, but relatively small economies for material cost, the inclusion of value added in the definition has the effect of increasing the m.e.s.[2] It is important to note that for this purpose value added is defined in terms of total costs (not sales) less the cost of materials, components and services.

For some products, costs do not fall continuously to a m.e.s. For example, in some engineering trades the main dimension of scale to which economies relate for products with low development costs is the size of batches. Once the batch size has risen above a certain level any further economies by increasing its size may be small, but, where output can be greatly increased it is sometimes possible to spend more on development, substitute more efficient techniques and set up special production lines. Once this level of output is reached there may be significant economies, representing more than 5% of total unit costs, to be achieved by a doubling of output. In this study the feasible range of output in relation to the U.K. has been considered when estimating the m.e.s. of production. It should be noted that there may be ranges of output below the m.e.s. over which total cost per unit fall slowly and at less than 5% for a doubling of scale, and that there may be ranges of output beyond those feasible in the U.K. where costs fall by more than 5% if scale is doubled.

VI. Strategies

Another difficulty when estimating the m.e.s. for an industry is that firms may follow different strategies. For example, some firms may not follow aggressive policies of development. Similarly firms often use different channels of distribution. Some firms sell to multiple stores while others concentrate on selling to independent stores and advertising their products.

---

(1) It is assumed that the range of operations performed by firms is not affected by scale. In practice the extent of vertical integration varies, and firms with a relatively large output of products tend to perform more operations, and buy out fewer operations.

(2) The definition should not be taken as an indication that we consider a reduction in total costs of less than 5%, or in value added of less than 10%, would not be a decisive advantage in a competitive industry.

For estimating the m.e.s. assumptions have to be made about the operations performed and the strategies adopted by firms. For the estimates of technical economies of scale given in this study, it is initially assumed that firms of varying size adopt the same strategies, but the effects of relaxing this assumption are discussed. The effects of introducing other costs – marketing, distribution and research – on these estimates of the minimum efficient scale are described and for this purpose it is generally assumed that firms adopt the strategies for marketing and research which are most favourable to their competitive position. For example it is assumed that firms with a small share of their market do not advertise.

In practice the 'minimum efficient size' of units depends on other factors besides the costs of production etc. These factors include the size of other firms in the industry and the extent to which there are market imperfections.

VII. Material costs

The cost of materials, services and bought-out components generally form a substantial proportion of costs, usually more than 50%, and in many trades the scale of firms does not greatly affect the price they pay for materials, etc. This does not necessarily reflect an absence of economies of scale for the production of materials.

Where scale economies obtained by a firm for the costs of material are small and material costs are included in unit costs, this damps down the effect of economies of scale on total costs, and if there are real effects, external to an industry, but internal to other industries, which are not allowed for in the estimates of material costs, then the estimates do not reflect the overall economies of scale for the production of products. Also there is a case for excluding material costs and assessing the effects of scale on labour and capital inputs alone, where the purpose of comparing costs is to indicate the effects of scale on the efficiency with which the national resources used in an industry are employed.

VIII. Alternative methods of measuring the economies of scale

In the Interim Report we discussed the alternative methods of measuring the economies of scale – cost comparisons and analysis of the changing structure of industries.[1] In view of the difficulties which we described in the Interim Report for measuring the economies of scale from costs for existing plant, no attempt was made to collect such data. But we examined Census data and the accounts of public companies to see if they provided any clues to the existence and size of economies of scale. Our analysis of this data is described in Appendices C and D.

In the Interim Report we described the limitations[2] of the 'survivorship' method of establishing whether scale economies exist by analysing changes

(1) p. 21

(2) p. 24

in the structure of industries through time. In our view this method is only useful for providing a very crude test of the results of other methods of measuring economies of scale. For example if other estimates showed that there were large economies of scale over the range of scale of existing plants, but the largest plants were being closed down, this would require explanation. However no such conflict exists between the changing structure of U.K. industry and our assessment that there are large economies of scale in many industries.

IX. A note on the presentation of scale curves

In the literature there has been much discussion about the shape of scale curves, but little discussion of the significance of the choice of axes for illustrating them in graphs. In fact the choice of axes can have a marked effect on the shape of scale curves as the example in diagram 2.1 shows. If log scales are used on both axes the reduction in costs appears to taper off more slowly and, though the curves drawn on normal axes would be described as 'L' shaped, those drawn on log scales could not. For purposes of considering the contribution of economies of scale to growth we want to know the proportional changes in costs attributable to proportional changes in scale, and for this purpose log scales are appropriate. However for purposes of comparing the competitive position of two firms of differing size at one point in time, differences in absolute costs are also relevant.

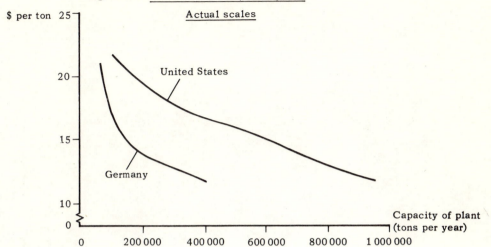

Diagram 2.1. Scale curves for cement plants

Actual scales

$ per ton

United States

Germany

Capacity of plant
(tons per year)

Source: Book 2, chapter 10.

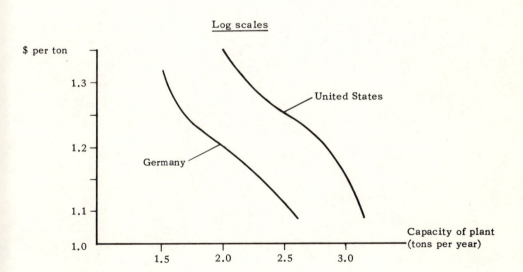

Log scales

$ per ton

United States

Germany

Capacity of plant
(tons per year)

Book 2. The Industry Studies

3. Introduction to the Industry Studies

The selection of industries

The industry studies cover a wide range of industries, which were selected in order that all the important types of industry, from a technical point of view, should be included. In addition the choice of industry was influenced by the importance of the industries to the economy and by a desire to include industries with differing structure.

The purpose of these studies was not to make detailed recommendations for changes to the structure of industries or to provide industrialists with a guide to the optimum size of factories. More detailed investigations would be required for this. The primary purpose of the studies was to provide a general picture of the real economies of scale.

Sources of information

The main sources of data for the industrial studies were the firms we approached and representatives of trade and research associations. In addition data published in Censuses and other official publications, trade papers, journals and books have been used. The number of visits made to firms in each industry depended on the data already available for the industry, the number of firms in the industry, the number of firms willing to cooperate, the diversity of output of an industry and the degree to which we were able to obtain information about the industry on our initial visits. For example in the case of the footwear industry twelve visits to firms manufacturing footwear were made, and discussions were held with machinery manufacturers and the industry's research and trade associations. In the case of machine tools eleven firms and two associations were consulted. For the study of the cement industry information was obtained from the three leading U.K. manufacturers, and for motor vehicles three U.K. and one European manufacturer provided data and advice.

The layout of the industry studies

There is so much variation between industries that it was not possible to apply a standard layout to each industry study, but as far as possible, we have used the plan which we now describe.

Each industry study is prefaced with a table giving a 'profile' of the industry derived from information published in the Censuses of Production. Unfortunately the main data about the size of establishments and enterprises relate to the 1963 Census, as the full results of the 1968 Census had not been published at the time of writing.[1] We then outline in a 'General Introduction' the salient features of the structure of each industry, the processes of production, the sources of economies of scale, and the dimensions of scale. The following section of each chapter provides an outline of the structure of costs.

The two 'background' sections on structure and costs are followed by sections dealing with the economies of scale. We deal first with initial costs and the economies of scale for products, we next consider the economies of scale for batches and production runs, and then for plants. Finally we discuss the economies of scale for firms; dealing first with economies for production costs associated with large firms, then with other sources of economies or diseconomies of scale — selling and distribution, research and development etc. At the end of each study we draw together any conclusions which emerge from the study. This plan has been adapted for each industry to take account of the varying importance of different dimensions of scale between industries, differences in the diversity of products produced by industries, the importance of the industry, the information we obtained, and whether the industry was included in the interim report.

Our estimates of costs are generally presented in terms of average costs, but in some cases we have added estimates of 'marginal costs'. This is the average unit cost for the output additional to the preceeding output for which we have estimated average costs.[2]

(1) We have shown those 1968 figures which are available, as percentages of the 1963 figures. It should be noted that the percentage changes indicated are influenced by short term factors affecting 1963 and 1968, as well as long run changes. Concentration ratios, the proportion of the output of products of each trade accounted for by the largest firms, are given in the profile tables.

(2) The following figures illustrate the method of calculation

Output (units)	100	200
Average cost	20	15
Marginal cost		10*

*[(200 × 15) − (100 × 20)] ÷ 100

4. Oil - An Addendum

Table 4.1. *Profile of the Oil Refining Industry*

	1963	% of all manufacturing industry	1968	% of all manufacturing industry	1968 as % of 1963.
Number of Employees ('000)	20.5	0.3	17.7	0.2	86
Sales (£m.)	509.3	1.8	829.5	2.1	163
Net Output (£m.)	63.9	0.6	102.9	0.6	161
Capital Expenditure (£m.)	11.9	1.2			

CONCENTRATION

Concentration ratio for the 5 largest firms in 1963 for Aviation and Motor Spirit — 98.5%

Size of Establishments and Enterprises (1963)

ESTABLISHMENTS   ENTERPRISES

Number of Employees	Number	% of Employees	Number of Employees	Number	% of Employees
1 — 299	7	4	1 — 999	4	10
300 — 2,499	8	34	1,000 and over	4	90
2,500 and over	4	61			
Total	19	100	Total	8	100

I. General introduction

In the interim report we described the structure of the oil industry in the U.K., and the economies of scale for refineries. Since the completion of the interim report in 1965 the main changes in the structure of the industry have been:

(a) the continued growth of the industry — since 1964 U.K. oil refining capacity has increased by 90% to about 100 m.t.p.a.

(b) the entry into the U.K. market of a number of American companies who have had to find markets for oil which they have discovered in the Middle East and Africa.

(c) the increasing scale of tankers and refineries. (The following figures illustrate the changing distribution of sizes of refineries.

33

Capacity in million tons	0–1	1–2½	2½–5	5–7½	7½–10	10–12½	12½–15	15–17½	Total
1962 (number of refineries)	7	2	3	1	2	1	0	0	16
1969 (number of refineries)	7	2	1	7	1	3	0	1	22

In 1969 four companies or joint ventures who did not operate refineries in the U.K. in 1962, each had refineries with capacities of about 5 million tons, and three more entrants to the U.K. market were building substantial refineries here).

(d) the increasing integration of petro-chemical production and oil refining.

II. Structure of costs

The main changes in costs since the preparation of the interim report have been the increases in labour and capital costs. On average the prices of oil products have not risen until very recently, and most of the increases in costs have been offset by cost savings over the whole integrated oil industry operation – production, shipping, refining and distribution. In addition profit margins per ton have fallen. A large part of the cost savings are attributable to economies of scale, but other sources of improvements in efficiency, such as operating process units with fewer staff, trimming safety factors when designing new plants as a result of experience, etc., have contributed to improvements in labour productivity and reductions in capital costs.

III. Economies of scale for refineries

In view of new estimates of economies of scale obtained from two companies it seems more realistic to concentrate on estimates showing larger economies than those used in table 5.9 of the interim report. A reason for the increased economies for refineries of 10 m.t.p.a. capacity, compared to those with 5 m.t.p.a., (table 4.2) is that distillation units with a capacity of 10 m.t.p.a., are being constructed for U.K. companies, though not for use in this country. In the industry it is expected that distillation units with capacities of 20 m.t.p.a. will be built during the 1970's. The revised estimates of costs for a refinery of 20 m.t.p.a. indicate that economies would tail off above 10 m.t.p.a., but it is possible that there would be larger economies for offsite equipment and down stream process units than the company which provided the estimates allowed for.[1]

(1) It is very difficult to generalize about the cost of offsite equipment. For example, at large scales it may be necessary to introduce cooling systems for water. At some locations companies can provide their own electricity, and can achieve economies by installing large units of generating plant, but at other locations the provision of electricity is regulated and firms cannot build their own plant.

34

Table 4.2. *Costs and Scale for New General Purpose Refineries* [a] [b]

Crude Refinery Capacity (million tons)	Interim Estimates of:		Revised Estimates of:	
	Refinery costs per ton	Ex-refinery costs per ton	Refinery costs per ton	Ex-refinery costs per ton
	(Indices of Costs)			
1	100	100	100	100
2	85	96	75	92
5	66	91	56	86
10	52	87	44	82
20			40	81

(a) Refinery costs include works fuel. It is assumed that there are no economies of scale for fuel and crude oil (included in ex-refinery costs). In practice a large refinery can be supplied by larger tankers or maintain lower stocks of crude in relation to its output.

(b) It is assumed that each refinery carries out the same range of operations. If a small refinery limited its range it could reduce its handicap. This point was discussed in the interim report.

Construction times

We also obtained additional information about the time required for the construction of refineries of varying size. It takes a period of anything up to 2 years to obtain planning permission, conduct site examination etc., for a refinery on a green field site, and the construction of the refinery takes a further two to three years depending on the complexity of the process units. It was estimated by one company that in the construction of new refineries of a similar type, there can be as much as a 30% increase in construction period between plants of 1 million and 10 m.t.p.a. throughput. The experience of this company was that little time was saved in expanding an existing refinery compared with construction from grass roots, unless the expansion was a minor one. Essentially this was because a refinery expansion necessitates full integration with existing equipment which has to be operated while construction work is taking place.

As it takes longer to build a large refinery this offsets some of the economies of scale because of the increased capital charges for unproductive capital during construction. An increase of 30 per cent in construction time is equivalent to an increase in capital cost of about 7%. The penalty would be greater if products had to be bought from other companies, or markets were lost during the interim period.

IV. Oil companies

1. Operation of a number of refineries

An oil company which operates a number of refineries in the U.K. or overseas can achieve economies by concentrating special plants at certain refineries, and by planning its capacity to concentrate expansion at different sites in turn in order to achieve economies of scale while maintaining high rates of capacity utilization. An independent refinery would have to buy and sell in the market to achieve a similar balance.

35

2. Vertical integration

In theory a firm need not integrate its operations back to prospecting and drilling for oil, but in practice there is no large scale independent refiner in the U.K. Once a company is in the prospecting business an important inducement to spread its operations is to reduce risk.

3. Marketing and distribution

The relationship between the scale of companies and their marketing and distribution costs was dealt with very briefly in the interim report. Companies with a large share of a market have an advantage for advertising and for distributing their product. Companies with a small share of the overall market for oil products may concentrate on a narrow range of products, motor oils for example, buying refined products from other companies for blending and distribution. The success of such companies depends on their selection of blends and their marketing. Companies with a limited share of the market for refined products may carry out the initial refining operation, but restrict their range of products by, for example, not making a wide range of lubricating oils. A firm with a small share of the market for such specialities would have high costs. Other ways of limiting costs are to market products without national advertising, and concentrate sales in areas near to a refinery to reduce delivery costs. In effect, firms with a small share of the market aim for a substantial share of a smaller market.

4. Entry to the market

As noted in the interim report the entry of additional firms into the U.K. market has been at the expense of economies of scale. But in this industry the new entrants usually build substantial plants. If they did not build refineries here they might import refined products instead, thus limiting any increase in the size of refineries operated by other companies in the U.K.

Table 4.3. *Summary of Minimum Efficient Scale for Oil Refining*

	Capacity of Refinery	% of U.K. Capacity	Percentage increase in costs at 50% of the 'm.e.s.'	
			total costs (inc. the cost of crude oil)[a] per unit	refinery costs[a] per unit
New General Purpose Refineries	10 m.t.p.a.	10%	5%	27%
Companies:	No estimates of the economies of scale for firms were obtained			

(a) The costs of marketing and distribution are excluded from these estimates.

5. Chemicals

Table 5.1. *Profile of the Chemical Industry*[1]

	1963	% of all manufact-uring industry	1968	% of all manufact-uring	1968 as % of 1963
Number of Employees ('000)	233.0	2.9	232.4	2.9	100
Sales (£m)	1,364.4	4.9	2,084.0	5.3	153
Net Output (£m)	581.3	5.4	830.9	5.2	143
Capital Expenditure (£m)	99.5	9.7	—	—	—

Concentration

Average concentration ratio for the 12 chemical sub-trades
distinguished in the 1963 Census   72%

Size of Establishments and Enterprises (1963)

	Establishments		Enterprises	
Number of Employees	Number	% of employees	Number	% of employees
Under 50	891	6	700	5
50–749	484	55	256	40
750–1999	42	24	15	8
2000 and over	10	15	16	47
Total	1,427	100	987	100

(1) The following census trades are included — general chemicals, fertilizers and chemicals for pest control, dyestuffs, synthetic resins and plastic materials, and explosives and fireworks. Enterprises which operate in two or more of the trades which have been aggregated may be included more than once.

I. General introduction

1. Products

The Association of British Chemical Manufacturers has defined the chemical industry in terms of products to include heavy chemicals, industrial gases, fertilizers, dyestuffs, medicinal and other fine chemicals, explosives, plastics and synthetic resins, but not the compounding of chemicals to make such products as paints, insecticides, sheep and cattle dips and pharmaceutical preparations.[1] The data shown in table 5.1 has a similar coverage.

One characteristic of many sectors of the chemical industry, particularly heavy chemicals, is the capital intensity (relative to labour) of production processes. Other characteristics of the industry are the relatively high expenditure on research and development, the rapid evolution of new products and processes which frequently result in existing products and processes being made obsolete and, partly as a result of the evolution of new products, the rapid growth of the industry. The rate of development of new products is illustrated by changes to the Classified List of Products Section of the *Directory* of the Chemical Industries Association. The *Directory* is published biennially and more than ten thousand products (including research chemicals but excluding varieties of dyes) are listed. Product for this purpose means distinct chemical formulations which are prepared for sale. About a thousand new headings are added in each new edition and approximately five hundred headings are deleted. Some recent estimates made by Hoechst, a German chemical company, also illustrate the rapid evolution of products. During the past ten years the company has introduced 3,000 new products and sales of these products now form one third of its turnover and produce a higher proportion than this of its profits.[2]

2. The structure of the industry[3]

The 1963 Census of Production shows that there were over 400 enterprises with more than 25 employees and in excess of 200,000 employees in the

---

(1) Association of British Chemical Manufacturers — Report on the Chemical Industry, London, 1949. (The A.B.C.M. has since been incorporated in the Chemical Industries Association.)

(2) European Chemical News, 16th May, 1969.

(3) For a more detailed description of the structure of the Chemical Industry, the reader is referred to 'The Chemical Industry' by W.B. Reddaway in Vol. I of *Structure of British Industry*, edited by Duncan Burn (Cambridge, 1958).

industry. Nevertheless because of a high degree of specialization there are only a small number of firms making most chemicals. Over 40% of the chemicals listed in the 1968 edition of the *Directory* of the Chemical Industries Association were made for sale by one firm only, many other chemicals were made by 2 or 3 firms only, and even I.C.I. makes only 4% of the chemicals listed.[1]

As the diversity of firms making chemical products in the U.K. is much greater than for many of the other industries studied, the best way to give some indication of the structure of the industry is to outline the operations of a number of these firms. This 'rag bag' approach has the advantage of illustrating the heterogeneous nature of the industry.

(a) I.C.I. is the leading U.K. chemical manufacturer and is the largest U.K. manufacturing company. It was formed in 1926 by a merger of four companies which between them manufactured a wide range of chemicals. The company is now a substantial producer of products in all the main sections of the industry (heavy chemicals, industrial gases, fertilizers, dyestuffs, other fine chemicals, explosives, plastics and synthetic resins) and a recent estimate of its contribution to U.K. chemical production was between twenty and twenty-five per cent, whether measured in terms of sales value or labour force.[2]

(b) B.P., Shell and Esso all manufacture basic petro-chemicals, such as ethylene, in the U.K. and, apart from the I.C.I., they are the only U.K. manufacturers of a wide range of basic petro-chemicals. The extent to which the oil companies have integrated forward their chemical operations varies, but a substantial part of Esso's chemical sales are basic petrochemicals and to a smaller extent Shell and B.P. also concentrate on the sale of basic and intermediate chemicals to other firms for further processing.

(c) There are a number of firms, including companies such as Albright and Wilson, Berk Chemicals and Laporte Industries, which produce substantial quantities of chemicals included in more than one section of the industry. These businesses were founded to manufacture a specialized product or to import or distribute chemicals and their manufacturing interests have developed over time. They buy some basic chemicals and quarry and manufacture others, and have also diversified into non-chemical interests.

(d) There are a number of companies which specialize in supplying certain markets e.g. companies which make dyes, pharmaceuticals or fertilizers. Some of the firms which manufacture dyes make a comprehensive range, while others manufacture a limited range from intermediate chemicals, and similar variations in the extent of vertical intergration occur in other sections of the industry. Also there are a number of

---

(1) The *Directory* includes laboratory and research chemicals which are produced on a small scale. It is possible that I.C.I. is not listed under all the chemicals that the company in fact produces.

(2) This estimate was provided by the company.

companies, and consortia formed by groups of major consumers, which were formed to manufacture, or have become associated with, the manufacture of a very limited range of products. Examples of such companies are British Oxygen, Borax Holdings (now part of the R.T.Z. group) and International Synthetic Rubber. This type of specialization may be associated with control over a particular source of certain chemicals, patents or accumulated expertise. Such companies, when independent, tend to diversify and grow over time to reduce their dependence on one product group, and to find additional markets, or to market new products that they have developed. But there are many small firms which specialize, and the consortia tend to remain restricted to their original field.

(e) The Distillers Company's chemical interests[1] originated from the sale of alcohol for industrial uses. Some coal, gas and steel companies have developed chemical interests from the sale of by-products. Also some firms including British United Shoe Machinery, have added the production of certain chemicals to their existing line of business where the markets are the same.

(f) Some companies have integrated backwards to the production of the chemicals which they use as raw materials, either by starting production of chemicals, or by taking over a firm which produces them. Courtaulds illustrates this type of entry into the industry.

(g) A number of overseas chemical companies including Union Carbide (U.S.), Monsanto (U.S.), du Pont (U.S.), CIBA (Swiss) and Geigy (Swiss) operate manufacturing subsidiaries in the U.K. Similarly, the leading U.K. companies operate overseas.

(h) There are a number of firms which make chemicals in very small quantities for laboratory and other uses. Such firms usually buy out basic chemicals, prepare and pack their products. The capacity of the equipment they use is very small compared to that used to make basic chemicals in large quantities.

3. The dimensions of scale

It is difficult to generalize about the dimensions of scale for such a heterogeneous industry, but the output of particular products over time, the size of plants and the size of firms are generally the most important dimensions of scale for purposes of achieving economies of scale. In addition, economies relate to the grouping of plants together to use common services and facilities, and linking the production of various chemicals in one plant to avoid reheating, to use surplus steam, etc. For some types of chemicals (mainly basic and intermediate chemicals), which are made in special continuously operated plants, the length of production runs is not a relevant dimension of scale, but the length of production runs is of importance for the production of many other chemicals, such as dyes.

(1) Distillers Company's chemical interests were taken over by B.P. in January, 1967.

40

II The structure of costs

Some general features of the structure of costs for the chemical industry are noted:

(a) For many production processes, particularly where scale permits continuous operation of special plants, direct labour costs are small compared with capital charges. (Data given below for types of chemical plant illustrate this point, e.g. table 5.2). However, when considering the industry as a whole there are a number of labour intensive activities, particularly research, testing and some packaging operations.

(b) For I.C.I., research and development expenditure of about £30m. a year represented approximately 3% of sales and 25% of profits, before tax, during the mid 1960's. For the U.K. chemical industry as a whole, research and development expenditure also represented 2.5% of sales in 1968 or 5% of the value added by the industry. For some sections of the industry, such as fine chemicals and pharmaceuticals, the proportion is substantially higher.

(c) Selling and marketing costs are also variable. Typically, for basic and intermediate chemicals they are low, but for some dyes, fibres, plastics, etc., they are a substantial element of costs, not only during the initial promotion, but in the form of customer service during the whole life of products.

(d) Transport costs again vary, not only with the varying properties of products but also with the geographic distribution of markets. The variability can be illustrated by data for fertilizers and dyes: transport costs represent 5.5% and 1.5% respectively of sales for these two trades. For heavy basic chemicals, they can rise to well over 10% of sales.

III. The sources of economies of scale for chemical plants[1]

Before describing case studies for individual chemicals and groups of chemicals, we deal in this section with some general information about the sources of economies of scale for plants — one of the principal sources of economies of scale in the industry.

1. Economies of scale for capital costs

(a) *The 0.6 rule.* There is a simple rule of thumb that is used by chemical engineers to relate fixed capital costs and scale. This is the 0.6 rule [2] However, the rule can only be applied as a very approximate guide. The exponent varies for different types of plants and over the range of sizes of individual types of plant.

A.B. Woodier and J.W. Woolcock in a paper on the 0.6 rule[3] have drawn

(1) Data published in five supplements of the *European Chemical News* dealing with Large Plants have been used in the preparation of this section of the chapter.

(2) The 0.6 rule states that if capacity is multiplied by a factor x, the capital cost is multiplied by $x^{0.6}$

(3) *European Chemical News* (Supplement of 10th Sept., 1965, p. 7).

attention to the danger of relying on such a rule except for illustrative exercises on hypothetical plants, and have described a more satisfactory method of preparing estimates of capital costs for plants of varying size. Where a breakdown of capital costs for one size of plant is available, or if a breakdown can be estimated, they suggest that the cost should be divided into the three categories listed below, and that the estimates of capital costs for plants of different sizes should be based on an extrapolation of this breakdown.

(i) Items of equipment e.g. the control room, the total costs of which are the same whatever the size of plant or are hardly affected by scale. Another example of expenditure falling into this group is design charges, although in practice the cost of designing a large plant is somewhat greater than for a small one, as designers tend to use more care in the case of a large plant because of the value of the materials used. (Exponent — say 0.0 – 0.4).

(ii) Items of plant which can be made bigger or smaller as required and for which the number is therefore independent of plant size. (Exponent — say 0.4 – 0.8). This economy of increased dimensions applies to columns, vessels, pipe work and usually to compressors and heat exchangers. The general concensus of opinion is that for plant of this type an exponent of 0.6 is probably the most suitable. The exponent only applies over the range of sizes of units of plant which are within the range of sizes normally built. If a larger unit has to be built there may be extra costs for designing it, and there may be initial difficulties in introducing it into service. Also there are limits to the size of plants which can be built, caused by increases in stresses which occur as the size of units is increased. These limits are pushed back over time as new materials and processes are invented and introduced. Again there are initial costs involved in introducing these new materials and processes.

(iii) Items of plant for which costs are nearly proportional to scale. An example of this type of plant is the furnace section of a large ethylene unit. Technical problems limit the size of individual cracking furnaces and, as a result, a large plant has many furnaces. (Exponent between 0.8 and 1.0).

It is of interest to note that the average exponent for the three groups is about 0.6.

If capital costs are classified into three groups in this way and an estimate of capital costs for plants of different sizes is prepared, the overall exponent will increase with scale, as the components of capital costs with a relatively high exponent (for which few economies of scale are obtained) form a progressively higher proportion of total costs. This division of costs also illustrates the importance of single stream plants — plants in which there is no duplication of equipment — for the determination of the economies of scale. As it becomes necessary to duplicate parts of a plant the economies of scale decline. In practice it is necessary to duplicate an in-

42

creasing proportion of plants as scale is increased, but for many processes it is now possible to construct predominently single stream plants with very large capacity. For other processes, e.g. those requiring very high pressures, the maximum scale is limited.

The scope for employing different techniques and processes as scale increases is a factor which is not allowed for in the type of calculation described. There are processes for which it is efficient to use different techniques for large scale plants, the use of centrifugal compressors, instead of reciprocating compressors in large ethylene plants provides one example. In practice, however, if both the feedstock and the proportions in which products are to be made are given, the scope for using different techniques is limited for many processes.

The main sources of economies of scale for capital costs are the use of indivisible items of plant and the economies of increased dimensions. Two factors which tend to raise the capital costs of large plants are the cost of transporting very large units to the site and, where this is impossible, the relatively heavy cost of fabricating plant on the site.[1]

John Haldi and David Whitcomb have collected evidence on the size of the exponent for units of process plants and for complete process plants.[2] Their estimates were based on data about the prices of units of plants given by companies in catalogues, news releases, trade publications etc. For plants most of the estimates were engineering estimates for hypothetical plants. The range of plant sizes to which the exponents in general relate were those built in the U.S. since 1945. The average exponent for the 662 types of units of plant listed was approximately 0.6, and for the 103 chemical plants (excluding rubber plants) approximately 0.7. The exponents varied within a wide range, from less than 0.4 to more than 1.1. For the units of plant, 71% were within the range 0.4 to 0.8, and for plants 75% were in the range 0.5 to 0.9. The exponent for plants may be less than for units of plant because there is more duplication of units of plant in large plants and/ or because the economies of scale for installation (setting up units of plant on the site) are smaller than for units of plant.

(b) *Forces which reduce the economies of scale for capital costs* The economies of scale for the capital costs of plants depend on the number of identical plants built. In some cases there may be a choice between building two or more small plants and one large plant. If two identical plants are built, the costs, including design costs, for the second plant are lower than for the first. For some types of plant the reduction in costs for the second plant, if it were a 'chinese' copy, could be as much as 20%, because

---

(1) New techniques may have to be developed for construction on the site to be possible e.g. in the case of very large forgings and castings, it has been necessary to forge or cast parts and develop new methods of welding at the site.

(2) Haldi & Whitcomb, 'Economies of Scale in Industrial Plants'. Jnl. of Pol.. Econ., Aug., 1967.

design costs would be avoided for the second plant, and there would be some economies for the construction of the second plant. (In making this estimate it is assumed that the orders for the two plants are placed with the same contractor and plant suppliers, and are placed simultaneously.)[1] In practice, if a firm decides to build two plants instead of one, it may obtain one slightly quicker, and, if it can delay the building of the second, it will be able to incorporate any advances in technology in the second plant. However it should be noted that the economies for 'chinese' copies are a source of scale economies only if a firm requires sufficient additional capacity to take advantage of them. Where a market is supplied by, say, two independent companies, they are unlikely to order identical plants at the same time.

Continuity of supplies of basic chemicals is essential.[2] The construction of large single stream plants, instead of a number of smaller plants, involves greater risks of disruption to supplies. These risks may be avoided by storing chemicals, but the cost of providing storage facilities offsets some of the economies of scale for capital costs. In some cases where other processes are dependent on by-products — for example steam from a sulpur plant — it can be expensive to provide alternatives in case of breakdowns[3] or interference with supplies of raw materials. However, care is again necessary when describing this as a factor reducing the economies of scale. There is no evidence that large plants within the range of plant sizes for which substantial experience exists, are more likely to break down than small plants. Indeed because 'down time' is more expensive for large plants, firms spend more to keep the plants in operation. For example more highly qualified and experienced engineers may be assigned to them.

Another factor reducing the significance of the economies of scale for capital costs, in relation to other costs, is the system of providing tax allowances or grants for capital expenditure. In this and other chapters these grants, which may represent as much as 40% of the cost of the hardware for a plant, have been ignored. These grants tend to reduce the optimum size of plants, but in practice they may encourage the construction of large scale plants to replace a number of existing small plants.

(1) This estimate is based on information obtained during a study of the economies of scale for chemical plant contractors. The size of the economies depends on the distinctiveness of the plant.

(2) The importance of continuity of supplies can be indicated for ethylene plants. The capital investment in the down stream production plants, for which ethylene is an input, may be more than £100m., compared with the capital cost of an ethylene plant, say, £25m.

(3) The likelihood of breakdowns can be reduced at some cost, at the design stage. Such breakdowns can seriously reduce annual capacity and it has been estimated that when single stream plants larger than previous ones are built, the effect of breakdowns can be to reduce rated capacity by as much as 40% in the first and 20% in the second years of operation. (Sir Ronald Holroyd, F.R.S., 'Ultra Large Single Stream Chemical Plants: their Advantages and Disadvantages'. Chemistry and Industry. Aug. 5th, 1967.) An advantage of very large companies when faced with the decision whether to build very large single stream plants is to construct one or more single stream plant and one or more with two streams.

Interest on working capital is usually ignored when making estimates of capital costs, but it must obviously be considered in estimating the economies of scale, because it is so important.[1] The main components of working capital are stock and net outstanding accounts, i.e. debtors less creditors. In general there are no economies of scale for outstanding accounts, but there may be economies for stocks of raw materials and of finished products. The need to hold stocks of products to insure against a breakdown may tend to result in proportionately larger stocks of finished products for large single stream plants, compared to a number of small plants, since risks of breakdown are spread with the latter. On the other hand a larger market could result in proportionately smaller fluctuations and hence smaller average stocks of finished products. In some cases, stocks of raw materials per unit of output can be reduced as scale is increased. On balance the economies for working capital are proportionately much smaller than for fixed capital.

Another possible source of diseconomies for the capital costs of large plants may be the length of construction time, but chemical engineers claim that the time allowed for building plants is not generally affected by scale *per se*. However, if a plant is larger than previous ones, and especially if it incorporates new techniques, there may be delays of twelve months or more in commissioning it because unforeseen difficulties may arise. These delays are caused by building new plants rather than building larger plants *per se*, but relatively large scale generally involves the use of 'untested' plant. Delays of a year or more are very significant in an industry in which the life of many plants is about ten years.

2. Direct labour, supervision and overhead costs

For most of the *European Chemical News* studies of plant scale economies for which estimates of operating labour costs were given, these were assumed to be constant or to increase marginally with scale. Maintenance costs were generally assumed to be proportional to capital costs, and works overheads, such as rates and laboratory expenses, where shown, were usually assumed to be equal to operating labour costs, or operating labour costs plus maintenance. It should be noted that most of the E.C.N. estimates were for single stream plants. Large plants of this type are now common in the production of many chemicals.

Haldi and Whitcomb collected estimates of the exponent for labour costs in addition to exponents for capital costs (see page 43). For 71% of the cases for which they obtained data (mostly engineering studies) the labour exponent was less than 0.4. The opinion of a U.K. petro-chemical company

(1) It may be noted that investment in working capital is less important for the chemical industry than for manufacturing industry generally. Net current assets represented 42% of net fixed assets in 1960, compared to 67% for all manufacturing industry. 'Income and Finance of Public Quoted Companies 1949-60'. Statistics Division. Board of Trade, London 1962. For certain types of chemicals the ratio is much lower.

was that 0.4 was a fair guide. Their experience was that, though on strictly technical grounds it was often not necessary to have more operating personnel for a larger plant, in practice unions insisted on this. Rates of wages were also higher for men operating larger plants.

3. Feedstock

The relative importance of feedstock varies for different types of process and with the scale of plant, but together with utilities it usually forms more than half, and in some cases more than 80%, of the costs for many large process plants. For the E.C.N. estimates it was generally assumed that there would be no economies of scale for these costs, but comparisons based on the assumption of constant feedstock costs, understate the advantages of large plants. There may be economies of scale which, though small as a percentage of material costs, are important because materials are so large a proportion of total costs. Also, where plants are included in a complex of units, the product of one process is often the raw material for another process and, as many chemical products are the result of a chain of processes, material costs have a much smaller dampening effect on economies of scale for final products than for a single plant.

4. Utilities

The E.C.N. estimate indicate few economies of scale for the cost of utilities. In practice, there are some small in-process economies for utility costs for some plants, but more important are economies for providing utilities. These may have been ignored in the E.C.N. studies because they usually relate to the total consumption of utilities at a site. A firm's total requirements of electricity, water etc. determine the price it pays for them or the size of the electricity generating plants it builds.

IV. Case studies for chemicals

1. Ethylene

A detailed estimate of the relationship between costs and scale for an ethylene (or olefins) plant is shown in Table 5.2 Ethylene is now of fundamental importance as a basic organic chemical from which many other chemicals are made; and output of ethylene has increased rapidly in recent years. Five companies, I.C.I., B.P., Shell, Esso and British Oxygen produce ethylene in the U.K., and they have a total capacity of about 1.5m. tons from 16 plants at 7 sites. The companies use a substantial proportion of the ethylene they produce in their own plants. The size of ethylene plants has increased; the first U.K. plant which used napptha as a feedstock was built in 1943 and had an initial capacity of 12,000 tons. Plants are now being built with a capacity to produce 450,000 tons of ethylene, although many of the older small plants are still being used. For such a well established basic chemical as ethylene, initial development costs are not now significant and have been ignored.

46

Table 5.2. *Ethylene Plants*

Size: annual capacity		000 tons	
Input of napptha	357	714	1,428
Output of ethylene (co-products excluded)	100	200	300
Total Investment Costs		£m.	
Plant	6.7	10.8	13.3
Offsite facilities	1.7	2.7	3.3
Total (excl. working capital)	8.4	13.5	16.6
Operating Costs per ton of ethylene		£	
Feedstock costs	35.7	35.7	35.7
Chemicals and utilities	5.5	5.5	5.5
Operating labour and supervision	0.8	0.5	0.3
Maintenance and works overheads	2.7	2.2	1.8
Depreciation	8.4	6.8	5.5
Interest at 10% on:			
Average fixed capital	6.3	5.1	4.2
Working capital	0.4	0.4	0.4
Total operating costs	59.8	56.2	53.4
less value of co-products:[a]			
Gasoline and fuel oil	13.0	13.0	13.0
	46.8	43.2	40.4
Other co-products (say)	15.6	14.4	13.3
Cost per ton of ethylene (Average Cost)	31.2	28.8	27.1
(Marginal Cost)		26.4	23.7

Source: Based on M.R. Wynn and G.H. Rutherford, 'Ethylene's Unlimited Horizons',
European Chemical News, Supplement of Oct. 16th, 1964.

(a) The product breakdown assumed, per ton of ethylene produced, is propylene 0.57 tons, butadiene 0.14 tons, gasoline 0.72 tons, other co-products 1.76 tons.

There are two special problems involved in preparing estimates of costs for ethylene plants. The first concerns the capacity of an ethylene plant. In the past, capacity has been measured in terms of the capacity to produce ethylene. Ethylene may, however, form as little as 25% by weight of the output of the plant.[1] The percentage yield depends on the design of the plant, the feedstock and the way in which the plant is operated, but it is not much affected by the size of the plant. The main co-products are propylene, butadiene, benzene, tuluene, gasoline and fuel oil. All the co-products except fuel oil have a market value above that of napptha, the feedstock. In Table 5.2 the capacity of 'ethylene' plants is described in terms of the input of napptha and the output of ethylene.

(1) For some of the latest plant designs the ethylene yield is claimed to be as high as 42%

The second special problem concerns the cost treatment of co-products. In the past, the procedure adopted in published studies has been to deduct from feedstock costs the value of co-products either at fuel cost,[1] or the cost of producing the products by the most efficient alternative process, or the market prices less the cost of any further processing required. The last procedure can result in a 'negative' feedstock cost, if market prices are high. For plants such as ethylene crackers, for which co-products are very important, this procedure is misleading as regards economies of scale. In table 5.2, therefore, we have included the full cost of feedstock and show economies of scale for the production of a combination of products. We then deduct a sum attributable to the production of co-products. Low value co-products – fuel oil, tail gas and gasoline – are deducted at their net market price. Other co-products are valued at the proportion of costs represented by the ratio of the market price of these co-products to the market price of ethylene.

Attention should also be drawn to the estimates of fixed capital costs. Shell have recently announced plans for the construction of an Olefins plant to produce 450,000 tons of ethylene a year, estimated to cost about £25m. One reason for the obviously greater cost is that the plant is to be built to use 'gas oil' as well as napptha as a feedstock, and it incorporates flexibility in its use of these feedstocks. This adds 15% to the capital cost. Given the high proportion of feedstock cost to total costs, this flexibility is very important.

Economies of scale apply to much 'offsite' equipment, but this equipment usually relates to a number of plants, rather than an ethylene plant alone. We have included estimates of costs for this equipment in order to provide comprehensive estimates of costs.

The data in table 5.2 shows that there are:

(a) large economies of scale for fixed capital costs. (The exponent is approximately 0.6.) But for plants of a larger size than the data cover, the exponent rises to 0.8 between 300,000 and 450,000 tons and 0.9 for plants over 500,000 tons. [2]

(b) in percentage terms even larger economies for labour costs, but direct labour and supervision costs form only 1% of overall production costs;

(c) economies of scale for maintenance and overheads of about the same size, in percentage terms, as those for fixed capital costs;

(d) no economies of scale for feedstock and utilities.

In practice, there would be some small in-process economies for utilities and some economies for supplies of both feedstock and utilities. These

(1) Fuel cost is based on the calorific content of products.

(2) The factors contributing to the increasing exponent are the rising proportion of the plant which has to be duplicated and the need to fabricate on site for very large plants.

last relate to total use at a site, not to one plant. Although no economies of scale are shown for these items, these could be absolutely important because they relate to two of the largest items of cost. There could also be some diseconomies, if, for example, above a certain size of plant, cheap supplies of water, or electric power from the firm's own plant, were to become exhausted, necessitating outside purchases at higher prices.

2. *Sulphuric acid*

For the ethylene study it was assumed that the proportions in which products are made are fixed. In practice there are alternative sources for many chemicals. Sulphuric acid provides an illustration. In the U.K. at the present time there are five main sources of sulphur for sulphuric acid production:

Source of Materials	% of U.K. production of Sulphuric Acid in 1968/69
Natural sulphur	59
Iron pyrites	9
Spent oxide	4
Zinc concentrates	8
Anhydrite	20
	100

There are more than twenty companies which manufacture sulphuric acid in the U.K. Laporte Industries, Albright and Wilson, Fisons, Courtaulds and I.C.I. are leading manufacturers and account for about half of total U.K. output (3m. tons of acid in 1969). About 70% of the acid produced in the U.K. is used at the manufacturer's own works.

The size of plants operating in the U.K. are indicated by the following data:

Output at site (000 tons per year)	0–50	50–100	100–300	300–500	Total
Number of sites	19	9	12	3	43
Output at sites by source of sulphur:					
Sulphur burning plants	14	11	7	1	33
Other	10	2	2	2	16

Note At some sites sulphuric acid is made from more than one type of material.

The economies of scale vary for different processes. For sulphur burning plants, operating costs and capital charges are small compared to the cost of the sulphur and utilities, and so the economies of scale, in terms of unit costs of production, for these plants are relatively small, i.e. there are economies for capital and operating costs, and they continue up to an output of at least 1m. tons of acid a year, but their significance is reduced by relatively heavy material costs.

The following estimates of economies of scale for sulphur burning plants were made by a firm of chemical engineers:

Annual capacity for acid production (thousand tons)	100	250	500	1000
Costs per ton of acid:	Indices of costs per ton			
Fixed capital costs	100	73	59	46
Operating costs (utilities and labour)	100	76	67	61
Sulphur	100	100	100	100
Total costs (including capital charges at 15% per yr.)	100	96	94	93

The capital costs per unit of output for plants using anhydrite are much higher and there are economies of scale up to a high level of capacity – at least 500,000 tons of acid per annum. The choice of process depends on the cost of raw materials, the value of the other products produced, including surplus steam, and cement, and in some cases on government policy to ensure supplies by using indigenous raw materials. [1]

Sulphuric acid is not an exceptional case. There are alternative processes for the production of petro-chemicals such as ethylene and acetylene, and, provided an attractive market is available, it may be economic to produce some by-products in relatively small quantities.

3. Dyes

The two chemicals considered so far, ethylene and sulphuric acid, are basic chemicals which are made in relatively large quantities. To test whether our conclusions that there are substantial economies of scale applied to chemicals made in smaller quantities, we consulted a company which manufactures dyes.[2] The experience of this company suggests that economies

(1) An estimate of the comparative costs of using sulphur and anhydrite as sources has been made as follows:

	Capacity – 200,000 tons per year	
	From Sulphur	From Anhydrite
Capital Cost of Plant £m.	1.1	5.0
	Cost per ton of Sulphuric Acid £	
Materials and Fuel	5.10	4.81
Processing Cost (less steam credit)	0.29	2.14
Capital Charges (22%)	1.21	5.55
	6.60	12.50
Less Credit for by-products		3.50
		9.00

Source: J.R. Potter, 'Economic Considerations in the Choice of Fertilizer Process Routes'. The Fert. Soc., 1970.

(2) The range of dyes and pigments is illustrated by the total number of different dyestuffs and pigments – some 7,000 in all. I.C.I. alone offers a basic range of 2,500 different products, excluding mixtures. N.B.P.I. Report No. 100. p. 5, (H.M.S.O. 1969).

of scale of the sort shown for ethylene also apply to the much smaller plants used for the production of dyes. The 0.6 rule, though not accurate for individual units of plant, appears to be generally applicable to the plants used. The exponents were said to vary between 0.4 and 0.8. A study of labour costs for the company's plants indicated an exponent of approximately 0.25 for these. Again this is in line with estimates for plants designed for the production of basic chemicals.

For ethylene and sulphuric acid, the dimensions of scale apart from size of plant were ignored. For dyes, because of batch production, the length of production runs is important. For new dyes the costs of development are an important component of costs, but there are many traditional dyes for which the original costs of development can be ignored. In a report on the industry, the National Board for Prices and Incomes has stated that a 'typical international manufactuer may spend as much as 5% of his turnover on R & D and 2.3% on technical service to launch his products and advise on their use'.

Dyes are generally made in batches,[1] and repeated batches of each dye are made. The main advantage of producing large batches is that the economies for large plants can be obtained. The advantages of preparing repeated batches of a dye are that:

(i) it is easier to produce dyes to match a specification by mixing a number of batches, rather than to mix one batch according to specification. (In effect this means that a smaller proportion of the product is rejected.)

(ii) the costs of cleaning out equipment can be spread over a greater output. (It takes about two days to clean out equipment. Some changes of products do not involve a full clean out — on average this is required for about one third of changes.)

Some estimates of costs for new plants for dye-making processes (not the manufacture of intermediate chemicals) are shown in table 5.3. The estimates are typical for dyes made in relatively large quantities. Costs for old plants are also shown: capital charges for these plants are ignored, as it is assumed that their resale value would be negligible. In practice old plants are not fully depreciated and there are some capital charges for most plants.

For the estimates shown in the first part of the table it is assumed that there are no clean-outs. The figures show substantial economies of scale for the production of dyes in large plants. For the second part of the table it is assumed that there are a number of clean-outs, and that for each run the quantity of product produced is not affected by the size of the plant i.e. that there are fewer clean-outs of the smaller plant. The estimates illustrate the economies which can be achieved by extending production runs. For example, if the number of clean-outs in a new plant of 0.75 X capacity

(1) Continuously operated process plants are not generally used for dye production because of the initial costs of designing and operating such plants. The difficulty of introducing continuous processing is attributable to the fact that the processes used in dye production are relatively complex. If the production of dyes could be greatly increased, it would be worth incurring the initial costs of designing more continuous processes.

Table 5.3 *Illustrative Production Costs for a Dye*

Capacity of plant	New Plant			Old Plant	
	1.5X	0.75X	X	0.5X	0.125X
Costs	Index of Costs per ton [a]				
Materials [c]	37	37	37	37	37
Energy and Services	5	5	5	5	5
Direct Labour	5	8	8	13	38
Maintenance	5	7	3	5	7
Works Overheads and Other Expenses	5	7	7	10	22
Capital Charges [b]	43	58	0	0	0
Costs assuming no clean-outs	100	122	60	70	109
Adjustment for clean-outs					
Average number of clean-outs per month					
(i)	4	2	2.7	1.3	0.3
Index of costs	121	134	65	77	110
(ii)	8	4	5.4	2.6	0.6
	166	151	72	80	111

(a) The total production costs for a new plant with a capacity of 1.5X, operating without clean-outs, are assumed to be 100. It is assumed that the proportion of product lost because it does not match specifications is not affected by scale.

(b) Capital charges are taken at 16.7% p.a. on the initial fixed capital. The capital charges for the old plant are assumed to be zero.

(c) It is assumed that the costs of materials and energy are not affected by the size or vintage of plant. Materials include intermediate dyes for which economies of scale could be obtained. These economies are ignored.

is reduced from 4 to 2 a month by increasing the length of runs, costs are reduced from 151 to 134 per ton. Similarly for a new plant of 1.5 X capacity costs are reduced from 166 to 121 if the number of clean-outs is reduced from 8 to 4. The table also shows that economies of scale for large plants decline as the length of runs declines and illustrates the relative costs for new and old plants; particularly for dyes made in short runs, the old plants have lower costs. Another point worth noting is that if a firm has to make a long run of a dye in a small plant, the economies of scale for a long run are small.

Finally the relatively high level of the charges for maintenance on the *new* plant call for comment. There is some divergence of practice in the process trades for deciding the degree of automation to install in new plants. The cost of maintaining complex electronic controls can be a significant item of costs, and some firms are less ambitious than others when designing the control of plants.

The effect of including initial costs of developing a new dye are illustrated in Table 5.4. The costs of developing new dyes vary, but no costings for dyes would be representative if development costs were excluded. For the purpose of this table we have assumed costs of 100 for an output of 1.5X of a dye per month which is made in a plant of this capacity. We have also assumed that 75% of total costs are production costs and that the economies of scale shown in Table 5.3 apply to these costs. It is assumed that for lower rates of output, correspondingly smaller plants would be used. Finally it is assumed that total development costs are not affected by the level of output, and that there are no economies for marketing etc.

Table 5.4 *Illustrative Initial, Production and Marketing Costs for a New Dye*

(a) Made in new plant

Capacity of Plant	1.5X	0.75X
Costs	Index Numbers of Costs per ton	
Initial development costs	10	20
Production	75	84
Marketing, packing, distribution and admininstration	15	15
Total average cost	100	119

(b) Made in old plant.

Capacity of Plant	X	0.5X	0.125X
Costs	Index Numbers of Costs per ton		
Initial development costs	15	30	60
Production	59	63	78
Marketing etc.	15	15	15
Total average cost	89	108	153

In practice plants are generally adaptable for the production of a number of products. New plants are built to make dyes which are made in large quantities, while dyes made on a small scale are produced in older plants. The data given in Table 5.3 is typical for dyes made in large quantities.

V. Transport costs

Transport costs are a potential source of diseconomies of scale for large chemical plants where increased scale is achieved by supplying markets farther from the plant. But there are economies for carrying chemicals in bulk, and concentration of output may reduce transport costs for raw materials and/or by-products. Also the number of sites at which some chemicals are used is small, and there is some flexibility for deciding where to site these plants.

The economies of scale for the bulk transport of liquid chemicals by sea are illustrated by the following data which are based on prices at the beginning of 1970. (Sea transport is, of course, only applicable for deliveries between coastal sites. Most, but not all U.K. chemical works are located near the coast.) The figures were obtained from a shipping broker.

Size of consignment (tons)	10	100	1,000	2,000	5,000	10,000	20,000
Freight cost per ton from:				£			
Tees to Rotterdam	10	5	1.35	1.00	1.00	0.95	0.70
Rotterdam to New York			2.50	2.30	2.08	1.67	1.56

For internal transport in bulk lorries there would be no economies for individual consignments above about 20 tons. Economies for rail transport extend to higher levels of output, and for movements by pipeline to much higher levels. There are also economies for regular consignments because this makes possible higher utilization of equipment.

In the case of sulphuric acid[1] and ethylene, the base chemicals discussed above, the cost of transport is relatively heavy. For sulphuric acid this is because the volume of the acid is about three times that of its sulphur content. For liquified ethylene, transport costs are also substantial because special tanks are required; a 200-mile haul in road tankers would add about 10% to the product price, while shipment to Europe over 500 miles would add about 20%. Shipment to the U.S. was estimated by one firm to add as much as 70% to the ex-works price. Two additional processes are required to convert ethylene gas to a liquid and to reconvert it, thus adding to costs of movement still more.

The importance of transport costs varies for different chemicals, depending on the value of the chemical per ton. Transport costs are an important factor determining the size and siting of plants to manufacture certain basic chemicals, such as sulphuric acid and ethylene, but for many chemicals they represent a very small proportion of total costs. In the case of dyes, they are about 2% of total costs for U.K. sales and 5% for sales to Europe. Economies of scale for the transport of dyes are in any event small, unless bulk transport can be substituted for transport in drums.

VI The control of plants

The evidence described shows large economies of scale for many types of chemical plant. For many chemicals, plants of minimum efficient scale would have an output equal to a substantial proportion of U.K. output, and often larger than the average annual increase in output. As demand increases through time, it is necessary to build a number of plants for making basic petro-chemicals, but the question arises whether there would be economies if one firm only controlled the building of all new plants for producing any particular group of chemicals. It could be argued that if one firm built and operated all the U.K. ethylene plants, for example, it could plan the construction of new plants to minimize transport costs and to make full use of its experience.[2] However, chemical plant contractors specialise on types of plant, and they transmit experience not only nationally but internationally. Competition may provide a stimulus to efficiency and may prevent exploi-

(1) Firms which operate sulphur burning plants in the U.K. have an Association which purchases sulphur and organizes the transport of the sulphur on a cooperative basis. Firms operating small works and receiving relatively small shipments generally pay the same price as firms operating much larger works.

(2) Another advantage to be achieved by concentration of the control of plants would be to enable firms to replace a number of existing small plants by one large plant where costs justified it.

tation — a point of some importance in an industry in which costing for joint products is inevitably arbitrary.[1] Although, therefore, there would be some technical economies if, say, B.P. and I.C.I. merged their basic petro-chemical interests, or if the government had the power to limit the entry of new producers of chemicals, there is a good case for several independent manufacturers.

It may also be noted that independent firms co-operate to avoid some of the possible disadvantages of divided ownership of plants. If the plant of one company breaks down, or if there is a delay in the completion of a new plant, other companies are usually willing to supply the chemicals to the company concerned. This is partly because of the chance that the next break-down may occur at their own plant. Also there is some collaboration regarding plans for expansion, with beneficial effects.

VII Economies for multi-plant complexes

There are potential economies to be achieved by concentrating a number of plants on one site. A number of plants can be controlled from one control room, and the introducion of computers is increasing the scope for this. The provision of engineering and laboratory services and off-site equipment, the elimination of transport costs where the products of one process are the raw materials for other processes, the use of surplus gases as fuel, the production of steam and electricity and the provision of water, effluent treatment, and transport for a number of processes simultaneously, are other sources of economies. Many of the potential diseconomies for isolated plants, located to take advantage of cheap raw materials etc., can be avoided or reduced by, for example, sub-contracting maintenance, or building the plant near other non-chemical plants which use electricity and steam. No estimates of these economies, which must depend on the type of plant considered, have been obtained.

A possible source of diseconomies for a multi-plant complex is the problem of providing adequate management, but managers of multi-plant complexes in the U.K. and Germany, with up to 35,000 employees, have expressed the view that any difficulties of managing such complexes can be overcome by delegation.

VIII The size of orders

A comparative study of manpower used in the chemical industry in the U.K. and the U.S.A. has drawn attention to the importance of the size of orders. This affects not only transport costs but costs of packaging and of processing also. In the U.S.A., it was found that the larger order size enabled relatively more goods to be shipped in bulk. For example if a plastic poly-

(1) An incidental effect of a merger between leading producers could be that customers would turn to other suppliers, including overseas suppliers, for some of their requirements, to ensure continuity of supplies in the case of a breakdown and also to test prices.

mer is sold in large consignments it is sometimes possible to move it in liquid, instead of solid form. Operations which are relatively labour intensive, and are not subject to economies of scale, can therefore be avoided.

IX Firms

There are economies for firms which operate plants at a number of sites, and for multi-complex firms, attributable to marketing, the joint provision of services, and the ability to finance a research and development programme and the construction of large-scale plants. We discuss these sources of economies of scale separately.

1. Research

We illustrated the importance of the development of new products for the chemical industry in the general introduction and we provided estimates of expenditure on R. & D. for this industry in Section II.

A distinction can be drawn between three aims of research — improvements to existing products or processes, new ways of producing existing products, and the development of new products. In some chemical trades, e.g., pharmaceuticals, research aimed to produce new products is very important. In other trades, e.g., heavy chemicals, the other types of research are more important — and are generally less expensive to undertake. Within each sector of the industry dyes, pharmaceuticals, fibres, plastics, etc., and for types of products, e.g., a fibre or chemicals for fire extinguishers, there are economies of scale for research. For example a firm with a large output can spread the costs of research to develop continuous processing over a large output.[1] A firm with relatively large overall output and expenditure on research can spread the costs of special research equipment over more experiments and output. Research to develop new products is risky and a firm with a large volume of research can spread its risks (on the other hand it loses some of the pressure to achieve results which applies to a small firm). Also, compared to research by a number of companies with small research budgets, a firm with a large budget should avoid duplicating research for new products and unproductive lines of research.

Where differences in scale are attributable to a wider spread of interest, the main scale advantage is greater scope for investing in research projects requiring large resources. It has been estimated that a new pesticide may take six to nine years, and cost more than £1m., to develop.[2] A new fibre may take as long to develop and cost £20m. In practice development costs are usually written off against current profits, and so a firm needs substantial profits, and hence scale, to develop certain products. However these are exceptional products. Many new products, new varieties of products, and new uses for products, can be developed for relatively small expenditure.

(1)   A firm with a large output of a product is likely to produce nearer to any technical barriers to increasing scale, and will have more incentive to develop plants of larger scale incorporating new techniques.

(2)   Royal Dutch Shell Group — 'Development of a New Pesticide', March, 1970.

Some small and possibly medium size firms can avoid heavy research and development costs by producing chemicals not subject to rapid developments, such as pigments for the food industry, and by copying developments made by other firms. Also licences for the production of some chemicals can be bought. It is in the interests of overseas companies to sell licences, if they are not going to exploit them in the U.K., and it is also in their interest to sell them at a price which will enable firms to compete in the U.K. But where a company is giving an exclusive licence, it usually favours a licensee with substantial capital and/or a leader in the field concerned. Also, as overseas companies increase their direct overseas investment, or amalgamate, and as tariffs are reduced, their desire to sell licences may diminish. It is doubtful whether a leading chemical company could survive without heavy expenditure on research. It would gradually lose its share of markets as new products were introduced. (This would affect its output of basic and intermediate chemicals as well as final chemicals.)

One very important effect of the organisation of the industry is on the extent of resources devoted to R. & D. In W. Germany and Japan, total expenditure on R. & D. is of the order of 100% and 50% respectively more than in the U.K. In both countries the chemical industry is more fragmented in terms of companies and it is possible that if the U.K. industry had been organised in a similar way, with more companies and with a good deal of specialisation, R. & D. expenditure would have been higher and progress faster. But there are many factors besides the structure of the industry affecting expenditure on R. & D. and the rate of progress, and it is not possible to go into them here.

2. Marketing

Large companies have advantages because of their greater experience in marketing and their ability to spread risks. The ability to spread the costs of developing a new market for a chemical provides large firms with advantages — only a large firm may be able to invest in the market promotion of a product previously produced only in small quantities.

The capacity to use or market co-products is also a very important source of advantage in some cases. But smaller firms are often able to buy out basic and intermediate chemicals to avoid the difficulties of marketing co-products, or they may get larger firms to market co-products for them.

3. General overheads

The ability of small firms to limit overheads is a possible source of strength in some cases. The overheads incurred by large firms for research, marketing and administration have to be recouped, and there may be scope for small firms with minimal overheads to undercut large firms for certain products.

4. Vertical integration

Vertical integration may occur between:

(i) oil refining and chemical operations. (Oil companies have an incentive to integrate forward to chemical production in order to control their outlets and to expand demand.)

(ii) the manufacture of basic chemicals and the production of other chemical products. (The motives for chemical companies to integrate forward are similar to those for oil companies.)

(iii) the manufacture of chemicals and the industries using them. (This type of integration is considered in connection with the production of man-made fibres, and is discussed in the chapter dealing with that industry.)

An advantage of vertical integration for small companies which use the chemicals they manufacture - backward integration - may be an absence of overheads. For example, a company making rubber and plastic products was able to set up a plant for mixing plastics[1] without increasing its costs of management and administration. In such a case, market demand may make the alternative of expanding output of rubber and plastic products an uneconomic way of utilizing such surplus management capacity, and a firm may be reluctant to cut its overheads by a reduction in the number of its staff. Similarly in some cases, firms using intermediate chemicals may not increase their overheads, or not expect to increase their overheads, by setting up plants for the production of these chemicals.

X. Conclusion

The result of all the conflicting forces, and of the multiplicity of different products and processes, is that it is not possible to specify any optimum size for a multi-product chemical company. A company of the size of I.C.I. clearly has advantages, but the net loss from dividing such a company into several more specialized independent companies might well be small in terms of economies of scale. Small companies can clearly compete in some circumstances and would not necessarily become more efficient by becoming a part of a larger company.

---

(1) This is not a chemical process within the definition given above. But similar situations occur which result in firms making chemicals.

Table 5.5 *Summary of Minimum Efficient Scale for Selected Chemicals*

	Output tons per year	% of UK output	% increase in total costs per unit at 50% of m.e.s.[a]	% increase in value added per unit at 50% of m.e.s.
New Plants				
Ethylene	(at least) 300,000	25	9	30—40
Sulphuric Acid	1,000,000	30	1	19
New Dyes (made in a new plant)	(a representative output)	100	22[b]	44
Old Plant				
Traditional Dye (made in an old plant)	(a representative output)	100	17	56

(a) No allowance is made for economies for the costs of raw materials or utilities

(b) Including initial costs.

Works: The minimum efficient scale of works is small because firms can specialize and buy out basic and intermediate chemicals. However there are large economies of scale where greater scale results in greater output of individual chemicals.

Firms: In this industry it is not possible to obtain estimates of the effects of scale of firms — the complexity involved is too great.

6. Synthetic Fibres

Table 6.1 *Profile of the Man-made Fibres Industry*[1]

	1963	% of all manufacturing industry	1968	% of all manufacturing industry	1968 as % of 1963
Number of Employees ('000)	37.3	0.5	42.5	0.5	114
Sales (£m)	209.7	0.8	344.5	0.9	164
Net Output (£m)	109.0	1.0	167.9	1.0	154
Capital Expenditure (£m)	11.7	1.1	-	-	-

Size of Establishments and Enterprises (1963)

	Establishments		Enterprises	
Number of Employees	Number	% of Employees	Number	% of Employees
25-499	11	8	4	2
500 and over	16	92	4	98
	27	100	8	100

(1) This trade relates to establishments engaged wholly or mainly in manufacturing continuous yarn and staple fibre by extrusion. Plants at which chemical materials for fibre production are made, but at which polymer is not extruded, are not included. The production of synthetic and other man-made fibres are not separately distinguished in the Census.

I. General introduction

1. Structure of the industry

The man-made fibres industry can be subdivided between cellulosic fibres (rayon) and synthetic fibres. For the purposes of this study we have concentrated on synthetic fibres. U.K. output of these fibres has been increasing very rapidly and, measured by weight, exceeded production of rayon for the first time in 1969. The three main types of synthetic fibre, polyamides (nylon), polyesters (terylene) and acrylics account for over 90% of U.K. consumption of synthetic fibres. Of the remainder, polypropylene and elastomeric fibres are the most important.

Six firms manufacture man-made fibres on a significant scale in the U.K., and of these Courtaulds and I.C.I. are the leading producers. Courtaulds produces nearly all the 260,000 tons of rayon in the U.K. each year. It is the second largest manufacturer of nylon, after I.C.I., and it accounts for about 60% of U.K. production of acrylic fibres (its main acrylic brand is Courtelle). The company has also started production of a polyester fibre. I.C.I. is the leading U.K. manufacturer of nylon and polyester fibres. British Nylon Spinners, until 1967 a company jointly owned by Courtaulds and I.C.I., and now a wholly owned subsidiary of I.C.I., produced all the nylon made in the U.K. until 1964, when British Celanese (since acquired by Courtaulds) commenced production of a slightly different type of nylon (nylon 6). I.C.I. now accounts for about 70% of U.K. nylon production. I.C.I. was the sole producer of polyester fibres until 1966 and now (in 1970) makes about 95% of total U.K. production. Both Courtaulds and I.C.I. manufacture synthetic fibres overseas.

Four subsidiaries of overseas companies also manufacture fibres in the U.K. British Enkalon makes nylon 6 and a polyester fibre, du Pont manufactures acrylic and elastomeric fibres. Chemstrand makes nylon 6 and acrylic fibres and Hoechst makes a polyester fibre. The production capacity of each of these firms is much smaller than that of I.C.I. and Courtaulds, but their significance for competition is more important than their U.K. manufacturing capacity suggests because they import fibres into the U.K. from their overseas plants, where they make a wide range of fibres, and their share of the U.K. market is growing.

Estimates of output in 1968 and planned capacity for each company at that time are shown in table 6.2.

Table 6.2 *Estimated U.K. Production of Synthetic Fibres in 1968 and (in brackets) Planned Capacity*

	Nylon		Polyester		Acrylic		Total	
			(th. tons)					
I.C.I.	80	(110)	60	(92)	—		140	(202)
Courtaulds	15	(25)	—	(10)	40	(80)	55	(115)
Chemstrand	10	(15)	—		22½	(35)	32½	(50)
British Enkalon	12½	(20)	2	(5)	—		14½	(25)
du Pont	—		—		0	(20)	0	(20)
Hoechst	—		—	(8)	—		—	(8)
	117½	(170)	62	(115)	62½	(135)	242	(420)

2. Production processes

There are three main groups of processes used for the production of synthetic fibres.

(a) the manufacture of the basic chemicals including ethylene, propylene, cyclohexane, para-xylene etc.

(b) the production of the polymer by a further series of chemical processes.

(c) the extrusion of the polymer. The liquid polymer is extruded through very fine holes in a nozzle called a "spinneret" or jet, and the threads or filaments so produced are solidified by cooling (melt spinning), by evaporation (dry spinning) or in a liquid bath (wet spinning). Continuous filament yarn is produced by collecting and slightly twisting together the filaments from the spinneret to form a continuous thread which is suitable for weaving or knitting into fabrics. Staple is manufactured by cutting a large number of filaments into short lengths, resulting in a soft fibrous mass. This is carded and/or combed, drawn, and spun into yarn in the same way as are natural fibres.

Two of the overseas manufacturers operating in the U.K. import polymer i.e. at present they do not perform (a) or (b) type operations in this country. Courtaulds buys chemicals and does not perform any (a) type processes for synthetic fibre production. I.C.I., but not Courtaulds, extrude some polymer at plants apart from those at which they produce polymer.

3. The dimensions of scale

The main dimensions of scale are the output of individual fibres and the varieties of fibres produced to which development costs and promotion costs relate, the length of production runs, the size of plants and the size of firms.

II. The structure of costs

1. The costs of production

Table 6.3 *Breakdown of Costs for the Main Processes Used for the Production of Fibres*

		Type of Process	Average for Nylon 6 and Polyester	
			Filament Yarn %	Staple Fibre %
Raw materials	(a)		25	41
Conversion to polymer	(b)		10	17
Conversion to fibre	(c)		65	42
			100	100

Source: based on information from industry sources

The purpose of quoting the estimates of costs given in table 6.3 is to convey to the reader the broad importance of the production processes in terms of costs. In practice the relative importance of the processes depends on scale, among other factors. The figures also illustrate the substantial difference in the structure of costs for filament yarn and staple fibres. The average cost per ton of staple fibre is about 60% of that for filament yarn because the conversion process is much cheaper.

2. Research and development and promotion costs

In the past, both R & D and promotion costs have been important for the industry. In 1968 R & D expenditure on synthetic fibres by U.K. producers was about £5m. and promotion costs, including advertising (but not discounts to buyers of fibres) in the U.K., was about £8m, of the order of 3% and 5% of net output. (Both R & D and promotion costs are a much smaller percentage of turnover for rayon). As synthetic fibres mature as commodities, advertising expenditure would be expected to diminish in importance.

It is of interest to compare expenditure by U.K. companies with that of U.S. companies. In 1968 total R & D expenditure on man-made fibres in the

U.S.A. was about £50m., and of this total du Pont's share was probably about £25m. Even when allowance is made for higher costs for R & D in the U.S., American expenditure is still very much greater than U.K. expenditure. R & D expenditure is devoted to improving processes, and inventing new fibres and varieties of fibres, and it may be that U.K. firms are spending relatively little on inventing new fibres. However in future new fibres may not displace existing textile fibres to the extent that nylon and polyester have done, although they may achieve an important place in special markets.

III. Initial costs

The main initial costs for new fibres and variations of fibres are R & D and promotion costs. Case studies of R & D expenditure etc. for new fibres were not obtained because firms were reluctant to provide the data and because the costs vary widely for different fibres and varieties of fibre. Nevertheless these costs are very important. Development costs were said to amount to more than £20m. for some new fibres introduced by an American manufacturer. Also, the long delay between initiating research on a new fibre or variety of fibre and selling it in large quantities, means that capital is tied up for long periods. In the case of nylon and polyester it took more than ten years to move from initial research to production, and the gap is still of the order of four years for a new fibre. There are also delays for new varieties of existing fibres.

During the early life of a fibre the initial costs build up - first the costs of R & D and then the initial marketing costs. Where possible the initial price is set at a high level in relation to production costs to recover the initial costs. The full initial costs for a fibre are borne by the firm which introduces the fibre. Other firms may buy a licence to manufacture it, or may start production when the patents have expired. For these firms initial costs will be lower, but the costs of acquiring expertise and bringing the quality of the fibre produced up to an acceptable standard are not negligible. In practice much will depend on the circumstances of the company, whether it is a broadly based chemical company or has strong marketing links, and the range of processes which it undertakes - extrusion only, or polymerization and extrusion.

The following figures illustrate the effects of spreading initial costs for a new fibre. Both the initial costs and production costs are for a hypothetical fibre: in practice there is a good deal of variation in the relative importance of the two groups of costs for different fibres. It is assumed that initial costs have to be recovered during the first ten years - a realistic assumption in present conditions. The bases of the estimates of production costs are described in later sections.

Average Annual Output of Fibre during first 10 years (m. lbs.)	10	20	50	100
R & D and promotion costs £m.	15	15	15	15
R & D and promotion costs per lb. £	0.15	0.08	0.03	0.02
Production costs per lb. £	0.30	0.24	0.20	0.17
Total costs per lb. £	0.45	0.32	0.23	0.19

Development costs for a new variety of fibre would be much lower, but the size of the market and the degree of market protection from other varieties of fibre would also be lower.

IV. Economies of scale for plants

The economies of scale for each of the main groups of processes can be considered separately.

(a) For the initial chemical processes which are usually performed in continuously operated plants, there are large economies of scale of the sort described in Chapter 5. (A source of advantage for a broadly based chemical company for the manufacture of fibres is that such a company may be able to use chemicals it produces as by-products. For nylon 6 it may be able to place the by-products of caprolactum which can be used for fertilizers.)[1][2]

(b) For the production of the polymer there are also substantial economies of scale. These processes are usually performed on a batch basis, but particularly for varieties of fibres produced on a large scale, continuous plants are used.[3] There are limits to the scale of single stream polymerization plants, and lines with a capacity of about 15,000 tons a year are the largest at present contemplated in the U.K.

(c) For the extrusion of fibres the economies of scale are smaller because the capacity of the machines used for extrusion is limited.

We have concentrated on the economies of scale for polymerization and extrusion as chemical processes were dealt with in Chapter 5.

1. Economies of scale for polymerization

Table 6.4 shows estimates of the scale effects for new polymerization plants. The scale effects are large for operating and capital costs, but are damped down by the assumed absence of economies of scale for material costs-

(1) A fibre company may be able to buy in the caprolactum or sell the by-products to a fertilizer manufacturer.

(2) Some choice of processes is available and it is possible to use a process which limits the production of by-products. A firm's choice of process also depends upon the availability of basic chemicals (benzene or phenol for nylon 6).

(3) Variations in fibres are introduced at the polymerization and extrusion stages of production. Colour changes are not important in this industry as colour is not added at synthetic fibre plants.

Table 6.4 *Polymerization Costs (Average for Nylon 6 and Polyester)*

	4	20	40	80
Annual Capacity (th. tons)	4	20	40	80
Number of lines [a]	1	5	5	5
		Indices of Costs		
Labour	150	100	50	26
Overheads	120	100	67	48
Capital Charges at 20% of the cost of fixed assets	118	100	75	57
Total (excl. material costs)	123	100	70	51
Material costs	100	100	100	100
Total	104	100	91	86

(a) As scale is increased some equipment is duplicated, but other plant is not. For example there are usually more autoclaves than dryers; drying is a batch process, and one dryer can take the output of a number of autoclaves. The figures for the number of lines are intended to indicate the average replication of plant.

Source: based on information obtained from industry sources.

For the purpose of making these estimates it was assumed that the number of production lines would increase in proportion to output, between 4,000 and 20,000 tons per annum, but that it would not increase between 20,000 and 80,000 tons.[1] In practice the number of lines does increase with scale. One fibre manufacturer suggested that as scale increased over time, the number of types of fibre increased by approximately the square root of the increase in output, and the increase in production lines required was about half the increase in types of fibre, i.e., if output increased four times, the number of types of fibre might double, and the number of lines increase by 50%. This suggests that for output between 4,000 and 20,000 tons economies are somewhat larger than those shown, and for outputs between 20,000 and 80,000 tons they are smaller. To take these factors into account, we have prepared the following revised estimate:

	4	20	40	80
Annual Output (000 tons)	4	20	40	80
Number of lines [2]	2	5	6	8
		Index Number of Costs [3]		
Costs excl. materials	140	100	80	65
Total costs incl. materials	112	100	94	90

A comparison of the two sets of estimates illustrates the importance of assumptions about the number of production lines which depend upon the length of production runs. An overseas producer setting up plant in this

(1) The estimates were based on these assumptions in order to place an upper limit to the economies of scale over the range 20,000 to 80,000 tons.

(2) For existing plants the number of lines is normally greater than shown for any given scale of output.

(3) Costs for an output of 20,000 tons a year have again been taken as 100, but absolute costs are not the same as for the output of 20,000 shown in Table 6.4.

country may be able to operate with fewer lines for a given size of plant because he can import special types of fibre. Also a new entrant may have proportionately fewer lines than an established producer who continues to operate older vintages of plant. Similarly a manufacturer making a limited range of a fibre in large quantities (e.g., some types of carpet fibres) requires fewer lines than a manufacturer producing a wide range. The important point is that a firm requires long runs of the fibres it makes relative to its competitors' runs for similar fibres. If a firm makes special products in small quantities, provided its competitors make equally small or smaller quantities, it should be able to produce at a competitive cost.

2. Economies of scale for extrusion.

The capacity of an extrusion line depends on the type of filament yarn or staple fibre produced. The range is from less than 100 tons a year of yarn or staple fibre, to over 500 tons of yarn or 2,000 tons of staple fibre. Given the need for replication of equipment, the scope for substantial economies for extrusion is limited. Nevertheless, in spite of it being necessary to duplicate machinery in order to increase capacity, some economies can be achieved. The following figures obtained from a company in the industry relate to the extrusion of a man-made fibre yarn in three plants. The economies in fixed capital costs which are based on the replacement costs of fixed assets, are accounted for by economies of scale for some subsidiary processes, the costs of buildings and other facilities. Sources of economies for operating costs are longer runs (involving proportionately less time for setting up machines) and spreading overhead costs over a larger throughput. The estimates provide some evidence of economies, even where a substantial part of a plant has to be replicated. But there are qualifications to estimates of this type because the product mix of different plants varies.

Table 6.5 *Fibre Extrusion Costs* (1966).

Capacity of Plant (000 tons of yarn per year)

	4	15	40
	Index of Costs		
Operating costs	108	100	86
Capital costs	114	100	82
Total costs (excl. polymer)	110	100	86
Cost of Polymer [a]	100	100	100
Total costs (incl. polymer)	106	100	91

(a) It was assumed for the purpose of this table that there were no economies of scale for polymer production or for materials consumption. If the length of runs were related to the scale of plants there would be some economies of scale for material costs, because yields are higher for long runs. For one manufacturer, yields varied between 86% for short runs and 91% for very long runs, but when assessing the costs of 'waste' material, allowance has to be made for reprocessing the material.

3. Economies of scale for polymerization and extrusion

Table 6.6 brings together our estimates of scale economies for polymerization and extrusion of yarn. It should be noted that in the first part of the table no allowance is made for the large economies of scale for the initial chemical processes. Nevertheless substantial economies are shown for outputs up to 40,000 tons a year. In the second part of the table we have allowed for economies for the production of the chemical materials.

Table 6.6 *Polymerization and Extrusion - Costs and Scale* [a]
(Averages for Nylon 6 and Acrylic Filament Yarn)
Capacity of Plant (th. tons of yarn per year)

	4	20	40	80
Part 1	Index Numbers of Average Costs			
Polymerization	140	100	80	65
Extrusion	112	100	90	89
Total (excl. materials)	117	100	89	87
Materials	100	100	100	100
Total (incl. materials)	114	100	92	90
Part 2				
Materials [b]	180	100	75	65
Total (inc. materials)	132	100	83	79

(a) A source of small economies, not allowed for in these estimates, is that a firm with a large output may be able to operate a recovery plant for chemicals from waste.

(b) These estimates are based on information obtained from industry sources. They do not allow for any economies of scale for the production of basic materials such as benzene or phenol. Economies of scale would apply for outputs above 80,000 tons a year for the production of materials.

The largest economies of scale are for the initial chemical processes, and a company can achieve these without undertaking polymerization and extrusion processes at the same site. Also, a company dividing its capacity for making polymers and extrusion between two plants with a capacity of 20,000 tons, instead of one plant with a capacity of 40,000 tons, would suffer a smaller cost penalty than these figures suggest because it could concentrate the production of different varieties of fibre at different plants, and thus not increase the total number of lines it operates.

4. Vertical integration of plants

Data on the costs of separating the production of chemicals and polymerization and extrusion processes were not obtained. The main costs would be any extra costs for transport and stocks. These would depend upon the distances involved and the location of the market. Some fibres, particularly those produced in large quantities, can be extruded without being solidified, i.e. the drying and melting processes are eliminated. If polymerization and extrusion are separated this short cut can not be used.

5. Production of a number of fibres

Polymerization plants for the production of different fibres are distinct i.e. a common plant cannot be employed. It is possible to extrude some fibres on plant designed for the extrusion of other fibres, but firms do not usually do this. The sources of economies for the production of a range of fibres, where this increases total output are that a larger factory is needed and that some factory and other overheads can be spread.

V. Size of firms

1. The overall costs of firms

No data were collected from firms to illustrate the importance of overhead costs which are affected by the size of firms, rather than the size of plants. But one clue that economies of this type could be important was obtained from a subsidiary of an overseas company operating in the U.K. It considered that taking up the under-utilized capacity in its service sections which could be achieved at a larger scale, was the principal source of economies for increasing the scale of its U.K. operations.

2. Research, development and promotion

The level of expenditure of the industry on R & D has been described above. It is worth noting a difference in the policy of the leading firms. I.C.I. spends more on research than Courtaulds and has a more aggressive policy for research and development. Courtaulds' spending is limited by its smaller output of synthetic fibres. A firm with a small share of the market might be able to avoid disadvantages of its size for R & D by association with an overseas company, or a major chemical company which could provide know-how.

The industry's promotion expenditure is aimed to build up consumer demand for new and improved fibres and to retain the markets once developed. It is possible that a firm with a relatively small output could sell substantial quantities of a synthetic fibre to the trade without promotion expenses once markets were developed, but it would be excluded from some markets because of the use of brand names. Alternatively a firm entering the market might be able to find a new use for the fibre or even develop a variety of the fibre with new and valuable properties. If the firm entering the market were a textile company it could itself use the fibre. Finally, the entry of a new firm may be facilitated because customers wish to have alternative sources of supply.

The four firms which manufacture on a relatively small scale in the U.K. are subsidiaries of overseas companies and avoid the full costs of R & D, but their overseas connections are of limited advantage for the promotion of their fibres in the U.K. market. One advantage which firms have, which an independent firm with a small share of the market would not have, is the ability to sell a range of fibres. The parent companies, or other subsidiaries, make fibres elsewhere which the subsidiaries market in the U.K. They can thereby offer a wider range of fibres, and this is claimed to be an advantage for spreading selling costs and providing advice to customers.

VI. Vertical integration

Courtaulds' man-made fibre interests developed from its interests in silk weaving, but by the 1920's the production of fibres for processing by other textile firms accounted for most of its production. However, during the inter-war period the company did acquire some textile firms to promote the use of rayon by example. In the past ten years there has been a much more marked trend towards vertical integration. Courtaulds has taken over and built up its textile interests, so that it now controls about 20% of the cotton and allied trades, and I.C.I. has promoted integration in the cotton industry by providing finance for a small group of textile companies. There has been a mixture of motives for these moves, including a desire to modernise and rationalise the textile industries, and to expand and control outlets for fibres.

The main sources of net economies and advantages for full vertical integration are:

(a) There is some scope for technical economies for integration achieved by planning and siting operations at the most efficient site. By siting new plant near fibre production units, transport costs are reduced. In practice the division of processing between independent fibre and textile companies is not necessarily the most efficient, but the scope for economies is very limited.

(b) Control of outlets was one factor which enabled Courtaulds to break into the nylon market held by I.C.I. and will facilitate its entry into the polyester market. It had a sufficiently large controlled market to enable it to commence production on a substantial scale, and its textile subsidiaries could not easily reject the products even if initially they were of inferior quality. (One of the initial costs for a firm starting production of a fibre is the low quality of the product). Even if it is conceded that control of outlets was a source of advantage for entry into fibre production, however, this is not argument for *permanent* vertical integration.

(c) Textile processing has been, on average, a less profitable activity (in terms of return on capital) than chemical processing. Synthetic fibre producers probably make substantial profits on the chemicals they manufacture, and on their fibre production. An advantage of vertical integration, or association, is that these profits (which are in part attributable to the oligopolistic structure of the fibre industry) may be used to speed up investment and innovation in textile processing. The advantages of this type of investment vary for different fibre producers. Some have more experience of textile processing than others, and can therefore control any textile companies they acquire more efficiently.[1] Another source of difference is in the scope for expansion elsewhere. A broadly based chemical company, such as I.C.I., generally has scope for expansion in many directions. It is also worth noting that future international competition may reduce the profitability of synthetic fibre production and hence the availab-

(1) Differences in the ability to control new subsidiaries are probably quite small. The fibre producers which have interests in textile processing do not usually replace the existing management.

ility of funds for investment in the textile industry, among others.

At this point it is well to relate the scale of the fibres industry to that of the British textile industries generally.

1968	£m.	%
Total sales of man-made fibres	300	20
Less exports plus imports	−30	−2
U.K. usage	270	18
Plus — cotton and wool	165	11
	435	29
Value added in the textile trades	680	45
Value added in the clothing trades	380	25
Total	1,495	100

(d) Some of the textile development of fibres affects textile processing - crimping is one example. If the fibre producer controls the textile processing stage he can retain all the profits attributable to developments he makes on this side of the business.

(e) There may be advantages if the firms engaged in making and processing fibres are under common ownership because they can reach agreements more readily.

(f) Another important advantage of vertical integration to a company is to give scope for manipulating prices. We have already shown that there are substantial economies of scale, and there are also large economies for increasing the degree of capacity utilization up to full capacity operation. A fibre producer who controls his customers can use differential pricing, and concentrate low prices — reflecting marginal costs — where there is most scope for expansion.

(g) The textile side of a vertically integrated firm could expect to receive a limited service from other fibre producers — thus reducing its selection of fibres. This provides a vertically integrated firm with an inducement to make a wide range of fibres, but this may involve a loss of economies of scale.

In addition to the points noted, there are effects of vertical integration which apply to vertical integration generally — improved stock control, some loss of the stimulus of competition, problems of management, etc.

VII. Conclusions

For those who attribute advantages to competition there is much in favour of the existing structure of the synthetic fibres industry in the U.K. Six firms compete, but the source of firms' competitive strength varies, I.C.I. had an early start and has a strong R & D position, Courtaulds has the advantage of controlling large markets for fibres, and the subsidiaries of overseas companies can draw on the experience and expertise of their parent organisations. But the competitive position of I.C.I. and Courtaulds against the major overseas producers, might possibly be improved by merger or cooperation. A larger share of world markets would facilitate I.C.I's policy of heavy expenditure on research.

Table 6.7 *Summary of Minimum Efficient Scale for Synthetic Fibres*

New Plants[b]	Output (tons per year)	% of U.K. market[a] A B	% increase in total costs per unit at 50% "m.e.s."	% increase in value added per unit at 50% of "m.e.s."
Manufacture of polymer	80,000 (at least)	33 66	5%	23 %
Extrusion of filament yarn	40,000 (at least)	16 33	7%	11%
Combined manufacture of polymer & extrusion	40,000 (at least)	16 33	7%	10%

Companies: Measures of the economies for large firms were not obtained.

(a) The figures are given in relation to 'A' the total U.K. market for synthetic fibres in 1968, and 'B' the U.K. market for nylon in 1968. Production of both yarn and staple fibre are included in each case.

(b) Initial costs are ignored. The inclusion of these costs would increase the economies of scale. Similarly selling and distribution costs are excluded. For the purpose of making these estimates, no account is taken of economies of scale in the production of materials. It is assumed that a range of polymers and fibres is made. For the production of single product, say, tyre cord, economies of scale would be greater over the range of output to about 20,000 tons a year and would then be smaller than the economies shown here.

7. Beer[1]

Table 7.1 *Profile of the Brewing Industry*[a]

	1963	% of all manufacturing industry	1968	% of all manfacturing industry	1968 as % of 1963
Number of Employees ('000)	86.6	1.1	86.9	1.1	100
Sales, including excise duty (£m)	723.5	2.6	1116.0	2.8	154
Net Output excluding duty (£m)	218.3	2.0	355.3	2.2	163
Capital Expenditure (£m.)	32.2	3.1	—	—	—

Concentration[b]

Concentration ratio for the 5 largest firms in 1963 — 50.5%

Size of Establishments and Enterprises (1963)				
	Establishments		Enterprises	
Number of Employees	Number	% of Employees	Number	% of Employees
Under 100	405	13	117	6
100 — 749	151	45	62	18
750 — 1,499	15	18	7	9
1,500 and over	11	24	10	67
	582	100	196	100

(a) The Census data includes malting.

(b) Brewing, excluding malting.

I. General Introduction

1. Structure of the industry

In 1967, U.K. output of beer was 31.2m. bulk barrels of which approximately two thirds was draught beer, and one third bottled beer. There were one hundred and ten firms in the trade, and they operated 240 breweries. In 1968 the seven largest firms controlled 75% of production.

The industry exhibits a high degree of vertical integration. Each brewery carries out both the production and the packaging of beer. The brewers themselves malt about one-half of their total annual requirements of malted barley, but their interests in the manfacture of other raw materials are negligible. All firms deliver some of their output with their own transport, and almost all own retail outlets. Slightly less than one-half of the total

[1] This chapter is based on a detailed study of the economies of scale in the U.K. brewing industry recently carried out by T.A.J. Cockerill, which is to form part of a forthcoming book.

number of licensed retail premises in the U.K.are owned by brewing firms, and these outlets account for two-thirds of the total annual volume of beer sales.

2. Production processes

Most brewery operations are of a process type — as for chemicals. At most breweries a batch system of manfuacture is employed, and the numbers, and types of beers produced, do not substantially affect the brewing process. Modern plants produce batches of beer on a 16 or 24 hour cycle, while older plants produce batches less frequently. At the packaging stage, flow-line production is possible using high-speed automatic equipment, particularly for bottling and canning.

3. The dimensions of scale

The main dimension of scale which affects production costs is the total annual output of a brewery. The number of beers produced and the length of production runs at breweries do not affect the unit costs of either brewing or packaging: vessels must be cleaned after the production of each batch, irrespective of the number of beers brewed.

II. The structure of costs

A breakdown of production, transport and excise costs is given in table 7.2. The table shows the importance of excise duty as a component of total costs; it forms well over half of total costs. Total costs for a new plant with a capacity of 0.5m. barrels are shown to be a little less than the typical costs for an existing brewery of the same size. The lower level of labour costs for the new brewery more than off-sets the higher depreciation charge; nevertheless the old brewery has the best return on capital employed because much less capital is employed.[1] It is also worth noting that the difference in labour costs between the old and the new brewery is large in relation to the economies of scale for labour costs shown in table 7.3. A reason for the old plant having higher labour costs, in addition to the greater labour productivity possible on new vintages of equipment, is that most existing plants were expanded through time, and so were not built to take full advantage of their scale, i.e. there was more replication than would exist in plants built to minimize costs, even if the plants incorporated earlier vintages of plant.

III. The economies of scale for breweries

Cockerill's estimates of economies of scale for breweries are summarised in table 7.3. The estimates show large economies of scale. The economies for capital costs result from the use of larger units of equipment at higher

---

(1) An important qualification to this argument applies where an old brewery occupies a valuable site in the centre of a town, and a new brewery is constructed on a relatively cheap site.

Table 7.2 *Structure of Costs for Brewing (1965)*

	Production. Excise Duty, & Distribution Costs[a]	Typical Production Costs[b] per barrel for Breweries with a capacity of 0.5m. barrel	
		Existing Brewery	New Brewery
	%	£	£
Brewery Materials	8.6	2.40	2.40
Direct Labour	7.2	1.53	0.33
Depreciation	2.8	0.45	1.43
Other Costs (including packaging & cleaning materials, power, rates, etc).	12.9	1.86	1.86
Total Production Costs excl. duty	31.5	6.24	6.02
Excise Duty	61.4		
Total	92.9		
Distribution Costs (incl. warehouse costs)	7.1		
Total	100.0		

(a) Source: N.B.P.I. Report No. 13.p.4. (H.M.S.O., 1966).

(b) Data obtained from firms in the industry.

scales of output and are greater for brewing than for packaging. Generally the relationship between the capacity and the cost of equipment follows the 0.6 rule and there is no reason to suppose that the economies for fixed capital costs are exhausted at the size of the largest plant considered. The fall in the index of unit labour costs to an annual output of 1m. bulk barrels reflects the increases in productivity as equipment size is increased, and the ability of employees to operate more than one piece of equipment, but as progressively higher output levels are reached, the behaviour of unit labour costs is erratic because of the need to duplicate certain types of plant.

The unit costs of raw materials depend primarily upon the strength of the beer produced and are not much affected by plant size, and this absence of economies of scale for material costs damps down the overall economies. A feature of the economies of scale in this industry is the extent to which they are also damped down by excise duty. Duty is related to the strength of the brew and is not affected by the costs of production or the price charged. It is also claimed that there are no significant economies of scale for the "other costs" item in table 7.2. (This includes packaging and cleaning materials and power).

IV. Transport costs

The N.P.I.B. figures given in table 7.2 show distribution costs, including warehousing, to represent as much as 7% of total costs including duty, and

Table 7.3 *Economies of Scale for New Breweries*[a]

(Indices of Unit Costs)

Annual Output Capacity				Total Costs (incl. materials) (excl. excise duty)		Total Costs (incl. excise duty)	
	Capital	Labour	Value Added				
(m. bulk barrels)				average	marginal	average	marginal
0.1	125	191	130	113	—	106	—
0.2	100	100	100	100	87	100	94
0.5	55	60	56	81	68	92	87
1.0	35	48	36	72	63	88	84

(a) The estimates of costs shown were based on information obtained from firms in the industry. The estimates exclude transport costs. For the purpose of making the estimates it was assumed that the output of the breweries was two-thirds draught beer and one-third bottled beer. Data obtained by Cockerill from U.S. companies suggest that scale economies continue beyond a capacity of 1m. barrels.

70% of direct labour costs and depreciation for production. In practice the main determinant of unit transport costs is the quantity of beer delivered per vehicle mile, and this is not systematically related to plant size. The level of unit transport costs incurred by any given plant depends very much upon the characteristics of the market (for example, if the market is highly concentrated, unit transport costs will be low). One of the chief benefits flowing from recent mergers has been the rationalization of distribution systems where breweries which merged served the same area. Transport costs are a source of increased costs where production is concentrated at fewer plants, but the increase in costs can be limited by moving beer in bulk.

V. The size of firms

Very little information about the relationship between the scale of firms and the costs of management, administration, advertising and promotion was obtained. But the main sources of economies for multi-brewery firms appear to be the scope for rationalizing distribution and production facilities, rather than economies for overhead costs.

1. Research and development

Expenditure by the large firms upon research and development forms a very small percentage of their turnover, and they do not seem to have derived any substantial advantages in this area.

2. Selling and advertising costs

Selling costs, excluding advertising, are not important for most firms since the majority of beer sales are through tied outlets. But advertising has become increasingly important in recent years, both in terms of expenditure and probably the effectiveness of advertising, as new beers and channels of distribution – particularly supermarkets – have been developed.

3. Vertical integration

The special features of vertical integration between brewers and tied houses are that:

75

(a) it limits competition and the scope for internal expansion,

(b) it has probably increased investment in houses, and increased total beer consumption.

Table 7.4 *Summary of Minimum Efficient Scale for Beer*

	Output per year	% of U.K. Market[a]	% increase in total costs per unit at 50% of "m.e.s."	% increase in value added per unit at 50% of "m.e.s."
New Breweries	1m. barrels	3%	3% (inc. duty) 9% (exc. duty)	55%

Firms: Estimates of the economies of scale for large firms were not obtained.

(a) Breweries enjoy advantages in their regions, because transport costs are important.

VI. Changes in the structure of the industry

The study of economies of scale in the brewing industry made by Cockerill suggests that there are substantial economies of scale for breweries and that there would be advantages to be obtained by further concentration of the industry through rationalizing production facilities and distribution systems. The extent of rationalization already achieved by concentration of firms in the industry was illustrated by data received from two companies. In one case the company had 4 breweries in 1955, it had acquired 11 more by 1970, but had closed 7 of them. It planned to close 2 or 3 more by 1975, and over the period 1955 to 1975 the average output of its breweries was expected to increase to three times the 1955 level. Another firm expected to increase the average output of its breweries to five times the 1955 level by 1975. This increase was attributable to closing three small breweries which had been acquired, and the expected increase in sales of 150% between 1960 and 1975 most of which was not achieved by take overs.

It is outside the scope of this paper to consider whether further rationalization is best achieved by mergers or by ending the tied house system. Unless the tied house system is abolished, competition alone would bring about rationalization very slowly. Even if the tied house system were abolished the basis for levying excise duty would slow down rationalization because it damps down differences in costs attributable to differences in efficiency.

8. Bread

Table 8.1 *Profile of the Bread and Flour Confectionery Industry*[a]

	1963	% of all manufacturing industry	1968	% of all manufacturing industry	1968 as % of 1963
Number of Employees ('000)	160.2	2.0	155.0	1.9	97
Sales (£m.)	381.1	1.4	475.7	1.2	125
Net Output (£m.)	159.8	1.5	215.9	1.3	135
Capital Expenditure	17.8	1.7	—	—	—

Concentration:

Concentration ratio for the 5 largest firms in 1963 — 71.4%.

Size of Establishments and Enterprises (1963)

Number of Employees	Establishments		Enterprises	
	Number	% of Employees	Number	% of Employees
Under 100	1,099	15	862	10
100 — 749	377	61	122	17
750 — 1,499	25	16	10	7
1500 and over	6	8	9	66
	1507	100	1003	100

(a) In this chapter we have concentrated on the economies of scale for bread baking; no data was obtained for flour confectionery. Consumers' expenditure on bread accounts for about 6% of total consumers' expenditure on food.

I. General introduction

1. Structure of the industry

In terms of the ownership of bakeries, baking is now a highly concentrated industry; the four leading companies and the Co-operative Societies control approximately seventy five per cent of the market. The concentration in the ownership of the industry has occurred since 1940, and has been motivated by the desire of the millers to secure outlets for their flour. This movement was triggered off by Mr. Garfield Weston who acquired a number of bakeries, and imported Canadian flour instead of buying it from British millers. Nevertheless in spite of the concentration of the industry there are still a large number of independent bakeries in Britain.

Although much of the industry is concentrated in terms of ownership, the industry is fragmented in terms of the number of bakeries. The large companies each own many bakeries, and at least two companies operate more than a hundred. The main reasons for the lack of concentration on large bakeries are that bread is a perishable commodity, it is expensive to transport, and there are heavy costs of replacing existing bakeries.

2. *Dimensions of scale*

The main dimensions of scale are the size of bakeries and firms. The initial costs of products are not important.

II. Structure of costs

Table 8.2 gives an average breakdown of the costs of baking. The table illustrates the importance of the costs of materials and of selling and delivery. "Other costs" include depreciation which for one company which operates a large number of bakeries represented only 2% of total costs when calculated on an historical cost basis.

Table 8.2 *The Structure of Costs for Bakeries (1964)*

	%
Flour	40
Salaries and Wages (excl. selling and delivery)	15
Selling and Delivery Expenses	27
Other Costs	15
Profit Margin	3
Total	100

Source: N.B.P.I. Report No 3 p. 6. (H.M.S.O. 1965).

III. Bakeries

Some approximate estimates of the capital costs and labour requirements for *new* bakeries were obtained from a multiple bakery group, and these estimates indicate substantial economies of scale. The data relate to the baking of bread, and exclude the cost of equipment for making other confectionery. For the purpose of making the estimates, it was assumed that the oven of a bakery with a capacity of 9/10 sacks would be hand operated while that for 18/20 sacks would be fully automatic. The number of operatives exclude overhead staff for whom there would be savings with increasing scale, and delivery staff. As a guide to the relative size of bakeries, a bakery with a capacity of twenty sacks an hour could produce sufficient bread for a population of 300,000.

There are two factors which damp down the economies for capital and direct labour costs, the costs of materials for which there are some small economies for bulk deliveries, and the diseconomies of scale for distribution costs. The larger the output of a bakery, the larger the area served, other things being equal, and so delivery costs tend to increase with scale.[1] The cost of flour and distribution represent 67% of sales revenue (see Table 8.2).

Comparative costs for new bakeries are especially hypothetical as the experience of one of the larger companies was that it lost money on all its

78

Table 8.3 *Costs and Scale for Bakeries*

Capacity of Ovens per hr. (Sacks of flour)	Approximate Potential Output per hr.		Index of Total Capital Cost	Index of Capital Costs per unit of output	Number of Operatives	Index of Direct Labour Costs per unit of output
	Sacks	Index				
9/10	7½	100	100	100	11	100
18/20	18/20	240/267	160/165	77/80	18	61—68
27/30	27/30	360/400	190/200	58/61	20	45—50

new bakeries in the early years of operation. The company only replaced bakeries where demand exceeded capacity or where a redevelopment scheme required the demolition of an existing bakery. Two explanations claimed for the relatively high costs of new bakeries were the provision of elaborate welfare facilities at new bakeries — required in part to attract and retain staff — and the inclusion of plant in new bakeries which ensures a consistently high quality of bread and which is not fully reflected in the price. The main explanation is the capital cost of a new bakery compared to the written down historical cost of an old one.

IV. Firms

1. The costs of administration

Some information about regional and national administration costs was obtained from a firm of multiple bakers. The costs which included the salaries of the accounts, sales and technical executives and advertising costs, represented only 1 per cent of total costs, or about 0.05p. per loaf. Off-setting this relatively small cost, there are advantages for such a group compared to an independent bakery, for the provision of technical expertise, and for the comparison of the operating performance of bakeries. Also the head office performs some functions, including the provision of finance, and the designing and planning of new or replacement plant which would otherwise have to be done at each bakery, or have to be bought out.

2. Buying

Multiple bakers are able to obtain materials and some items of plant and vehicles at a lower cost than independent bakers. However, flour is the main raw material and, as two of the largest groups are controlled by millers, it is difficult to make any meaningful comparisons of costs for this item.

3. The position of independent bakeries

In this industry there are a number of forces enabling independent firms

(1) Where a bakery can increase its share of a market, for example by increasing the number of homes in a street to which it delivers, there are likely to be economies for distribution costs.

with small bakeries to compete. Independent firms can operate profitably by using written down plant, by providing fewer fringe benefits such as pensions schemes, increased holidays for long service, five day weeks, sick-pay schemes, protective clothing, canteens etc. for employees. Most of the independent firms have 'tied' outlets, shops and/or delivery rounds, and in some cases they can charge a higher price for their bread because of quality differences.

Table 8.4 *Summary of Minimum Efficient Scale for Bakeries*

Scale		% of U.K. market	Increase in costs per unit[a] at 50% of the ''m.e.s.''		
			including materials and delivery costs	excluding delivery, including materials	excluding materials and delivery costs
New bakeries	30 sacks an hour (suffici- ent to serve a population of 500,000 people)	1%	7.5%	15%	30%

Firms: it was not possible to quantify the effects of the scale for firms.

(a) It is assumed that there are no scale effects on materials or delivery costs.

9. Soap and Detergents

Table 9.1. *Profile of the Soap and Detergents Industry*

	1963	% of all manufac- turing industry	1968	% of all manufac- turing industry	1968 as a % of 1963
Number of Employees (th)	21.8	0.3	16.8	0.2	77.1
Sales £m.	140.8	0.6	184.9	0.6	131.3
Net Output £m.	56.4	0.4	68.2	0.4	120.9
Capital Expenditure £m.	4.2	0.4			

Concentration

Concentration ratio for the five largest firms in 1963 — 82.7%

Size of Establishments and Enterprises (1963)

Establishments			Enterprises		
Number of Employees	Number	% of Employees	Number of Employees	Number	% of Employees
Under 100	156	14.2	Under 100	143	12.2
100 — 299	13	11.0	100 — 299	11	9.7
300 — 1499	9	30.3	300 — 749	3	5.6
1,500 and over	4	44.5	1,000 and over	4	72.5
	182	100.0		161	100.0

I. General Introduction

1. Structure of the industry

The importance of, and degree of concentration for the main groups of products made by the industry in 1965 are shown in table 9.2. The only major product groups which are not dominated by the two leading firms are toilet soaps and liquid detergents, and the third leading company, Colgate Palmolive, now has a substantial share of the market for these products.

2. The processes of production

The first step in the traditional sequence of operations for soap production is the boiling of fats in a 'kettle'. The fats are then separated by the addition of salt into neat soap, and a residue which contains glycerine, a by-product.[1] These processes have a cycle time of about 24 hours. The neat

---

(1) A continuous process can now be substituted for the batch kettle process.

Table 9.2. *The Structure of the Soap and Detergents Industry*

Product Group	% of industry sales in 1965[a]	% of the market held by Unilever and Proctor & Gamble
Hard soap and flakes	10	90
Soap powders	30	95
Toilet soaps	15	50
Synthetic powders	30	95
Synthetic liquids	15	60
	100	

Source: N.B.P.I. Report No. 4 (H.M.S.O., 1965.)

(a) Since 1965, sales of synthetic liquids have increased as a proportion of total sales, and sales of synthetice powders have increased relative to soap powders.

soap is next run off into a 'crutcher', or mixing machine, where 'builders', colouring, and perfume are added. During the final processes the soap is dried, extruded into bars, cut and shaped as tablets of the appropriate length and packed. There are about fourteen firms in the U.K. which make neat soap for the manufacture of toilet soaps. The many other firms which make toilet soap buy neat soap and carry out the mixing, extrusion and packaging operations.

The sequence of operations is similar for other soap and detergent products, but for liquid products, the relatively expensive drying processes are avoided, and for some products for industrial uses the production processes are simpler because the quality specifications, as to the size of the granules of powder and the ingredients, are not as high. These differences in processes are reflected in the structure of the industry: there are many more firms making liquid detergents and products for industrial customers, than firms making synthetic powders for domestic use.

3. The dimensions of scale

For production and marketing the main dimensions of scale are the output of each product, the output of groups of products for which the same machinery can be used and/or to which advertising costs relate, the size of factories, and the overall size of firms.

II. The structure of costs

The following is an approximate breakdown of the costs of a synthetic detergent powder made on a large scale. The costs shown are representative for the heavily promoted products sold by the industry, but the margin for company overheads and profits varies for different products and through time. The leading companies sell some brands without heavy promotion costs and many of the smaller firms compete without heavy promotion expenditure. Also for products sold to industrial customers, including laundries, promotion expenditure is a relatively small item of costs.

	Approximate percentage breakdown of costs of a synthetic detergent powder (1967)
Materials incl. packaging materials	38
Other production costs	5
Distribution	5
Advertising and other selling costs	20
Company overheads, inc. R. & D., and profit	12
Total — Manufacturer's Price	80
Retailer's Margin	20
Price to the Consumer	100

The outstanding feature of costs for the industry is the high level of selling costs. The National Board for Prices and Incomes found that in '1964 the cost to the two market leaders of advertising all their products under reference was around 12 per cent of their total net selling price, a further 6 per cent was accounted for by promotional expenditure.'[1]

Expenditure on Research and Development represents of the order of 1% of the total world sales of the international groups, but expenditure on R. & D. in the U.K. forms a rather higher proportion of U.K. sales because certain of the groups concentrate some of their R. & D. in the U.K.

III. Initial costs

The development of new products has played a vital part in determining the share of the market held by firms. Proctor and Gamble's share of the U.K. market for soap and detergent powders increased when the firm was first to introduce white synthetic powders, then blue synthetic powders and later enzyme products. Innovations have also affected the shares of the market for other products. The initial R. & D. costs for products are variable and are difficult to isolate, but for very few individual innovations are the specific R. & D. costs more than £100,000. The R. & D. costs for introducing enzyme powders were less than £200,000, and for blue detergent powders they were negligible according to one firm. But another firm commented:

In fact, the introduction of these product categories did involve substantial research and development costs. Successful product innovation, in our experience, normally requires a completely integrated new product concept, and this was so in both these cases. In order to take account of research evidence on changing consumer needs related, amongst other factors, to changes in washing habits, washing machine development and fabric trends, major changes to existing detergent formulations were in-

(1) N.B.P.I. Report No. 4, P. 13. In terms of net output-sales less purchases of materials and fuel-advertising represented 35% of the output of the industry in 1963. (Census of Production 1963). For some products the percentage was much higher.

volved. In other words, it would be wrong to assume that blue colour or the enzyme ingredient, was simply inserted into existing basic formulations with little research effort.

In addition to developing the ingredients for a new product, firms incur initial costs for testing the product, deciding the best size, colour and shape of pack to use and the weight of the contents, and for advertising the product. Initial marketing costs for new products launched by the leading firms are generally much greater than the R. & D. costs, but the launching costs depend upon the policy of the company launching a product, whether the product is given a new brand name or an amended version of an existing name, and whether it is a new type of product. An illustration of launching costs is provided by the recent introduction of enzyme brands: the leading firms have each spent more than £1m. advertising an enzyme brand.

One estimate of initial marketing costs obtained was that it would cost a new entrant about £1m. to 'buy' a 10% share of the synthetic detergents market in the U.K., and for each successive new entrant the costs would rise because of the reluctance of retailers to stock additional brands. It was not possible to obtain an estimate showing the relationship between advertising expenditure and the share of the market obtained — the advertising expenditure required to buy a 5%, 10% or 20% share of the market. But if a firm attempts to win a limited share of the market for an existing type of product, it is plausible that there are increasing returns for advertising up to the level at which sufficient customers are asking for a product for a substantial proportion of retailers to stock the product. (It may be more realistic to say that a substantial proportion, perhaps 80%, of potential retailers of the product, may have to be convinced that the promotional expenditure will be sufficient to attract enough custom for them to stock the brand, in order to get the best return from advertising).

At least in theory it would be possible to launch a new type of product with little advertising, but this would mean a slow build up of demand, and leave greater scope for other firms to capture a large share of the market. If a firm were launching a new brand of an existing product it could attempt to market it by charging lower prices or selling 'own brands' to large retailers or voluntary retail chains, instead of advertising. But in this industry the leading manufacturers compete for this market: they sell their advertised products at lower prices when sold without their brand names. In certain trades, domestic appliances is one example, some of the leading firms are unwilling to do this.

IV. Production

The main dimension of scale which affects production costs is the output of products which can be made in a plant. The production of a range of brands does not substantially increase production costs because most distinctions, such as colouring, fragrence and enzymes, can be introduced late in the sequence of production.

We obtained the following estimates of costs for some items of new soap and detergent plants.

Table 9.3. *Costs for Soap and Detergent Plant (1967)*

Output tons per year	Vacuum Dryers & Mixers for Soap Plants		Spray Dryers for Detergent Plants	
	£(th)	Capital charges[a] per lb. assuming 70% capacity utilization (p.)	£(th)	Capital charges[a] per lb. assuming 70% capacity utilization (p.)
2,500	23	0.5	23	0.5
5,000	30	0.4	26	0.3
10,000	43	0.3	34	0.2

(a) Capital charges are assumed to be 20% of the capital cost.

The costs exclude much of the plant required for making soap, including plant for the initial processes and for processing glycerine a by-product, but there would be economies of scale for most parts of a new soap plant up to an output of at least 10,000 tons — 3 per cent of U.K. output of soap. There would also be economies of scale for direct labour up to this level of scale.

If costs for new soap plants with say 10,000 and 50,000 tons a year were compared there would again be economies for capital and labour costs, but because these costs would form a rather small element of costs for a plant with a capacity of 10,000 tons — about 2p. per lb — the economies of about 0.5p. would also be small in absolute terms, and would represent about 2% of the retail price of heavily promoted toilet soaps.

In practice firms use much old equipment and even the leading firms use kettles, etc, which were installed before 1940. Both the capital charges and economies of scale for this plant are smaller than the estimates given so far. Firms with a relatively small output generally have more to gain by continuing to use relatively old plant, and they can buy neat soap from other manufacturers to avoid the processes for which capital costs are highest, and for which the economies of scale are largest.

Table 9.4. gives estimates of the economies of scale for the production of synthetic detergents in new plants. These estimates are based on information obtained from detergent manufacturers and manufacturers of detergent plant. Above 30,000 tons the economies for labour would be small because most of the labour would be operating parts of the plant which would be duplicated above this scale. The absence of substantial economies for warehouses (about 25% of the costs for a new plant with a capacity of 30,000 tons) and for some other parts of the plant, would also limit the economies for capital costs beyond this scale.

A feature of the estimates in table 9.4 is the relatively low level of costs attributable to labour and overheads. In view of the small proportion of costs which are direct labour and for factory overheads, it is unlikely that economies of scale for production costs are more than a supporting factor contributing to the very high degree of concentration in the industry. It is also

Table 9.4. *Production Costs and Scale for Detergents*

Output of detergent powders (th. tons a year)	10	30	70
	Percentage of Costs.		
Raw materials	91	90	89
Direct labour	4	2	1.8
Overheads incl. capital charges	13	8	6.5
Index of factory costs	108	100	97.3

worth noting that if the position of a new entrant and an established producer are compared, if the new entrant can jump to a position of holding, say, 15% of the market, by advertising, the size of the units of plant which he installs might not be much different from those of an existing producer with a larger share of the market (who built up his capacity over a period of time.)

V. Distribution

Distribution costs represent of the order of 3% of sales of soap and detergents, and a higher percentage for domestic detergent powders. There are economies of scale related to the size of deliveries to individual customers and a firm with relatively popular brands, or a large number of brands, will obtain more of these economies. But the scope for delivering to wholesalers and the warehouses of large grocery chains limits the importance of economies for delivering to shops. Also a firm may be able to deliver soap and detergents with other products, while for special toilet soap and industrial products, distribution costs form a smaller percentage of sales.

VI. Firms

1. Marketing

Besides creating a market by advertising, the leading firms advertise heavily to retain their shares of the market. Firms repeatedly advertise many of their products and incur heavy promotion expenses partly because purchases of soap and detergent products are made frequently. [1]

Where advertising is essential in order to maintain a share of the market, it forms a source of substantial economies of scale, because there are initial costs of advertising which have to be spread, there are probably increasing returns to promoting an existing brand similar to those for launching a brand which were discussed earlier, and firms which advertise heavily obtain some discounts from the media.

(1) It has been suggested that advertising may reduce other selling costs, that retailers may accept a lower margin for advertised products, and that sales representation can be reduced. This may be true, but to attempt to establish this point by comparing distribution costs and margins for detergents and ice cream, which is a seasonal product, has to be frozen and is sold in relatively small lots, as some writers have attempted, is misleading. It is also claimed that promotion expenditure increases total sales of the type of product to which it relates

2. Research and development

The importance of new developments for changing the share of markets has already been mentioned. Firms with a small share of the market cannot spend as much on R. & D. as the leading firms, who can spread their expenditure over their sales in many countries. The smaller firms have two options. They can virtually cut out R. & D. expenditure and rely on the technical expertise of material and machinery suppliers. This type of strategy is appropriate for some manufacturers of toilet soaps, for which development is slow, and some industrial products. Alternatively the smaller firms can spend a limited amount on R. & D. If a firm which adopted this strategy recruited staff from the leaders and made use of suppliers' expertise, it could probably match many developments made by other firms without much of a time lag, and might occassionally initiate developments itself. It is promotion costs which really prevent firms entering the 'domestic' market with this strategy. Although technically they could follow the leaders' innovations, many firms cannot meet the launching costs, or are reluctant to do so. Also in some cases, such as enzyme powders, patents prevent them from following the leaders.

Table 9.5. *Summary of Minimum Efficient Scale for Soap and Detergents*

	Annual Output	% of U.K. market	Percentage increase in costs at 50% of the 'm.e.s.'	
			total costs per unit [a]	value added per unit [a]
New plant for manufacturing detergent powders	70,000 tons	20%	2.5%	20%
New soap plant	at least 10,000 tons if all processes carried out [b]	3%	n.a.	n.a.

(a) The costs of marketing and distribution are excluded. It is assumed that there are small economies for purchases of materials.

(b) If a firm bought out neat soap, the minimum efficient scale would be less than 10,000 tons.

10. Cement

Table 10.1 *Profile of the Cement Industry*[a]

	1963	% of all manufacturing industry	1968	% of all manufacturing industry	1968 as % of 1963
Number of Employees ('000)	14.2	0.2	14.0	0.2	99
Sales (£m)	84.3	0.3	105.4	0.3	125
Net Output (£m)	40.8	0.4	49.4	0.3	121
Capital Expenditure (£m)	11.2	1.1	–	–	–

Concentration

Concentration ratio for the 5 largest firms in 1963 — 89%.

Size or Establishments and Enterprises (1963)

	Establishments		Enterprises	
Number of Employees	Number	% of Employees	Number	% of Employees
Under 25	15	1	15	1
25–299	37	38	8	5
300–399	7	17		
400 and over	10	44	6	94
	69	100	29	100

(a) The Cement trade as defined for census purposes includes aluminous cements and cement based paints, besides the production of Portland cement.

I. General introduction

1. Structure of the industry

The data given in Table 10.2 show that the cement industry is highly concentrated: one company controls 60% of U.K. output and three companies together control 90% of output.[1] A feature of the structure of the industry as shown in the table, is that Associated Portland Cement Manufacturers Co. (A.P.C.M.) has not in the past operated larger plants on the average than its rivals, in spite of its large share of total U.K. output.

2. Production processes

There are two products in cement manufacture — clinker and cement itself. Clinker is the fusion of chalk or limestone and clay which emerges from a rotary kiln fired by pulverised coal or oil. The clinker-making process (a process-type operation) is continuous and kilns are worked 24 hours a day

---

(1) The extent of concentration is not much affected by international trade, as both imports and exports of cement are very small compared with U.K. output.

Table 10.2 *Structure of the Portland Cement Industry in 1968*[a]

Manufacturer	Home Deliveries of Portland Cement in 1968		Number of Works	Average Output per works
	'000 tons	% of total		'000 tons
Associated Portland Cement Manufacturers Ltd. (A.P.C.M.)	10,435	59	33	316
Tunnel	2,394	14	5	479
Rugby	2,327	13	7	332
Aberthaw (26% owned by A.P.C.M.)	629	4	2	315
Ribblesdale (owned 50/50 by Tunnel and Ketton)	691	4	1	691
Ketton	610	3	1	610
I.C.I.	486	3	2	243
	17,572	100	51	345

Source: N.B.P.I. Report No. 133 (H.M.S.O. 1969)

(a) The larger number of enterprises shown in the Census data is attributable to the wider definition of the trade used for the Census.

with breaks only for maintenance and relining. The clinker is subsequently cooled and stored, to be later ground with a small quantity of gypsum into the fine powder known as cement. The grinding of the clinker into cement can be arranged to coincide with off peak electricity loads. In addition to the clinker-making and milling operations, quarrying and packaging operations are performed at cement works. At most cement plants in the U.K. the full range of operations is carried out, but at a small number of works, clinker is ground but not produced at the site.

3. The dimensions of scale

At nearly all U.K. cement factories a single product — Portland cement — is manufactured. For the bulk of production there is therefore no question of economies arising from reducing variety and achieving long production runs and large outputs of individual products, since variety does not exist. The main dimension of scale for determining economies is simply the output capacity of cement factories.

II. The structure of costs

The costs shown in table 10.3 are for existing works: for new works, capital costs would be higher and labour charges lower. A point worth noting about the costs of production is that raw materials (apart from fuel) are a relatively small part of total costs. In the table they are included in 'other costs'. Material costs are low because the main raw materials used in the production of cement, chalk or limestone and clay, are obtained on the site at most U.K. works. Another feature of costs is the relative importance of fuel and distribution costs. Research, development and advertising expenditure are relatively insignificant for this industry.

Table 10.3 *Average Costs for U.K. Cement Manufacturers in 1966*

	Average Costs per ton		As % of Manufacturing Costs	As % of Total Costs
Manufacturing Costs	£	£		
Kiln fuel	1.01			
Electric Power	0.45	1.45	32	25
Wages & Salaries		0.65	14	11
Maintenance Materials		0.48	11	8
Works Overheads		0.34	8	6
Depreciation		0.30	7	5
Interest at 10% on capital employed[a]		0.70	16	12
Other Costs (including materials)		0.58	13	10
Total		4.49	100	76
Delivery Expenses		1.01		17
Sales Expenses & Containers		0.40		7
		5.90		100

Source: based on data given in N.B.P.I. Report No 38 (H.M.S.O. 1967)

(a) Our estimate of capital employed was based on the book value of capital shown in the companies' accounts.

III. Economies of scale for factories

1. *Estimates of scale economies*

Estimates of economies of scale for cement plants have been published in a United Nations study. Table 10.4 shows the main relationships between costs and scale: substantial economies of scale for labour, fixed capital and overhead costs per unit are indicated, but no economies for materials and fuel. We should expect proportionately small in-process economies for fuel and power, some small reduction in unit costs by spreading the fixed charges for power, and possibly some reduction in costs for fuel to reflect economies in transporting it. We should also expect the overall demand for fuel by a firm to have some small effect on the price paid for fuel. The reasons for expecting these economies were discussed for chemicals, and the same conditions apply to cement.

The following up-to-date estimates of capital costs for new 'green field' cement plants in the U.K. were obtained. The capital costs exclude the cost of offsite equipment and equipment for quarrying. It is also assumed that plants have a single kiln and mill.[1]

(1) Fuel consumption is lower for new plants. Compared with dry process plants of the same size built about 1950, fuel consumption might be as much as 20% lower for a new plant. The improvement in fuel consumption for wet process plants has been smaller of the order 5—10%. Fuel requirements for a new dry process plant are about 20% less than for a wet process plant of the same size, but electric power costs are higher for dry process plants. The reductions in fuel requirements achieved since 1950 are attributable to improvements in design.

90

Table 10.4 (1) *Costs and Scale for Cement Factories*

	Capacity of Works (000 metric tons p.a.)						
	33	66	100	200	400	500	1,000
Fixed investment per ton of capacity [a]							
W. Germany $	48	35	29	24	19		
(index)	(200)	(146)	(121)	(100)	(79)		
U.S.A. $			65	54	45	43	30
(index)			(120)	(100)	(83)	(80)	(56)
Labour Requirements							
U.S.A. Number per 100,000 tons			75	48	32	30	15
(index)			(156)	(100)	(67)	(63)	(31)
Unit Costs per ton of capacity							
W. Germany $	21	17	16	14	12		
(index)	(150)	(121)	(114)	(100)	(86)		
U.S.A. $			22	19	17	16	12
(index)			(116)	(100)	(89)	(84)	(63)

(a) There is a substantial difference between the U.S. and German estimates of capital costs which is accounted for in part by the exclusion from the German data of the costs of land, land clearing, the costs involved in opening up the quarry, the cost of power generating equipment, additional equipment for dust collection, highly automated systems for measuring raw material inputs, and elaborate conveying equipment and storage facilities. These are included in the American figures.

(2) *Breakdown of Unit Costs for two Hypothetical U.S. Works*[b]

Cost	120,000 tons	1,000,000 tons	Difference in Costs per ton	% of Total Savings
	($ per ton)			
Direct labour	3.70	0.90	2.80	32
Direct material and water	0.67	0.67	—	—
Power	2.10	2.10	—	—
Fuel	2.37	2.37	—	—
Indirect labour and overheads	3.37	1.61	1.76	20
Depreciation on fixed capital	4.93	2.53	2.40	27
Interest on fixed capital	3.89	2.00	1.89	21
	21.03	12.18	8.85	100

(b) These American estimates are, of course, based on American relative prices. If it were assumed that U.K. wage rates were about half the American levels, and that this was the only difference in costs — a very crude approximation — then the effect on the index would be quite small because labour costs are a small component of total costs for U.S. plants.

Source: Studies in the Economics of Industry 1. United Nations, New York, 1963.

Capacity (th. tons p.a.)	100	300	600	1,200
Capital Cost £m.	3	7½	12½	22
Capital Cost per ton £	30	25	21	18

The following tentative estimates of the relationship between scale and costs for new U.K. works were based on the U.N. estimates and our discussions with firms in the industry. The importance of the assumptions about the number of kilns and mills installed in works should be emphasized. Also it is assumed that the 2 million ton works is sited on the coast. It would be uneconomic to transport 1 million ton units to an inland site.

Table 10.5 *Estimated Costs*[a] *for New U.K. Cement Works*

Capacity (000)	100	200	500	1,000	2,000
Number of Kilns and Mills	1	1	2	2	2
			Indices of Costs		
Fuel, Power and Materials	100	98	97	96	95
Wages and Salaries	100	70	55	40	35
Depreciation and Return on Capital	100	80	70	58	47
Overheads	100	90	82	75	70
Average Total Costs	100	85	77	69	62
Value Added	100	80	69	58	49
Marginal Cost		70	72	61	55

(a) The costs of transport and selling are excluded.

2. Changes in the technical economies of scale

The technical economies of scale in the cement industry have increased as maximum capacity of new kilns, the most important item of capital equipment, has risen from 150,000 to 1 million tons during the past ten years.[1]

3. Construction times

We obtained some information about the length of time it takes to construct cement works. One firm estimated that the minimum time required to plan and construct new cement works on green field sites is about 2 years, including 5 months for obtaining planning approval. It was claimed that the time needed is not much affected by the size of the works although the experience of this firm did not extend beyond works with a capacity of 600,000 tons. Thus building a larger plant on a green field site does not apparently involve a penalty in terms of interest on capital tied-up in plant in the course of erection. However it is generally possible to expand the capacity of an existing works more rapidly than to build on a green field site. One company was able to expand the capacity of one of its works from 300,000 to 600,000 tons in only 8 months.

(1) It is the general experience in process industries that it is desirable to have at least two units of such items of equipment as kilns and furnaces to provide flexibility for contingencies, such as breakdowns and relining. In the cement industry itself, time lost through breakdowns etc. represents 5% of capacity per annum.

IV. Distribution costs

Distribution costs represent as much as 17% of total costs for cement (Table 10.3) When considering the relationship between unit costs and scale the following points are relevant.

(a) As the raw materials for cement production (apart from fuel) can often be obtained locally, the increased costs of supplying distant markets from a large works are not offset by lower transport costs for raw materials, as occurs in oil refining and many other process industries. But some offset to higher transport costs for a single large plant may be obtained by siting the the single plant so as to use the raw materials which are of the highest quality, and are most accessible. Account also has to be taken of the effect of the choice of a site on fuel costs. There are important differences in fuel, and particularly coal, prices at different locations.

(b) An approximate guide to the costs of transporting cement is that for large regular consignments of 500 tons, the rail freight is approximately 15/- per ton per 100 miles. This rate excludes the cost of loading and unloading. (The use of small tankers to deliver from a coastal works to a market which can be reached by sea reduces transport costs in some cases.)

Transport costs are an important factor influencing the location and size of cement works. If the industry were to be rebuilt from scratch, these costs would justify the siting of works at, say, 5 sites spread across the country but in practice capacity is built up over time as demand increases. Nevertheless, for the purpose of achieving the technical economies of scale, the production of cement should be concentrated on not more than 10 sites in the long run.

V. Firms

1. Past performance

There are two sources of data on the past performance of companies. Evidence submitted to the Restrictive Practices Court and data from company accounts.

Some evidence submitted to the Restrictive Practices Court suggests that differences in costs for firms are not related to scale. It was stated that 'the range of costs in the industry is small, there being a 3% difference between the highest and lowest average costs of the six largest manufacturers. Moreover the makers who have the highest costs vary from year to year: no one maker appears always as the highest cost producer nor does any one maker always appear as the lowest cost producer.[1] Similarly the comparison of return on capital[2] which we made did not show any consistent relationship with scale.

(1) Restrictive Practices Reports 2, 1960–61.

(2) The rates of return on capital were calculated from data in published company accounts. For this purpose capital was taken at the valuation shown in the accounts. The period covered was 1958 to 1968.

It might be expected that comparisons of this type would reflect the existence or absence of economies of scale in this industry because it produces a relatively homogeneous product and prices are controlled by agreement. The comparisons are therefore relatively free of differences attributable to differentiation of products and price differences. There are, however, other important factors influencing costs and profitability besides the size of firms, and these differences may obscure any relationship between size and profits.

(a) The company with the largest share of the market has a less than average output per works (Table 10.2). (There might be economies for managing and operating a number of plants, but some of the smaller companies may have offset these economies by operating larger plants.)

(b) With price agreements operating throughout the country, the smaller firms can concentrate output in areas with a relatively high level of demand, while the A.P.C.M. continues supplying less concentrated and less profitable markets.[1]

(c) Freedom from restrictive practices imposed by employees has been a source of advantage for some of the smaller firms in the past.

(d) For at least one firm new plants were the least profitable in terms of return on capital (measured in book terms). The main reason for this was that the capital cost of the older plants had been largely written off. This reduced the annual charge for depreciation and interest on capital. (The resale values of some old plants is low, but in other cases the land is valuable for redevelopment purposes). A firm which expands relatively rapidly might thus be expected to have a relatively low average return on the book value of its capital, other things being equal.

These factors influencing comparisons[2] mean that past estimates of costs and return on capital cannot be used to provide a guide to the economies of scale for large firms in this industry. The absence of a positive relationship can be explained by other factors obscuring any relationship with size.

(1) Although a 'basing point' system of pricing is employed in the industry, there is in effect a transport subsidy for the more distant customers. Cement Makers' Federation Agreements. Restrictive Practices Court Reports 2, 1960—61 p. 242.

(2) Yet other factors which affect the comparisons are that Tunnel Portland Cement is part owned by a Danish Cement company and the Ketton Portland Cement Co. is a subsidiary of a company operating in the engineering and metal industries. These links may provide some advantages of scale for acquiring technical knowledge, managerial experience and raising finance. A.P.C.M. revalued its fixed assets in 1960 and Rugby has made substantial acquisitions of other companies in recent years. An additional qualification to the comparisions of return on capital, in this case, is the inclusion of investment in overseas countries. The return on these investments depend partly on political and other factors in the countries concerned, and the geographical distribution of investment varies for the three main companies.

2. Non-technical factors

The information we obtained about non-technical factors was limited, but marketing and R & D expenditure are relatively small in this industry.

3. The future

The A.P.C.M. is at present constructing a plant with a capacity of 4 million tons a year, and it plans to phase out at least nine of its existing works. Thus it will in future be taking advantage of its large share of the market to obtain the technical economies of scale for large plants — the main source of economies of scale in this industry.

VI. Summary

Table 10.6 *Summary of Minimum Efficient Scale for Cement*

	Output (tons per year)	% of U.K. Market	Percentage increase in costs at 50% of 'm.e.s.'	
			total costs per unit	value added per unit
Plants	2 million	10	9%[a]	17%[a]

Firms: We have been unable to measure the extent of economies of scale for firms.

(a) Transport costs have been excluded: these are substantial and are very important for determining the location and size of plants. The differences in costs for plants of 1 and 2 m. t.p.a. capacity are based on the assumption that there are two kilns at each plant. If there was only one kiln at the plant with a capacity of 1m. tons, the economies would be smaller.

ADDENDUM

Information obtained from the A.P.C.M., since the manuscript was sent to the press, confirms that there are large technical economies of scale for new cement works. Significant economies for capital, fuel and operating costs extend to new plants with a capacity of 4m. tons.

11. Bricks

Table 11.1. Profile *of the Brick Industry*[a]

	1963	% of all manufacturing industry	1968 (Estimate)	% of all manufacturing industry	1968 as % of 1963
Numbers of Employees ('000)	35.9	0.5	38.0	0.4	92
Sales (£m)	72.1	0.3	96.7	0.2	134
Net Output (£m)	44.9	0.4	58.9	0.4	131
Capital Expenditure (£m)	4.4	0.4	–	–	–

Concentration

  Concentration ratio for the 5 largest firms in 1963 — 51.9%

(a) The data included in the profile is for Flettons and non-Flettons which are not distinguished in the Census and is for firms with 25 or more employees. Separate details of the size of establishments and firms in the brick trade are not available from the Census.

I. General Introduction

1. Structure of the industry

The brick industry is similar to the cement industry in several respects: the market for its product is the construction industry, process operations are used and the cost of transporting products to customers is an important item of costs. Also international trade in bricks is negligible. On the other hand the variety of bricks produced is greater, and the industry is much more fragmented. About 8,000 m. bricks are produced annually in the U.K. and the production of clay bricks, 93% of the total, is divided between 'Flettons' and 'non-Flettons' in the ratio of three to four. The raw material for Flettons is Oxford clay which has a unique combination of properties ideal for mass producing bricks of normal building quality, but the main advantage is that less external heat has to be added in the kiln — the normal fuel requirement is 1½ cwt. of coal per 1,000 bricks compared to about 6 cwt for other types of bricks. Fletton production is highly concentrated, in terms of the number of companies and works, compared to the production of non-Flettons. London Brick Co. produces 70 per cent of the Fletton bricks and two other producers make the remainder. In 1967 the ex-works price of Fletton 'common' bricks was £5 per 1,000 and for Fletton facing bricks £9 and upwards — the difference in costs is probably smaller than the difference in price implies.

  In this chaper we have concentrated on the production of non-Flettons. There are approximately 400 firms manufacturing non-Fletton bricks in the

U.K. and there are more than 500 non-Fletton brickworks. The largest 23 firms accounted for nearly 50% of production in 1967.[1] In 1967 the price of non-Fletton common bricks was about £9, and non-Fletton facing bricks ranged in price from £12 to more than £25 per thousand.

2. Processes of production

The main processes of brick production are the formation of bricks by extrusion, pressing, or moulding, and the firing of bricks in a kiln. There are also subsidiary processes for quarrying, preparing clay, mixing in any colouring and for transporting the clay and the bricks. The type of clay, the colouring added, the temperature, the atmospheric condition in the kiln, and the position and length of time in the kiln are the main sources of variation in quality of bricks. But the increase in costs for making a variety of bricks at a brickworks appears to be marginal as the first copy costs are negligible for different types of bricks, and the set up costs for a change of brick are generally small.

3. The dimensions of scale

As the output of individual products and length of runs do not significantly affect costs, the main dimensions of scale for purposes of considering the economies of scale are the output of brickworks and firms.

II. The structure of costs

The costs of production for two works are shown below in some detail because they illustrate differences caused by the age of plant. Such differences occur in all industries but they are particularly marked for such industries as bricks and cement because for new works, capital costs represent a large proportion of total costs, and because technical progress has not made existing plants uneconomic.

Table 11.2. *Brick Production Costs*[a] (Including depreciation and excluding interest on capital)

	Old Works[b]	New Works[b]
	%	%
Claygetting	2.6	2.6
Fuel and Power	31.5	28.6
Wages etc.	41.4	20.1
Repairs	9.6	10.5
Rates	2.6	2.8
Works Office Expenses	5.5	5.6
Depreciation	6.8	30.0
Total Works Costs	100.0	100.0

(a) Total works costs per unit are approximately the same for the two works.

(b) The new works has two kilns and a capacity three times that of the old works which was built some forty years ago.

Source: A company in the industry.

(1) N.B.P.I. Report No. 47, H.M.S.O., 1967

The main points to note about costs are the low level of material costs and the importance of wages, fuel and power, and, for the new plant, depreciation. If a charge was included for interest on capital, costs for the new plant would be much higher than for the old plant.

III. The economies of scale for brickworks.

Kilns are the most expensive single item of plant in new brickworks[1] and largest new non-Fletton kilns at present being installed have a capacity of about 25 m. bricks a year, a very small percentage of the industry's capacity. If a number of kilns are sited at a works this provides some flexibility; for example, when a kiln has to be slowed down or shut down for maintenance, and to allow an even flow of work. Bricks are in the kiln for from three days to four weeks depending on the quality of the clay and the type of kiln and, if there are a number of non-continuous kilns, these can be loaded and unloaded in turn. For continuous type kilns, two kilns would be sufficient to provide most of the advantages of flexibility but, if the kilns were not continuous, and some kilns of this type are still being built, at least three kilns are required to enable an even flow of production to be maintained. In practice many small firms operate with only one continuous tunnel kiln.

The capacity of most of the other plant and machinery for making bricks is limited. Most works have at least two extrusion plants; and these plants have a maximum capacity of 15 m. bricks a year. There is also replication of pressing plant which has a maximum capacity of 1.5 m: bricks a year. However there would be some economies for capital costs for quarrying plant and for handling plant at large multi-kiln works, but costs for these operations form a small proportion of total costs.

A study of labour requirements made during the early post-war period[2] suggests that there are economies of scale for labour costs up to an output of at least 25 million bricks a year. Estimated minimum labour requirements for three brickworks making wire-cut bricks in a tunnel dryer were:

Output m. bricks per year	5	10	25
Number of Employees	20	33	66
Man hours per 1,000 bricks	10.5	8.5	6.7

Since these estimates were made labour productivity has improved and for new tunnel works, labour requirements of 1.5 men per million bricks produced per year are not uncommon — this is equivalent to 37 men for a works with a capacity of 25 million bricks. There are economies of scale for labour costs because it is possible for operatives to control a number of extrusion lines, pressing machines, etc. simultaneously. Similarly it would not be necessary to duplicate the management if extra kilns were added to a works.

(1) The capital cost of kilns represents about 30% of the capital cost of new brick works of a conventional type. For tunnel kiln works they represent a higher proportion.

(2) National Brick Advisory Council, Paper 1. Brickmaking, Labour Requirements. H.M.S.O. 1947. p. 59.

Some estimates of the minimum efficient scale as defined in chapter two for new brickworks were obtained from Miss P.L. Cook.[1] The estimate for non-Fletton works was 25 m. brick a year. This is a conservative estimate as the figures given below show. The maximum capacity of kilns has risen since Miss Cook made her study, and in the U.S. kilns with a capacity for 100 m. bricks a year have been built.[2] Even for outputs above this level, there would be some small economies of scale for some on-site transport operations, preparing the clay and for management costs.

The following estimates obtained from a leading manufacturer confirm that substantial economies continue up to an output of at least 25 million bricks a year for new kilns.

Table 11.3. *Costs for New Tunnel Kilns*

	10	25
Capacity per year million bricks		
Capital cost of	£th	£th
Kiln	125	200
Associated Works	59	96
Total	184	296
Cost per 1,000 bricks	£	£
Fuel and Power	1.78	1.50
Labour	1.27	0.86
Capital Charges at 15% of the initial fixed capital cost	2.76	1.78
	5.81	4.14
Marginal cost		3.03

The estimates show similar economies of scale to those for process plants discussed in earlier chapters. A point of particular interest, however, about the estimates which were obtained from a very reliable source, was the significant economies for fuel costs.

IV. Flettons

For the production of Flettons the costs of firing bricks in the kiln are much lower and economies which can be achieved for large scale quarrying are relatively more important. Examples of economies which can be obtained for quarrying operations are that the cost of over-burden removed at a large fletton works was about 4p a cubic yard in 1967, against 18p, or more, a cubic yard when done by an outside contractor for a small works. The economies are attributable to the use of very large excavators on double shift working, as against scrapers brought in for a limited period. Similarly the most economical drag-line excavator available at that time had a capacity equivalent to an output of 300 million bricks a year.

(1) Miss P.L. Cook of the University of Sussex made a study of the brick industry during the period 1961/62.

(2) Economies are understood to extend to these larger sizes of kiln but estimates of the size of the economies were not obtained.

Unfortunately no overall estimates of the economies of scale for Fletton production could be obtained.

V. Transport costs

Transport costs also affect the structure of the industry. The additional transport costs for carrying Fletton bricks twenty miles from a works by road would amount to about 20% of the ex-works costs, and to transport them fifty miles would increase costs by about 40%. Transport costs provide some protection for non-Fletton production outside a radius of from 100 to 150 miles outside the Fletton belt which stretches from Bletchley to Peterborough. Transport costs also provide some protection for non-Fletton works when competing with each other, but for expensive non-Fletton facing bricks, the equivalent figures for additional transport costs may be as low as 5–12½%, and 10–20%, and so transport costs are a less important source of protection.

VI. The survival of small works

There are a number of factors besides transport costs which make the continued use of small works economic. Perhaps the main one is the use of old plant and equipment: the cost advantage this can confer is illustrated by the costs given in table 11.2. Also access to clay which gives an attractive finish to bricks, makes it possible to charge a substantially higher price than for bricks with a less attractive finish. The price of some facing bricks is several times that for plain Flettons. There is a local demand for some high cost facing bricks to repair, or make additions, to existing buildings and for new buildings to blend with existing buildings. In some cases it is possible to apply pressure to local authorities to support 'local rural industries' and better liaison with local builders and architects can, it is claimed, be achieved. Apart from local demand there is a demand from architects to use high cost facing bricks when designing some public buildings, etc. In these cases there is scope for architects to take account of aesthetic considerations when making specifications, and the costs of an outside skin of bricks may be small relative to the total cost of the building. Finally there is a demand for some types of bricks for engineering purposes e.g. to line kilns and furnaces (for these uses strength and low porosity are required).

However in spite of these factors which aid the small works, the share of the total market for bricks held by the Fletton manufacturers who operate the large scale works is increasing, and the total number of brickworks in the U.K. has declined from about 1,500 to 550 since 1938. There will clearly be economies and increases in productivity to be achieved by a continuation of this trend.

VII. Firms

The main source of economies for multi-works firms is the spreading of overheads. Evidence obtained from one multi-works company suggested that there are economies for these costs which represented of the order of 7½%

100

of the total costs for this company. The company reduced its central over-heads, including head office administration and selling costs, per unit of output, by 25% when it doubled its output by the take-over of another company. Overheads may increase in stages: once a firm has reached a scale at which it has to carry a number of specialists, there may well be economies for further expansion, but a small firm may simply avoid the overheads such as a company secretary, and a Board Room. It may also avoid some of the 'costs' a large firm may incur in order to grow e.g. making surveys for new sites for quarries and brickworks.

Another advantage of very large scale is that a firm can set up a network of distribution centres to be supplied by rail, but such an operation has to be on a very large scale to justify deliveries by train loads which is necessary to reduce transport costs to competitive levels. Only for the leading Fletton manufacturer is it economic to distribute in this way, and it may be noted that the number of bricks transported by rail has declined in recent years.

A factor aiding small firms is that they know the prices charged by the larger companies and can sometimes be more flexible in their pricing policy for individual contracts. They can take advantage of shortages by raising their prices, and can cut their prices when there is a surplus, but their scope for cutting prices is often very limited because they operate with low profit margins – profits as a ratio of sales. Small firms also claim greater flexibility, and it was suggested that the managers, often the owners of small works, are in some cases more cost conscious – rejects are more carefully selected, defective clay is avoided – and, if special sizes, colours or quantities of bricks are required in very small quantities, their production can be organised more easily at a small works.

Vertical integration

The Coal Board supplies some of its brick works with materials and some steel companies, builders and builders merchants own works and use, or distribute, some of the bricks produced at their brickworks. However, these tied markets represent a very small proportion of the output industry.

VIII. The significance of economies of scale and possible changes to the structure of the industry

In this industry a works of minimum efficient scale is relatively small in relation to the total output of the industry, but there are many existing works below this scale. There are many factors enabling the smaller works to compete, but economies could be achieved by a continuation of the trend towards concentration. Governmental action could assist the brick industry to take advantage of these economies in several ways. It could perhaps limit the number of types of facing brick or the price of the bricks that architects can specify without obtaining special consent when designing public buildings, although such restrictions might conflict with aesthetic considerations. It could provide a subsidy to encourage some of the smaller firms to close their works earlier than they would otherwise close them, along the lines of schemes which have been used in the cotton textile industry. Finally, with the nationalisation of a number of brickworks owned by steel companies, about 10% of the industry's output is within the public sector (including coal). A separate board to control these interest, if this were found desirable on more general grounds, would be able to test fully the advantages and economies of multi-works operation.

Table 11.4. *Summary of Minimum Efficient Scale for Bricks*

	Output	% of U.K. Output	Percentage increase in costs at 50% of the 'm.e.s.'	
			total costs per unit	value added per unit
New Non-Fletton Brickworks	at least 25 m. bricks per year	0.5%	25%	30%

Firms: The economies for multi-works firms depend on the circumstances. Where a specialist firm operates a single brickworks there may be few economies if it was made a part of a larger group, but where large groups merge or grow, there may be significant economies.

12. Steel - An Addendum

Table 12.1 *Profile of the Iron and Steel Industry* [a]

	1963	% of all manufacturing industry	1968	% of all manufacturing industry	1968 as % of 1963
Number of Employees ('000)	269.5	3.4	262.0	3.2	97
Sales (£m)	1,310.4	4.7	1,646.8	4.2	126
Net Output (£m)	405.8	3.7	511.1	3.2	126
Capital Expenditure (£m)	101.6	9.9	—	—	—

Size of Establishments and Enterprises (1963)

	Establishments		Enterprises	
Number of Employees	Number	% of Employees	Number	% of Employees
Under 100	290	4	214	2
100 – 999	194	22	96	12
1000 – 3999	45	34	17	14
4000 – 7499	11	21	4	8
7500 and over	4	19	10	64
	544	100	341	100

(a) The production of tubes, drop forgings, iron castings and wire are excluded.

I. Introduction

Since the interim report was prepared we have obtained additional information about the economies of scale for steel production from the British Steel Corporation, other steel manufacturers, and the manufacturers of 'steel plant. Also a detailed study of the economies of scale for steel production, including finishing operations, [1] has been published.

Before discussing the new evidence on the economies of scale we have outlined the changes in the structure of the industry which have occurred since we published the interim report. We have not described the processes of production or discussed the dimensions of scale because these were dealt with in the earlier report.

Structure of the Industry

Fourteen companies which accounted for 90% by weight of U.K. output of iron and steel products were nationalized in July, 1967, and the British

(1) A.H. Leckie and A.J. Morris, 'The Effect of Plant and Works Scale on Costs in the Iron and Steel Industry', Journal of the Iron and Steel Institute, May, 1968.

Steel Corporation (B.S.C.) was formed. B.S.C. first organized its capacity on a regional basis and has now reorganized on a product basis, with four steel divisions for general steels, special steels, strip mills and tubes. When it was set up, B.S.C. operated 39 crude steel producing plants and many other works producing pig iron, iron castings, and finished steel products, and has since followed an active rationalization policy.[1]

By value the private sector still accounts for one third of the output of the steel industry. There are more than 100 companies and 180 works in the private sector, and its main interest lie in stainless steel, other alloy steels, (these are the fastest growing sections of the industry) and some finished carbon steel products, e.g., bright steel bars, light sections, cold rolled strip and wire rods.

We deal first with the economies of scale for the production of crude steel.

II. Economies of scale for crude steel production

The following estimates of the economies of scale for crude steel prod-uction[2] in blast furnace plants and steel furnaces, supersede the data given in table 4.9 of the Interim Report. The estimates are based on calculations made in 1967. The main source of the economies is the use of larger furnaces as scale is increased, but for steel production there are also economies of scale attributable to higher utilization of furnaces in relation to installed capacity. It is assumed that the size of ingots increases with scale up to an output of 2m. tons, but not above this level. Where the size of ingots is not affected by scale, the economies of scale for forming ingots, and for inspecting and storing them would be small.[3]

The estimates shown in Table 12.2 have already been superseded by the construction of larger blast and steel furnaces. As a consequence of these changes, the maximum annual capacity of new blast furnaces has increased from 1 million tons to about 3 million tons and L—D furnaces to 3m. tons. Our revised estimates, based on information obtained from manufacturers of

---

(1) At first the scope for closing works was limited by the high level of demand for many steel products, and because it takes time to plan reorganization and make investments. In addition there are political and social pressures to keep plants going in certain depressed areas.

(2) The estimates were prepared by Mr. A.J. Morris. They were based on the data collected for the paper by Dr. Leckie and Mr. Morris.

(3) In practice larger ingots tend to be made at the larger works. However, the main factor determining the size of ingots is the use for the ingots — ingots for blooming mills are seldom as large as those for slabbing mills. Also some small works produce some very large ingots, for example for forgings. The size of ingots affects the cost of making ingots and the yield of finished steel as the 'end loss' for large ingots should be less.

Table 12.2 *The Economies of Scale for the Production of Crude Steel*

	Output of Plant — 000 tons per annum				
Output of Iron	250	1,000	2,000	5,000	10000
Number of blast furnaces	1	1	2	4	7
	(Index Number of Costs per ton for Sinter and Blast Furnace Plant)				
Materials [1]	100	70	68	67	67
Net Fuel [2]	100	100	100	100	100
Operating Charges	100	63	62	60	58
Capital Charges [3]	100	57	55	50	48
Total (average cost)	100	83	82	80	79
Output of Steel	250	1,000	2,000	5,000	10,000
Number of steel furnaces:					
Installed	2	2	2	3	6
Operating at one time	1	1	1	2	4
	(Index Numbers of Costs)				
Materials [4]	100	84	81	80	79
Operating Cost	100	67	61	60	60
Capital Charges [3]	100	68	52	41	40
Total (average cost)	100	80	75	73	72
(marginal cost)			74	74	73

(1) The blast furnace material costs decline with increasing size of plant because it is assumed that a small works would receive a number of small ships, rather than a few large ships — this assumption may not apply. For example a small works may be near a quay which can take large bulk carriers, and which is used to supply other works not necessarily steel works. For the purpose of these calculations it is also assumed that special ore selection is practised at small works. No allowance was made for a reduction of port charges for small scale operations. (If a quay would have to be built this could cost as much as £20m., and would be a source of economies of scale. If capital charges were 10%, spreading the capital charges for such a quay over an output of 5m. tons instead of 2m. tons, would reduce costs per ton of steel by about 2%).

(2) There is no evidence that the N.C.B. supplies coal to large works at lower prices than to small works. The costs of making coke and by-products would be slightly reduced as scale increased, and there would be small economies for fuel costs for large furnaces, but no allowance is made for these economies. For some overseas plants there are substantial economies for transporting and buying fuel in large quantities.

(3) Capital charges, depreciation and interest on capital, are included at 15% of the initial capital employed. (Working capital would form a small proportion of the capital for a new plant — less than 20 per cent.)

(4) Materials for steel include iron, scrap, oxygen and other materials. The iron/scrap ratio is assumed to be 70:30. The iron required for a steel plant with an output of, say, one million tons would be approximately 780,000 tons. Materials costs for steel do not move in step with the costs of iron from blast furnaces because there are assumed to be no economies for purchases of scrap — this damps down the economies — and because of of discontinuities attributable to the optimum size of capacity of blast furnaces — about 1.5 million tons when these estimates were prepared.

plant, of the economies of scale for larger installations built in the next few years are:

Output of Iron (m. tons per annum)	2.2	6.5
Number of blast furnace plants	1	2
Size of furnaces	38'	46'
Output of steel (m. tons per annum)	2.9	8.7
Number of steel furnaces		
Installed	2	3
Operating	1	2
Capacity of Furnaces (tons)	265	400
Index of:		
Material costs per ton	100	90 – 98
Operating costs per ton	100	65 – 75
Capital charges per ton	100	65 – 75
Total costs per ton (including capital charges at 20%)	100	82 – 90
(Marginal costs)		73 – 85

A range of estimates for material costs has been given. The estimates showing large economies of scale are for a plant which uses imported ore and coal, and obtains economies for the use of large bulk carriers.[1] The estimates which indicate small economies are for a plant using home produced coal and for which special dock facilities are not provided. The range of estimates for operating and capital costs are attributable to the uncertainty involved in making such estimates.

Some economies for the construction of coke ovens and sinter plants were included in the estimates. Although coke ovens and sinter plants are replicated in a large plant, there are economies of scale for ancillary plant and for installation.

The choice of tonnage for the comparisons effects the economies of scale. If a plant with a capacity to produce 4.3m. tons of steel, instead of 2.9m. tons, was compared to a plant of 8.7m. tons, there would be no benefits through using larger blast furnaces for the larger plant. The reduction in costs per ton of steel between 4.3m. tons and 8.7m. tons would be about half the reduction between 2.9m. tons and 8.7m. tons.

It is important to note that the estimates are based on levels of performance achieved in Japan, where 80 'heats' a day from three L–D furnaces have been obtained.[2] In the U.K., the best rates achieved so far are about half the Japanese rate, but U.K. performance is relatively close to U.S. rates. Japanese performance is better than U.K. (and American) performance because:

(1) It is assumed that material costs are the same for the smaller size of plant whether ore and coal are imported or not. This is an assumption which would not apply in practice.

(2) The number of heats obtained from furnaces is inversely related to size for large furnaces.

106

(a) the materials, coal, iron ore and refractories used in new Japanese works are of superior quality, [1]

(b) the higher level of general efficiency achieved in Japanese steelworks because of their greater experience of operating new plants, a more plentiful supply of adequately trained graduates, and a more adaptable labour force,

(c) the longer product runs common in Japanese steelworks.

If lower levels of output are assumed because of inefficiency and/or shortage of demand for products, this has the effect of increasing the economies of scale because the weighting of operating and capital costs is increased. If it were assumed that best U.K. performance will be two thirds of the Japanese performance, costs for the two plants would be:

Output of steel based on Japanese performance (m. tons)	2.9	8.7
Output of steel based on assumed U.K. performance (m. tons)	2.0	6.0

Indices of:

Material costs per ton [a] (say)	102–106	93–99
Operating costs per ton [a]	150	100–112
Capital charges per ton [a] [b]	150	100–112
Total costs per ton [a]	120–124	96–104

(a) Indices for a plant with a capacity of 2.9 m. tons of steel if operated at Japanese levels of efficiency, are taken as 100.

(b) No allowance has been made for the U.K. plant having a longer life. In Japan process plants tend to be operated at a higher rate and are replaced earlier than in the U.K.

For the smaller plant capital charges would be more than £7 per ton. If there were delays in bringing the plant into production this would again increase capital charges. It is worth noting that the balance of advantage between old plants for which the capital has been written off, and new plants, is affected by the efficiency with which plants are operated — the incentive to replace old plants is reduced if new plants are operated inefficiently, even if plants of older vintage are also operated inefficiently.

It is claimed that the performance of an L–D steel making plant declines if more than three furnaces are included because of the problems involved in materials handling. Thus a steel plant with an output of about 9m. tons given Japanese performance, appears to be the minimum efficient scale for steelmaking with blast furnace plant and L–D furnaces. An output of 18m. tons would be required for the duplication of plants and even at this level of output the reduction in costs, compared to costs for a plant of 9m. tons capacity, would be small.

A qualification to the existence of large economies of scale for steel production, in the future, is the production of steel from pellets — concentrated iron — in electric furnaces. At the present time the cost of pellets and electricity, relative to the costs of ore and coal, mean that this is not a competitive process for the production of steel in very large quantities.

(1) The quality of materials affects the performance of blast furnaces particularly.

If it were, the optimum size of steel plants would be reduced because the maximum capacity of electric furnaces is much smaller than for blast and oxygen furnaces. Even now, costs for direct reduction may be lower than for blast furnace plants for outputs of less than 1 million tons, and so our estimates in table 12.2 exaggerate the economies of scale between a scale of 0.25m. tons a year and a scale of 1 m. tons a year. Also the points made for chemicals that construction of new sizes of plants involves design costs, that other things being equal fewer plants of a large size will be built, and that, if more smaller units were built, there would be economies for producing them, apply to steel. Effects of this type have not been incorporated in the estimates given above.

Another point which is worth noting is that advantage may be taken of the large scale of furnaces when expanding or replacing capacity at existing plants, i.e., a blast furnace plant and two extra L—D furnaces may be added to a works to provide 3 million tons of extra capacity. For expansion the ratio of installed to operating capacity of steel furnaces may not be as high as for plants on green field sites, because existing capacity may be used to even out fluctuations in the availability of plant. Also existing plants have advantage for capital costs because of their depreciated plant, including plant for subsidiary operations. However, the large economies of scale are important when steel plants have to be resited to take advantage of cheaper materials and/or large increases in capacity are required.

III. Economies of scale for finishing

1. Rolling

The economies of scale for finishing are dependent on the type of products produced, which determines the type of finishing process (casting, forging or rolling) used, and the type of equipment employed. In this chapter products involving rolling operations only are considered, but these account for more than 95% of the output of the industry, in terms of tonnage. Some aspects of the economies of scale for forging and the production of steel castings have more in common with the maufacture of iron castings, discussed in the following chapter, than with steel rolling. The optimum size for actual new plants depends, of course, on the available market for any particular group of steel products, besides the economies in costs which can be achieved by large scale operations. Table 12.3 gives estimates of the maximum outputs of rolling mills (either for actual or planned installations) in the U.K. or in the World. Figures for the World are given because the large total outputs of the U.S.A., Japan and Russia are less serious obstacles to the use of large plant. (For readers not fimiliar with the industry we should, perhaps, mention that many products are made by a succession of rolling operations).

Table 12.3 *The Optimum Scale for Rolling Mills*

Type of Mill	Product	Capital Cost per annual ton of capacity for Rolling Mills (Mechanical equipment only)[a] £	Annual Output of largest mill (m. tons)[b]		Total U.K. output (1965)
			U.K.	World	
Slabbing mill	slabs	1.2	4.0	4.5	7.5[c]
Blooming mill	blooms	1.25	3.0	4.0	10.5[d]
Continuous casting machines	slabs	3.1	1.0	1.0	7.5[e]
Continuous casting machines	blooms	3.4	0.5	1.0	10.5[e]
Billet mill	billets	3.1	3.0	5.5	6.0
Hot strip mill	hot—rolled wide strip	4.0	3.5	6.0	4.3
Cold strip mill and temper mill	cold—rolled sheet in coil	3.8	1.0	2.0	3.0
Tinplate mill and temper mills	tinplate base	8.3	0.6	0.6	1.2
Narrow strip mill	hot—rolled strip up to 18″ wide	5.3	0.5	0.5	1.8
Heavy plate mill	plates	11.0	1.0	2.4	2.4[f]
Beam and section mill	beams and sections	14.5	0.6	0.75	2.9
Rod mill	bars and rods in coil	6.0	0.14	0.6	1.8
Bar mill	light sections and bars	9.0	0.4	1.0	2.8

(a) The estimates of capital costs for the mechanical equipment of mills are included to provide a very crude indication of the capital costs for each type of rolling mill. As an extremely crude guide these costs form of the order of a quarter of the installed capital cost of mills. The ratio varies for different types of mill. The costs given for mechanical equipment are for large mills and are approximate.

(b) Actual or contemplated.

(c) Including slabs for plate mills.

(d) The total output of blooms is not recorded as much of it is immediately re—rolled, and the figure given is an estimate.

(e) Only a small proportion of the U.K. output of slabs and blooms is made by continuous casting.

(f) Excluding plate from strip mills.

Generally there are technical economies for the use of larger capacity rolling mills of each type, up to the maximum sizes shown in table 12.3 (providing, of course, the capacity of large rolling mills can be utilized). These economies of scale for rolling mills were illustrated in the interim report. The following data obtained from a manufacturer of rolling mills, provide a further illustration, in this case for slabbing mills.

Capacity m. tons p.a.	1	4
Costs	£ per ton	
Labour	0.50	0.17
Capital [a]	0.56	0.25
Other operating costs	0.60	0.56
Total	1.66	0.98

(a) Another source suggested that this estimate of economies of scale for capital costs was higher than they would expect.

Nevertheless, the output figures for overseas works give a rather exaggerated indication of the size of works required to achieve the main economies of scale. An advantage of large outputs of similar products is that mills can specialise. Where mills specialise those which roll products with a relatively heavy weight per foot run will have a higher output measured in tonage, and other mills will have a lower output. Some of the overseas mills included in table 12.3. specialise on relatively heavy products and some other mills in those countries have a correspondingly lower output. [1]

During the 1960's demand for steel products did not increase rapidly, and for most groups of products, the growth of U.K. demand was less than the outputs of plants listed in table 12.3. In the U.K. steel industry it has only been possible to install the most efficient sizes of rolling plant, if old plant was replaced and/or new capacity was operated at less than full capacity for extended periods, and/or a substantial part of the extra capacity was used to produce steel for exports for which the ex—works price was generally lower than for steel sold on the home market. [2]

A consequence of the relatively slow growth of U.K. output, in relation to the capacity of new mills, is that the steel industry usually has to install rolling mills of a new design often incorporating new techniques for control and/or new sizes of mill, each time it builds a new plant, and this results in problems similar to those described in Chapter 5 for chemicals. Unforeseen problems occur when the new plants are built, and these result in delays. However rolling mills usually cause less initial problems than crude steel plants. Delays in introducing new plant are one reason why the pay off from new plants has not been as high as was expected.

2. Inspection and other finishing operations

In terms of costs, and particularly labour costs, other finishing operations

(1) Demand for different sizes of products etc. is also affected by pricing policy and differences in consumer tastes in different markets. For example American and Japanese steel manufacturers sell more wide sheet than U.K. mills, partly because American car manufacturers produce more cars with wide dimensions, and partly because their steel producers charge different relative prices for their products.

(2) For strip mills this problem was exacerbated by the political decision to build two mills with capacities of 1.5 and 2 million tons during the early 1960's.

including inspections, dressing, pickling, grinding, and shearing are significant, and for some products the costs for these operations are of the same order of magnitude as for the rolling operations themselves. For these finishing operations economies of scale are generally smaller, although there are some opportunities for using different techniques and spreading fixed capital costs as scale is increased, especially for handling and inspection.

One important determinant of costs is the extent of wastage; yields range from less than 55% for forgings to nearly 80% of the ingot tonnage rolled for heavy sections. Where economies of scale are achieved by substituting automatic rolling machinery a possible offsetting source of higher costs is increased wastage because scope for eliminating defects during rolling are reduced. Also as the size of ingot or billet rolled increases, it is claimed, that wastage may increase because defects are less likely to be eliminated. On the other hand the end loss for a large ingot or billet should be proportionately less. There are many factors determining yields and, though scale effects, particularly the length of product runs, could be important, we have no detailed evidence showing this.

3. Economies of scale for steel production and finishing

The minimum efficient scale (m.e.s.) of steel plants is greater than the maximum capacity of any type of rolling mill, and so, if the full economies of scale for steel production are to be achieved in steel plant of the m.e.s., this has to feed a number of rolling mills. In practice it must also be a multi-product works because increases in demand at any one time are unlikely to justify the duplication of any one type of rolling mill. We discuss later the possible scope for separating steel production and rolling.

IV. The economies of scale for steelworks

In order to specify a minimum efficient scale for steelworks a number of assumptions have to be made. The first of these assumptions concerns the choice of steel making process, for example whether steel is to be produced from ore and scrap via blast and oxygen furnaces, or from scrap in an electric furnace. The relative costs for the two methods of production are heavily dependent on the price of scrap which is in part determined by the number of works using scrap as their raw material. If the B.S.C. attempted to greatly increase its production of steel from scrap in electric furnaces, it would have to increase the U.K. supply of scrap, possibly by increasing its price, and/or import more scrap, at prices higher than those for U.K. scrap.[1] The scrap available for the B.S.C. to build plants based on scrap is limited, but the B.S.C. and independent companies could build such plants in the U.K. In Germany a company has built a small new steel works using scrap as raw material, and it rolls reinforced bars. The plant has a capacity

---

(1) The price of imported scrap is more than twice the U.K. price at the present time (June 1970).

of about 150 000 tons a year. A number of plants of this type have been built in America, and one is planned for the U.K. Such works do not suffer a substantial loss of economies of scale on their processes — conversion of scrap in electric furnaces, continuous casting and rolling bars. Also the capital costs for such a mini—works can be low — about £40 a ton; one way of keeping down the capital costs is to buy second hand rolling mills. A mini—works may be sited near sources of scrap and the only market it is intended to serve, and so save on delivery costs, compared to mills serving dispersed markets. A mini—works situated in London might save of the order of a £1 a ton on transport costs for scrap, and £1 or so for transporting finished products, assuming it could sell most of its output in the London area. In the case of a developing country without a steel industry the saving on transport costs would, of course, be much greater if the products of the mini—works could be absorbed within the country. However, the favourable economies of small scrap based works are limited to products such as reinforcing bars for which the economic size of mill for making the product is still quite small.

Leckie and Morris in their paper on the 'Effects of Plant Scale' illustrate the importance of a second assumption — the product mix. They estimate the return on capital for a hypothetical plant that is developed in four stages as it is not possible to compare costs at each stage of development because the product mix changes. The relationship between return on capital and output depends on the order in which development are implemented. If a wide strip mill is installed to start with, the first major peak return of 20% on capital employed, is not reached until the crude steel output is 4m. tons a year, but, where an integrated works starts with billet and medium section mills, the first major peak (19%) is reached at an output as low as 1½m. tons a year. [1]

A third important assumption concerns the extent of vertical integration. It may be possible to avoid the disadvantages of small scale for steel production by buying out ingots or having ingots transferred from another works. Another example of vertical separation is the division of rolling and wire drawing. For the production of wire, steel is first rolled into billets and then rods, and wire is produced by a succession of drawing operations. The capacity of many wire drawing machines is quite small — several thousand tons a year, and so the achievement of the technical economies of scale for these operations requires relatively small tonnages compared to the production of crude steel or the rolling of billets or rods.[2] Thus the minimum

(1) The authors point out that since the paper was written, individual unit capacities have greatly increased, and minimum capacity for peak returns are now considerably higher than at the time that the paper was written.

(2) For some operations involved in the production of wire, there are substantial economies of scale, e.g. for pickling, annealing and for galvanising. In terms of costs the importance of these operations varies. For example many wire products are not galvanised. Overall a very crude estimate obtained suggested that substantial economies of scale exist for approximately half, measured in terms of costs, of the operations performed in a large wire works.

efficient scale in terms of tonnage, for converting rods to wire is very small compared to that for an integrated works making steel and converting it to wire.

Another important determinant of the optimum size of plants is the overall output of a company. It may be economic for a firm with a large output of sheet, but which is short of capacity on a wide strip mill, to build a narrow strip mill. An independent company might specialise on producing narrow strip and operate a mill for this purpose, and it may have lower costs for these products than a firm making the same products on a wide strip mill. Also the cost of iron ore and other materials is affected by the overall size of a company's requirements, besides demand at a single works. It will be possible for the B.S.C. to transport ore in very large bulk carriers and by transferring ore to smaller carriers in the U.K., it could supply some of its smaller works with low cost ore. A small independent works may pay more for its materials.

A possible advantage of buying in large quantities is that ore can be assembled from a number of sources, and a more consistent quality of ore can be fed to blast furnace plants.

V. Production runs

Two aspects of the economies of scale for which no detailed estimates were given in the interim study were the economies for large outputs of individual products and long production runs. For most rolled steel products the spreading of initial or first—copy costs, which is very important in many other industries, is relatively unimportant, but the fact that some companies in this country and abroad have entered into agreements to enable the length of production runs for rolling mills to be increased by redistributing their orders, suggests that there are economies of this type. The main economies are achieved by reducing the time required for resetting mills and by increasing the roll life. (A factor limiting the economies of long runs in certain cases is the use of different qualities of steel ingot for single runs.)

The importance of economies for long runs varies for different types of product. For rolled sheet it is claimed that the economies for longer runs would be small because changes in specification can be achieved without significant loss of output in the mills. Also, for the production of plate wear on rolls, rather than the length of runs, is generally the limiting factor on the time between roll changes. But for section rolling there is a much greater loss of production caused by changing specifications, primarily because differences in specifications are much greater. The type of control systems used for sheet rolling cannot be incorporated in section mills, but plant designers are now designing new section mills with capacity for changing rolls much more rapidly.[1]

An example of the effects of extending the length of runs was obtained for two billet mills. The first operated three shifts a day and had approximately three roll changes a week, and the second operated one shift a day and had thirty roll changes a week. The rolling costs for the second were £20 a ton compared to £10 a ton on the first.[2] For other finishing operations differences in costs were not reckoned to be significant.

The extra cost of making 'specials' should be noted. For products requiring metal specifications outside those normally made by a firm, or different sizes of ingot, costs are substantially higher than those for 'standard' products.

The B.S.C. can achieve significant economies by rationalizing the rolling of sections, but a limitation to the extent of these economies is exemplified by the fact that the steel companies, when independent, used to vary the length of their runs according to the state of trade. When trade was slack they were prepared to make small quantities of a size, but when trade was good runs were extended and customers had to wait for deliveries if necessary, i.e. short runs concealed spare capacity which was required for boom periods. Even if the B.S.C. extended runs during slack periods, it could not dispense with the spare capacity. Another temporary limitation on the benefits of rationalization is that a substantial increase in *rolling* capacity brought about rationalization may not be usable because steel making capacity cannot be increased in the short run at the same works, but it may be possible to obtain steel for rolling into sections, either from other

---

(1) The length of time required for changing rolls when changing the size of sections varies from 30 minutes to 10 hours. A number of roll changes can be avoided for certain changes of section being rolled, but not for others, so shapes are rolled in a sequence or 'campaign', to minimise roll changes. Both the output of individual sections and the size of campaigns can be increased by rationalization. Other types of rolling are also organized in campaigns. If the sequence of a campaign is disrupted (for a rush order of a special size) the extra costs are substantial.

(2) It is difficult to distinguish the effects of the length of run and the number of shifts operated. If there are many changes of rolls, these can often be made during non—operating time, if a single shift is worked. In practice short runs, single shift working and the use of old plant tend to go together.

114

U.K. works or from overseas.[1] In the long run there will be substantial economies to be achieved by installing new mills each producing a limited range of products, and this will apply to section, plate and strip mills. In the past, each independent company tried to maintain a part of each part of the market for sections, plates, etc., and so when investing in a new mill there was a tendency for such a mill either to be able to roll a vast range of products, or to be designed so that the range of products could be increased. This resulted in compromises in mill design and increased operating costs.

Apart from the technical economies of long runs, there are other possible sources of economies — for stockholding and management, but no quantitative estimates of these were obtained. However, there are also some advantages to be gained from rolling a combination of products because this spreads the wear on rolls.

VI. Vertical integration of works

There are possible economies in fuel, transport and maintenance[2] costs to be achieved by the integration of processes in one works. In part the addition to costs caused by operating separate works will depend on the proximity of a supply of hot metal or semi-finished steel. Also if the finishing costs are relatively important, the diseconomies of separate works are comparatively less important. (For all finished products, finishing costs are a substantial part of total costs, but for some products they form a much higher percentage than for others).[3]

For some steel products there are natural breaks in the processes of production — i.e. the steel is allowed to go cold — where it would be less costly to divide processes geographically. The points at which these breaks occur vary for different products. In the production of hot—rolled strip, slabs are normally allowed to go cold for dressing, classifying etc., so, that the next stage of reheating and rolling could be separated. Practice varies, but at some plate mills, slabs are also allowed to go cold. However, for both of these products, division of processes would mean considerable transport problems as both hot—rolled strip and plates are usually made on

(1) For a discussion of the effects of the length of run for section rolling see A. Woodall, K.H. Sanders, and J.A. Walker 'Model Building with Particular Reference to the Use of Productive Capacity', Jnl. of The Iron & Steel Inst., May 1970.

(2) Economies for fuel costs occur if surplus heat can be used for subsequent processes, or if the reheating of the steel can be avoided. It may be possible to achieve a more effective utilization of service and maintenance labour at an integrated works.

(3) Finishing costs as a proportion of total costs vary between 1/7 and 1/4 for billets and 1/4 to 1/2 for finished steel products. In general the finishing costs are a higher proportion of costs when the material is of a low chemical analysis and vice versa, but the complexity of the rolling process is also important.

a large scale. Separation of works might also result in the inability to use surplus heat and fuel produced in the earlier iron and steel—making processes, but this would not be important if a proportion of the steel made at a works were finished at another works, or if the surplus fuel could be used at other plants in the locality. In practice where hot—rolled strip is further processed into cold—rolled sheets or tinplate these processes are often separated from the main producing works.

There are no natural breaks in the production of heavy sections, beams and light sections. The heat is retained in the ingot, and the steel is passed straight on to the heavy section mill from the primary rolling mill. On the other hand for the production of bars, rods, or narrow strip, though the ingot heat is retained for primary rolling and the bar goes straight through the billet mill, the steel is then allowed to go cold for inspection, dressing and classifying, and it is quite feasible to have the production of bars, rods, etc. apart from the main steel works.

Where division of works necessitates reheating, the fuel cost for reheating depends on the product and varies between 5/- and 10/- a ton compared to the cost of crude steel which is about £30 a ton. The cost of reheating is at least partly offset by a reduction in the imperfections of the final product made possible by inspection of the cold steel, and this is important. The high rejection rates have been mentioned above, and a reduction of these rates of wastage results in substantial savings.

Division of processes between works may result in additional transport costs. The costs for carrying steel billets in quantities of 50,000 tons a year over distances of 100 miles would be a little as £1 per ton for some products, but there would also be costs for loading and unloading the steel. These transport costs might be offset, or partly offset, by reduced costs carrying finished products. Although the economies of each case have to be considered separately, there could be technical and management economies to be achieved by concentrating crude steel production and primary rolling, and to continue to use some existing finishing capacity with supplies of crude steel from other steel works, as the heating and transport costs, the main additional costs, are relatively small. Also the finishing operations are generally the most labour intensive, and so this division would have the advantage of limiting the redeployment of labour required.

VII. Special steels [1]
Special steels include alloy steels, steels in which elements other than iron and carbon are included for a specific purpose, and carbon steels which

---

(1) The main manufacturing operations for special steels are:
   1. melting. (Cold pig iron and/or scrap are heated and refined in an electric furnace. The alloys required are added at this stage).
   2. cogging. (The ingots produced from the electric furnaces are heated and rolled or hammered).
   3. heat treatment, dressing and inspection, and reheating for rolling.
   4. rolling to shape the product.
   5. inspection, finishing and testing.

116

have a low degree of surface defects. (Annual U.K. output of each of the two groups of special steels is about 2m. tons.) Special steels have distinctive properties such as hardness, resistance to wear, resistance to corrosion, springiness, strength, shape, etc. which are attributable to the combination of ingredients and/or the methods of production used for their manufacture.

On an a priori basis, the economies of scale might be expected to be smaller for special steels because the costs of materials (including nickel and other ingredients) are higher, but, although material costs are higher for some types of special steels, labour and capital costs per ton are also much higher.

Both the firms which we consulted about economies of scale for special steels operated a number of electric steel furnaces and rolling mills, and this replication of plant was attributable to the wide range of products made. If costs for *new* plants were compared and it was assumed that the range of products made was not affected by scale, there would be considerable economies for producing special steel in large quantities. These economies would be gained by using large capacity furnaces and rolling mills, and more specialized rolling mills as scale increased.

The following estimates illustrate the economies for large furnaces:

Capacity of furnaces	7 cwt	15 tons	110 tons
Cost per ton	£	£	£
Materials	20.00	20.00	20.00
Direct Labour	13.00	0.93	0.15
Electric power	41.00	3.35	2.50
Other costs		15.02	11.20
Total	74.00	39.30	33.85
Index of costs excl. materials	280	100	72
Index of costs incl. materials	188	100	86

Some furnaces with a capacity of only 5 cwts. are operated in the industry for the production of qualities of steel required in small quantities.

Apart from economies for producing steel in larger furnaces and using larger capacity rolling mills, there would be some economies for inspection, organizing production etc. if longer runs were achieved. Also the length of runs is one factor determining the choice of techniques. An important example is provided by hammer cogging. In terms of costs hammer cogging is an important process, and where rolling can be substituted for long runs, it reduces costs by as much as 80% of the costs of hammer cogging. There is some dispute about the relative merits of hammer cogging and rolling, but some authorities claim that most, though not all, types of steel at present hammer cogged could be rolled without loss of quality.

Control of wastage is particularly important for special steels where yields of less than 50% of the ingot tonnage are not unknown. Again, lower wastage rates may be a source of lower costs for some types of low capacity mills which can be adjusted to take account of the quality of billets.

In practice many firms use much old plant and because the capital charges for this plant are low, total unit costs for old plant are often lower than for new plant. When discussing the economies of scale with firms in the trade this relationship tends to dominate businessmen's views about the relationship between scale and costs — increased scale would require expensive new plant. However economies of scale operate for new plants.[1]

In chapter 5 we provided estimates of economies of scale for producing bulk chemicals and for dyes which are made in relatively small quantities. In that case economies were proportionately larger for dyes. The same applies to steel. For producing special steels economies are larger than for bulk carbon steel, and, though we have not provided figures to show this, the same probably applies to rolling special steels compared to bulk carbon steels.

VIII. Large orders

There are economies for processing and delivering large orders. One firm estimated that the delivery costs for large orders — involving regular deliveries by two or three specially designed lorries a day — over distances of 100 miles, would cost about 14/- a ton, compared to costs of about £3 a ton for special consignments transported similar distances. However the delivery cost for small consignments delivered locally in the area of the works was only about 5/- a ton. In addition to the extra delivery costs small orders involve extra costs for preparing records.

IX. Firms

(A) The British Steel Corporation

1. Technical economies. There are a number of possible advantages associated with the ownership of a number of works by one firm, and for this

---

(1) Where output of special steels alone does not justify the use of large capacity plant, the production of general carbon steel on the same plant may do so. For example some billet mills are used for both general carbon and special steels.

industry it is appropriate to consider the sources of advantage of the British Steel Corporation, compared with the fourteen independent companies which were nationalised.

(a) The main potential sources of technical economies in the relatively short run were to be achieved by planning production so as to operate the most efficient plants at a higher level of capacity utilization, to scrap plants with capacity no longer required, and to achieve long runs. We say in the 'relatively' short run because it is necessary to build up a planning organization to get these benefits. Information has to be collected and checked, and production planning and marketing have to move in step. Also the cooperation of employees is vital to the success of such reorganisations.

(b) In the longer run there is scope for concentrating expansion and capacity to take advantage of the economies of scale for new plants. (In theory many of these advantages should have been achieved by the industry before nationalisation, because of the special arrangements for planning and cooperation which then existed. In practice the need to achieve expansion inspite of the reluctance of some companies to expand capacity, and political intervention, prevented efficient planning for expansion.) Also there is greater scope for the B.S.C., than the independent companies, to utilize the production capacity of new plants quickly. [1] Indeed the minimum efficient scale of new steel plants and wide rolling mills is so large that consideration is being given to joint ventures between the B.S.C. and European steel manufacturers.

2. Vertical integration. The technical advantages of integrated plants were discussed above, here we deal with an advantage for vertically integrated firms. An interesting example of the benefits of vertical integration was provided by a steel company before nationalization. It had found that when steel was transferred between works in the group, the yield was almost always better than for sales outside the group, because outside customers demand a more perfect product. The system of pricing is involved in assesing this point, but it may be easier to achieve an optimum solution when works are owned by one firm. The formation of the B.S.C. has not greatly affected the extent of vertical integration because the largest steel companies which made most of the steel they rolled were nationalized.

In the past some representatives of the industry have been concerned with another dimension of scale — the extent to which the firms own or control firms converting steel to finished products. Before nationalization

---

(1) The alternative strategy for fully utilizing the capacity of large new plants is to export the product. The Japanese aided by low costs have used this strategy but it also requires a degree of ruthless price cutting which in part depends on low production costs, and which it may be difficult for the B.S.C. to achieve. Capital costs for Japanese large scale plants are substantially below those of U.K. plants; of the order of £50 per ton of capacity compared to £80, or so, in the U.K. Reasons for this difference include, more experience of building new plants, the construction of larger new plants, possibly lower wages and greater efficiency in construction, and (it is claimed) because less is spent on anti—pollution devices.

some of the largest steel producers were companies which were also engaged in engineering industries. In addition some steel companies owned subsidiaries using steel for bridge building and construction, while others entered the market for prefabricated housing. The main economic advantages to be achieved by further vertical concentration of this sort are to ensure that old and new markets for steel are fully developed, to make possible a reduction of stock—building cycles and to ensure that the consequences of the decisions of consumer industries for steel producers are taken into account. It is conceivable that these objectives could be achieved by other methods such as close cooperation between steel producers and consumers, and by the steel companies subsidising product development. On the other hand a disadvantage to the economy as a whole of formal ownership by steel companies of consumer firms is the possible reduction of competition between steel producers and the manufacturers of possible substitute products, such as plastics.

3. Marketing. Selling costs form a very small proportion of total costs of steel, but it is nevertheless important to the success of an organisation, particularly in export markets. The main possible sources of disadvantage for the centralization of control involved in the new organisation of the B.S.C. are

(a) that it is more difficult to synchronize selling with production requirements. (For example an individual company might make special concessions to win an order which fitted in with its production plans. It is more difficult, though not impossible, for a centralized organisation to achieve this sort of flexibility. Similarly it may be more difficult to keep sales representatives aware of changes in qualities which can be offered, and steelworks acquainted with customers' requirements.)

(b) centralization of selling may result in fewer approaches to individual buyers. (Instead of several companies seeking orders, one selling organization may approach buyers, but concentration may result in approaches to more customers, especially overseas, and improved capacity for meeting delivery dates.)

The technical economies to be achieved by centralization may swamp these marketing difficulties, if, indeed they do exist.

4. Research development and services. There should be greater scope for spreading the costs of providing R and D and services within the B.S.C. On the other hand there are costs involved in obtaining information from subsidiaries etc., but in the long run the economies for providing specialist services should exceed the extra costs of control.

5. Conclusion. A return of the B.S.C. to private enterprise organised as fourteen separate firms would result in an immense loss of economies of scale and is impracticable. But it is worth, briefly, considering the scope for dividing the B.S.C. between, say, two, or three separate groups, whether these remained nationalized or were wholly or partly returned to the private sector. The most appropriate division would probably be along geographic lines with separate Welsh, and possibly Scottish, Steel Companies.

This division could not be a rigid one, but it is possible that there would be advantages for morale in sticking as closely as possible to such a regional breakdown. If division along these lines occurred, the extent of competition between the groups would be limited because the works in Wales concentrate on sheet, and capacity for the production of sheet in the English steel industry is at present limited. Certain finishing and special steel works could also be transferred to the private sector. It is outside the scope of this paper to consider arguments for these changes of organisations in detail, but they need not necessarily result in a significant loss of technical economies of scale. However such a reorganisation would cause disruption, and the planning and financing of very large new works (9m. tons) would be made more difficult. For the time being, increasing efficiency to get more output from existing plant, expanding some existing works, and fully utilizing increases in capacity, are probably more important sources of increased efficiency than economies for giant new works built on green–field sites, for which it will be difficult to achieve a high level of capacity utilization. But there is no evidence that these alternative sources of increased efficiency would be achieved more rapidly if the B.S.C. were divided, and in the long run the construction of large new works could result in important advantages.[1]

(B) The survival of small firms

There are a number of factors contributing to the continued existence of many small firms in the steel industry. In the past, the maintenance of effectively fixed prices during recessions may have limited the penetration of efficient, large scale producers. Many of the smaller firms make special products and alloy steels, and are not competing directly with the large companies. Some perform a limited range of operations, particularly finishing operations. Some use old plant and equipment which has been written off. Another factor which enables a small scale producer to compete is the use of different techniques and raw materials; for example, by making steel from scrap in an electric furnace rather than from pig iron. Finally, superior control of yields can significantly affect costs, and small firms may simply avoid heavy overheads for management, selling, market research, personnel management, etc., and minimize their labour force.

Although there are sources of competitive advantage for small firms, the existence of economies of scale will make survival increasingly difficult for these firms.

(1) Increasing efficiency in the U.K. steel industry requires technical improvements in iron and steel making, and much research and experimentation in production plant will be required to do this. It would be expensive to duplicate this research.

Table 12.4 *Summary of Minimum Efficient Scale for Steel*

	Output tons per year	% of U.K. Capacity	% increase in average total costs at 50% of 'm.e.s.'	% increase in average value added at 50% of 'm.e.s.'
Crude Steel Plant for conversion of iron ore to steel in blast and L.D. furnaces	9m	33	5–10	12–17
Integrated Steel Works producing a range of rolled products including wide strip	4m[b]	80	8[a]	13[a]
Types of special steel	The m.e.s. is large in relation to U.K. output.			
Steelworks	The m.e.s. is small in relation to U.K. output because of the scope for specialization on the production of steel from scrap and rerolling.			

(a) Based on estimates given in interim report, adjusted to allow for new data for steel making.

(b) Economies of scale would extend beyond this level, but, though we have obtained estimates of economies for producing steel on a larger scale, we have not estimated the economies of scale for rolling steel in substantially larger quantities.

13. Iron Castings

Table 13.1. *Profile of the Iron Casting Industry*

	1963	Percentage of all manufacturing industry	1968	Percentage of all manufacturing industry	1968 as % of 1963
Number of Employees ('000)	113.2	1.4	102.6	1.3	91
Sales (£m.)	309.1	1.1	345.5	0.9	112
Net Output (£m.)	143.9	1.3	163.3	1.0	113
Capital Expenditure (£m.)	12.1	1.2	—	—	—

Concentration

Concentration ratio for the 5 largest firms in 1963 — 33%

Size of Establishments and Enterprises (1963)

	Establishments		Enterprises	
Number of Employees	Number	% of Employees	Number	% of Employees
Under 100	965	22	891	20
100–999	216	57	150	36
1000 and over	15	21	17	44
	1196	100	1058	100

I. General introduction

(1) *Structure of the industry*

At the end of 1969 there were about 920 iron foundries in the U.K. with a total of 101,000 employees. Although the number of foundries has fallen by more than half since 1945, production of iron castings is still a relatively fragmented industry. Output is concentrated at the larger production units, and nearly two-thirds of all iron castings are made at the 78 foundries producing more than 10,000 tons of castings a year: while 168 foundries had an output of less than 200 tons in 1969. In terms of firms, the B.S.C. controls 12% of the sales of the industry, and the ten leading companies, including the B.S.C., account for 42%. (In terms of tonnage they account for 54% of the output of the industry.) Another feature of the structure of the industry is the extent of vertical integration;[1] about 30 per cent, by weight,

(1) There are advantages of vertical integration, such as control of supplies from a tied foundry, and also possible difficulties, such as the provision of specialised managers for foundry operations. The advantages and dis-advantages of vertical intergration were not studied for iron foundries, but were considered in more detail for some other trades.

123

of all castings are made by 'tied' foundries — foundries owned by firms which themselves machine or assemble the castings made. [1]

This study is based on the experience of foundries making castings for the motor vehicle and engineering industries. Vehicle castings account for about a quarter of the total output of castings by weight, and with the castings made for other engineering products, they represent about half of the output of the industry.

2. The processes of production

The main processes of production used in a foundry are:

(a) the making of pattern equipment, including patterns and pattern plates, coreboxes, running systems, core assembly fixtures, and checking gauges;

(b) the preparation of sand for moulding and coremaking;

(c) the formation of moulds; [2]

(d) the preparation of cores; [3]

(e) the melting of iron in a cupola or furnace;

(f) the casting of molten metal in the mould;

(g) knocking-out the casting from the mould;

(h) de-coring and 'chipping';

(i) cleaning, i.e. fettling, grinding and shotblasting;

(j) ancillary operations such as heat treatment.

The products of a foundry vary in size, complexity, the metal used, the number of castings produced, the techniques of production employed, the precision of the castings and the extent to which they are finished. These differences are inter-related; for example the type of pattern used and the technique employed to produce the mould, depend on the complexity, size, precision and quantity of the castings.

3. The dimensions of scale

Foundries specialise, some make long runs of certain types of vehicle castings while others concentrate on work involving short runs. They also specialise according to the size of castings, as this affects the type of

(1) The data given in this paragraph was obtained from the Joint Iron Council.

(2) For this operation a pattern plate, with the pattern or patterns fixed to it, has a moulding box placed on it, which is then filled with sand. The sand is jolted, squeezed, or otherwise pressed in the box against a squeeze head leaving an impression, or several impressions, in the sand mould. This can be done mechanically up to about two hundred times an hour, and each operation makes from one to thirty impressions depending on the size of the castings. The complexity and size of the casting i.e. length, depth, breadth, and amount of coring, influence the type of machine used, and therefore the speed of output. Typical vehicle cylinder blocks are made with single impressions at rates of from 60 to 100 per hour, and with multiple impressions at rates up to 300 moulds per hour.

(3) In order to form castings with internal hollow sections, cores are inserted in the mould.

handling equipment required, and the technique employed. However at some foundries a wide range of castings is made and this often involves the use of different techniques of forming moulds. Thus there are many dimensions of scale for the industry including the total output of each product, the length of production runs, the extent of specialisation of production at a foundry, the size of foundries and the size of firms.

II. The structure of costs

Compared to the steel industry which we discussed in the previous chapter, and particularly the production of sheet steel, the production of iron castings is relatively labour, as opposed to capital, intensive. For large new plants capital costs per ton of sheet steel and iron castings are about the same, but the labour input per ton of castings is about ten times that for sheet steel.

The relative importance of types of costs varies according to the castings made at a foundry and the vintage of the foundry. Material costs represent of the order of 50% of the costs of foundries, patterns about 5%, and selling and distribution costs 5% or so.

III. Initial costs

For castings produced in small quantities one of the main economies to be achieved by increasing output of individual castings is the spreading of pattern costs, but the relative importance of the costs of patterns depends on the size and complexity of the castings. For small quantities of a casting, the ratio of pattern costs to production costs may be of the order of 1 to 1 for a box, and 50 : 1 for a complex casting. [1]

The effect of spreading pattern costs for *short runs* is illustrated by the data shown in Table 13.2. For the purpose of making these estimates it was assumed that the castings were made in one run.

(1) One source of flexibility for pattern costs is the material used for the pattern. The cost of a wooden pattern for a very short run would be about 25 per cent of the cost of a metal pattern. Also the use of different techniques provides some flexibility for certain castings; for example, the relative costs for shell and green sand moulding vary for different scales of output. However, the main determinant of the technique used is the type of casting made, rather than the number of castings.

Table 13.2. *The Relative Importance of Pattern Costs (1967)*[a]

Number of Castings	1	10	100
Simple Conveyor Casting (wt. 7 lbs.)		£	
Pattern cost	3.0	3.5	22.0
Production costs per unit	0.53	0.45	0.35
Total cost per unit	3.53	0.80	0.57
Gear Box Casting (wt. 2 cwts.)			
Pattern cost	100	110	140.0
Production costs per unit	15.0	13.5	12.0
Total cost per unit	115.0	24.5	13.4
Tailweight casting (wt. 15 cwts.)			
Pattern cost	60	75	110.0
Production cost per unit	75	65	55.0
Total cost per unit	135	72.5	56.0

(a) The estimates of costs given in this table were obtained from a firm which makes engineering castings. The figures for pattern costs were lower than those quoted by other firms, and it should be noted that patterns frequently cost several thousand pounds.

A guide to the overall importance of pattern costs was obtained from a manufacturer of machine tools who made a wide range of tools on a batch production basis. In this case, pattern costs represented about 5% of the costs of the firm's castings. Also the cost of patterns represented about 5% of total costs for a jobbing foundry, but for vehicle castings made in large quantities pattern costs are much smaller. [1]

In addition to pattern costs there are other costs which relate to each product — records have to be made for each 'job' and some learning effects may relate to the output of each casting.

IV. Production runs

The production of castings is organised on a batch basis. Usually a casting is required repeatedly and the custom of the trade is for foundries to work to delivery schedules of a certain number of castings a week or month. In the past firms were reluctant to hold substantial stocks of castings because of the cost and difficulty of raising finance, and because faults in castings could go undetected while many castings were made if they were held in stock.

The length of production runs affects costs in a number of ways. Firstly, a change of pattern means that a pattern has to be obtained from the stores and the new pattern has to be set up in the mould forming machine. This takes up to half an hour, but if changes are infrequent it may be possible to synchronise such changes with lunch breaks etc., so that the working

(1) In passing it may be noted that patterns are sometimes bought from specialist firms and that customers often own the patterns.

time of operatives, not involved in making the change, is not lost. Also, for some types of machine with 'butterfly' or 'pattern shuttle' systems, a change-over can be made in less than a minute, though it takes considerably longer to set up a new pattern on a wing of the 'butterfly'. The subsequent processes need not be delayed by changeovers, as a stock of moulds can be built up, but a change from producing long runs to making a series of short runs would result in a lack of balance for different operations.

Changes in products should not materially effect the cost of preparing sand and iron melting, provided that the type and quality of iron used does not change, nor should it affect the cost of pouring the iron into the moulds,[1] but it does affect the finishing processes. A switch of products involves operatives performing different operations which are subject to a learning process and it is claimed that this learning process is associated with the length of individual production runs, rather than the overall output of a product, although this also has a slight effect. It is not only the time lost in learning a new routine but also the decline in quality that increases unit costs. At one foundry it was found that inspectors had to spend a disproportionate time on checking short runs and that rejects were of the order of two per cent compared to one per cent for long runs.

Reliable estimates of the relative costs for short and long runs of the same castings are difficult to obtain because foundries which make long runs do not generally accept work involving short runs, though they are more flexible when trade is slow. The estimates for production costs shown in Table 13.2. which are based on the assumption that the castings are made in one run, indicate the effect on costs of the length of run up to 100 units. These figures illustrate the effect of increasing the length of run at a foundry where the average length of run is short. They do not include the effect on costs of increasing the average length of run at a foundry. A substantial increase in the length of runs would increase the scope for using more efficient machinery. An estimate of the effects of extending longer runs was obtained from a foundry making vehicle castings. It was estimated that an increase in the length of run from 1,000 to 10,000 units a week could reduce the cost per unit by 5 per cent, excluding the advantages of automating production which might be made possible by longer runs. In both cases it was assumed that the length of run did not affect the level of capacity working of the foundry.

V. Size of foundries

(1) *Materials*

On average, iron and steel scrap forms about 70% of the ferrous materials used by iron foundries, and an economist who collected some data on the cost of scrap to foundries found that the larger companies had an 'edge' for buying, but very small foundries were at both extremes, some buying

---

(1) Where castings of varying size are made in turn there may be some difficulty in utilising the full capacity for iron production.

127

relatively cheaply while others paid the highest prices. In some cases large consumers have to pay an extra charge to merchants for agreeing to supply large quantities of scrap regularly, while small foundries sometimes obtain local supplies cheaply. There are some discounts for bulk deliveries of coke bought from the National Coal Board, and for electricity, which small foundries — those with an output of less than about 5,000 tons a year — cannot fully exploit, and the larger firms are able to negotiate discounts on some of their other supplies. Nevertheless the overall economies for large scale buying are small in this industry, and the absence of substantial economies of scale for purchases of materials damps down economies for other costs.

(2) *Capital and operating costs*

The total output of a foundry is an important factor determining the cost of sand preparation, iron production and air conditioning and it also influences the extent of mechanisation and automation. The substantial economies to be achieved for large scale production of *steel*, through the economies of large dimensions of furnaces, were described in the interim report.[1] These economies also apply to iron melting over the much lower levels of throughput achieved in this industry. But the cost of furnaces for iron melting forms a smaller proportion of capital costs for iron foundries than for steel rolling and steel castings. The depreciation charge related to the melting shop for one jobbing foundry was as little as 2% of the total depreciation charge, but for foundries making long runs and/or with new furnaces the capital charges for melting are more important. Economies of scale for capital and operating costs would also be expected for sand preparation, air conditioning, the formation of moulds and coremaking.[2]

(3) *Summary of costs for foundries*

Estimates of the effects of scale on costs for new foundries are shown in Table 13.3. These estimates were prepared by a firm which operates a number of foundries, including large foundries. The estimates indicate considerable economies of scale up to outputs of 50,000 tons a year for a foundry making cylinder blocks[3] and to 10,000 tons for a foundry making a range of small castings.

---

(1) *Op. cit.*, p. 67.

(2) For the formation of moulds and for coremaking the economies would depend on the relationship between scale and the range of products made.

(3) Equivalent to an output of about 1 million cylinder blocks.

Table 13.3. *Costs and Scale of New Foundries*

A — Foundry making cylinder blocks

Output per year (th. tons)		10	25	50	100	200
Number of cylinder blocks		1	1	1	1	1
Number of cupolas		2	2	2	4	6
Number of sand preparation plants		1	1	2	2	3
Number of moulding lines		1	1	2	4	4
	Weight[a]	Index of costs per unit of output				
Capital cost (index)	15	150	120	100	90	85
Labour cost (index)	40[b]	130	115	100	95	90
Material and fuel cost (index)	40[b]	108	102	100	98	96
Transport and selling costs	5	100	100	100	100	100
Total	100	123	110	100	96	92

(a) for an output of 50,000 tons a year

(b) including an apportionment of overheads.

B — Foundry making small castings

(Index of Total Unit Costs including materials)

Output and capacity of the foundry (th. tons)	Average number of different castings made per month		
	20	100	200
	Index of costs		
2.5	100	120	140
5.0	94	110	120
10.0	89	100	110

(4) *Other factors affecting the competitiveness of foundries*

There are many forces which determine the competitiveness of foundries besides the economies of scale. As in other industries a foundry may use depreciated buildings, plant and machinery, and there have been periods of excess demand for castings which have aided marginal foundries. In addition there are differences in managerial efficiency and in wage rates. Another factor enabling some small foundries to compete is their close links with local engineering firms which require a reliable supply of castings.

It is sometimes claimed that some of the smaller foundries have an advantage because working conditions are not maintained at a high level. However, foundries are subject to inspection, and it has been claimed that some larger firms more effectively resist the enforcement of factory legislation. (The cost of providing good working conditions is substantial in this industry. In one case, 20% of the capital costs of a new foundry were accounted for by the cost of air conditioning, ventilation and heating.)

Nevertheless, in this industry the main reasons for the competitiveness of units of varying size is the range of products made, and the varying length of production run. Even some vehicle castings are made in short runs for spares, for some types of commercial vehicles, and at times when there are shortages of capacity. For many types of engineering castings short runs are inevitable. The advantages of the larger foundries for this type of work are small, and the managers of small foundries may be better able to provide the close supervision and flexibility required for such work, without incurring heavy overheads.

(5) *The future*

Our estimates suggest that the concentration of the output of the industry in fewer foundries which has taken place in recent years should have increased efficiency, and that there is scope for achieving further economies of scale. We obtained no quantitative estimates to show the benefits of specialization on castings for different trades at foundries, but these are clearly important, and we should expect a move towards greater specialization in the future, and that this will also result in economies.

VI. Firms

(1) *Research and development*

There are a number of multi-foundry firms in the industry. The main advantages of these companies are their ability to finance research, to compare the results of different foundries, and to employ highly qualified staff. But these advantages are probably not of great importance for most types of castings. Much of the industry's research and development work is done for iron foundries by the Research Association for the industry, sponsored by the Department of Trade and Industry, and the results are universally available to the whole trade. Nor is the expenditure for developing and designing new products of much importance compared to engineering industries.

(2) *Selling and distribution*

In some industries large firms have an advantage for selling costs, but engineering castings are sold to firms which are expert in assessing quality and the selling costs for foundries are relatively slight. Selling and transport costs together representing 5% or so of total costs for foundries, and transport costs are the main component.

(3) *Specialisation*

A firm operating a number of foundries may be able to obtain some technical economies by distributing its production so that each of the foundries can specialise on a type of casting, but some independent foundries achieve a high degree of specialisation.

Table 13.4. *Summary of Minimum Efficient Scale for Iron Castings*

	Output per year tons	% of U.K. Output of all Castings [c]	% increase in average total costs at 50% of 'm.e.s.'	% increase in average value added at 50% of 'm.e.s.'
Products [a]	No estimate			
Foundry making cylinder blocks [d]	50,000	1	10%	15%
Foundry making small engineering castings [b][d]	10,000	0.2	5%	10%

(a) The output of products varies greatly and a general estimate of the m.e.s. for products is not possible, but economies continue up to the level of U.K. output of many castings.

(b) It is assumed that the length of runs does *not* increase with scale.

(c) The percentages would of course be much higher if outputs of foundries were related to the output of similar products.

(d) The estimates are for new foundries.

14. Motor Vehicles

I. General introduction

(a) Structure of the industry

The British motor industry consists of firms producing cars, commercial vehicles, tractors, and components and accessories for these. This chapter is concerned principally with the manufacture of cars and commercial vehicles, especially the former.

The industry produces nearly two million cars and half a million commercial vehicles annually. Peak production of cars was achieved in 1964, while 1964 and 1969 were peak years for commercial vehicle production. In 1969, some 45% of car production was exported and 39% of commercial vehicle production. Imports have been rising, especially of cars. In 1969 they represented about 10% of new registrations of cars.

Four firms dominate the industry. They are British Leyland and three subsidiaries of United States manufacturers – Vauxhall (General Motors), Ford and Chrysler (formerly Rootes). In 1969 these firms accounted for over 99% of the cars produced and some 98% of the commercial vehicles. There are several independent manufacturers of high quality and sports cars and heavy commercial vehicles, but their total output is very small. British Leyland's share of car production in 1969 was over 48% while that of Ford was nearly 30%. British Leyland accounted for 40% of commercial vehicle production in 1969, as against 27% for Ford and 24% for Vauxhall.

As a consequence of its development by mergers, British Leyland's production facilities are fragmented. In all it has 60 manufacturing centres spread throughout the U.K. It assembles cars at seven separate sites in the U.K., but assembly of the cars it produces in large quantities is concentrated at two sites. The other three major companies each has two main production centres, one in each case being in a development area.

(b) Processes of production and sources of economies of scale

The main processes of production performed by motor manufactures are the casting and forging of components such as engine blocks, the machining of components for engines, gear boxes etc., the production of bodies by pressing operations, and the assembly of sub-assemblies into the final products. The four main U.K. motor manufacturers all press bodies, make engines and assemble cars and commercial vehicles but the extent to which they make castings, forgings and other components varies.

Processes of this sort can give rise to considerable economies of scale. The manufacture of car bodies, for example, is particularly subject to initial fixed costs economies, while the machining of components gives much scope

132

Table 14.1. *Profile of the Motor Industry*

	Production of cars, taxis and chassis with engines. [1]		Total Motor Industry [2]				
	1963	% of all manufacturing industry	1963	% of all manufacturing industry	1968	% of all manufacturing industry	1968 as % of 1963
Number of Employees ('000)	149.0	1.9	444.9	5.6	466.2	5.8	105
Sales (£m.)	1038.3	3.7	2059.6	7.4	2770.7	7.0	135
Net Output (£m.)	327.1	3.0	736.6	6.8	995.7	6.2	135
Capital Expenditure (£m)	49	4.8	88	8.6	—	—	135

Concentration

Concentration ratio for the 5 largest firms in 1963.

Cars 91.5%

Commercial Vehicles 84.1%

Size of Establishments and Enterprises (1963)

	Establishments		Enterprises	
Number of Employees	Number	% of Employees	Number	% of Employees
Less than 100	905	5	762	5
100 – 999	254	18	160	11
1,000 – 3,999	70	29	28	11
4,000 – 7,499	18	22	6	8
7,500 and over	8	26	10	65
	1255	100	966	100

(1) Firms with more than 25 employees, only.

(2) Motor vehicle manufacturing as defined for m.l.h. 381, including the production of cars, commercial vehicles, tractors, and certain parts for vehicles.

for economies through specialisation of plant. Casting is less important as an area for economies of scale, as is assembly. Both can, however, benefit from initial fixed cost economies, together with economies in working capital and specialisation of labour.

(c) The dimensions of scale

The two main dimensions of scale for the motor industry are the output of particular models and the overall capacity of firms. The latter gives rise to economies in selling and in research and development. Besides the output of individual models and the capacity of firms, the output of a range of models which incorporate common components, the capacity of individual plants and the extent of vertical integration are other important dimensions of scale affecting costs of production.

II. The structure of costs

The following breakdown of the cost of sales to outside buyers, including sales of spare parts, for the Vauxhall Motor Co. is typical for the industry: materials and services 61%; wages, salaries, etc. 25%; special tools and depreciation 9%; tax, interest and profit 6%.[1] Fixed capital overheads have increased as a percentage of total costs in recent years. This trend reflects heavy investment by the companies in highly mechanised techniques, and increased vertical integration. Operation below full capacity, because of low demand and strikes, has also increased the burden of fixed costs.

A feature of the cost structure is the rather high proportion of bought out materials and services. Although the extent of this has been reduced by the increased vertical integration in the industry, materials, components and services bought out still represent about 60% of sales for U.K. manufacturers. Selling costs (included in the breakdown of costs for Vauxhalls given above under both services bought out and wages and salaries) are a relatively small proportion of total costs for this industry. The main item on the selling side is publicity, including advertising, which accounts for around 2% of sales turnover. The costs of warranties and of transport are other significant items of costs, but the latter is usually paid for separately by buyers of new cars.

III. Initial costs

The total output of particular models is clearly an important factor determining costs because of the initial tooling costs, particularly for body pressings. There are other substantial initial costs for models, including the costs of design, the building of prototypes and the disruption caused by the introduction of a new model. The suppliers of special components for models incur similar costs. There is some difficulty in specifying the initial costs for cars because:

(1) Vauxhall Motors Limited, Operating Review, 1968.

(1) the costs depend on the extent of variation from other models in a firm's range. Firms use the same basic engine for a number of models and may be able to use the same components (though in practice designers even within the same firm often select different components for different models of a similar size).

(2) firms frequently publish figures purporting to give the capital cost of introducing new models, but it is often difficult to distinguish the cost of introducing a new model *per se*, from the costs of expanding (or replacing) capacity which would otherwise have been incurred.

(3) there are economies of scale for introducing new models. If a firm introduces new models frequently, it can build up a team of designers, make use of ideas for styling in a number of models, learn by experience, and so on.

(a) Body costs

We deal first with body costs because the body is the most distinctive feature of models, and because tooling costs for bodies account for a substantial part of total tooling costs. An American estimate published in 1965 gave the minimum tooling costs for a new steel body as £2–£2.5m.[1] Two U.K. companies have suggested that the tooling costs of a new body would be much higher. One of these firms, for example, has estimated tooling costs for a new car body to be about £3m, with a further £¾m for a shooting brake or van (£1 million for both) based on the same model. This gives a total of £4m, and is based on the assumption that costs are tightly controlled. It was estimated that the figure of £4m. could be reduced by about £½m if a short run were expected.[2] Also a firm may reduce costs by tailoring the new design to make use of tooling for a previous model.

In practice a firm may introduce several variations of a model e.g. 2 and 4 door versions, and designers may indulge in relatively expensive tooling: thus in the event body tooling costs may well exceed £5m for a model aimed at a substantial share of the market.

Table 14.2. shows some estimates made by a motor company of the effects of increasing the output of a model on the costs of steel bodies. The main economies are achieved by spreading tooling costs,[3] but there are also economies in the use of materials and labour which are allowed for in the main

(1) R.S. Morrison, 'F.R.P. Stalks the Car Body Field'. S.A.E. 2nd April, 1965. This figure should probably be increased to £3–4 m. to allow for subsequent price rises.

(2) Where a short run of a model is expected some savings in tool costs can be made by using fewer, though larger, body pressings. But if this policy is used the buyer's maintenance costs are increased because damage to a large panel is less easily dealt with than that to a small one.

(3) The main cause of wear on body tooling is the number of times the dies are placed in the presses rather than the number of bodies which are stamped. A substantial proportion of tooling would still be usable after an output of a million units, if spread over five years but the cost of repairing tooling would increase.

part of the table and are also shown separately in the last two columns of the table.

Table 14.2. *Index of Costs for Body Shells* [a]

Annual Output ('000)	Index of body costs			Unit Material Costs	Unit Operating Labour Costs
	Expected Life of Basic Model				
	2 years	5 years	10 years	(2 year life)	(2 year life)
25	100	78	70	100	100
50	86	70	66	100	97
250	64	58	57	97	90
500	57	56	55	96.5	80
1000	56	55	54	96	80

(a) The costs include tooling, materials, labour, depreciation and other works overheads, and are for the production of body shells, i.e. they include the cost of assembling panels. For the purpose of making these estimates, it is assumed that the total output of the factory at which the body is made is not affected by the output of this model. No allowance is made for interest on capital.

The table illustrates an important feature of initial costs. These can be spread either by making many units during a short period, or by extending a model run over a longer period of time. The figures indicate that an output of a million units, whether spread over two years (500,000 per annum) or five years, (200,000 per annum), is required to achieve the main economies of scale for body production costs: costs which represent about 15% of the ex-factory costs of cars produced in large quantities (see below).

The spreading of body costs by high rates of production per annum or over runs of long duration are not, of course, equally attractive options: for example, the retention of an unchanged body for an extended period may involve marketing problems. These are discussed below.

(b) *Engines and other parts*

Engines are changed less often than bodies, and much machinery for manufacturing engine blocks can be adapted for the production of different engines. However, if a radically new engine is to be introduced, new machine tools and transfer equipment are usually acquired for its manufacture. Similarly new tools and equipment may be required for other parts, depending on whether existing components are used or new ones introduced.

(c) *Total initial costs*

We now consider total initial costs for models. For the purpose of illustrating the effect of spreading initial costs we have assumed that:

(1) the life of the model is 4 years [1]

(2) the capacity of the engine is 1500 ccs

(1) In the past U.K. manufacturers, have changed their leading models at intervals of more than 4 years.

136

(3) the body is a new one

(4) extra presses and factory space are not required. [1]

Given these assumptions, the initial costs would be of the order shown:

Output over 4 years	200,000	1,000,000
If a new basic engine is not required:		
Total initial costs (incl. development, tooling and disruption costs.)	£m 8–12	12–18
Initial costs per car	£ 40–60	12–18
If a new basic engine is required		
Total initial costs	£m 11–16	16–26
Initial costs per car	£ 55–80	16–26

The main initial costs are for design, testing and tooling. By synchronising a change-over of models with the annual holidays, a firm might aim to limit the loss of output to the equivalent of two weeks production of the model, costing perhaps £1m. for a production rate of 100,000 cars a year, and £2.5m for a rate of 250,000 a year. However the loss of production equivalent to six week's output is not unknown.

A range of costs is shown for each rate of output because initial costs of models vary between companies. They are also affected by the policy of a company. For example, if a company wishes to increase its share of the market by introducing a completely new model, it may have to spend more on initial costs to make a more appealing model. The initial costs for an output of a million units are shown to be 50% more than those for an output of 200,000 units. This increase occurs because the range of variants produced may increase with output, progressively more tooling has to be duplicated as the rate of output is increased, and disruption costs are approximately proportional to scale.

The estimates of initial costs given so far do not include initial costs borne by suppliers. These are substantial for many components. In some cases motor manufacturers pay separately for initial costs e.g. dies; in others they are included in the price per unit paid by the motor manufacturer for components.

An offsetting source of economies for initial costs is that when a new model is designed and new tooling has to be bought, advantage can be taken of technical progress in new and improved materials and techniques to reduce the costs of the new model. For example if metals with improved qualities have been introduced, it may be possible to reduce the weight of materials used or substitute different materials. Any savings are of course proportional to output. If similar changes were made for existing models, this might necessitate changes of tooling.

---

(1) If presses and additional factory space are required, this will add greatly to the capital expenditure for the new models.

IV. Production costs[1]

(a) A single basic model (with variations)

As a part of the description of initial costs, estimates of production costs for pressing operations were given in table 14.2. The main production processes not dealt with so far are casting, the machining and assembly of components such as engines and gear boxes, and assembly.

(1) *Castings and forgings.* The most detailed analysis of the technical economies of scale for the U.K. motor industry previously carried out was by Maxcy and Silberston.[2] For castings they estimated that an output of 100,000 cars a year was sufficient to enable a manufacturer to avoid any serious competitive handicap. The production of castings was discussed in the previous chapter. The information we give there suggests that economies for outputs substantially greater than those suggested by the earlier study may now exist. Economies of scale for forgings which are more important than castings in terms of costs are similar to those for castings.

(2) *Engines and transmission equipment.* The following estimates of the capital and operating costs for new lines to machine engine blocks were obtained from a U.K. motor company.[3] It is assumed that the life of the engine would be about ten years.

Annual capacity (thousands)	25	100	250	500	1,000
Capital cost £m	0.65	1.5	2.25	4.5	9.0
	Index Numbers of Costs per Engine				
Capital charges	173	100	60	60	60
Operating costs	129	100	80	80	80
Operating costs and capital charges	155	100	64	64	64

The estimates indicate large economies of scale up to an output of 250,000 units a year, but economies exhausted at that level of output. However there is an important qualification to this assessment; machinery has to be duplicated for outputs above about 250,000 units a year,[4] and for outputs above this level there is an increase in costs until sufficient output is again reached to fully utilize the duplicate plant. Also it is important to note that in practice firms generally have separate lines for different basic

---

(1) For the estimates given in this section, it is assumed that production is concentrated in one complex.

(2) George Maxcy and Aubrey Silberston. 'The Motor Industry', Allen & Unwin, London, 1959.

(3) Two recently introduced techniques which increase the flexibility of engine lines and/or reduce the economies of scale for engine production are the machining of engines with a varying number of cylinders on the same equipment, and the use of shell moulding techniques to make more accurate castings which, it is claimed, reduce the machining required.

(4) The maximum capacity of a single line depends on the number of shifts worked and other factors.

engine, so these economies relate to the output of each type of engine rather than a firm's total output of engines.

The economies of scale for the assembly of engines are proportionately smaller than for machining engine blocks. A comparison of assembly costs for vehicle diesel engines showed labour costs between 20 and 25% lower for engines made at a rate of 100,000 a year compared with an engine made at a rate of 2,500 a year.

Detailed estimates of costs for transmission equipment were not obtained, but the picture is broadly similar to that for engines. There are large economies of scale up to outputs of about 400,000 units a year for a single model, and above this output lines have to be duplicated.

(3) *Assembly.* For assembly Maxcy and Silberston again give a figure of 100,000 cars a year for the output required to enable a firm to use the most efficient techniques of assembly. The main development which has taken place since the Maxcy-Silberston study is the introduction of more automated tools for assembly. The following table gives recent estimates of the effects of capacity on labour requirements for assembly.

Annual Output (thousand cars)	60	125	300
Index of labour requirements	125	100	90

Source: The Automobile Industry of Western Europe 1965–1970, by Eurofinance.

A U.K. manufacturer provided the following estimates of labour and capital costs for assembly lines:

	15	30	60	80
Capacity of line per hour	15	30	60	80
Output per year assuming two shifts (thousands)	55	110	220	294
Labour costs per unit (Index)	125	100	90	88
Capital costs per unit (Index)	130	100	82	72

For rates of output above 80 cars per hour it was suggested that the efficiency of a single line would be affected by the increasing speed at which the track would have to move. However higher rates of output are achieved in the U.S. where lines with a capacity of more than 120 cars an hour have been built. But it is worth noting that for one of the leading European producers the maximum rate of production per hour on assembly lines is only 16 units. [1]

A U.K. manufacturer also estimated that the effects of putting a mix of models on its existing line reduced capacity by about 8%. If a firm operated a line for a single model, it could redesign parts of the line and increase capacity. For some operations it would be economic to substitute capital for labour and this process of substitution applies generally not to assembly alone. The economies of scale for assembly operations will be seen from

---

(1) Other estimates of maximum output per line per hour for this manufacturer were machining engine blocks and transmissions 64 per hour, assembling engines 33 and painting 32.

this to be proportionately small, as is the case with the assembly of engines. Assembly operations are relatively labour-intensive. For U.K. car manufacturers, assembly operations including the assembly of engines, account for some 45% of total direct labour costs.

(4) *Bought out materials and components.* Costs of materials and components are the largest group of costs for car production. For many items e.g. steel, tyres and much electrical equipment, the reductions in unit price paid for outputs of more than 25,000 units a year of a model are small. This is because the total industry output of standardised products is large. For other items including castings, forgings and electrical components special to a model, there would be economies of scale attributable to spreading the costs of dies and the use of more efficient techniques for outputs above 100,000 units a year. For all materials and components there would also be some economies of scale for suppliers' overhead costs, and for many items there would be economies for transport costs. Another source of economies as requirements increase is that firms can benefit by buying from a number of suppliers. One firm commented that 'for a volume of 25,000 (of a model per year), we would only use one source of supply, for a volume of 100,000 to 500,000 we may use two or three sources of supply. By bringing in competition, there is usually a price advantage. This could be as much as 10%'.

(5) *Production overheads.* For outputs much above about 250,000 units of a model, the economies of scale for direct production costs are relatively small, as the engine transmission, painting (which we have not dealt with separately above) and assembly lines have to be duplicated.[1] It is difficult to determine the effect on production overhead costs for power, purchasing departments, general management, the provision of other services etc. at higher levels of output. Important economies certainly exist for some of these costs and we have allowed for some economies for these costs in the following summary of the economies of scale for producing one model in varying quantities. Also large firms may spend more on buying, testing and research and this may reduce the costs of materials etc. An important item of overhead costs is for warranties; these can amount to 3%, or more, of costs. [2]

(6) *Summary of the economies of scale for the production of one basic model.* Table 14.3. shows our estimates of costs for a firm producing a single model at varying levels of output at one site. The costs are based on U.K. prices in 1968. It is assumed that the firm makes only one model

(1) There are of course discontinuities i.e. for outputs of 400,000 units of a range of models, two lines would be required for engines and assembly, but not transmissions, and unit costs for some operations would be higher than for outputs of 250,000 units. The experience of one company was that it was only for rates of output of 250,000 units a year, or more, that a satisfactory paint plant to meet their standards of quality could be installed.

(2) If the quality of control declines at higher scales of output because it becomes proportionately more difficult to control production at high rates of output, the cost of warranties will be a source of diseconomies of scale.

and that its total output changes with the output of the model. Costs are based on those for firms using a mix of vintages of plant which has been built up over time i.e. it is not assumed that the firm is using entirely new plant. If all new plant were assumed to be used, this would increase the economies of scale, because capital charges for which economies of scale are proportionately greater than average would be increased relative to other costs.

Table 14.3. *Illustrative Estimates of Costs and Scale for the Production of One Basic Model and its Variants*[a]

Output (thousands a year)	100	250	500	1,000
Initial costs for model £m.	15	20	28	38
	Costs per Vehicle £			
Initial costs	38	20	14	10
Materials and components bought out[b]	265	250	240	235
Labour (direct and indirect)	102	90	86	83
Capital charges for fixed and working capital	60	53	50	48
Total ex-works costs	465	413	390	376
Index	100	89	84	81

(a) A production run of 4 years is assumed, and the basic model is assumed to be in the range — 1,000–1,200 ccs.

(b) The estimates of economies for material and component purchases which we obtained from firms varied. Some estimates suggested that these economies would be smaller than those shown and others that the economies would be greater. It is assumed that the total output of suppliers is not affected by the purchases of the firm considered.

Source: The estimates in this table and in table 14.4. are based on the data given above and our discussions with firms in the industry.

The estimates indicate that the largest economies of scale are achieved over the range 100,000 to 250,000 units. It is assumed that the engine and assembly lines would be duplicated for outputs of 500,000 units and that there would be four lines for an output of a million units. The economies in operating costs for outputs above 250,000 units are attributable to pressing operations, the production of components, operating a number of lines in parallel and for overheads. In practice a firm with an output of a million units of one model could operate three engine, transmission, painting and assembly lines, and possibly only two lines. If so the economies would be larger — equivalent to another £10 per car over the range 250,000 to 1m. units a year.

(b) *A range of models*

The main source of higher costs for a firm making a range of basic models, and the same total output as a firm making a single model, would be the higher level of initial costs although other costs would also be raised. [1]

(1) Higher stocks of spare parts at the factory and at distributors is another important source of higher costs, and the need for capital to finance these stocks may present problems apart from the cost of finance.

Our tentative estimates of costs for a firm making a range of three basic models are shown in Table 14.4. It is assumed that one model is made in greater quantity than the other two. For example that at an output of 250,000 units a year, the firm makes 150,000 units of a model of about 1,300 c.c's, 50,000 units of a model of about 1,000 c.c.'s and 50,000 units of a model of about 1,800 c.c.'s (for each model there would be body and engine variants). The proportional division of output at each scale is assumed to be the same.[1] The economies of scale are greater for the models produced in smaller quantities as economies, in proportional terms, decline as scale increases (see table 14.3).

It was also assumed, for the purpose of preparing this table, that models have a life of four years. In the past U.K. companies have changed their models at longer intervals than four years, but as an offset to this, British Leyland in particular has many more than three basic models in production, the rate at which models are changed seems likely to speed up in the future.

Table 14.4. *Illustrative Estimates of Costs and Scale for a Range of Models (consisting of three basic bodies with variants, and five basic engines)* [a]

	100	250	500	1,000	2,000
Output (thousands a year)	100	250	500	1,000	2,000
Initial costs for model £m.	40	50	60	80	110
	Costs per vehicle £				
Initial costs	100	50	30	20	14
Materials and components bought out	290	270	255	247	240
Labour (direct and indirect)	120	100	92	87	84
Capital charges for fixed and working capital	75	65	58	53	48
Total ex-works costs	585	485	435	407	386
Index of average costs	100	83	74	70	66
Index of marginal costs		72	65	66	62

(a) Costs have been 'standardised' to be comparable with those in Table 14.3. If the range of models included large and sophisticated models this would, of course, raise average costs per unit, but we have ignored this factor.

The estimates shown in Table 14.4 suggest substantial economies of scale for the production of cars if the range of models does not increase with scale. There are however a number of important factors which have not been allowed for when preparing these estimates which tend to increase the economies of scale.

(a) Large firms are able to spread the costs of introducing new techniques and of improving the supply of materials over a larger output. This gives them a greater incentive to incur expenditure on innovation.

(b) Since large firms can increase their capacity by relatively large

(1) If it were assumed that the output of models made in relatively small quantities increased more than proportionately with scale the economies would be greater.

142

absolute amounts, they have greater opportunities for introducing new plant of the optimum size and of fully utilizing it quickly.

(c) Costs per unit for new plant are likely to be lower for large firms, since they can spread the costs of designing plant over more plant. They are also likely to have greater knowledge of the equipment etc. available.

(d) Large increases in vehicle output lead to substantial increases in output for material and component suppliers. These can then achieve economies of scale in excess of the reductions in material and component costs shown in Table 14.4.

V. Commercial vehicles

Separate estimates of the economies of scale for commercial vehicle production have not been obtained. However, most light commercial vehicles are variants of cars, the bodies are relatively simple, and they are not subject to as rapid evolution as cars. Also engines and chasis are usually common to both light commercial vehicles and cars.[1] The main scale effects of producing light commercial vehicles for a car manufacturer are to obtain:

(a) the benefits of spreading the special initial costs of commercial vehicles. (The number of each model of light commercial vehicle produced is much smaller than that of car models. This offsets the fact that the special initial costs are much smaller.)

(b) the economies of scale for common components by increasing total output of these components.

For heavy commercial vehicle production, we should expect there to be economies of scale for the production of components and engines, and the assembly of chassis. When comparing economies of scale for cars and commercial vehicles there are two conflicting forces. The annual output of commercial vehicles is relatively small and, as the economies of scale diminish at the margin as scale is increased, we should expect large economies of scale for commercial vehicle production. On the other hand, the relatively high cost of material inputs tends to damp down the economies of scale. A leading U.K. manufacturer estimated that direct labour costs for a sixteen ton truck were only 3% of total factory costs, as compared with more than 8% for a car. There are generally relatively small economies of scale for material costs, which are proportionately more important for commercial vehicles.

VI. Factories

Estimates of the effects of fragmentation of production facilities in different factories were not obtained. If individual factories are so small that operations for individual models have to be duplicated at a number of sites, this

---

(1) It is also interesting to note that companies buy out many diesel engines. A number of manufacturers use the same diesels made by specialist manufacturers. In this way economies of scale for engine manufacture are gained.

143

will clearly increase production costs. In the past, fragmentation in the U.K. has resulted in vertical disintegration of production, and the separation of the manufacture of different models, rather than in the duplication of facilities for producing the same model. The main costs of vertical disintegration are the extra costs of transport and loss of flexibility. Extra transport costs are serious if bodies and/or chassis have to be moved. Moving car bodies over short distances, of, say, 30 miles may cost as much as £2 a body.[1] As regards loss of flexibility, if production is concentrated, redundancy created by new investment can be handled by reallocation of work, and space no longer required for one operation can be used for another operation. Where production facilities are geographically separated, however, flexibility is reduced. The division of production between a great many sites may also involve loss of control and management problems, especially if labour relations are indifferent and/or good management is scarce. Although it is difficult to quantify the effects of fragmentation of production facilities, these may be important.

An important dimension of scale is the operation of plants in a number of countries. When overseas plants are first set up they are usually assembly plants, and are built to get within tariff barriers or to reduce costs of transport. In time, local operations often expand vertically and local supplies are obtained. The economies achieved by adding overseas plants are that:

(1) during the early years, the demand from the overseas plant may enable the company to operate its U.K. plant at a higher rate of capacity utilization than it would otherwise achieve (for this to apply it has to be assumed that the overseas market could not be supplied entirely from U.K. production. The importance of this effect is probably exaggerated in practice because firms underestimate the extent to which some markets can be supplied from the U.K., and the speed with which vertical integration will in fact take place at the overseas plant).

(2) an increase in output enables economies to be achieved, e.g.

(a) technical economies for the production of components or models which are centralized. For example, although British Leyland makes a range of models at its Australian plant, it exports sports cars to Australia from the U.K. Ford is using engines made in the U.K. for cars assembled in the U.S., and is planning to centralize the production of automatic gear boxes for its European plants.

(b) where the plants duplicate production facilities, there are economies for design work and some overheads.

A point worth noting about overseas plants for a study of the economies

(1) This estimate is for transport costs alone. In addition there are costs for loading and unloading, for damage caused by transporting the bodies and for loss of control. Also if the extra costs are added to the price then purchase tax and dealers' margins further increase the effect on the final price.

144

of scale, is that U.K. firms have usually had a smaller share of the markets in which their overseas plants operate than of the U.K. market. The overseas markets themselves are expanding, and the economies of scale to be obtained by merging overseas operations have therefore become proportionately larger in relation to their U.K. operations.

VII. Firms

The production economies of scale for manufacturing cars on a large scale have been described above. In this section we outline the advantages of vertical integration for a firm, and the effect of scale on the non-technical factors determining the success of firms of different sizes.

(a) *Vertical integration*

The main advantages of vertical integration for firms in this industry are:

(1) increased control over production

(2) improved flexibility for planning

(3) the ability to take a view of the total effect of its decisions.

These factors are important in an industry which is subject to cyclical variations in demand. Also, it is supplied by industries themselves subject to substantial economies of scale, whose costs are very sensitive to levels of capacity utilisation e.g. sheet steel producers. Where vertical disintegration involves body and chassis production, as it did in the past for B.M.C., there could be serious differences between the interests of the assembler and of other firms involved in vehicle production. Now an overall view is taken, so pressure to fill capacity by exporting etc. is greater, thus tending to increase capacity utilisation and hence efficiency.

(b) *The non-technical forces*

C.E. Edwards[1] analysed the non-technical forces affecting the competitiveness of American manufacturers. He showed that the major manufacturers had important advantages, apart from the technical economies of scale, and that for obtaining these advantages the total output of a firm was more important than the output of particular models. These advantages are now discussed.

(1) *Distribution costs.* Distribution costs, including transport costs, form a larger proportion of costs for U.S. motor manufacturers in their home market than for U.K. producers with their more concentrated market. In the U.S., the three largest firms operate a number of widely scattered assembly plants and this has given them an important cost advantage compared to the smaller 'independent' companies who have to transport finished products. Similar advantages can be obtained by large scale British manufacturers in export markets which in 1969 accounted for 45% of car production. There are also substantial economies of scale for supplying

(1) C.E. Edwards, 'Dynamics of the U.S. Automobile Industry' (COLUMBIA, 1965).

overseas markets in large quantities. The following estimates illustrate these economies.

Number of cars sent from U.K. to Canada per year (thousands)	5	10	60
Index of transport costs per car [a]	100	85	70

(a) Unit costs for transporting 5,000 cars a year would be about £40.

(2) *Marketing*. One of the marketing advantages enjoyed by the three leading American car manufacturers, to which Edwards draws attention, is the spreading of advertising expenses. (Expenditure on advertising accounted for about ½% of U.K. manufacturers' sales in 1963). Another advantage claimed was the confidence of consumers in the products of the leading manufacturers. This is particularly important for products such as cars which form a substantial item in family budgets, people are less likely to be ready to take a risk. Also, a small scale manufacturer is not in a good position to spread the risks involved in style changes. A large scale manufacturer can adopt a number of styles simultaneously, and can afford to change an unsuccessful style comparatively rapidly.

An important marketing factor is the maintenance of an adequate dealer network. Edwards found that there are economies of scale which are partly attributable to advertising at this level of marketing. There are also economies for supplying spare parts and trained service engineers. Edwards estimated that in the U.S. a market of 400,000 units per year is required to achieve an efficient dealer network unless franchises can be duplicated. The need for widespread points of sale and service facilities are part of the explanation.[1] A final marketing scale advantage is that success may breed further success in marketing. A firm with a large share of the market tends to set the style, and the fact that its cars sell in large quantities is itself an advertisement. On the other hand, if people like a distinctive car, this tends to give small firms an advantage.

Marketing costs are related to the output of models as well as the total output of firms. Particularly when introducing a model, firms advertise a model rather than their range. A firm with a large share of a market has an advantage when introducing a new model because it is likely to have more and better distribution outlets. Other things being equal, it will therefore win a larger share of the market for its new models.

Another important factor affecting the success of firms is that exported mass-produced cars generally sell at lower ex-factory prices than cars sold on the home market. A relatively small firm might thus offset some of its scale disadvantage by sticking to the home market, although this has not

---

(1) One difference between the marketing of cars and tractors on the one hand and heavy commercial vehicles on the other, applies to the provision of servicing facilities. Commercial vehicles travel much greater distances in such markets as the U.S.A., and the E.E.C., and it is necessary to build up comprehensive servicing facilities if the vehicles are to be sold in any part of the market. Cars and tractors can be marketed in parts of these markets with less complete coverage of servicing facilities.

been buoyant in recent years. In practice, the percentage of cars exported by the leading companies is approximately the same, but a higher proportion of B.M.C.'s exports are special models which it does not sell overseas at lower ex-works prices. It therefore sells a relatively smaller proportion of mass-produced cars in export markets than other major manufacturers, and thus benefits as far as export discounts are concerned.

(3) *Research and development.* Another advantage of large scale producers is the ability to spread the costs of research and development (apart from the costs of developing new models), although these costs have represented a very small percentage of the turnover of the independent U.K. groups in recent years. Subsidiaries of U.S. companies have an advantage in being able to take advantage of research and development work carried out by their parents. They can also make use of their parent's experience of investing in new techniques and more capital intensive techniques.

(4) *Labour relations.* A recent study[1] of labour relations in the motor industry has suggested that there is not a consistent relationship between the size of the firms and the quality of their labour relations. The authors found that there were considerable variations among both the large and the small companies in this industry. But the number of firms compared was inevitably very small: too small to support firm conclusions about the effects of size. Also the study was principally concerned with strikes and the causes of strikes, rather than the incidence of restrictive practice among labour.

VIII. The survival of smaller scale firms

Companies manufacturing cars on a relatively small scale can reduce the disadvantages of high tooling costs by concentrating on a limited range of models, preferably for types of cars for which the overall market is limited, so that they have a substantial share of the specialist market. Jaguar and Rover (now a part of British Leyland), Rolls-Royce, Volvo and American Motors all operate in such markets. This policy is likely to be more effective if the size of engine required for the specialist product is outside the range of those mass produced by the large-scale motor manufacturers. A higher price can then be charged for a non-competing article. When independent, the Rover Co., and particularly Jaguar, achieved returns on capital comparable to, or better than, the leading car manufacturers by this type of specialisation.

Another way in which a relatively small firm may be able to reduce initial costs is by keeping the same basic model in production for a long time by attracting customers with conservative tastes, or buyers who are not fashion conscious. Alternatively, it might accurately foresee trends in design and be the first to produce new designs, thereby achieving longer runs. Or a company with a small share of the market may not aim to attract

(1) H.A. Turner, G. Clack and G. Roberts, 'Labour Relations in the Motor Industry', Cambridge, 1967.

customers who frequently change their model of car every time they buy a new car. A company with a large share of the market needs to attract repeatedly customers who may change their car every year but do not wish to buy the same basic model year after year.

Another way in which a firm with a relatively small output may be able to reduce its costs is by buying out a higher proportion of its product. For example, it may buy out engines and/or bodies and thereby obtain the advantages of scale enjoyed by its suppliers.

A marketing strategy of producing for special markets is not limited to the smaller firms. British Leyland in particular has inherited this policy. The 'Mini' is smaller than any cars produced by Ford or Vauxhall, and British Leyland also produces a wide range of sports and quality cars. There are two possible disadvantages of this strategy. Production of special types of car might affect the efficiency of producing other cars in large quantities. Even with delegation, it may not be possible for a firm to be expert in a wide range of sub-markets. Other difficulties may be created; for example piece rate negotiations may be complicated if, measured in terms of units produced per employee, productivity varies greatly between employees because of wide differences in types of model and their scale of output. Also it may be difficult to achieve different standards of quality, and reputation for quality, within one organization. The other problem concerning this strategy is that it might become increasingly difficult to find new niches in the market.

It is worth considering very briefly the sources of economies of scale when firms such as Rover and Jaguar merge with larger firms. If, as is usually the case, production facilities are not rationalized, economies for production costs are limited; the main sources would be for some common components and for material costs. If the company taken over produces products outside the range of the firm which acquired it, economies may be limited even if production is concentrated, because separate lines may have to be set up for engines, transmissions and assembly. However, there may be some economies for distribution and a larger enterprise may be able to supply more finance to its subsidiaries than they could raise if independent.

IX. Conclusions

We have attempted to estimate technical economies of scale for this industry, and have found that these are considerable. We did not attempt to quantify non-technical economies of scale, but our discussion of these suggests that, if anything, they add to the overall advantages of scale in the industry, particularly because of marketing economies. Our conclusions on technical economies can be summarised as in Table 14.5.

The estimates make clear that there are substantial economies which U.K. firms cannot exploit because of their size. Even when production for both home and export markets is considered, this is still true: total U.K. car output was only 1.7 million in 1969. In the case of subsidiaries of U.S. companies, there is scope for reductions in costs by international inter-

Table 14.5. *Summary of Minimum Efficient Scale for Cars*

A firm making	Annual output[a] 000's·	% of UK market	Percentage increase in average total costs at 50% of 'm.e.s.'	Percentage increase in average value added at 50% of 'm.e.s.'
One model and its variants	500	50[b]	6	10
A range of three basic models	1,000	100	6	13
Size of works	No estimate made			

(a) A life of four years is assumed for models. The estimates of economies for the production of one model are based on those for a firm making only one model. If a firm made a range of models the economies would be smaller. On the other hand the assumptions are based on conservative assumptions about the number of engine and assembly lines used.

(b) The output is related to U.K. output of models in the range 1,000 c.c.'s to 1,300 c.c.'s.

gration of their activities, although tariff and other barriers inhibit this. In the case of British Leyland, there is also some scope for intergration with overseas operations, but again there are barriers in the way of this.

For commercial vehicles, the smaller scale of production makes the achievement of scale economies even more difficult, but intergration of car and van models is helpful here.

The possibility of achieving a scale somewhere nearer the m.e.s. in the U.K. rests mainly on an expansion of home and export markets. Firms themselves can make a contribution by reducing model variety and by keeping particular models in production over a long period of years. This is how the small manufacturers have to behave, although they are helped by being able to buy standardised components at relatively low prices. Unfortunately for the larger manufacturers, keener international competition in recent years has increased pressure for greater model variety and shorter model life. Success in introducing new models may, indeed, now be of much greater value to a firm than the reduction in costs that longer model runs can bring.

With the market completely dominated by three U.S. subsidiaries and one British firm, the scope for further rationalisation by mergers among companies operating in the U.K. seems to be very limited. Pressure for rationalisation within firms, in spite of market forces to the contrary, is the main hope for further economies of scale, together of course with a general expansion of the market. More remote possibilities are some form of merger between British Leyland and another European (or Japanese) firm to take advantage of the scope for spreading initial costs for models and using common components, and a merger between Chrysler U.K. and another manufacturer.

15. Aircraft

Table 15.1. *Profile of the Aircraft Manufacturing and Repair Industry*

	1963	% of all manufacturing industry	1968	% of all manufacturing industry	1968 as % of 1963
Number of Employees ('000)	254.6	3.2	229.1	2.8	90
Sales (£m)	573.9	2.1	851.0	2.2	148
Net Output (£m)	324.7	3.0	490.4	3.1	151
Capital Expenditure (£m)	11.4	1.1	—	—	—

Concentration

Concentration ratios for the largest firms in 1963
Aircraft (5 firms) — 98%
Aero-engines (8 firms) — 97%

Size of Establishments and Enterprises (1963)

	Establishments		Enterprises	
Number of Employees	Number	% of Employees	Number	% of Employees
Under 100	144	3	108	1
100—999	100	15	54	7
1,000—3,999	49	41	12	9
4,000—7,499	9	20	4	8
7,500 and over	5	21	7	75
	307	100	185	100

I. General introduction

(1) *Structure of the industry*[1]

Inspite of some contraction of the aircraft industry in recent years, it still employs nearly a quarter of a million people — 1% of the entire working population. The bulk of the British aircraft industry has been concentrated into four groups, two fixed wing airframe builders, British Aircraft Corporation and Hawker Siddeley, one engine manufacturer, Rolls Royce, and one helicopter manufacturer, Westland.

(2) *Processes*

The industry is like the motor industry in some respects: the processes of

---

(1) The Plowden Report (Report of the Committee of Inquiry into the Aircraft Industry HMSO, 1965) provides a comprehensive description of the structure of the industry and some information costs.

150

production – the pressing and machining of components and assembly – are similar, and firms assemble parts supplied by many other firms and industries. Also engines are used in a number of distinct types of airframe. But there are important differences. The degree of precision required is much greater for aircraft, technical progress is more important and faster, and the output of individual types of aircraft is much smaller than for models of cars.[1] For example, only 1,545 Hawker Hunters and 444 Vickers Viscounts were built. The output of other types of military and civil aircraft built in the U.K. during the period since 1955 has been much lower than for these two aircraft. For example 52 V.C. 10's were built, a total of 82 Tridents have been ordered, of which 13 orders were from overseas, and 190 BAC 1 – 11's have been ordered, 122 for export. In contrast, about 750 Boeing 707's had been sold by 1969.

(3) *The dimensions of scale*

Two recent studies[2] of the economies to be achieved by producing large numbers of the same type of aircraft have been published. They show that these economies, which are achieved by spreading design and development costs, and by learning from experience as more aircraft of one type are built, are very substantial. Apart from the output of types of aircraft, the other important dimensions of output for the industry are the rate of production of each type, the size of firms and the overall size of the industry. The construction and assembly of aircraft can be subdivided between different plants so that the size of individual plants is perhaps of less importance, than in some other industries. We have collected no data dealing with this point.

II. The structure of costs

We did not collect any information from firms about the structure of costs. The main feature of the structure of costs is the heavy cost of R & D – 19% of sales and 33% of value added in 1968.[3]

III. Types of aircraft

(1) *Development costs*

The main economies to be achieved by large outputs of one type of aircraft are obtained by spreading launching costs, the costs of designing, planning and development, and the cost of the special jigs and tools. This last item

(1) For an entertaining account of the differences between car and aircraft production see 'Over to Bombers' by Mark Benney, London, 1942.

(2) S.G. Sturmey, 'Cost Curves and Pricing in Aircraft Production', Economic Journal, Dec., 1964. K. Hartley. 'The Learning Curve and its Application to the Aircraft Industry', Jnl. of Ind. Econ., March, 1965.

(3) 'Statistics of Science and Technology', Min Tech. H.M.S.O. 1968.

is, in part, dependent on the number of the model of aircraft which a firm *expects* to make. Table 15.2. shows some illustrative figures for the relationship between launching costs, other costs, and average total unit costs for a plane.[1]

Table 15.2. *Costs and Output of an Aircraft Type*[a]

Number of Aircraft	Average Labour Cost[b]	Average Production Cost[b]	Average Launching Cost	Average Total Cost
1	2.43	9.6	200	209.6
10	1.54	7.1	20	27.1
50	0.98	5.7	4	9.7
100	0.8	5.2	2	7.2
200	0.65	4.7	1	5.7

(a) The costs are in terms of 'units'. For a small aircraft, for example a DC.3 replacement, each of these cost units would represent less than £20,000: for a large jet transport each unit would represent about £200,000. Thus (c. 1963) average launching costs for a large jet transport would be 200 times £200,000 i.e. £40 million.

(b) The basis for estimating labour costs and production costs is discussed below.

Source: Based on S.G. Sturmey, op. cit., p. 969, and on the Plowden Report.

The data in Table 15.3. show the rapid increase in the relative importance of R & D costs during the post-war period. Part of the increase is attributable to smaller production runs, but this in turn is partly attributable to the increased efficiency, size and speed of the later aircraft which has resulted from increased development costs.

(2) *Production costs*

Both Sturmey and Hartley provide measures of the learning effect on direct labour costs — the learning curve.[2] This relates average man hours per unit to the cumulative output of a type of aircraft. Sturmey presents evidence

(1) The output figures given in Table 15.2. can be compared to the output of the following aircraft made in the U.K.

Aircraft	Number (built or on order by 1.8.65)	For U.K. Use Civil	Military
Hawker Hunter	1,525	—	1,045
Gloster Javelin	428	—	428
Vickers Viscount	444	84	—
Bristol Britannia	82	37	23
Comet 3 and 4	75	33	6

On *average* U.S. output of types of military aircraft was 3½ times the U.K. level during the period 1955-61, and for transport aircraft 4½ times the U.K. level. (Source: Plowden Report p.9 and 121 et seq).

(2) For a graphic account of the learning effect in operation, and for the reasons why it is particularly important in aircraft production, see 'Over to Bombers' by Mark Benney.

that average man hours of direct labour per airframe fall by about 20% with each doubling in output, and this relationship was assumed in estimating the average labour costs shown in Table 15.2. The sources of the economies through learning have been discussed by Nicholas Baloff.[1] He emphasises the role of indirect staff in facilitating increases in productivity, as well as the increase in productivity achieved by direct labour through learning by experience.[2] He also refers to evidence which shows that the effects of learning vary for different aeroplanes.

Table 15.3. *Research and Development Expenditure as a Percentage of Total System Cost*

System	Percentage	System	Percentage
B-36	2	F-86	1
B-47	3	F-100	3
B-52	5	F-105	21
B-58	18	F-108	23
B-70 (Small fleet)	30		
B-70 (Large fleet)	12		

Source: H.O. Stekler, The Structure and Performance of the Aerospace Industry, (Univ. of California Inst. of Business and Economic Research), p.19.

An economist with experience of aircraft engine manufacture has claimed that, after a production run lasting eighteen months, his firm had found that there was very little further reduction in costs through learning. Baloff gave conflicting evidence for the existence of a steady state phase of this sort. He concluded that 'it may very well be true that the steady-state phase is typically irrelevant in a particular industry, but to assume *a priori* that this condition always holds may occasionally result in rather dubious applications of the learning curve'. It has also been suggested that the learning effect is greater for assembly work than for machining. An indication of the difference is that the effect of the learning process on machining operations is only about half that for assembly.[3]

The Plowden Report referred to evidence obtained from the Ministry of Aviation that the learning effect applied to costs other than direct labour costs, but that the effect was smaller. They estimated that, for every doubling of the length of production run average unit production costs, including direct labour costs, in the British aircraft industry fall by 9% and in the U.S. industry by 12½%. The former estimate has been used to calculate the average production costs shown in Table 15.2.

(3) *Marketing*

Sturmey also refers to the marketing advantages to be achieved by long

(1) Nicholas Baloff. 'The Learning Curve — Some Controversial Issues'. Journal of Industrial Economics, July, 1966.

(2) In so far as the learning effect reflects the introduction of new techniques, rather than a more efficient use of existing techniques, it is not, of course, a true economy of scale.

(3) Winifred B. Herschmann. 'Profit from the Learning Curve'. Harvard Business Review, Feb. 1964.

runs. The second hand price of aircraft produced in large numbers is likely to be higher partly because servicing facilities will be better and more widespread: a case of success breeding success.

(4) *Limitations to the size of economies of scale*

There are several qualifications to the estimates of economies of scale given so far. The relative importance of development costs, the main source of scale economies, depends on the complexity of the aircraft, and, if it is tent to which it differs from earlier aircraft. Also engines, and many other components, are used for a number of different types of aircraft and if it is not necessary to develop a new. engine for an aircraft, this will reduce development costs. It may be noted that the cost of engines represents about a third of the total cost of an aircraft, if replacement engines are included. In addition, a firm which is aiming to obtain a small share of the market only, may be able to spend less on development partly by introducing a plane later than planes made by competitors, and possibly by producing a simpler product. A firm which expects to produce small numbers of an aircraft can also limit initial costs by using fewer special jigs and tools, but this will be at the expense of extra production costs.

IV. Output per unit of time

Another variable affecting unit production costs is the time taken to produce the total output of a type of aircraft, and it is necessary to distinguish between the effects of changes in the planned rate of production, and the effects of subsequent departures from the planned rate. The latter is not relevant to an overall economic assessment of economies of scale for aircraft production as it reflects the underloading or overloading of planned resources. (A reduced throughput with the same plant will increase the unit allocation of fixed charges, and may prejudice the continuity of labour requirements in particular trades, while increased throughput may bring problems of interference between different operators working in congested areas.)

If one turns to the effects of changes to the planned rate then there are two principal factors to be considered, tooling and learning. As regards the effects on tooling, probably the best published source of information is an estimate by Levenson and Barro.[1] This suggests that the tooling hours (and hence costs) are proportional to $R^{0.4}$ where R is the production rate. There are quite plausible explanatory factors for an index substantially less than unity (i.e. for tooling costs to be less than directly proportional to rate of production). Some of the tooling costs are for tool design which would be largely independent of rate of production if increases in rate are achieved by multiplication of jigs and tools. There may be some 'learning' effect in producing additional examples of jigs and tools, and there may not

(1) Levenson and Barro. Cost-Estimating Relationships for Aircraft Airframes. Rand Corporation Memorandum RM-4845-PR, May 1968.

154

be a need to increase the numbers of some tools. (Jigs and tools may be continuously utilised but it is unlikely that they all would be.)

The second factor, 'learning', is somewhat more problematical. Such information as is available suggests that the learning process is not appreciably slowed up by multiplication of jigs. Much of the 'learning' is obviously due to information which is readily (and sometimes necessarily) conveyed from line to line or to all lines simultaneously, either by physical transfer of operators or by changes in instructions on drawings or planning sheets. A U.K. company provided an estimate of the learning curve for an assembly made on five jigs. The twenty third set produced was the first set from the fifth jig, but the man hours for this set were similar to those made on the other four jigs at the same time. These were by then producing their eighth, sixth, sixth and fifth sets. But this evidence does not show whether a greater learning effect would be achieved if a given number of units were produced on, say, one line, rather than two lines.

V. Firms

The evidence suggests that, if the U.K. aircraft industry is to produce advanced transport aircraft, the concentration of the industry in recent years is justified on the basis of economies of scale for models of aircraft. A demand from the home market for fifty aircraft of an advanced civil type is the likely maximum. More than one airframe manufacturer can only be justified if firms produce aircraft for different sectors of the U.K. market — e.g. short haul, long distance transport or military aircraft. If export markets are included, the position is less clear cut. Even greater concentration of engine manufacture is justified because of the fact that variants of an engine can be used in several airframes.

Even if firms develop products for different markets, there are likely to be some economies from concentration. A firm developing and producing a succession of types for different markets should be able to maintain a higher rate of utilisation of design teams and production units. There should be some saving in overheads and it would be possible to eliminate some duplication in research and development. Sturmey also describes the advantages conferred by marketing a range of aircraft, especially if they incorporate engines made by a single manufacturer.

There appears to be no reason why a relatively small firm should not produce a relatively small, simple aircraft, but the size of the U.K. market for such planes compared to the U.S. market, may be an important obstacle to the successful development of such a business.

VI. Summary

Table 15.4. *Summary of Minimum Efficient Scale*

	% of U.K. Market	% increase in average total costs at 50% of the M.E.S.	% increase in average value added at 50% of the M.E.S.
A Type of Aircraft such as the B.A.C. 1-11	100	> 20%	> 25%
Size of firm which manufactures aircraft	There are substantial economies for firms which manufacture a range of aircraft, but no measure of these economies has been obtained.		

16. Bicycles

Table 16.1. *Profile of the Bicycle, Tricycle and Motor Cycle Trades*[a]

	1963	% of all manufacturing industry	1968 (Estimate)	% of all manufacturing industry	1968 as % of 1963
Number of Employees ('000)	17.5	0.2	14.3	0.2	82
Sales (£m.)	38.9	0.1	41.8	0.1	107
Net Output (£m.)	17.8	0.2	19.9	0.1	112
Capital Expenditure	0.3[b]	0.0			

Concentration:

   Concentration ratio for the 5 largest firms in 1963 — 89.0%.

(a) Separate data for bicycles alone are not available. The data given are for large firms only, those with more than 25 employees, and exclude firms making parts only.

(b) Before deducting sales of property.

I. General introduction

This industry was included in the study partly in order to see if the concentrated structure of the industry reflected substantial economies of scale. Another reason for the inclusion of bicycle production was that bicycles are relatively simple products, compared to the other engineering products discussed.

1. Structure of the industry

Raleigh Industries, a subsidiary of Tube Investments, dominates the U.K. cycle industry and produces about 80% of the bicycles made in the U.K. — nearly two million a year during the 1960's, of which 60% were exported. In 1963, eleven other firms shared the remaining production. The overall size of the industry is indicated by total employment which was approximately 10,000 in 1969 — less than 0.1% of the labour force.

2. Production Processes

The operations common to Raleigh and most of the manufacturers who operate on a smaller scale are the production of frames and forks, the enamelling of frames and the assembly and finishing of bicycles. The extent to which a firm can make components efficiently increases with scale. For example, it is economic for a manufacturer to make hubs for annual outputs of more than 100,000 units and, at an output several times this level, it would pay a firm to make rims, but even at an output of a million units a year it pays a

manufacturer to buy out components such as lamps and tyres. The differences in the proportion of bought out parts are substantial, and where a
manufacturer's range of operations is limited to enamelling, assembly and
finishing, his operations would represent only an eighth of those performed
by the large scale manufacturer - measured in terms of value added by the
large scale manufacturer.

3. The dimensions of scale

The dimensions of scale for bicycle production which we have considered
are the output of particular models, the length of production runs, the size
of factories and firms.

II. The structure of costs

A detailed breakdown of costs was obtained from only one firm — a firm
which assembled, enamelled and finished bicycles. Their costs during the
final year of production, 1965, when they assembled about 20,000 bicycles,
were:

	Cost per bicycle £
Components	8.00
Direct Labour for Assembly	0.25
Other Manufacturing Overheads	0.75
Total ex-works cost	9.00

This breakdown of costs is of some interest because it indicates the limited
scope for a manufacturer producing on a large scale to achieve lower costs
than smaller firms if they can buy components at competitive prices. [1]

III. Models and production runs

The wide range of models made by firms is illustrated by the catalogue of
one firm (not Raleigh) which included more than twenty distinct models. But
in this industry the initial costs for a new model are comparatively small.
If production on a large scale is planned, say 20,000 units a year, initial
costs for a *radically* new model may amount to £20,000, but if a smaller output is expected initial costs can be drastically reduced.

The diversity of styles, sizes and colours of bicycles produced means
that the manufacture of cycles is generally organised on a batch basis,
though the production of some components is standardised. There are some
economies for long production runs, but most of the machinery and plant
employed is readily adaptable for different models, and the economies to be
achieved by say doubling or quadrupling the length of runs are not substantial. If the character of demand for cycles changed and was concentrated on
one type and size of cycle, substantial economies could perhaps be achieved

---

(1) The company ceased to manufacture bicycles because of the decline in U.K.
    demand for cycles and because the two managers of the cycle manufacturing
    department were approaching retirement.

158

by mechanisation and automation, but it is unrealistic to think in terms of such a change. The trend is towards greater diversity as increased attempts are made to encourage buyers of cycles to be *fashion* conscious. Nor do exports at present provide an opportunity to standardise production because the demand in each market is different, and tastes for bicycles in these markets are often conservative. But in the future there may be increased conformity in different markets, especially for new designs.

IV. Factories

No data about the economies of scale for factories were obtained. A large firm could produce components at separate factories without significant loss of economies of scale, but the reader is referred to a brief discussion of the effects of division of production between separate factories on efficiency for motor vehicle production as the effects are likely to be similar for bicycles.

V. Firms

1. *Operations common to Raleigh and the smaller manufacturers*

As it is not possible to standardize production, a manufacturer with an annual output of more than 100,000 bicycles has to duplicate many of the operations involved in constructing frames (bronzing, tubing and enamelling) and assembling cycles. However a manufacturer producing a million units a year has some scope for employing different techniques, for example for enamelling, and by the use of more conveyor belts. Also assembly operations can be further broken down and output of types can be concentrated on different assembly lines. But the economies which can be achieved by each of these changes are small in relation to the total cost of the group of operations common to Raleigh and the smaller manufacturers, and the overall cost of a bicycle.

In the past similar considerations have applied to the development of new techniques, such as ring brazing, which have been made by the large scale manufacturer in this industry. These techniques reduce costs and often improve quality, but because the cost being reduced in each case is relatively small, compared to the total cost of a bicycle, the savings in costs are not competitively significant.

2. *The manufacture of components*

Economies of scale for the manufacture of many components are greater than for assembly, partly because there is not so much diversity. An important source of these economies is the use of different techniques. For example, as the scale of production of hubs increases, forging can be substituted for machining and, at a still higher level of output, cold flow press-work can be employed economically. In one case, the use of cold press-work, instead of forging, cut the metal requirements by half. Similarly the use of automatic equipment for the assembly of pedals can be justified if the output is in excess of 2 million pairs a year.

159

Two illustrations of the economies of scale for the production of components were obtained. The cost for the first batch of 50 units of a new component for a folding bicycle was £6 each. The next production batch, even though only 5,000 were required, justified a press tool, and were produced at 5s. each including the cost of the tool. For hubs it was estimated that if the cost for 1,000 hubs was taken as 100, the index of unit costs for 100,000 would be of the order of 85. For making this very approximate estimate it was assumed that for a run of 1,000 hubs a capstan lathe would be used and for 100,000 hubs, presses and automatic lathes would be employed. A very tentative estimate of the breakdown of costs at each scale of output was also obtained. This indicated that economies in material and labour costs would be partly offset by higher overheads reflecting the increased capital intensity of production.

Table 16.2. *Economies of Scale for the Production of Cycle Hubs*

Output per year	1,000	100,000
Cost	Index of Costs for Hubs	
Materials	55	45
Labour	22½	10
Overheads	22½	30
Total	100	85

3. Overheads

A large scale producer has an advantage for employing and spreading the cost of specialist staff. For example a qualified chemist can be employed to advise on the enamelling operations and qualified engineers and designers can be continuously set new tasks to improve methods of production. A small scale manufacturer has to rely much more on his own or external expertise, or he is faced with heavy overhead costs.

4. Overall estimate of the effects of the size of firm and costs of production

As mentioned above there is a large gulf between the leading U.K. manufacturer and the others, both in terms of total output, and operations performed, and the question of differences in costs for two firms producing say 100,000 and a million units a year, and performing the same operations, is therefore hypothetical. However, an estimate was obtained from one company on the basis that the smaller firm itself manufactured all the components which it was economic for the larger manufacturer to produce. (It was not assumed that the smaller firm would necessarily use the same techniques.) The very tentative estimate was that the difference in costs might be of the order of 10%. One important factor contributing to this result was the cost of materials and components, which would represent 50-60% of the costs of the larger plant, and for which it was assumed there would be few economies for large purchases.[1] If account is taken of the fact that the smaller firm

(1) The position is complicated by the largest firm in the industry supplying components to the smaller manufacturers. The supplier in these transactions presumably takes some profit on these sales and it was significant that a small manufacturer thought that the large firm took its profits on the sale of components (i.e. he assumed that Tube Investments made the same profits whether they sold the components, or assembled the bicycle) even if this was not in fact true.

could in practice buy out the components for which it had a disadvantage, the actual economies of scale are clearly not large in relation to the cost of the finished product.

5. *Marketing and distribution*

The costs of marketing and delivery to the home market are of less significance for the bicycle industry than for motors. There is more flexibility in marketing because the product can be distributed through merchants and through a wider range of retail outlets including specialist shops, department stores, and mail order houses. Also as the cost of the product is much less, consumers can more readily afford to experiment and so customers are not so tied to certain manufacturers. But, if the industry was a great deal more fragmented, there would be duplication of sales forces and significant extra costs.

6. *Other factors affecting competition*

In addition to the absence of substantial economies of scale for some of the processes involved in making cycles, there are a number of other factors tending to enable a small manufacturer to remain in the industry. They can make specialist products such as racing models and perhaps charge a higher price for their product. In the past if they avoided export markets they increased the average price they obtained as the ex-factory price for exports was about 15% less than for the home market *before* devaluation. The importance of export markets to the industry as a whole is shown by the proportion of cycles exported which has been about 60% in recent years. Also it is possible to buy components overseas and at 'special' prices, from East European countries. A small scale manufacturer who buys out components has more flexibility for taking advantage of such supplies at least in the short run.

VI. Conclusions

This industry is dominated by one company and so a change in its structure in the direction of greater concentration would not result in a significant lowering in the costs of production of bicycles or increase in labour productivity. On the other hand greater fragmentation of production would increase unit costs.

Table 16.3. *Summary of the Minimum Efficient Scale for Bicycles*[a]

	Output of Bicycles per year	% of the U.K. market
A firm manufacturing a range of bicycles	< 100,000	10%

(a) No overall estimates of the increase in costs at lower scales were obtained, but, if the firm with the smaller output limited the range of its operations, the difference in costs would be small.

17. Machine Tools[1]

Table 17.1. *Profile of the Machine Tool Industry*

	1963	% of all manufacturing industry	1968	% of all manufacturing industry	1968 as % of 1963
Number of Employees (’000)	74.4	0.9	77.1	1.0	104
Sales (£m.)	196.8	0.7	258.9	0.7	132
Net Output (£m.)	104.5	1.0	146.6	0.9	140
Capital Expenditure (£m.)	7.1	0.7	—	—	—

Concentration:

Concentration ratio for the 5 largest firms in 1963 — 25%.

Size of Establishments and Enterprises (1963)

Number of Employees	Establishments Number	Establishments % of Employees	Enterprises Number	Enterprises % of Employees
Less than 100	338	15	276	11
100 to 999	155	65	101	45
1,000 and over	9	20	12	44
	502	100	389	100

I. General introduction

(a) Structure of the industry

The machine tool industry is small in relation to the economy as a whole. It employs less than ½ per cent of the labour force and it is not a capital intensive industry. However, the techniques of production used in the industry, and the range of models made by machine tool firms, are typical of many other engineering industries — particularly the manufacture of woodworking, textile, hosiery, tobacco, coal cutting, footwear and rubber and plastic-processing machinery — and so a study of economies of scale for the machine tool industry is of importance as a guide for a large section of the mechanical engineering industry. Also the machine tool industry is particularly important because it supplies machines which affect the productivity and performance of the engineering industries.

In spite of the recent spate of take-overs in the industry it is still relatively fragmented, and there are more than 200 firms making machine tools

---

[1] This chapter is a revised version of a paper published in the Journal of Industrial Economics in February, 1971.

162

in the U.K.[1] Firms in the industry specialize to a varying extent depending partly on their size. There are three sorts of specialization — according to product (lathes, boring machines etc.), the size and degree of complexity of products, and the demand for products. The following indicates the scope for this specialization.

(a) A recent analysis listed seven groups of products — including lathes, drilling and boring machines and grinding machines — and a total of forty-four classes of tools within these seven groups.[2] Even within the forty-four classes of tools there are ranges of models and variations of models. The Machine Tool Trades Association lists 400 separate headings in its classification code.

(b) An indication of the varying size and complexity of machine tools is provided by the range of prices, which varies from £200 to more than £100,000.

(c) Finally some models are 'standard' machine tools for which U.K. demand runs into hundreds a year, and for a few machine tools, thousands a year; while at the other extreme are tools made on a one-off basis.

The company with the largest output of machine tools, in terms of value, in the U.K. is Alfred Herbert Ltd., which has more than 11,000 employees, most of whom are employed in the industry. The company makes a wide range of models which are included in five of the seven groups, and twenty of the forty-four classes of tools mentioned above.[3] Similar details for some other leading British companies in the industry are given in a footnote.[4]

The smaller firms in the industry each specialize on a small number of classes of tools, but even so most of them produce a range of models. For a firm with 200 employees to have five basic models currently in production represents concentrated production, while a company with 500 employees

---

(1) An indication of the degree of concentration of the industry is that the largest twenty firms accounted for 70 per cent of the output of the industry by value in 1969.

(2) Some tools can perform a number of the operations which are distinguished, e.g. drilling, boring and milling.

(3) This is a very imperfect guide to the range of a firm's products because a firm may specialize on sophisticated or standard products, and this specialization may cut across the classification according to groups and classes of products.

(4)

	Number of employees (thousands)	Number of groups of tools	Number of classes of tools
Staveley Industries	7.2	6	19
Tube Investments	5.0[a]	5	13
John Brown (Wickmans)	3.0[a]	3	4
B. Elliott	3.6	5	11

a   Estimated.

163

may make forty or so different basic models a year.[1] Because of the multiplicity of models, production in machine tool factories has been organized on a small batch basis, but recently a number of firms have pioneered the use of flow production for some machining operations and assembly.

The horizontal concentration of the industry can be considered in terms of the number of firms making each class of tools. This again varies – there are twenty manufacturers of centre lathes and more than ten manufacturers of multi-spindle and tape controlled drills, mechanical power presses, and horizontal and universal milling and surface grinding machines, but on the average there were six U.K. manufacturers of each of the forty-four classes of tools.[2] [3]

All the larger firms in the industry and many of the smaller firms operate a number of factories. Alfred Herbert, Staveley Industries and B. Elliott each operate ten or more factories. In the past different models of tools were made at different factories, rather than each factory specializing on different stages of production, but recently there has been some movement towards greater horizontal specialization.

There are differences in the extent of vertical integration in the industry. For example, some companies make many of the castings which they use, while others buy out all castings. Another area of diversity for vertical intergration is selling. Some firms, including Herbert, Tube Investments and Wickman, sell to users not only their own tools, but tools made by other manufacturers in the U.K. and overseas. Other firms sell exclusively or partly through merchants, or sell their own tools only direct to users.

A number of sources of variation between machine tool firms have been described. This is not an exhaustive list. A particularly important source of variation is the quality of management. Management is important in all trades, but in the machine tool industry there is a combination of factors, including the erratic changes in demand, the labour intensive type of production, the need to build up, and hold together, a balanced team of highly skilled personnel, and rapid technical development, which make the quality of management very important.

(b) The stages of production

The main stages of production for machine tools are:

(a) the conception of a new or improved tool. (In the smaller firms this is the task of the entrepreneur of the firm, assisted to a varying extent by

---

(1) Some firms have more specialized production. For example, one firm with 700 employees makes only 3 basic models.

(2) Some of the models made by firms in each class are not directly competitive for many uses because of differences in size and performance.

(3) When considering the degree of concentration of the machine tool industry, account has to be taken of international trade in tools which represents a substantial proportion of U.K. production and demand. In 1968 U.K. exports of machine tools amounted to £59m., and imports £46m.

his staff. In the larger firms there are specialist departments and com-mittees to initiate and develop ideas for new tools, but even for these firms the costs attributable to this very important activity are negligible in re-lation to total sales.)

(b) the design of new tools or models, the building of prototypes and the preparation of special patterns, jigs and tools for production. (These are the main initial costs for a machine tool.)

(c) the production of the machine tool. (The main production processes are the machining of parts and the assembly of the machine tool. In terms of costs the machining of parts is the more important, and the average ratio of labour and overhead costs for the two types of processes is of the order of 2 to 1.)

It is of interest to compare the techniques used for machine tool pro-duction with the manufacture of motor vehicles, for which we have shown that substantial economies of scale exist. The materials and components bought out are similar and the technical processes are the same. The out-standing difference is the quantity produced: the annual output of machine tools is measured in terms of tens, hundreds and occasionally thousands, while popular car models are produced in hundreds of thousands, and con-sequently flow production techniques can be employed much more generally for the manufacture of cars. Also pressing operations which are the source of the largest technical economies of scale for motor cars are relatively unimportant for machine tools.

(c) The dimensions of scale

The main dimensions of scale for machine tool production are:

(a) the output of particular models;

(b) the size of batches;

(c) the size of factories;

(d) the size of firms.

II. Costs of production

For the machine tool industry as a whole, the 1963 Census of Production shows that purchases of materials, components and fuel represented ap-proximately 35 per cent of sales, and that wages and salaries accounted for a further 37 per cent of turnover. The Census does not give figures for capital employed or depreciation of fixed assets, but figures for de-preciation can be obtained from published accounts, and these show that depreciation accounts for only a small proportion of turnover — between 2 per cent and 6 per cent for most companies. As in other industries, the breakdown of costs varies for different firms depending on the proportion of parts, e.g., castings, bought out, the type of products made, and whether firms sell direct to users.

Two features of firms' costs require special attention. First, the effect on costs of the use of existing buildings, plant and designs. Examples of the importance of this were obtained from several firms. One firm had obtained estimates of the cost of replacing its existing factory which was valued for resale at £150,000. The cost of a new factory of the same capacity was estimated to be about £500,000: the saving in costs attributable to a modern factory were considered to be less than the additional depreciation and interest charges. At another firm it was estimated that the substitution of new machinery for the existing plant would quadruple the depreciation charge. A very approximate estimate was that 75% only of the increase in costs would be offset by reductions in other costs.[1]

The other feature of costs is the high proportion of overhead costs — total costs excluding the cost of bought out materials and components and direct labour. The main components of overhead costs are works overheads, including depreciation, maintenance, inspection and power; initial costs of new machine tools, including the costs of design, development and special jigs and tools; selling costs and the cost of general administration. The relative importance of these costs varies considerably for different firms, but a very approximate guide is that direct costs average about 60 per cent of total costs; works overheads more than 20 per cent; initial costs less than 10 per cent, and selling and administration about 10 per cent.

III. Models

The main sources of economies for increasing the output of particular models is the spreading of design and development costs, the cost of patterns, special jigs and tools, and the cost of introducing new models into a firm's production programme.

Estimates of the costs of designing and developing individual tools were obtained from eight companies. The tentative conclusions about design costs based on estimates obtained from these firms were that:

(a) The cost of development up to the stage of producing a prototype for a standard tool is generally about £100,000.[2] A qualification to this estimate of the costs of developing a new standard machine tool was the experience of one of the smaller companies which had designed two models to the prototype stage at a cost of about £40,000 each. This company had made extensive use of university engineering departments for testing and improving its designs, and it had collaborated with an American company

---

(1) For this exercise capital charges were taken at 15% of book value for existing plant, and of cost for new plant, and it was assumed that the new plant would be operated on a mutiple shift basis.

(2) Firms usually spend more on the development of general purpose tools which are intended to be produced in large quantities than on special purpose tools. If a firm aims to get an edge over its competitors on all features of a general purpose tool the development costs are relatively heavy. Also, if a substantial market is to be obtained, costs of development are increased by the need to design developments to extend the range of operations performed by a machine. Also more extensive market research is required.

which supplied a part of the design.

(b) On the basis of the experience of two firms which make large sophisticated tools selling at about £10,000 each, the initial costs for models of this type are of the same order of magnitude as for standard tools. One firm had developed a new tool which incorporated numerical control for £120,000. The other firm had spent £200,000 in developing a model to the prototype stage.

(c) At a number of the factories visited, examples of tools costing much less than £100,000 to develop were described. These tools were less sophisticated and/or more like existing models than those considered in (b). Estimates of development costs of from £5,000 to £20,000 were mentioned at several factories, and in one case a figure of £1,000 for a particular model was given.

Estimates of the costs of special patterns, jigs and tools for a new model ranged from 20 per cent of development costs up to prototype stage, for a firm which made extensive use of numerically controlled machine tools, up to 100 per cent of these development costs. Other costs, including the cost of employees learning to machine components and assemble a new model, and the costs of negotiating new rates of wages, are also incurred when a new model is introduced. One of the firms visited had made a detailed study of these costs. Their estimate was that the costs of disruption, etc. were of the same order of magnitude as the cost of developing a tool to the prototype stage, in their case about £200,000; but this firm introduced new tools infrequently. The firm included in disruption costs the extra labour and overhead costs for the initial batches. Another way of assessing these costs is to compare costs for successive batches of a product. At one firm it was suggested that the costs for the initial batch produced may be as much as three times the average costs of a machine tool after it had been in production for eighteen months or so. Another 'rule of thumb' suggested was that the average cost for the first production batch could be reduced by more than one third. (In practice the size of batches usually increases as firms acquire experience of production.)

For motor cars initial disruption caused by the introduction of a new model is quickly overcome, and the reduction in costs attributable to learning are generally achieved within a few weeks. This is because a major engineering effort is made to achieve efficient production quickly. This could also be done in the machine tool industry, but a greater engineering effort, than at present, would have to be spent on preparing for production i.e. the initial costs would be greater. A similar difference was found to exist between the production of radio and television sets and electronic capital goods.

In order to assess the relative importance of the initial costs, it is necessary to estimate the total cost of machines, the rate of output for models and the life of designs, as initial costs per unit can be reduced by increasing the rate of output of the tool per unit of time or the life of the tool. Some representative estimates of the total production costs and the demand for tools are given in Table 17.2. The expected life of new designs has fallen in recent years and is now claimed to *average* about 7 years. For some designs a firm may have a clear run for less than this — 2 to 4 years — and may aim to recoup its initial costs during this period.[1]

Table 17.2. *Development Costs for Machine Tools*

		Demand per year	Average Production costs (excluding initial costs) (£) per tool	Total initial costs (£'000)	Initial costs as percentage of average production costs (excluding initial costs) over this range[a]
Standard tool	A	500-1,000	500	200	11.4-5.7
Standard tool	B	200-500	1,000	200	14.3-5.7
Sophisticated tool		20-50	10,000	200	14.3-5.7
General tool	A	25-50	400	10	14.3-7.1
General tool	B	10-25	2,000	40	28.6-11.4

(a) A life of 7 years is assumed.

The following factors would tend to reduce the importance of initial costs as shown:

(a) The initial costs are for completely new models. The initial costs for a development of an existing model, or a modification of an existing model, or a tool that made use of an earlier design (e.g. for a numerical control unit) could be much less. Also economies on these levels of costs are possible for a completely new machine, if demand is expected to be limited. But economies for initial costs may raise production costs, e.g. less may be spent on special jigs and tools, but this would increase machining costs.

(b) No allowance has been made for revenue obtained by selling the prototype(s).

On the other side no allowance had been made for interest on the capital tied up in the initial costs. Inclusion of interest on development costs would substantially increase the initial costs.

Another indication of the relative importance of initial costs is the proportion of these costs to total costs. Firm's development costs generally vary within the range of from 1 per cent to 6 per cent of turnover, with firms which do not attempt to compete by introducing innovations — and some firms producing standard tools in large quantities, at the lower end of the range, and firms which concentrate on sophisticated tools or which are rapidly expanding their range of tools at the upper end.[2] The cost of special

(1) In practice, many firms write off all, or a large part, of the initial costs as they are incurred, against profits on existing machine tools, and thus reduce their tax liability.

(2) A way of avoiding development costs is to obtain a licence to make a model designed by another firm, usually an overseas company. The cost of a licence is normally made up of a price for an initial set of drawings, perhaps £200, and a royalty varying between 5 and 10 per cent of sales revenue, depending, in part, on the proportion of components which are bought from the licensor.

jigs and fixtures represents from 1 per cent to 3 per cent of total costs, but in years in which new products are introduced this expenditure may be significantly higher. In addition there are costs of disruption and interest on capital used for development and tooling, which firms do not usually distinguish in their accounts.

IV. The size of batches

Although some firms have introduced flow production for assembly and some machining operations, all firms machine parts and most assemble tools in batches.[1] The main determinant of the size of batches is the rate of output of models per unit of time i.e. if a high rate of output is achieved then the size of batches will be correspondingly large. But the relationship between batch size and rate of output is not precise, because the extent to which common components are incorporated in a number of models varies, and the size of batches of parts does not necessarily correspond to the size of batches for assembly, as it is economic to produce some components in large batches and stock them until they are required for assembly.

There are three main sources of economies for large batches.

(a) Economies in overhead and direct costs achieved for machining by spreading the cost of setting up machines, and, particularly for assembly, by increasing speed and reducing wastage as a result of learning. Some economies for assembly are attributable to improvements in the accuracy of successive batches of machined parts as the experience of assembling parts is used to improve the specifications for parts.

(b) Economies in overhead costs attributable to spreading the costs of planning, controlling and recording production over more·units in large batches.

(c) As the size of batches is increased it is possible to substitute different types of more specialised machine tools for machining components in order to reduce costs per unit.

The only really satisfactory method of estimating the economies of long runs would be to conduct a series of experiments varying the programme of manufacture at a number of plants and comparing the differences in costs. In practice this is not possible, and for this study four types of information have been used.

1. Some data on the effects of the size of batches on the costs of machining parts were obtained.

2. Several managers in the industry were asked to estimate the effects of changing the length of run. Such estimates have the virtue of being based on experience, also they are often the basis for decision taking.

3. More detailed estimates were obtained from two firms, although all

(1) Even firms which employ flow production for assembly, assemble batches of different models or variations of models in turn.

the managers who provided estimates had made some study of the effects of runs, as two of them had changed their policy on runs in recent years, and another had published an article on the effects of increasing runs.

4. Finally some information about the effect of producing tools in very long runs was obtained from four firms which had introduced methods of flow line production for assembly.

(a) Economies for batches of components

The most efficent type of machine tools — standard, numerically controlled or automatic — for a machine tool manufacturer to use for making a particular part, depends on the total output of the part *and* the size of batches, as the initial costs of tooling and/or programmes can be spread over the total output, and set up costs incurred before each batch is produced have to be spread over the number of units produced in each batch.[1]

The following estimates for turning a typical component illustrate the economies of scale for this type of operation. It was assumed that batches are made over a period of 5 years. Turning operations account for of the order of 50% of machining in machine tool factories.

Size of Batch (number of units)	Type of Machine Tool used	Index of Turning Cost (excl. Materials)	Index of Least Cost
5	Centre lathe / N.C. lathe	100 / 65	65
15	Capstan lathe / N.C. lathe	80 / 40	40
30	Multi tool automatic / N.C. lathe	45 / 35	35
60	Multi tool automatic	30	30
120	Multi tool automatic	25	25
240	Multi tool automatic	22½	22½
1,100	Automatic	20	20

Estimates for other machining operations suggested smaller economies. There was less scope for substituting different techniques for these operations. Again these estimates probably understate the economies of scale because full account is not taken of the effects on overhead costs of longer runs.

There are substantial economies for machining large batches of parts, but if the machinery used is not affected by the size of batch, the economies, which are attributable to spreading set up costs, diminish as the size of batch increases. Where the technique of machining can be varied with the size of batches and the total output of components, then economies

---

(1) The shape of the part, the machining operations required, and the machine tools available to a firm would, in practice, all affect the tool used.

170

continue indefinitely, as more specialized machinery is introduced, but, even though potential economies continue indefinitely, there are wide ranges of output for which the economies for larger batches are small.

(b) Estimates made by managers

The following estimates of the economies for assembling large batches were obtained from a manager of a firm making a wide range of models:

Batch size for assembly	5	10	20	50
Index of production costs	100	95	93	90

These estimates were based on three assumptions:

(a) The total output of the model is not affected by the size of the batch. This assumption means that the initial costs per unit of output are not affected, and that overhead costs which relate partly to the number of models in production are not reduced.

(b) The size of batches for components increases in proportion to the increase in the size of batches of tools.

(c) The level of capacity utilization and the capital equipment of the plant are not affected by the size of batches.

A manager of a firm which made batches of up to twenty-five machines suggested that economies of about the above size would be achieved, and a manager of a firm making batches of between ten and fifty estimated that the savings in costs by doubling the size of batches within this range would not be more than 5 per cent.

(c) Detailed Estimates

One firm which makes large sophisticated machines provided a more detailed study of the effects of the size of batches and this is summarized in Table 17.3. The three estimates of costs for machine B, which are based on different assumptions about batch sizes, again indicate that economies for making a given annual output of a model in larger batches results in small economies. However, a comparison of costs for machines A and B suggests that there are substantial economies for operating costs for increasing the annual output of a model. One of the main problems for making these estimates was the treatment of overheads which were in fact allocated in proportion to direct labour costs. As the main effect of changing the length of runs would be to change total potential output, and, as this would affect the output over which both direct labour and overhead costs could be allocated, this crude assumption probably gives a satisfactory first approximation – if anything it tends to under-state the effects of long runs because of the 'first unit' costs for organizing production of a batch of tools.

Another firm provided the following estimates of the effects of batch size. These estimates were based on more detailed estimates than the earlier estimates. This firm organised assembly so that wherever possible men specialized on one machine throughout the year, rather than making different models in turn.

171

Size of Batch for Assembly (monthly)	1	2	5	10	25	50	100
Index of Assembly Cost per Unit	150	110	100	95	90	87	85
Size of Batch for Machining (quarterly)	3	6	15	30	75	150	
Index of Machining Costs (including materials)	135	115	100	90	85	82	
Combined Index	140	113	100	92	87	84	

Table 17.3. *Batch Size and Unit Costs for Machine Tools*

Model[a]	Number made per year	Size of batches[b] for machining	for assembly	Index number of costs[c] materials	operating costs	total
A	4	4	1	100	100	100
B	22	22	7 or 8	96	73	83
B	22	11	4 or 5	96	75	85
B	22	5	3 or 4	96	80	87
B'	3	3	1	96	90	93

(a) Model A is assumed to be a radically different model from model B, but of the same size and complexity. Model B' is a variation of B with many common parts.

(b) The figures for batch sizes indicate the sort of flexibility for determining batch sizes which exists in practice. If a small number of a machine are made each year, components will be machined in one batch; where larger quantities are made, more than one batch of components may be made. The cost estimates for machine B illustrate the effects of the decision about batch size, but the estimates of costs do not include any charge for holding stocks, which would be higher for long runs.

(c) Costs exclude initial and selling costs.

(d) Large Batches

Four of the firms visited were using methods of flow production rather than batch production for some machining operations and for assembly. The scope for using flow production depends upon the output of particular models and the total output of standard tools, i.e. a firm can either use a special line if it has an output of more than 30 units of a model per week (one firm suggested as few as 15), or it can assemble a range of models on one line. One firm suggested a minimum of 100 units of a model per year for assembly on such a line.

The experience of the four firms showed that there are substantial economies to be achieved by switching to flow production methods when demand for a tool is sufficient. One firm had calculated that it had made a saving of 18 per cent of the assembly costs by switching to flow production.[1] The average time taken to assemble tools was reduced from a month to one day and stocks and work in progress were reduced by 7 per cent — a reduction of 2 per cent in the capital employed.

Before giving our tentative estimates of the economies for large batches, the effects of scale on the cost of materials and bought out components

(1) Another firm claimed to have saved as much as 46 per cent of the labour costs for assembly by switching to flow production, but much of this saving was offset by increased costs for machining.

should be mentioned. Economies for these costs relate to both the output of models and the output of firms, but the latter is generally more important. The scope for negotiating reductions in prices of materials and parts as the size of batches alone is increased would be limited to materials and components which are special to the model. In practice an additional important source of economies for buying when producing standard tools in very large quantities is that it is economic to search for cheaper substitutes for existing materials and components.

Our conservative estimates of the economies to be achieved for large batches of a standard tool are shown in Table 17.4. In practice firms would probably make smaller batches at each level of output than those shown, and this would increase operating costs and thus the economies of scale for larger scales of output.[1]

Table 17.4. *Output of Model of Machine Tool and Unit Production Cost*

Output of tool per year	5	10	20	50	100	200	400	800
Size of batch for assembly	5	5	10	20	33	50	(flow assembly)	
Cost of bought out materials and components per tool	100	98	96	94	93	93	92	92
Operating costs per tool	100	92	86	79	76	70	65	62
Production costs per tool	100	95	91	86	83	81	78	77

For the purpose of making these estimates, the following assumptions were made:

(1) The costs exclude design and development costs.

(2) The level of capacity utilization of the plant and the size of the factory were not affected by the length of runs.

(3) Different techniques of machining parts would be used as output was increased.

The above estimates exclude initial costs. These are included in the estimates for a standard model given in Table 17.5.

Table 17.5. *Output of Model and Unit Ex-Factory Costs*

Output of model per year	10	50	100	800
Inifial costs (£'000)	100	133	167	300
Initial costs per tool (£)	1,430	380	240	40
Production costs (£)	1,150	1,050	1,020	960
Total ex-Factory costs (£)	2,580	1,430	1,260	1,000

The life of the model is assumed to be 7 years. If a firm producing 10 or 50 units a year is to sell in direct competition with a firm producing much larger quantities, it would clearly have to reduce its initial costs below the level assumed by using old designs or by making machine tools with

---

(1) The size of the batches made by firms is affected by demand for the model, as it may not be possible to keep customers waiting, and the state of demand generally. If demand is heavy in relation to capacity, manufacturers may be more inclined to let orders for models accumulate and make larger batches.

different characteristics.[1]

Table 17.6. shows similar estimates for special tools, model A is a small tool and model B a large sophisticated one. Again lives of 7 years were assumed.

Table 17.6. *Additional Examples of Output of Models and Unit Ex-Factory Costs*

	Model A			Model B		
Output of model per year	10	50	100	5	10	20
Initial costs (£)	8,000	10,000	12,000	100,000	125,000	150,000
Initial costs per unit (£)	110	30	20	2,860	1,790	1,070
Production cost per unit (£)	400	370	350	15,000	14,400	13,800
Total ex-factory costs (£)	510	400	370	17,860	16,190	14,870

V. Size of factories

For estimating the economies of scale for both factories and firms, increases in scale brought about by increasing output of a constant range of products, i.e. increasing the size of batches, and by increasing the range of products made are distinguished, though in practice increases in scale are often achieved by a combination of these increases. If the size of batches were positively related to the size of factories, economies for large batches, described in the previous section, would be associated with large factories, but a firm could achieve most of these economies if it divided its production among a number of factories. Similarly, where standard tools are produced in large quantities it is difficult to specify any technical economies for large factories, because the machining of some components and the assembly of sub-assemblies could be carried out at a separate factory without significantly increasing costs. It is therefore more appropriate to consider the economies for a firm producing a narrow range of tools in increasing quantities, whether it operates one or more plants.

However there is scope also for considering the economies of scale for operating large factories, as the larger firms have some choice between building tools in large factories or in a greater number of smaller factories. In the rest of this section the economies for factories at which tools are made in batches of up to 50 machines, and where scale is increased by expanding the range of models made, are described.

The main sources of technical economies of scale for such increases in scale are the spreading of the cost of special tools and equipment,[2] and limiting the range of operations performed on machinery and by operatives.

(1) There are many factors which determine the competitiveness of models. A firm cannot ensure a market merely by spending heavily on development. Improved performance and the fact that a machine tool has been redesigned are selling points, but the fact that a machine tool has been in production for a number of years may also aid sales.

(2) These economies would be substantial for new factories, but for long-established units the economies would not be as significant because much of the plant and equipment would have been written off. Existing small units are able to reduce their cost disadvantage or achieve a cost advantage by using old equipment.

Also there would be scope for spreading some overheads as scale increased. However, if a firm operates a number of factories, especially if the factories are close together, these economies will exist, but they relate to a firm's total capacity, rather than its capacity at any one factory. For example, a firm can site special items of equipment at one factory and centralize the operations to be performed on it.

Offsetting the economies for large factories, there may be some diseconomies of managing a larger unit. Two illustrations of this tendency were obtained from managers. In one case, a manager claimed that when he had about 200 employees at his factory, he could rely on the staff ensuring that products were up to the standards required without detailed inspection. The products might not meet the specifications in some unimportant respects but where, through experience, they had found that high standards were required, this was achieved. It was claimed that this informal flexibility was difficult to achieve in a much larger factory. Another illustration of the flexibility of small units was the opportunity for the manager of a small unit to know the abilities of his staff to carry out difficult machining operations, as this could reduce the need for specialized machinery. Again it was claimed that this was more difficult in a large factory.[1]

Two managers suggested that the optimum size of factories for batch production was about 300 employees. In each case the firm's main factory had expanded beyond this level, but it was shortage of labour, particularly skilled labour, and incentives to operate factories in other regions, which had caused them to build elsewhere. Two other managers emphasized the importance of being able to employ more expensive plant at larger factories and considered that problems of management could be reduced by reorganizing management methods as scale increased. Nevertheless economies attributable to larger factories appear to be small in relation to other factors affecting performance.

VI. Size of firms

The final dimension of scale considered was the size of firms. This important dimension of scale is dealt with briefly because it was not found possible to obtain measures of many of the effects of scale. The technical economies for firms making a constant range of standard tools are considered first, and then the economies for firms for which differences in scale are attributable to the range of products made.

(i) Increasing scale for the production of a narrow range of products

Apart from our discussions with managers, the only sources we had for obtaining a guide to the effect on costs of increasing scale by producing a narrow range of tools in larger quantities was to obtain a breakdown of costs over time, for firms which had increased their output of such a range

---

(1) It was suggested by two multi-factory firms that where the degree of precision required for the production of tools varies, it is preferable to make the tools in different factories.

of tools, and to compare the movement of prices charged by such firms with the movement of prices of other firms' products. These comparisons suggested there were substantial economies, but these economies were not all attributable to economies of scale in the traditional sense;[1] they included economies attributable to learning through time and the introduction of new techniques which were partly attributable to the sustained output of a narrow range of products. Our very tentative estimates of costs at different levels of output of standard tools are shown in Table 17.7.

Table 17.7. *Output of a Range of Models and Costs*

Number of tools produced per year	800	1500	3000	6000
Cost of materials and components per tool (index)	100	98	96.5	95
Operating costs per tool (index)	100	93	88	83
Total Production costs per tool (index)	100	95.5	92.5	89
Production costs per tool (£)	1000	955	925	890
Total initial costs (£'000)	600	650	700	750
Initial costs per tool (£)	110	60	30	20
Total ex-factory costs (£)	1110	1015	955	910

For the purpose of making these estimates it was assumed that the firm made four standard models, i.e. the economies of longer runs were achieved at higher scales of output. The economies shown are based on the assumption that firms with different levels of capacity design their plants to produce their outputs at minimum cost, i.e. they do not build surplus capacity for some operations to allow for expansion.

(ii) *Increasing scale by extending the range of products made*[2]

The main potential areas for economies are:

(a) *Development and design.* An important part of the operation of machine tool firms is the development of new tools. These may be improvements of existing tools or new tools incorporating new techniques or of a new size or to meet a new demand because of changes made by user industries. The advantage of a large firm compared with smaller firms is that it can pool the special skills of a number of experts, but if a manager, or someone else, in a small or medium-size firm has a flair for initiating new designs for which there is an opening in the market, the firm will not necessarily be at a disadvantage compared with large firms. Also there are limits to the advantages of specialization in this industry because familiarity with many

---

(1) The traditional economies of scale were achieved by the use of special purpose machines and equipment, etc., at different scales of output. In this connection it is worth noting that there was very little duplication of plant and processes throughout the machining and assembly shops of the firms which made standard tools in large quantities. Other sources of advantage were the employment of a higher proportion of unskilled labour — this is particularly important where skilled labour is in short supply — and the ability to concentrate on cost reductions through time.

(2) In this section, references to 'small' firms means firms with 300 or less employees, medium-size firms from 300 to 1500, and large firms those with more than 1500 employees.

176

aspects of a business is helpful. For example when selecting new tools to manufacture, account needs to be taken of how they will fit in with the production programme, as well as customers' requirements and the strength of competing manufacturers. Also a small firm may be able to stick to existing designs, obtain assistance on technical matters from university engineering departments, buy out designs from overseas firms, design machines in collaboration with an electronics firm or copy features of designs introduced by other firms, and thus avoid being at a disadvantage compared to larger firms. The success of a small firm depends upon the ability of its managers, the extent to which it specializes and the speed of advance in its field.[1]

The next stage of development is the design prototypes. Usually the design staff of the larger firms are divided into teams for each type of model and there is only a limited interchange between them. Small firms can generally avoid any disadvantages at this stage, but this may involve collaboration with other firms and the temporary hiring of designers if there are peaks in design work. Also the problems of bringing new tools into production tend to increase with scale and increased specialization.

(b) *Economies for production costs.* The total output of a firm and the extent of standardization determine the degree to which firms can employ special plant and machinery. A change that has increased the scope and importance of this is the increased standardization of parts for different models achieved by some firms. This has enabled the firms to install expensive equipment to machine parts, such as heavy castings for a range of products. However, in relation to all the factors affecting the success of a business, these advantages are not generally very important, and small firms may avoid a disadvantage by excluding from their range of products tools requiring special machining equipment i.e. development policy can be used to facilitate production planning.

(c) *Economies for buying and selling.* There are economies for buying in large quantities, and at one firm which had expanded very rapidly, partly by taking over smaller firms, it was suggested that the difference in unit costs of materials for small firms, compared with the largest groups in the industry, was of the order of $5-10$ per cent, equivalent to $2\frac{1}{2}-5$ per cent of total costs.[2] On the basis of our discussions with other firms in the

(1) It is not intended to belittle the importance of research and development and technical advance. These are clearly important and are becoming increasingly so. Nevertheless some firms can succeed without concentrating resources on technical development and others can concentrate a small and effective development effort on a narrow range of products.

(2) It is difficult to obtain reliable information about economies for buying because, though firms know the prices they themselves pay, they have little information about the prices paid by other firms. In the case referred to the large firm had taken over other firms, and could compare prices. An indication of the problem was provided by a firm which took over another four times its own size. For some important materials the firm making the bid obtained discounts of 20 per cent compared with discounts of between $7\frac{1}{2}$ per cent and 10 per cent obtained by the larger firm.

industry and suppliers such as steel stockholders, these estimates seem to be rather high.

The market for many machine tools is now international. In order to obtain the maximum economies of large outputs of models, firms have to export, and if they export a substantial proportion of their output, this provides stability against fluctuations in the U.K. market.[1] For selling costs it is possible to point to areas of advantage for large firms, such as the provision of technical service and representation in export markets. But the smaller firms can sell to users through merchants or possibly manufacturer distributors both in the U.K. and overseas. Also advertising costs are generally low, though representation at exhibitions is costly, and formed 2 – 3 per cent of costs for one medium sized firm. For sophisticated tools the number of potential customers is small, so manufacturers can go direct without incurring heavy costs, and some customers buy tools after themselves making a very detailed survey of the machine tools available.

(d) *Risk taking*. A source of advantage for the larger companies is their ability to finance and accept the risks involved in designing new machines, setting up new factories, concentrating the output of a factory on a limited range of products or type of development e.g. tools for machining a new type of aero-engine. Their advantage is to be able to deploy large quantities of additional capital and expertise at one time, but though they have this advantage it is not always used wisely. These advantages of large firms should not be exaggerated as small firms, with less than 500 employees, in the U.S.A., Germany and the U.K. have introduced many competitive new tools, pioneered the use of flow production techniques, and expanded very rapidly. It might be argued that a number of independent small firms can manage rapid adjustment to changing circumstances more easily than a large firm, and they may be able to improvise and organize production changes at less cost.

The only information available on the relationship between the size and performance is the data from Company Accounts, but Accounts for a run of years are only available for the quoted public companies. For the companies for which accounts are available a comparison of recent profitability is not favourable to the large companies, but Alfred Herbert,[2] Staveley and Elliotts have all been substantially reorganized during the last few years.[3]

(1) The increased size of market provides sufficient demand for the development of specialized machines which would not be justified for one national market.

(2) It may also be noted that in their 1968 accounts, Herberts stated that 'With effect from the beginning of the current financial year, therefore, the twenty-three operating companies that previously functioned separately, and with considerable overlap of products, have been reorganized into seven'. In view of the type of organization employed in the past, it may be that the company did not achieve all the economies of scale available to it.

(3) Staveley and Elliotts have expanded rapidly and have taken over a number of firms in recent years. It is possible that the prospects of the companies which were taken over were not as good as those of the companies which retained their independence.

Also the industry has had to adjust to increased international competition and faster technical development in recent years, so it is even more difficult than usual to draw any final conclusions about the long run effects of scale from the data in Company Accounts.

VII. Conclusions

This chapter has provided some illustrative estimates of the economies of scale for the production of machine tools. It has emphasized the economies for large outputs of individual models. The extent of these economies depends partly on the size of development costs in relation to the costs of production, and for many tools significant economies continue up to outputs which represent a large proportion of total U.K. demand for the particular type of machine tool, and in many cases exceeds it.

Conclusions about the importance of economies for large firms are difficult to draw. A firm with a single factory and with a small output in relation to that of the industry, say ¼ per cent, could manufacture machines for which the market is small without being at a substantial disadvantage compared with larger firms. Even to produce a limited range of standard tools in large quantities, a firm requires only 1 or 2 per cent of the value of the industry's total output of all types of machine tools at the present time.

Table 17.8. *Summary of Minimum Efficient Scale for Machine Tools*

	'M.e.s.' output	% of U.K. output	Increase in costs at 50 per cent of m.e.s.	
			Total Costs	Value Added
Models of machine tools	This depends upon development costs and other factors	For many models more than the total U.K. output (of models with similar specifications)	Say 5%	Say 10%

The m.e.s. for factories and for firms is less than 1% of U.K. output.

179

18. Diesel Engines[1]

I. General introduction

1. Structure of the industry

There are about thirty firms which manufacture diesel engines in the U.K. and these firms have a total labour force of between thirty and forty thousand engaged in making diesels. A feature of the industry is that approximately 75% of its output is exported directly or indirectly in tractors or other products. The output of firms varies from the production of a few large marine diesels made on a one—off basis to the mass production of more than 100,000 vehicle diesels a year. A possible division of the industry is on the basis of the size of engine:—

(a) 1 to 300 b.h.p. This category covers engines designed for vehicles, industrial applications such as electricity generating and pumping sets, trawlers, yachts and as auxiliary engines for larger vessels.

(b) 300 to 3,000 b.h.p. This range includes engines used for power stations, locomotives and small ocean going ships. Detailed information about economies of scale for this section of the industry was not obtained.

(c) 3,000 to 30 000 b.h.p. Engines of this size are built for ship propulsion and for electricity generation.

2. The processes of production and the dimensions of scale

The processes of production and the dimensions of scale are similar to those for other engineering industries. The machining of parts and then assembly are the main processes of production, and economies relate to the output of basic engines and varieties of engines, and the overall output of firms.

Estimates of the effects of scale for the production of 'small' engines are described first.

Small diesels

II. Introduction

1. Structure of the industry

About ten firms, including the main commercial vehicle manufacturers,

---

(1) A profile table is not given for this trade because the coverage of census trades does not correspond to the range of firms from which we obtained data.

make engines in the range up to 300 b.h.p. The manufacturer with the largest output of this size of engine is F. Perkins Ltd., a subsidiary of Massey Ferguson, a Canadian company which is the leading U.K. manufacturer of tractors. About one third of Perkins output is sold to members of the group.

III. Structure of costs

The information we obtained about the structure of costs for small diesels was limited. However two points can be made.

(1) The cost of bought out materials and components represents of the order of 60% of total costs. (In all some 800 firms supply materials and components such as castings, pumps, starters, generators, lubricating oil, etc. to the industry.)

(2) Sales of spare parts by manufacturers, on average, represent more than 25 per cent of the sales of new engines by value, and profits are concentrated on the sale of spare parts which are a tied market.

IV. Initial costs

Data for small engines was obtained from two firms. One of these firms manufactured small diesels for industrial and marine uses. In 1967 the firm estimated that initial costs, including design and special jigs and tools, for an engine which it expected to make at a rate of 2,000 units a year for ten years, would be of the order of £0.25m. This figure excluded the cost of machine tools. A similar estimate by a firm which made diesels in much greater volume was that the initial costs for an engine made at a rate of 100,000 units a year would be about £4m. This estimate included the cost of new machine tools, but not the cost of a new factory etc., and both estimates excluded the costs attributable to disruption.

V. Production costs

The firm which made engines on a large scale manufactured different 'basic' designs on separate production lines at widely differing levels of throughput. Production was organised in this way because much of the equipment for machining engine blocks was designed for particular engines. Also when a new engine was introduced, sales of the engine were in practice partly additional business and partly replaced sales of existing engines, and as the reduction of sales of existing engines did not occur in the right magnitude or at the right time to release facilities for the new engine, new facilities usually had to be built.

The experience of the firm illustrated another aspect of the economies large scale production. The cost of materials represented more than two-thirds of the firm's direct costs of manufacture, and it operated with only five days supplies of parts for the engines produced on a large scale, compared with much greater supplies of parts for diesels produced on a small scale. In the case of one engine made in small quantities these stores represented three months production.

Some estimates of the economies of scale for production costs were obtained from another firm. Two thousand units of a basic engine per year was the highest level of output this firm had achieved. Production was not arranged on separate production lines for each engine and the engine blocks etc. were manufactured on a batch basis. They were machined on a number of machine tools on each of which only one operation was usually performed.

An estimate had been prepared of the costs of manufacturing one engine at a higher scale of output, 5,000 units a year, and these estimates indicated that unit costs would fall by about 15%. It was intended to use numerically controlled machine tools to perform the machining operations for the model, as this level of production was not sufficient to justify the firm setting up a line with special machine tools and automatic transfer equipment. The estimate overstates the economies of scale as some of the economies were attributable to the use of new tools which could have reduced costs if used for the existing output, but no credit was taken for any reduction in the cost of bought out parts which were expected to form two thirds of costs at an output of 5,000 units a year. The firm's experience during the preceding three years, when total output had increased by about three times, and the prices of components had been kept constant in spite of inflation, suggested that there were economies to be achieved by increasing the quantity of components purchased. Estimates were also made of the costs of increasing output to 10,000 and 15,000 units of the engine per year by shift working, and these indicated further economies in total costs, 3% for increasing output from 5,000 to 10,000 units, and a further 1% for increasing it to 15 000 units. Again it was assumed that there would be no effect on the cost of the bought out parts. The effect on these costs would, of course, be very important.

It is of some interest that the prices charged by firms making a somewhat different engine on a much larger scale — about 100,000 units a year — indicated that, if output was increased to this level, costs could be reduced by, of the order of, 20%, compared to unit costs with an output of 5,000 units a year. [1] But such comparisons are a very crude method of assessing the economies of scale.

The second firm also made some types of engine at a rate of less than 2,000 a year. It had found that, if output of an engine was below 2,000 units a year, the main source of increased unit costs was the burden of development costs, rather than increased production costs.

Our very tentative estimates of the economies of scale for the manufacture of a diesel engine in the range 25–100 b.h.p. are:

---

(1) The prices charged by the larger scale manufacturer were adjusted to allow for his profit margin in order to compare costs.

Capacity (Engines per year)	1,000	2,000	5,000	100,000
Initial Costs (1967) £th.	200	250	350	4,000
Initial costs per engine [a] £	20	12.5	7.0	4
Index numbers of costs per engine:				
Initial costs	290	180	100	60
Material & components	110	105	100	90
Labour and capital costs [b]	104	102	100	60
Total	112	105	100	80

(a) A design life of 10 years is assumed.

(b) It is assumed that for outputs of 1,000 to 5,000 engines per year the firm makes a range of engines, and that the output of one engine does affect the type of machinery used, or the utilisation of the machinery.

The estimates of technical economies of scale which we were able to make for this industry were very tentative. The costs of materials and components are about 60 per cent of total costs, and we were unable to obtain a firm guide to economies of scale for these costs.

VI. Firms

(a) Output of a range of engines

The economies for the production of a range of engines are difficult to estimate. At low levels of output the total output of a range of models would affect the type of machine tools used and the extent to which the machine tools are utilised. Also there would be benefits for spreading some overheads and for acquiring materials, components and services. Although it is very difficult to assess these effects, they could be important.

(b) Marketing

Selling costs are not a substantial item of cost for many manufacturers in the industry, as they either transfer many of their engines to other companies in the same group, or sell them in large numbers for inclusion in vehicles or railway engines. Captive markets provide a source of strength in 'free' markets as firms with a tied market can recoup their development costs etc. on sales within the group, and do not face as great risks as firms which rely on entirely 'free' markets.

For 'free' sales the experience of one firm suggested that there were few economies of scale for selling costs, as it had had to increase its sales force and other marketing costs in line with its increased output. But some small economies would be expected for a firm if it extended the range of its products.

Large Marine Diesels

VII. Introduction

1. Structure of the industry

There are seven manufacturers of large 'slow speed' marine diesel engines in the U.K. and the design of these engines is even more concentrated. Three firms, led by the Swiss firm, Sulzer, designed 80 per cent of the diesel engines installed in ships over 2,000 tons launched in all the non communist countries during 1969.[1] Most engines built in the U.K. are built to designs by Sulzer or Burmeister and Wain, a Danish company.[2] The manufacturers of slow speed diesels compete with the producers of turbines and medium speed diesels, but no U.K. firms make either of these types of engine in the same plant as they make slow speed diesels.

VIII. Structure of costs

Two points which have been made for other engineering trades apply to the production of large marine diesels.

(a) The breakdown of costs is very dependent on the extent of vertical integration. For a firm which itself machined most of the components for its engines, materials and components bought out, cost of the order of 50 per cent of production costs. For a firm which bought out crankshafts the average was about 60%.

(b) Costs for different vintages of plant vary greatly. A crude estimate by one manufacturer was that if it replaced its existing plant with current vintages of machinery, this would reduce factory labour requirements by 60 per cent, and increase fixed capital charges to ten times the existing level. Another firm estimated that the cost of replacing its plant and machinery would be £7m. The existing plant had a book value of about £1 m., and the annual saving in labour costs attributable to replacing the existing plant was estimated to be about £200,000, 15% of total labour costs.

IX. Initial costs

The charges made by the firm which design engines represent of the order of 5 per cent of the ex—works price of engines. The firms of designers base their charges on the total h.p. of the engines produced, and so there are no economies of scale for design charges unless large scale manufacturers can negotiate a lower rate. (It is doubtful whether there are significant differences in these rates between firms with different outputs.)

A firm which designs engines gave an estimate of £0.5m. for the costs of designing and developing one of its engines, but commented that R & D expenditure for a radically new engine might involve expenditure of £3m. or more. The leading designers each spend of the order of £3m. a year on R & D. Large marine diesels cost from about £0.25m. to more than £0.7m.

Patterns, dies, jigs and tooling for a new design of engine costs of the order of £50 000. (This figure depends on the differences between the new and earlier designs and the lengths of runs expected). In addition new

---

(1) Source: Sulzer Ltd.

(2) In terms of b.h.p. the distribution of the current U.K. order book is Sulzer 47% B & W 39% and Doxford (a U.K. company) 14%.

machine tools, handling equipment and testing plant may be required. If the new design is for a larger size of engine it may be necessary to enlarge buildings to assemble the engine for testing. If a new assembly and testing bed for large engines is required this can cost £0.5m. and the costs of machine tools for a new design which is larger than earlier designs may be similar. But it is usually possible to make do with existing plant, although this may mean testing sections of an engine in turn,[1] and some bottlenecks for machining operations.

X. Production costs

(1) Designs

In addition to spreading initial costs over the output of a design, there are learning effects which relate to the output of an engine. These economies might be expected to be smaller in this industry than for, say, the heavy electrical industry because many development problems are solved by the licensor and because there is a great deal of similarity between designs of engines. Also, compared to machine tools, there is much more replication of machining operations for individual engines. But any reductions in time for assembling an engine attributable to learning may be swamped by delays in moving completed engines. If a firm has no space for storing completed engines, these take up assembly space until they can be transported to the ship.

One firm provided the following tentative estimates of the economies for learning based on records for two series of engines which had been built in recent years.[2]

Number of production unit	1	2	3	4	9
Index Numbers of Costs of successive units					
Materials and components	100	100	100	100	100
Labour and Overheads	100	91	86	82	78
Total costs (excl. initial costs)	100	96	94	92	90

The firm also expected some economies for material and component costs but these could not be quantified.

(2) Batches

Another potential source of economies for large engines is the size of batches of indentical engines. These are attributable to spreading set up times for machining components over larger batches and to learning. One firm estimated the economies for a batch of 8 engines of a design compared

---

(1) In practice designs are usually built by the designers and are thoroughly tested before licencees build them, and so testing sections of an engine in turn is satisfactory.

(2) These estimates were based on the assumption that the engines were built in rapid succession. If they were built at longer intervals the economies would be smaller.

to a batch of 4 engines to be at least 2.5% of average costs for 4 engines. Another firm suggested that the economies attributable to differences in the size of batches would be smaller.

(3) *The total output of factories*

The Geddes Committee on Shipbuilding suggested that an annual capacity of 300,000 h.p. per annum is required to obtain the full benefits of scale for the production of diesel engines and turbines. The report does not specify what size of engines such a works would manufacture or the vintage of plant it would use. Given that a firm concentrates on a range of diesel engines of about 10,000 h.p., it would seem to be able to achieve most of the economies of scale at an output of 100,000 h.p. or, say, ten engines a year, if much of its plant is not of recent vintage. If engines with more power are made, but the extra power is achieved by adding cylinders, then the minimum efficient scale is not affected.

If a completely new engine plant were built some economies for capital charges for machining and testing operations would extend well beyond 100,000 h.p. a year. New machine tools and testing plant increase the capital employed and have a greater capacity than earlier vintages. However it is possible to use excess capacity on some machine tools for sub—contracting work, and this reduces the output of engines required to fully utilise machinery.

The construction of a range of engines including larger engines, would not significantly alter the scale required to achieve the main economies, as nearly all the machine tools are adaptable for the production of different designs. But if production of each design increased with increasing scale there would be economies for larger batches.

Capital charges for stocks and work in progress are very important as stocks, etc. may represent more than 50% of the annual turnover, and because a larger output facilitates faster production there would be economies for stocks. A firm with a larger output may use faster operating machine tools and speed up assembly. Certainly a firm which *increased* its capacity by buying new machine tools would buy machine tools which operated faster. Possible effects on costs, through lower stocks are illustrated by the following figures:

Output per year (number of engines)	10	20	40
(100,000 h.p.)	1	2	4
Sales £m.	5	10	20
Stocks and Work in progress £m	3	5	8
Interest at 15% on stocks and work in progress as percentage of sales	9	7.5	6.0

XI. Firms

1. *Administration*

The costs of administration for one of the firms visited was about 6% of total costs, or 15% of value added. (Selling costs which are very small were included in this estimate of administration costs). These costs were

186

an important source of economies of scale for this firm. It had not increased administration costs while nearly doubling output, and had achieved substantial economies by centralising the administration (accountancy, buying, etc) of three factories.

2. Vertical integration

At present there is a fairly high degree of vertical integration for the production of engine components, such as crankshafts. One aspect of the scale of production of designs of engines, and the overall output of firms is the effects on the speed of production partly because the pace at which ships are built is increasing. [1] A higher output facilitates and usually means faster production. Also defective components can be replaced more readily from parts for later engines of the same design, and a firm with a large total output of an engine is in a better position to make or order some components on 'spec', and can use them for rush orders or replacements. (U.K. firms do not generally do this.) Some of these advantages for components might be achieved if engine builders bought them from specialist manufacturers who could then produce them on a larger scale. This is the practice in Japan, and some U.K. manufacturers now buy their crankshafts from Italy and Japan. A crankshaft for a large engine weighs of the order of 150 tons, and costs about £40,000 — £266 a ton. (The price of crude steel is about £30 a ton and the price of special steels of the sort used in crankshafts about £100 a ton.) Crankshafts are made by forging and machining, and very large economies of scale would be expected for these operations. A firm with a large output (one Japanese firm has an output of one crankshaft a day) can spread the cost of efficient machine tools. The only way in which a firm with a small output (12 a year in the case of one U.K. diesel engine manufacturer) can make them competitively is to use old, written down machinery. A disadvantage of reliance on outside suppliers claimed by firms which make their own crankshafts is the loss of control of deliveries. This would be serious if the production programming of suppliers was not reliable, but this is not the experience of firms which buy out. [2]

3. Marketing

The licencing agreements by which firms manufacture diesels control the export of diesels, and for a number of manufacturers markets are limited to

---

(1) This will be very important when the shipbuilding industry has to operate without a large backlog of orders.

(2) Manufacturers are also reluctant to be at the 'mercy' of one manufacturer of a component, although there is some international competition for the supply of components.

the U.K. There are now about six potential customers — U.K. shipbuilders[1] for large slow speed diesels in the U.K. and marketing costs are negligible.

Table 18.1 *Summary of Minimum Efficient Scale for Diesels*

	Minimum Efficient Scale	Percentage Increase in costs at half the m.e.s.	
		total unit costs	value added per unit
Engines of 1–100 b.h.p.	Annual output of 100,000 units of a design[a]	4[c]	10[c]
'Slow Speed' Marine Diesels	An output of 100,000 h.p. per year[b]	8[c]	15[c]

(a) This output represents of the order of 10 per cent of U.K. production of diesels, but 100% of U.K. output of most sizes of engine.

(b) For this estimate it was assumed that plants use a good deal of old machinery. An output of 100,000 h.p. a year respresents about 10 per cent of U.K. production. If a firm used new machine tools for the heavy machining operations, the economies of scale would be much greater.

(c) Approximately.

(1) Some diesel engine manufacturers maintain contacts with shipowners to influence their choice of engines. Although shipbuilders generally contract the purchase of engines, shipowners usually specify the engine builder. Also shipowners buy spares from engine builders for whom this is a very important market.

19. Design of Chemical Plants[1]

I. General introduction

1. Structure of the industry

Four groups of firms are involved in ordering, designing and constructing chemical plants.

(1) The chemical manufacturing company who orders the plant and usually specifies the product, including the by-products, the proportions in which these products are made, the concentration of the products, the rate of output, the feedstock, the process to be employed[2] and the target date of completion.

(2) The chemical engineering contractor who designs the plant and who may also select or help select or design the process to be used. This firm will design the plant to fit the particular site, to meet the specification as to the degree of concentration of the product etc., and the price. In addition it is usually responsible for ordering the components of the plant, and in some cases checking that it operates in accordance with the design.

(3) The construction contractor who builds the plant.

(4) Equipment fabricating and other firms who make parts and machinery, such as pressure vessels, columns heat exchangers, tanks, etc.

In this chapter the economies of scale for chemical engineering contractors are considered. In most engineering industries, design work of this type is not separated from the firms which make the hardware. This division of functions for chemical plant enabled us to make a special study of the design function.

There are twenty or so substantial firms in the U.K. which specialise in designing chemical plants and they employ a total staff of about 15,000. About half of these firms are subsidiaries of overseas firms.

2. The dimensions of scale

The dimensions of scale for engineering contractors are the number of each type of plant which they build, the overall size of firms, the extent of vertical integration and diversification.

---

(1) The design of chemical plants is not included in the Census of Production and so there is no profile table for this trade.

(2) Most chemical processes are the property of major chemical and oil companies but designers of chemical plants acquire considerable knowledge and expertise in connection with particular processes.

II. The structure of costs

The margin chemical engineering contractors receive represents of the order of 20% of the price of plants. The work of the contractors is labour intensive: they use little fixed capital and are able to rent their premises, but access to substantial reserve finance is useful because of the risks involved. The remaining 80% of costs is for materials about 60% and construction approximately 20%.

III. Repeated building of similar types of plant

There are economies for contractors to be achieved by specializing on types of plants and the repeated construction of similar types of plants. These economies are attributable to learning by experience and spreading costs of improving designs etc. Examples of the benefits of learning are:
(a) Costs can be forecast more accurately for the purpose of making tenders.
(b) Experience will lead to modifications and improvements to designs. This is more important than reductions in design costs attributable to experience.
(c) A team of reliable contractors and suppliers can be built up.
(d) The risks involved can be more accurately assessed.[1] (This is probably the most important benefit.)
Examples of costs which can be spread over a series of plants are:
(a) The costs of preparing computer programmes for designing plants.
(b) Expenditure on research and development work. Although contractors do not generally invent new processes, some spend substantial amounts on process development. (For example one contractor spent £¾m. on a pilot plant.)

The scope for building identical plants (chinese copies) is limited because of technical progress which occurs through time, differences in sites, differences in the ratios in which products have to be made, etc., and because of these differences, the average costs of preparing designs for tendering and for construction are not greatly reduced, as the number of a type of plant designed is increased but there are some economies. Estimates made by firms suggested that costs of preparing tenders and designs for a plant for which a firm had no experience would be of the order of 20% higher than the costs for a firm which has such experience. (The costs of preparing a tender may amount to as much as 1% of the contract price.)

Surprisingly, contractors would seem to obtain few economies for the costs of parts and machinery used when building two plants of the same type. The view of an official of one company was that the ordering of two sets of parts etc. would only be likely to enable a firm to negotiate a discount on the price, if trade was slack, while another firm thought it might

(1) If a firm tenders for plants outside its specialist field, it runs the danger of winning contracts at uneconomic prices, as it is likely to win those contracts for which it submits relatively low bids. When it submits tenders there is scope for considerable errors in forecasting costs.

190

obtain some small discounts. However fabricators and suppliers of
special plant themselves incur design costs in respect of the plant they
sell and much of the plant used by chemical construction companies is
made on a one-off basis. [1] Besides savings for design costs, fabricators
can achieve economies through learning by experience, and the total economies to be achieved for special components by building a second identical unit would represent at least 10% of the costs of the first unit and
probably 20% in some cases. These estimates of economies are based on
the assumption that the components for the two plants are ordered at the
same time. The longer the delay in ordering the second plant the smaller
will be the economies for components. The economies of the type achieved
by duplicating a plant also apply if additional plants are built. Although
advantages of spreading design costs become progressively less important,
there are other sources of economies. [2]

Our tentative estimates of the effects on costs of the number of plants of
a design built each year are shown in table 19.1.

Table 19.1 *Number of Chemical Plants and Costs*

Number of plants of a type built per year	1	2	4	8
	(Index of average costs)			
Costs of materials etc.	55	52	50	48
Costs of construction	20	20	20	20
Chemical Engineering Contractor:				
Costs of tendering, design ordering components etc.	17½	15½	13½	12½
Profit margin	7½	7	7	6½
	100	94½	90½	87

The following points have to be taken into account when interpreting table
19.1

(a) The relative importance of different costs depends on the complexity
of plants: if the plant is complex or of a new design, design costs are relatively high.

(b) The extent to which there are economies depends on the similarity of
plants: for the purpose of preparing this table it was assumed that plants
are similar but not 'chinese copies'.

(c) It is assumed that the number of plants built each year is constant.
If in one particular year a relatively large number of plants are built, this
may push up costs because of difficulties of obtaining staff, materials, and

(1) In the case of one firm which fabricates parts for chemical plants, design costs
represented as much as 20% for items ordered on a one off basis.

(2) A firm which manufactured compressors and boilers said that it would achieve
few economies for making two units rather than one, but if, say, ten boilers of
a size were ordered it could achieve substantial economies by spending more
on designing products in order to reduce production costs, and by using more
special jigs. Also a large order would facilitate full utilization of the plant.

components, i.e. there are important economies for maintaining an even flow of orders from year to year.

(d) Chemical engineering contractors aim for a substantial profit margin to compensate for risks. It is assumed that these risks are related to the costs of completing contracts and that they decline with the number of plants built. It is not implied that in practice firms would lower their absolute profit margins if they were building a number of each type of plant a year.

The following figures show the completions of ethylene and sulphuric acid plants in U.K. and the rest of Europe in recent years. They show that for these plants there is very limited scope for competition in the U.K. market alone if firms are to achieve the benefits of specialization. This also applies to many other plant, indeed we should expect a smaller number of plants to be built for the production of special products and for products for which demand is not increasing rapidly.

Table 19.2 *Estimated Completions of Chemical Plants*

Year	1962	1963	1964	1965	1966	1967
			Ethylene [1]			
U.K.	1	1	—	—	2	2
Rest of W. Europe	4	9	2	3	10	2
			Sulphuric Acid			
U.K.	2	2	5	6	2	4
Rest of W. Europe	5	13	11	11	27	24

(1) The capacity of ethylene plants :increased during the period.

IV. The size of firms

1. Horizontal scale

(a) *Management.* A very small firm may perform one contract at a time and the manager will be in charge of it. As the size of a firm increases, and it carries out a number of larger projects simultaneously, responsibility for contracts is delegated, and staff are allocated to each contract, but eventually this system tends to break down because of the difficulty of controlling staff as the demand for specialists on the various contracts varies and because of the inability of the manager to supervise all the contracts. It was suggested by one firm that this system operates effectively until the total staff exceeds 250 and the individual contracts are for more than £500,000.

The next stage of development involves the setting up of departments for each speciality-process, mechanical, electrical, civil, and chemical engineering etc. and service departments for sales and personnel etc. With such a structure the control of staff is partly the responsibility of the heads of the specialist department and partly of managers of particular contracts. This system involves higher overheads and at least one firm operating it has set up a separate department to tender for the smaller contracts. This department operates rather like a one man business and illustrates a way of eliminating the disadvantages of large-scale — the overheads — for contracts where there are no advantages accruing to a larger organisation. Larger firms tend to employ more highly qualified and more highly paid engineers whose employment for small and often relatively simple contracts cannot be justified.

(b) *Specialization.* The advantages of the larger firms depend on the size of contracts and the scope for employing specialist staff and experience on the contracts. An advantage of a large firm is its ability to concentrate staff on a big contract. Two estimates of the maximum staff required to work on a large contract for an individual plant, not a complex of plants, were, about, 70 and 100. One firm provided an estimate of the build up of staff on a contract for the construction of a small refinery and these estimates are shown in Table 19.3.

Table 19.3 *Staff Requirements for a Small Refinery Contract*

	Period After Signing the Contract in Months				
	3	6	12	18	24
	(Number of staff employed)				
Engineers	6	8	8	2	—
Draughtsmen	—	4	50	10	—
Purchasing staff	—	4	8	8	—
Contract Supervision staff	—	—	2	12	12
Total	6	16	68	32	12

It was estimated that if additional engineers were available a further six could be employed on the contract during the first six months and this would speed up progress, but that it would be difficult to use additional staff for the other stages of the project. The type of engineers employed varies during the course of a contract, the balance shifts from chemical engineers to specialist process, mechanical and electrical engineers. A firm with a staff of between 500 and 1,000 can of course carry out a number of projects simultaneously and it is doubtful whether a larger firm would obtain much advantage from concentrating staff on individual contracts, but such a firm would have advantages for a very large project such as a major oil refinery.

(c) *Capital.* In effect plant designers sell the skill of their staff and it is possible for them to operate with negligible financial resources by relying on progress payments. The limited capital required is illustrated by the capital of two subsidiaries of U.S. companies operating in the U.K. In 1964, Stone and Webster had an issued capital of £5. In addition it had undistributed profits of nearly £400,000. The issued capital of Lummus, another company controlled from overseas, was £1,000. Again there were ploughed back profits, and in this case, inter-company balances. For the two companies profits before tax were £750,000 and £217,000 — both companies had a return on capital of more than 100% on the capital employed. The advantage of access to substantial capital is to enable a firm to survive heavy losses which are possible on individual contracts, rather than for day to day use. These risks are illustrated by one company which recently lost more than £1m. on one overseas contract, and another which lost £12m. on a refinery contract.

(*d*) *Tendering.* One advantage of greater concentration of firms in this industry would be some reduction in the number of tenders submitted i.e. if firms merged they would not submit two tenders for the same contract.[1] Tendering costs of the order of 1% of the contract price. This is an example of selling costs being reduced by concentration and larger scale. Independent firms could possibly obtain the same benefits by agreements.

2. Vertical integration

The advantages and disadvantages of vertical integration between chemical manufacturers and engineering contractors and between hardware manufacturers and engineering contractors have been discussed in a recent article. The most important factors for a consideration of economies of scale are that vertical integration gives the advantage of control over operations, but that it interferes with the economies of specialization described above.

3. Diversification

The main advantages of diversification through building different types of plant, apart from economies through increases in scale, are to reduce the effects of changes in demand for particular types of plant and to provide scope for growth. Contractors diversify, particularly when demand for chemical plants is slack, but they generally attempt to stick to the process industries, such as brewing and food processing. In practice it is difficult for the contractors to switch rapidly to other specialist fields, such as steel plant, as the steel firms like to buy from companies with experience of building their type of plant. Also it is claimed that it is difficult for mechanical engineers to switch from making one type of plant to another though draughtsmen[3] and other specialists can generally do so. Another factor making it difficult for contractors to diversify profitably is that engineers with experience of the chemical industry tend to be paid more than other engineers, and some engineers with experience of one type of plant are reluctant to switch to another.

---

(1) In some trades e.g. stone quarries, firms which have merged sometimes continue to submit multiple tenders.

(2) Chemical Processes Plant: Innovation and the World Market. Nat. Inst. Econ. Rev. Aug., 1968.

(3) Many draughtsmen are self employed and can be hired for particular contracts. This provides some flexibility for contractors for whom demand fluctuates.

V. International groups

Another dimension of scale is the extent to which U.K. firms are controlled by groups operating in other countries, usually the U.S. One source of advantage for international groups is the scope for pooling knowledge about designs. The U.S. parent of one firm has a computer programme to adapt the basic designs for one type of plant to particular sites etc., and the U.K. subsidiary has made use of this. Another advantage of U.S. control claimed by the firm was that it helped them to obtain finance from New York for contracts. Also as the U.S. parent firms are generally larger than U.K. firms they could perhaps in theory back their subsidiaries financially to enable them to beat independent U.K. firms.[1] Finally the U.K. subsidiaries can make use of American experience and this is of some importance as the U.S. dominated the industry up until the post-war period. Since then it has been a case of the independent British firms entering the market and attempting to catch up with the Americans.

Ownership by a U.S. firm does not necessarily help the U.K. subsidiary to avoid cycles in demand. In one case the U.S. parent only made use of the U.K. subsidiary for sub-contracting design and engineering work when they had insufficient capacity, and the U.K. subsidiary claimed that it could not afford to sub-contract work to the U.S. during booms as costs there are much higher. In theory it should be profitable for the U.S. company to sub-contract work to the U.K. subsidiary, and in some cases for chemical companies to make it worthwhile for contractors to use the resources of their U.S. head office to break bottlenecks.

There are clearly advantages, in terms of costs of engineering plants, to be achieved by close links between U.K. and U.S. chemical engineering contractors. The disadvantage for the U.K. is the cost in foreign exchange of these relationships if the U.K. firm is owned by an American firm, but as the U.S. subsidiaries win some overseas contracts which would not be won by U.K. firms this cost may be offset. British groups could achieve similar advantages by building plants in the U.S.A. for which they have special expertise.

VI. Conclusion

As there are important economies for designing plants of each type and the demand for plants within the U.K. is small, the pressure for firms to specialize on an international scale is clear. The economies for large firms making a range of plant are also important, though not as important as the economies of specialization.

---

(1) Some British contractors are subsidiaries of larger groups.

Table 19.4 *Summary of Minimum Efficient Scale for Chemical Plants*

	Number of Plants per year	% of U.K. Market	% Increase in Average Total Costs at 50% 'm.e.s.'	% Increase in Average Value Added at 50% of 'm.e.s.'
A type of chemical plant (e.g.)				
Ethylene plants	2	100	(about) 5%	(about) 10%
Sulphuric acid plants	4	100		

Firms

It is not possible to specify any m.e.s. for firms in this industry, nor the magnitude of economies of scale for firms, because firms of different sizes can specialize types of plant.

20. Turbo Generators and Electric Motors[1][2]

Turbo generators

I. General introduction

1. Structure of the industry

In this chapter we consider the economies of scale for two groups of products out of the wide range of products made by the electrical industry — turbo generators and electric motors. Two firms, G.E.C., and Reyrolle Parsons, make all the turbo generators produced in the U.K., and between them control the heavy electrical interests of four firms which operated independently in the early 1960's.

Turbo generators are produced in 'sets'. The main customer is the C.E.G.B. which standardised on 500 M.W. sets in the mid-1960's and 660 M.W. sets for installation in the 1970's. Each of the two groups mentioned above can produce generators with a total capacity of the order of 6,000 M.W. a year, but their 'capacity' depends on the size of the sets ordered, and the length of runs — if orders are for standardised large sets, they can produce more than if they make an assortment of smaller units. In addition to their sales to the C.E.G.B. whose orders amount to about 5,000 M.W. per year at present, they sell to overseas customers and to firms which produce electricity in the U.K. for their own use. A much greater range of sizes of turbo generators is sold to the 'other' customers.

2. Techniques of production and the dimensions of scale

The main processes of production are the machining of components and the assembly of components and products.[3] Some of the machining operations involve the use of expensive specialised machine tools, but many of the assembly operations are labour intensive. The main economies of scale relate to the output of each design, the rate of output of a design, the total output at a factory and a firm's total output.

---

(1) The production of turbo generators is not distinguished in the Census of Production, but the total number of employees engaged in their production in the U.K. is of the order of 30,000.

(2) Most of the data used for preparing this chapter was provided by the C.E.G.B.

(3) Pressing and other metal shaping operations are also used.

II. Structure of costs

The price of a 660 M.W. set with auxiliary equipment is between £8m. and £9m. Of this total £5–6m. is for the turbo generator alone. The costs of production are made up of about 45% for materials and components, (including forgings and castings, copper extrusions, steel etc.), and 55% for labour and other costs. The costs of transport and erection of turbo generators at sites form about 10% of total costs.

III. Initial costs

The main initial costs are for developing a new design, for jigs and tools for production, and for getting a new design into service. The costs for developing a new design depend on the variation from other designs. For moving from sets of 500 M.W. to 660 M.W. sets the development costs were estimated to be between £½m. and £1m. As each of the two manufacturers may expect orders of from 15 to 30 of these sets, worth over £100m., these development costs form a small proportion of total costs. However, the change from 500 to 660 M.W. requires modifications rather than complete redesign. The importance of this for development costs can be gauged by comparing the costs for designing 660 M.W. sets with an estimate of the costs of designing 1,300 M.W. sets approximately £3m. The £3m. is not attributable to the change in size alone, but also to the introduction of technical modifications.[1] Both the estimates given exclude the costs of making good faults in generating equipment, and the costs of new machine tools and balancing machines which may be required for the production of a new size of set.

The manufacturer generally has to make good any faults which occur during the first year of operation and these costs form an important category of initial costs, but the manufacturer is not usually responsible for the full extent of any consequential losses — which can be substantial — to the generating authority of any failures.[2] The extent to which new designs can be tested by using models is limited, and partly for this reason faults in design may only become apparent when a design is introduced into service. All the companies which built 500 M.W. sets incurred costs for correcting faults and it is understood that for the four firms concerned, these ranged from some £100,000 to £3m. The quality of design work is clearly an important factor determining the success of a firm. A way of reducing the effects of teething troubles for a new design is to allow a time interval between the production of the prototype and the remainder of the sets.

A problem involved when quantifying development and other costs associated with a new design is that these are variable. Differences in the costs

(1) At present the C.E.G.B. policy is to place contracts with each of the two firms to carry out the development work when it is decided to develop larger sets for the C.E.G.B.'s system.

(2) During shutdowns electricity authorities have to use less efficient plant or simply fail to meet demand.

198

of making good faults in designs is one source of variation, there are many others. If a firm is to build a much larger size of set, it may be necessary to strengthen roads and bridges to get the sets to a port. (This cost is only partly borne by manufacturers in the U.K.) Also development costs can be reduced by producing a more inefficient design in terms of operational efficiency [1] the costs of construction, or the costs of getting it into service. Conversely expenditure on development can reduce the costs of construction, the number and seriousness of faults which occur when the machine is introduced into service, and the efficiency with which it operates. (A firm with a relatively large output of a design can either reduce development costs in terms of outlay per set produced, or spend more in total on development and reduce other costs per set).

In addition to initial costs specifically related to one design, firms carry out research and development related to their range of products, and the development of one design affects other designs. In all, the C.E.G.B. and the two companies are spending of the order of £6m. a year, or 6% of sales including export sales, on R and D.

IV. Production of a design

The main sources of economies for producing large numbers of a design are:

(1) spreading the initial costs,

(2) spreading the cost of special purpose machinery,

(3) a reduction in the proportion of time required for setting up machinery,

(4) the benefits of learning,

(5) the use of more efficient techniques.

The first source of economies has been dealt with in the previous section. Much of the plant at present used by U.K. manufacturers is not specific to one size of set. When firms began to build sets of 500 M.W., plant had to be replaced, but most of the new plant can be used for sets of more than 500 M.W. [2] The spreading of set up time provides some economies for repeated production of a design but these economies are limited. (For each unit there is a good deal of replication for many operations). There are also benefits of learning which relate to the output of a design over time and the rate of output of a design. Finally, where the sustained output of a design is anticipated, more efficient techniques can be used for insulation and also for machining, because expenditure on more special jigs and

---

(1) A firm may be forced into some economies in design costs because of limitations on its resources. A company may have too few engineers to redesign a set and simply scale up some parts. Such methods may result in extra costs of production and/or faults in designs.

(2) The latest vintages of machine tools are more efficient than older vintages, and when firms introduce new tools this generally results in some increase in capacity.

tools can be justified. If a rate of production of 8 or more units a year was achieved, a semi continuous production line might be adopted for some operations.

One firm provided the following tentative estimates of the reduction in time required for successive generators.

Production	1st Unit	2nd Unit	3rd Unit	4th and later Units
Index of labour time per unit	100	90	80	75

Clearly there must be a great deal of variation about these figures. Some new designs are introduced relatively smoothly, and the learning effect depends on the rate of production. For these estimates it was assumed that the rate of production was 4 units a year. Also the learning effect depends on the degree of similarity between different designs.

A reduction in the time required for producing a machine, effectively increases the capacity of a works, although bottlenecks may occur for processes for which productivity does not respond to learning as sharply as the average for all processes. Very approximately, it can be assumed that, provided the extra capacity can be utilized, the economies for factory overheads will be similar to those for labour inputs.

There are also economies for increasing the rate of output from, say, two to four units of a design a year. If only two units a year are made, the learning effect for the first four units will be smaller than those shown i.e., more than four units will have to be produced to get labour requirements down to 75 per cent of those for the first unit. If the rate of production was increased to eight units a year, it was estimated that man hours per unit would be reduced by not more than 10 per cent of the labour requirements for a rate of output of four units a year.

If man hours and factory overheads decline by 25 per cent, this is equivalent to about 10 per cent reduction in unit costs. But other overheads, such as research and design, would also be affected by increased output of a model, and so the overall effect on costs would be nearer 15 per cent.

V. Output of a plant

The main sources of economies of scale for a large throughput at a plant are:

(1) spreading the cost of special purpose plant,

(2) spreading overhead costs for management and research and development.

In order to assess the scope for economies at, say, twice or four times the output achieved in the U.K., it would require detailed study which the firms cannot justify because such a scale of operation does not appear feasible at the present time. But, if costs for hypothetical *new* plants were compared, they would be likely to show appreciable economies extending to outputs of more than 6,000 M.W. a year.

VI. Output of a firm

There are two main sources of economies for a multi plant firm.

(a) It can duplicate production facilities and attempt to spread R and D costs, but it is claimed that it is difficult to separate design and production because continuous close co-operation between designers and production employees is required for efficient production.

(b) Alternatively, different plants can specialise on different parts of turbo generators. There are inevitable transition difficulties when firms merge because different plants use different methods with which their own staff are familiar. But in the long run, the main economies of scale can be achieved in this way.[1]

VII. Economies for large generating stations

Economies of scale for large power stations is a subject outside the scope of this chapter, but it is worth mentioning some points about these economies to place the production of different designs of turbo generators in perspective. There are substantial economies for large power stations. The cost of much of the equipment per M.W. declines with scale, and even where the turbo-generators have to be duplicated, as in the case of 1320 M.W. stations with two 660 M.W. sets, there are still some economies. The C.E.G.B. provided an estimate of 10% for the reduction in average capital costs per M.W. of capacity for a station of 1320 M.W. with two turbo-generators, compared to a station of 660 M.W. capacity. This reduction was attributable to spreading the cost of capital equipment and buildings which did not have to be duplicated. An offsetting source of extra costs for large power stations is the need for larger movements of electricity through the transmission system.[2] Also the length of time required for overhauls is somewhat longer for large plants.

A consequence of the increase in the size of units, from 120 M.W. in 1960 to 660 M.W. in 1970, and the much lower labour requirement per M.W. for the large sizes, is that, though demand for electricity has increased, it has not kept pace with the increasing capacity of the heavy electrical engineering industry. Over capacity has also been caused by somewhat erratic ordering of equipment by the C.E.G.B. in the past.

VIII. Conclusions

There are substantial economies of scale for the production of turbo generators and the concentration of the industry which has taken place can be

(1) One of the U.K. manufacturers has concentrated most of its production of turbo-generators at a single site, and the other is in the process of concentrating production at three sites — making turbine components at two sites, and generators at the other.

(2) If more smaller stations were built they could be built nearer the sources of demand. If the electricity to be transmitted is greatly increased, a new larger grid may have to be constructed.

justified by the existence of these economies of scale. The difficult question that remains is whether concentration should be carried further. At present facilities are being rationalised by the two remaining producers and some of their plans would be changed by a merger. Briefly the main arguments for retaining two suppliers of turbo generators are that the firms compete to meet the C.E.G.B.'s requirements, and the existence of two firms may ensure greater flexibility to meet the C.E.G.B. demands which must inevitably be subject to some fluctuation. Also if the firms merged, the C.E.G.B. might import equipment to introduce some competition and flexibility.

The advantages of a merger would be to take further advantage of the economies of scale. For example one group of works could produce all the 660 M.W. sets or other standard machines for the C.E.G.B., and the other could produce for export markets and special sizes for the home market.

Other ways in which advantage could be taken of the economies of scale for generating equipment for the home market are:—

(a) more co-operation between U.K. manufacturers on research, development and the production of components,[1]

(b) agreements between European generating authorities to standardize the generating equipment they use where this is feasible[2] and co-operation on research and development between the U.K. firms and other European firms.

Electric motors[3]

IX. General introduction

(1) Structure of the industry

Three firms account for most of the U.K. output of motors in the range 1 - 100 h.p. (The recent mergers between G.E.C. and English Electric and Hawker Siddeley and Brook Motor reduced the number from five to three). As a result of growth through mergers both G.E.C. and H.S. each operate two factories for the production of motors in the range 1 - 100 h.p.

One manufacturer has estimated that his company makes 40,000 distinct types of motors, but this includes motors outside the 1 - 100 h.p. range and differences involving very minor distinctions. A better guide to diversity of production is that another firm makes about 15 'frame' sizes and about 600

---

(1) The existing practice has the advantage, however, that alternative approaches to development are adopted.

(2) At present the C.E.G.B. and the generating authorities in France, Germany and Italy buy most of their generating equipment from their national manufacturers. If this practice were to change the structure of the turbo generator industry might be changed also.

(3) Census data for electric motors are not available, as the trade is not distinguished in the census. The total number of people engaged in making electric motors in the range 1-100 h.p. is about 5,000.

variations based on these frame sizes. In addition it makes some 'specials'.

2. Processes of production

Electric motors consist of two end brackets, a stator case, stator and rotor cores and coils. The end brackets and the stator case are usually made by machining iron castings or aluminium die castings.[1] Apart from casting and machining, the main operations used are the pressing of components, winding wire coils, assembly and testing.

3. The dimensions of scale

As for other engineering industries there are a number of important dimensions of scale, including the output of products, production runs, the capacity of factories and the output of firms.

X. The structure of costs

The following breakdown of *costs* is for a popular motor.

Table 20.1. *Cost Breakdown for an Electric Motor*

Materials	%
Copper[a]	16
Electric Steel	19
Other	22
	57
Direct Labour	7
Total direct costs	64
Other variable costs	18
Fixed costs	18
Total costs	100

Source: N.P.I.B. Report No. 139, p.9. H.M.S.O. 1970.

(a) Mostly copper wire

For processes apart from casting and die casting, the breakdown of direct labour costs is approximately 25% for machining, 50% for winding and 25% for assembly and testing, and this provides a crude guide to the relative importance of processes.

XI. Initial costs

The rate of development of electric motors is not rapid compared to some of the other engineering products we discuss, but firms improve their models and have to change them to conform to changes in performance specifications set by the British Standards Institution. There have been a number of changes to the B.S.I. specifications since 1955, but in 1970 an international agreement was reached to maintain specifications unchanged for a period, probably until 1980. In addition special products have to be designed.

(1) Certain manufacturers fabricate some motors and do not use castings.

When a new range is developed the costs are substantial. One firm estimated them to be £0.5m., about 7% of this firm's annual turnover. For another firm the costs of design and development during the period when the 1966 changes in standards were being introduced was about 2% of total costs – 4% of value added, and the cost of special tools etc., was about 4% of total costs, but this level of expenditure was higher than usual. For 1969 the percentages were design 1.2% and tooling 2.9% of total costs. About 30% of this firm's output was of special motors, and a substantial proportion of the initial costs related to these models.

When motors are redesigned this can result in significant reductions in costs,[1] and it is possible that firms with a larger output than those now operating in the U.K. would redesign their motors more often to take advantage of these economies.

XII. Production runs

Economies of scale for long runs can be achieved for all the main processes – casting, machining parts, winding and assembly – these economies are attributable to substituting more efficient techniques as scale is increased and to learning. The extent to which firms equip with special purpose machinery for shaping parts, for winding and for testing is, primarily, determined by the length of runs. There are very substantial economies for substituting different techniques. For example, winding machines which are justified for outputs of a frame size of more than about 100 a week, reduce the time required for winding a motor from 25 minutes to 5 minutes.[2] For outputs of 2,000 a week this might be reduced to 1½ minutes by the introduction of more sophisticated equipment. For casting, metal patterns can be substituted for loose patterns for outputs above about 200 a week, and for outputs above 2,000 a week die casting can be used and this greatly reduces machining costs, because of the increased accuracy of the castings.

Another source of economies is learning. For winding and assembly, there are significant economies for batch sizes up to at least ten units and for larger batches the costs of learning on the first ten units can be spread over a larger output. For machining there are economies for spreading set up costs.

The number of units produced declines as the size of motors increases. Annual outputs of frame sizes of less than 10 h.p. are measured in tens of thousands and for motors of more than 50 h.p. in hundreds. There are very substantial differences in prices for different sizes, and by making approximate allowances for differences in material content and work input attributable to the size of motors, it is possible to isolate the effect of scale. Such calculations again suggest substantial economies for high rates of output.

(1) The N.B.P.I. refers to a case where redesign reduced the material content of motors by half and direct labour costs by 40%. Report No. 139. p. 10.

(2) At lower levels of output hand winding is used.

XIII. Factories

The main source of economies of scale for factories, apart from economies for long runs which we dealt with in the previous section, is the increasing scope for the use of specialized machinery. For example as scale is increased semi-automatic and automatic tools can be introduced for machining.

The following very crude estimates of the effects of scale for new factories each with a foundry were based on our discussions with one firm. (The capacities of the factories represented 15 and 30% of U.K. output of motors 1-100 h.p., and it was assumed that the range of products made was not affected by scale). These estimates include the effects of longer runs; if the range of products were to increase with scale,[1] the economies would certainly be smaller.

Table 20.2. *Tentative Estimates of the Economies of Scale for Electric Motors.*

COST	% of Total Costs	Effect on Average Cost of Doubling Capacity
Materials	50	Nil
Other production costs (including initial costs)	40	Reduced by 25%
Selling and distribution costs	10	Nil
Total	100	Reduced by 10%

The results of a more comprehensive exercise carried out by another firm gave the results in Table 20.3.

Table 20.3. *Estimate of the Economies of Scale for Electric Motors*

Output (% of U.K. output)	30	60
	Index numbers of average costs	
Materials	100	90
Direct labour	100	80
Factory overheads	100	75
Production costs	100	85
Development, selling, administration and other costs	100	78
Total	100	85

The main source of the substantial production economies was longer runs, rather than the overall output of the factory. For materials, the sources of economies were greater purchasing power for wire, which would enable suppliers to make economies, and the substitution of different methods at higher scales to reduce requirements of materials.

A third company suggested that the economies of scale would be smaller than those shown, but it provided no detailed estimates of the scale effects. Also it is worth noting that the economies of scale do not apply continuously

(1) This could occur if a firm which produced a small range of motors increased its output and range of motors. The three leading manufacturers already produce a wide range.

as scale is increased. If the output of a manufacturer producing special sizes of motor on a small scale were doubled, this could well have few effects on the methods used and so provide only small economies.

XIV. Firms

1. Material prices

The prices of most materials are affected by the output of models and the size of firms rather than the capacity of factories. The economies of scale for purchases of materials such as electric steel, ore and scrap are negligible, but there would be significant economies for wire and castings if the output of models was positively related to the scale of firms.

2. Selling and Distribution

Selling and distribution costs represented of the order of 10% of total costs for one firm, attributable to selling and distribution in about equal proportions, and rather less for another firm. These costs are heavier for overseas sales than domestic sales, and can be very low for U.K. business, particularly where large numbers of motors are sold for use in machines. Indeed one firm went so far as to comment that it was 'usually approached by firms with orders'. There are some economies for selling and distribution. For example there are economies for selling and transporting motors to overseas markets and for selling larger quantities of motors to individual customers.

3. Research and development costs and specialist skills

Although R. and D. costs are not high compared with many other industries, a large firm can spread the cost of its R. and D. over a greater output. A smaller firm can sustain the same rate of expenditure, but incurs a penalty in terms of costs. Alternatively the smaller firm can cut its R. and D. expenditure and in the long run suffer a penalty because of the quality of its product.

It is possible that a large diversified engineering or electrical group may be able to supply management and engineering skills for its electric motor factories more readily than specialist producers can hire or develop such skills. Also, in theory, the large groups can use their overall buying power to reduce the price paid for materials. However, these are not in practice important sources of adavntage.

206

Table 20.4. *Summary of the Minimum Efficient Scale for Turbo Generators and Electric Motors*

	Dimension of Scale	Minimum Efficient Scale	Percentage of U.K. Market (M) or Output (O)	Tentative Estimates of the Increase in Average Costs at 50% of the m.e.s.	
				Total cost per unit	Value added per unit
Turbo Generators	One Design	4 units a year	100 (M)	5	10
	Factories	An output of at least 6,000 M.W. a year	50 (O)		
Electric Motors[c]	Factories[a]		60 (O)	15[b]	20[b]

(a) For estimating the minimum efficient scale for factories making electric motors, we have used the second set of estimates shown in section VIII. These were the more satisfactory estimates, though they may somewhat overstate the economies of scale. It is assumed that a wide range of motors is made at the factory.

(b) These estimates are based on the assumption that the range of products made at a factory does not increase with scale. In view of the wide range of models made by the leading firms, this assumption is realistic.

(c) For firms making a wide range of motors, the minimum efficient scale is similar to that for factories.

21. Domestic Electrical Appliances

Table 21.1 *Profile of the Domestic Appliances Industry*

	1963	% of all manufacturing industry	1968	% of all manufacturing industry	1968 as % of 1963
Number of Employees ('000)	72.3	0.9	71.7	0.9	99
Sales (£m.)	215.9	0.8	270.2	0.7	125
Net Output (£m.)	104.7	1.0	133.4	0.8	127
Capital Expenditure (£m.)	5.5	0.5	—	—	—

Concentration

Concentration ratio for the 5 largest firms in 1963 —

Cookers	56%
Washing Machines	85%

Size of Establishments and Enterprises (1963)

	Establishments		Enterprises	
Number of Employees	Number	% of Employees	Number	% of Employees
Under 100	157	6	133	4
100 – 999	63	34	50	27
1,000 – 1,999	11	25	3	8
2,000 and over	6	36	8	61
	237	100	194	100

I. General introduction

This chapter deals with a part of the domestic appliance industry – that concerned with the production of 'white goods', cookers, refrigerators, laundry equipment, dishwashers etc. These accounted for about 55% by value of U.K. production of domestic appliances in the mid 1960's. This chapter is based on a study made by John Hatch in 1964 and 1965.[1]

1. Structure of the industry

At the time Dr. Hatch's study was made, there were 26 firms engaged in the final production and assembly of white goods in the U.K., their total output was of the order of 2.5 million units a year, and they had a labour force of

---

(1) Dr. J.H. Hatch prepared a study of the economies of scale in the appliance industry while in residence as a research student at Cambridge University from 1963 to 1966. It was embodied in his dissertation for the Ph.D. degree.

27,000 employees.[1][2] Of the firms making 'white goods', only two oper-ated more than one plant for the manufacture of these products in 1965. One of the two firms, Hoover, made motors and components at one plant and assembled products at another, and A.E.I., the other firm, made a different range of products at each of its two plants. Most of the firms in the in-dustry produce other products in addition to 'white goods', but generally these are made at separate factories.

A characteristic of the firms with a relatively small output, those with less than 1,000 employees making appliances, was that they generally con-centrated on producing one type of appliance, in most cases laundry equip-ment. In contrast to the small firms, half of the firms with over 1,000 em-ployees from whom data were obtained, made more than one type of product.

2. Production processes

The manufacture of cookers, refrigerators and laundry equipment is basic-ally similar. The box-like cabinet, normally of sheet steel, is character-istic of the three appliances, and the manufacture of the appliances is centered upon the production of these cabinets. The main sections of a white goods factory are the press shop, where sheet steel is cut in guillo-tines and shaped in presses, the welding and machine shop where a great variety of welding and metal finishing operations are performed, the finish-ing shop where the various parts are painted or enamelled, and the assembly shop.

It is possible to integrate the production of the three types of appliance. One major manufacturer produced all three types of appliances at one fac-tory — the products followed a common path through the press, welding and finishing shops, but there were separate lines for the final assembly of pro-ducts.

3. The dimensions of scale

The main dimensions of scale for the industry are:

(a) total output over time and the rate of output for each particular appli-ance;

(b) the range of appliances manufactured;

(c) the 'depth' or degree of vertical integration of a firm's production — the extent to which it manufacturers the components which it assem-bles;

(d) a firm's output of white goods, and also its total output.

II. The structure of costs

The unweighted average of the raw material and component costs as a

(1) By 1970 the number of independent firms had fallen to about 18, and total annual output was between 2.5m. and 3.0m. units. Three firms, British Domestic Appliances, Hoover and Philips produced about 70% of the industry's output.

(2) Information was collected from 19 of the 26 firms, and in addition data were obtained from several firms which had previously operated in the field.

proportion of production costs was approximately 70%. The proportion of
the product bought out was relatively large for the smaller firms and also
for sophisticated products such as automatic washing machines. Besides
making a higher proportion of components themselves, some of the large
firms also supplied components to the smaller firms.

The direct costs for departments are affected by the proportion of the
product bought out, the actual products made, and the age of the plant. The
data in Table 21.2 provide an indication of the relative importance of departments, but there is a great deal of variation between firms.

Table 21.2 *Direct Costs by Departments of Domestic Appliance Factories*

Department (Shops)	Total	Press	Machining and Welding	Finishing	Assembly
		(Total Direct Costs = 100)			
Labour Costs	66	9	18	15	24
Machinery Costs	34	8	9	12	5
Total	100	17	27	27	29

Both tooling costs — the main initial costs for new models — and advertising, are important for this industry. Figures for average expenditure by
firms for tooling are not available, but costs for models are shown below.
In 1963 advertising expenditure represented 5.1% of sales: this is substantial compared with many other trades which manufacture consumer goods.

III. Initial costs

Some estimates of tooling costs, the largest component of initial costs are
shown in Table 21.3

Table 21.3 *Tooling Costs for Various Products and Various Depths of Production*

	Bought-out content as % of Ex-works costs		
	Less than 50%	50–70%	70% and over
	(Estimates of tooling costs)		
Cookers			
Standard models	40	80–120 60–80 75	70+
Luxury models		150+	
Washing Machines			
Simple non automatic		75	8
Automatic		100+ 200	12
Refrigerators			
Small—4 cu. ft. and less	42	40 40+	
Large—4 cu. ft. and more	90	60	

The data in Table 21.3 show that initial tooling costs for firms are dependent on depth of production[1] and on the type of model: sophisticated models are more expensive. Tooling costs are also affected by expected output. However it was estimated that the saving in costs would not be more than 15–20% if a relatively short run were expected by a firm. Differences in accounting practice may account for some of the differences in initial costs, but the data suggest there are considerable differences between firms in expenditure on initial costs for models.

The effect of spreading tooling costs are illustrated in Table 21.4. For comparison, U.K. output in recent years has been approximately one million refrigerators and washing machines and half a million cookers.

Table 21.4 *Tooling Costs and Effects upon Ex—works Costs for Various Length of Model Run*

	Tooling Costs £'000	Output of Model		(000 p.a.)	Assumed Ex—works cost at output of 50,000 p.a. £
		10	50 100	500	
Cooker	80				
Tooling cost per model £		8	1.6 0.8	0.2	
Index of total production costs [a]		119	100 98	96	35
Washing Machines (twin tub)	90				
Tooling cost per model £		9	1.8 0.9	0.2	
Index of total production costs [a]		124	100 97	94	30
Refrigerator, 4 cu. ft.	50				
Tooling cost per model £		5	1.0 0.5	0.1	
Index of total production costs [a]		120	100 97	95	20

(a) In estimating production costs, it is assumed here that there are no economies except those achieved by spreading tooling costs.

IV. Economies of scale for factories

1. *Performing a constant range of operations*

One difficulty encountered in estimating the economies of scale by analysing the techniques performed in each department — the method used by John Hatch — was that the estimates were limited to the range of output of existing factories. It is likely that substantial economies might be achieved by the introduction of techniques such as flow line production in the press shop and automatic welding processes. These are not economic for firms even when operating at the highest scales achieved in the U.K. It is possible only to make a guess at the impact of these techniques.

(1) If a firm buys out components, suppliers meet the initial costs, or the firm selects standard components for which there are no additional tooling costs.

An analysis of the processes of production employed suggests that, over a range of output up to 150,000 units a year, the main economies would be achieved in the press shop, through better utilisation of press capacity, and the finishing shop, through the automation and mechanisation of processes, although there would also be some economies in other departments. At higher levels of output, from 150,000 to 500,000 units a year, the main economies would be achieved in the press and welding shops through automation and mechanisation. The following estimates of the technical economies of scale for a firm buying out a constant proportion of the product (60 per cent), and making a constant product mix were based on estimates of the effects of scale on costs for the various shops, and on estimates of scale economies made by some of the firms taking part in the enquiry.

Table 21.5 *Economies of Scale for Factories making Domestic Appliances*

Output (units per year)	('000)	$10^{(1)}$	50	150	500
				(150,000 = 100)	
Unit costs of bought out materials and parts	(Index)	110	105	100	95
Unit costs for value added	(Index)	118	106	100	88
Unit costs of production	(Index)	113	105	100	92

(1) Below this figure costs rise rapidly.

When considering these estimates of economies of scale for production costs, it is important to note that:
(a) the costs of tooling are excluded;
(b) the estimates for outputs of more than 150,000 units a year are speculative;
(c) the estimates are based on the accounting costs of firms with a mix of different vintages of plant. If economies of scale for factories equipped with new machinery were calculated, they could well show appreciably larger economies of scale.

2. *Producing a wider range of models*

Some illustrative calculations of the effects of varying assumptions about the level of output, and the number and life of models, are shown in Table 21.6. The figures are illustrative, but those suggested for annual outputs between 10,000 and 150,000 units a year were representative for firms in the British appliance industry in 1965.

212

Table 21.6 *Economies of Scale and the Production Range*

Annual Production (thousands)	Unit Production cost with constant range [a] (Index)	No. of basic models assumed	Life of models assumed (years)	Unit Production costs (Index) [a]	Unit Initial costs (Index) [b]	Total Ex—works costs (Index) [c]
10	113	1	8	107	92	99
50	105	5	3	103	100	102
150	100	10	2	100	100	100
500	92	10	2	92	93	85

(a) Excluding tooling costs and assuming a constant proportion bought out.

(b) This index is for initial and production costs, but no allowance is made for economies for production costs. The estimates allow for the spreading of initial costs which are assumed to be tooling costs plus 40% for research and development and for disruption and other costs attributable to introducing new models. No adjustments are made for economies for tooling costs made by firms with short production runs, or for firms which introduce many models.

(c) The estimates allow both for the spreading of initial costs and for economies of scale for production costs.

The estimates suggest a substantial advantage for firms with a larger output and the same range as their competitors, but they also illustrate ways in which smaller firms can remain competitive – by limiting their range and/or by changing it less often. This would apply within the range 150,000 to 500,000, as well as below 150,000. Firms can do this either by producing a product which is not directly competitive with the appliances of the large scale manufacturers – because, for example, it is smaller or larger than competitors' models – or they may compete on price with a model which is out of date technically or not abreast of fashionable design trends. Or they may introduce a new type of appliance (at one time dish washing machines provided an example of a new type of appliance sold by a relatively small firm.) Finally a firm may simply capture a large share of the market with a single model – Hoover's automatic washing machine provides an example.

3. *Varying the depth of production*

The estimates shown so far assume a constant proportion of the product bought out. They therefore exaggerate the economies of scale available for firms operating large factories, as the smaller firms can reduce their handicap by buying out a higher proportion of the product. Estimates of the size of this effect were not obtained.

4. *Division of production between a number of factories*

It was noted in the introduction that only two firms operated more than one factory for the production of white goods when the study was made, and this suggests there are economies for concentrating production in large factories. If the production of a firm were divided between factories, the effects on the

economies of scale shown above would be:
  (a) most of the economies for bought out materials and parts would be retained;
  (b) there could be a substantial loss of economies of scale if the operations were divided vertically;
  (c) there would be increased costs if the operations were divided horizontally. The main sources would be additional transport costs and the effects of diminished managerial control.

V. The size of firms

1. *Production of a range of products*

Apart from raising a firm's overall output of 'white goods', and so enabling it to achieve technical economies, the production of a combination of appliances may help to dampen seasonal fluctuations in output.[1]

2. *Marketing*

Marketing is a very important factor determining the success of firms in this industry. Important potential sources of scale economies are the spreading of advertising expenditure and spreading the cost of servicing facilities. But a special feature of this trade is that Area Electricity Boards are the largest distributors, and at least two of the smaller firms sell a substantial proportion of their output to Area Boards which advertise these products with their own brand names. The future of these firms is committed to the Area Boards, as they would have great difficulty in finding alternative markets quickly, if they were to lose their contracts to supply the Boards. Some other firms are reluctant to sell goods without their own brand because of the danger of this undermining their advertised brands.

One leading manufacturer operates a fleet of service vans, and the firm obtains economies for providing this service, both because it has a large share of the market for white goods and because it makes a wide range of domestic appliances, apart from white goods.

3. *Diversification*

It is difficult to assess the net advantages of diversification. The large diversified electrical companies can supply many of the components used by their appliance divisions. They claim to transfer them at the same prices at which they sell to outside firms, but there may be some advantages to a group to be achieved through using standardised components and gaining better control of production. Another illustration of the economies to be achieved through diversification is the centralisation of design and development. One diversified engineering group which manufactures white

(1) Sales of refrigerators reach a peak during the summer, with 75% of sales being made during the period April — September. The market for laundry equipment shows a less marked seasonal trend with sales building up slightly towards the end of the year.

goods on a relatively small scale has centralised the design, development and production of prototypes of all its products. This concentration avoids the need to employ specialist market research experts, designers and draughtsmen who would be required at infrequent intervals, perhaps every three years, to prepare a new appliance model. However, the larger diversified companies do not centralise the design and development of products, e.g., white goods and electrical motors; this is carried out by their subsidiaries. Another source of advantage for being a part of a large diversified engineering group, rather than completely independent, is for purchasing materials such as steel.

VI. Addendum

The merging of the domestic appliance business of E.M.I., A.E.I., G.E.C., and English Electric into British Domestic Appliances, together with other mergers since the mid-1960's, has resulted in much greater concentration of the white goods industry. In order to assess whether there have been any substantial changes in economies of scale, we asked for further information from one of the leading companies. The main points to emerge in our discussions were that:

(1) The life of basic models has increased and is more than two years. Five years would be a better average, with two or three 'face lifts' during the life of a model. The initial costs for both face lifts and additional brands are of the order of 10 to 20% of the initial cost of the basic model. Separate brands have to be maintained in order to retain the share of the market, and are likely to be a source of cost disadvantage for a firm which grows by mergers, compared with one which grows internally.

For the purpose of preparing table 21.6, it was assumed that the life of models made by firms with a large output was 2 years. If lives of five years were assumed, this would reduce economies of scale for outputs between 150,000 and 500,000. It would also reduce the advantage in terms of costs, achieved by the firm with an annual output of 10,000. However, the cost of face lifts have the same effect as the initial costs of products and would offset 30–50% of the reduction in initial costs.

(2) For the firm consulted, other initial costs, apart from tooling costs, were estimated to be of the order of 40 – 50% of tooling costs. The main component of the other initial costs was research and development costs. The firm managed to make changes in models with very little loss of output, but there were costs for testing which were included in the research and development budget. This estimate provided support for the estimates given in table 21.6.

(3) The firm estimated that tooling and other initial costs had not increased substantially in relation to other costs since the mid 1960's.

(4) The company also provided the following 'guesses' of the relative costs of large 'green field' plants to manufacture 'white goods'.

Annual Output (millions)	0.5	1.0
	Index of Costs	
Materials	35	35
Other Costs	65	55
Total	100	90
Marginal Cost		80

The firm had not considered building large new plants, and so the comparison of costs was for hypothetical plants. However it had built a pilot plant incorporating new techniques and a high degree of automation, and this provided some guidance.

(5) The firm had reduced the number of its factories making white goods from eight to four and was moving towards rationalizing production so that the remaining factories specialized in different appliances. Also the firm expected substantial savings in R & D costs once the special development expenditures required as a result of the merger were passed.

(6) It would perhaps be misleading to complete this addendum without mentioning the extent to which the firm consulted deprecated the advantages of scale in relation to other factors affected by mergers. The factors mentioned by the firm as making scale advantages relatively less significant in determining the overall success of a firm were:—

(a) the detrimental effects on the morale of employees caused by rationalization after mergers.

(b) the need to maintain profitability, which may conflict with increasing scale.

(c) the advantage of private companies in being able to plough back their profits into investment and/or their not having to aim for as high a rate of profits to pay dividends.

(d) the existence of substantial differences in the availability and cost of labour in different parts of the country.

(e) the problem of gaining sufficient control of markets.

However, though there are qualifications to the advantages of increased scale brought about by mergers, there are significant economies. Alternative ways of bringing about concentration — such as forcing the weaker manufacturers to cease production — may be very slow to operate. To increase its share of a market without a merger, a firm needs to innovate in marketing its product in addition to, or as an alternative to low production costs. This was the source of John Bloom's temporary success, and of the increasing share of the refrigerator market held by Lec Refrigeration, whose refrigerators the Area Electricity Boards sell under their own brands. Also market shares are more likely to change when there is costly technical development of models as with the introduction of automatic washing machines.

VII. Summary

Table 21.7 *Summary of Minimum Efficient Scale for Domestic Appliances*[a]

	Output units per year (thousand)	% of U.K. market[b] 'A'	'B'	% increase in costs at 50% 'm.e.s.'	% increase in value added at 50% of 'm.e.s.'
Manufacture of a range of 10 appliances which are changed every 2 years[c]	500	20	50	+8	+12

(a) The economies of scale for production in a new plant may be appreciably larger than those indicated.

(b) The figures are given in relation to 'A' — U.K. output of all white goods — and 'B' — refrigerators or laundry equipment only.

(c) The estimates of economies of scale shown are speculative because at the time the study was made no U.K. firms produced 500,000 units of white goods a year.

Firms with a small share of the market can reduce their handicap by making a smaller range of products, and this does not necessarily impose a marketing handicap.

22. Electronic Capital Goods

Table 22.1. *Profile of the Electronic Capital Goods Industry*

	Electronic Computers[1]		Radio, Radar & Electronic Capital Goods	
	1963	1968	1963	1968
Number of Employees ('000) (1968 Census)	10.4	18.1[2]	75.2	75.2
Sales £m. (1968 Census)	40.1	119.2	175.6	244.8

(1) The trade covers Minimum List Heading 366, manufacturing digital, analogue and hybrid electronic computers and related equipment, including peripheral equipment for computing systems and data transmission equipment.

(2) International Computers (Holdings) Ltd., alone had 34,000 employees in 1969. The low census figure may be attributable to problems of classification.

I. General introduction

(1) Structure of the industry

Electronic capital goods are the main users of research and development work in the electronics industry, and in many ways can be regarded as providing the dynamic drive behind its expansion. Whereas entertainment markets[1] in the U.K. have been more or less satiated for the past decade, and markets are mainly those of replacement, the capital goods sector has achieved continuous growth and advance, as the possibilities for the control of processes in industry have been extended, and as new equipment has been substituted for existing types. While radio and television sets show evidence of fairly slow technical change, apart from the introduction of colour television, capital goods have changed very rapidly. The movement forward has been accelerated by the fact that a large quantity of electronic capital goods is produced on Government account as part of general provision for defence. Speed of reaction, range of action, small size of equipment are elements which defence needs imply: and such advances easily spill over into civilian production.

The rapid advance of technique implies that the life of equipment to obsolescence is fairly short, and that improvements in equipment may be extremely rapid. In terms of sales, the most important type of electronic equipment is the computer: computers tend to arrive in 'generations': that

(1) The market for radios, T.V. sets etc.

is a new type or family of computers arrives which becomes standard for a period, but is then obsolescent and is replaced by a further type, faster in its working, and probably of smaller dimensions and greater capability. The life of a computer generation is regarded as about five years. In the less glamorous parts of the market, the onrush of technical progress may not be so evident to the outsider, but, in general, it is felt in the industry that a product which has remained on sale for five years can be regarded as reaching obsolescence. This is not only because of research and development undertaken by the capital goods manufacturers themselves. Work which takes place on the improvement of components — more particularly the 'active' components, valves, tubes and semiconductors — forces manufacturers to reconsider their designs frequently. A particular example of this sort of reconsideration being forced onto manufacturers is the rapidly increasing availability of integrated circuits, in which whole circuits can be reduced to a tiny chip of silicon. Once these become commercially available, the opportunities available to capital goods manufacturers to improve their designs, making them more adaptable, of better quality and less bulky, are very great, and the competitive nature of the industry forces them into this reconsideration very rapidly.

The industry is, however, extremely diverse. Alongside huge computers are such items as walkie-talkie radios, scientific instruments and so on, each existing in a multitude of guises. Similarly, the length of production runs is variable: some installations (e.g. huge broadcasting transmitters) are made in small numbers, some less sophisticated items (e.g. oscilloscopes, mobile radios) may be produced in runs of many thousands per annum.

For its 'bread and butter' lines the industry is dominated by large groups, including Plessey, G.E.C., Phillips-Pye, I.C.L., S.T.C., Decca, I.B.M., and Honeywell. Oligopoly, or in some cases fairly clear market sharing structures, are common. None of these giants can afford to stay still however: the history of the industry (particularly in the U.S.A.) contains enough examples of rapid expansion of small firms to imply that continuous development is a *sine qua non*. Most of the small and medium size firms, of which there are a great many in the industry, operate as sub-contractors, or as suppliers of specialized equipment.

As computer production is an important and growing part of the industry, we have concentrated here on this part of the industry. I.C.L. is the only U.K. company producing computers on a large scale. In 1969 it accounted for about 40% of deliveries of computers to the U.K. market and over 50% of U.K. exports of computers. I.B.M. has about 30% of the U.K. market, and three other U.S. companies, Honeywell, N.C.R., and Burroughs, share most of the remainder. Imports by I.B.M. represent about 70% of their sales in the U.K. market and of their exports from the U.K. Total deliveries of computers to the U.K. market in 1969 were approximately £140m.[1]

(1) The information given in this paragraph was obtained from industry sources.

(2) *Production processes*

The main stages in the production of electronic capital goods are:

(a) the development of a new item of equipment or generation of equipment, and the construction of prototypes;

(b) the manufacture of components, many of which can be bought out. The production of many active components now involves the use of chemical-type processes. The production of passive components involves the pressing of metal parts, wire winding and assembly;

(c) the assembly of the product.

(3) *The dimensions of scale*

The principal dimensions of scale are the total output of particular items, the length of production runs, the range of equipment made, the output capacity of plants and the output capacity of firms.

II. The structure of costs

The main feature of costs for the industry is the high level of research and development expenditure: this averages about 10% of sales.[1] Another feature of costs is the labour intensity of production, particularly for the production of active components and the assembly of products. About 50% by number of all employees are women engaged in assembly work. One reason for the labour intensity of this type of work is the relatively short length of runs.

III. Initial costs

The main initial costs are for research and development. The N.I.E.S.R. has assembled some estimates of research and development costs for electronic capital goods and this is the main source of the data used in this section. Their estimates are shown in Table 22.2.

The estimated development costs for products are minimum estimates, as it is assumed that the development costs are for firms following a defensive policy and not attempting to set the pace. The lead times are the time it takes to develop products. The estimates of minimum annual expenditure are derived from the first two sets of data, and are intended as a guide to the minimum annual R and D expenditure a firm must be able to sustain if it is to remain competitive. If a firm cannnot incur expenditure at this rate, competitors who can will achieve a dominant market position unless the firm can avoid or reduce R and D costs by buying-out designs.

Substantial costs are also involved in the setting up of production lines

---

(1) This figure is based on data supplied by five companies in the industry, including two companies which make components as well as capital goods. On average R. & D. costs are a higher proportion of costs for capital goods production than for the production of components. Data for R. & D. are also complicated by the international relationships between companies; in particular U.K. subsidiaries may make use of research and development carried out by their U.S. associates.

Table 22.2. *Development Thresholds and Lead Times (c 1965)*

	Notional development cost	Notional lead time	Derived annual R. & D. expenditure
	£'000	Years	£'000
Radio communication receiver	80—150	2	40—75
V.H.F. transmitter	240—360	4	60—90
Laboratory oscilloscope	300—450	3	100—150
Marine radar set	100—200	3	33—66
Machine tool control equipment	300—600	3	100—200
Small scientific computer	1,000—2,000	3	333—666
Research satellite	500—1,500	4	125—375
T.V. colour camera	1,600—3,000	4	400—800
Large fully electronic telephone exchange	6,000—9,000	4	1,000—1,500
Range of E.D.P. computers, software and peripherals	8,000—16,000	4	2,000—4,000

Source: National Institute Economic Review, November 1965.

for new products, but there is no hard and fast relationship between R. & D. costs and the costs of setting up production lines for a product. A computer manufacturer suggested a relationship of 3 : 1 between R. & D. and set-up plus learning costs, while a manufacturer of telecommunications equipment gave the following examples:

	R. & D. costs £'000	Set-up Costs £'000
Product 1	60	11
Product 2[a]	3	25

(a) Product 2 was an improved version of an earlier product.

Our industry sources suggested that set-up costs are of the order of 2-3% of total sales, indicating total initial costs of the order of 12-13% of industry sales, or 20% of value added by the industry. But there is a wide variation around this average for firms and products. Officials of the two firms which provided information for this section, regarded initial costs as invariable with expected output of a product. In practice, however, there appears to be some flexibility.

IV. Production costs for runs

(1) Components

The economies of scale for the production of components were discussed in a recent O.E.C.D. report.[1] The report also illustrates the steep reduction in the costs of components which is achieved over time. The case used for illustration was integrated circuits. For prototypes, costs were about $500 per unit, but within 10 years the cost was below $1.00, and the price

(1) Gaps in Technology — Electronic Computers, O.E.C.D., Paris 1969.

of an integrated circuit is now less than $0.50. The reduction in costs is attributable to inventing production techniques for the mass production of new components — if low cost methods of production were not developed, the new components would not replace existing components on a large scale. In the case of integrated circuits, much of the development of production techniques was financed by the U.S. Space Programme. Annual output of integrated circuits in the U.K. and the U.S. is measured in terms millions of units. Economies of scale for producing these circuits are understood to exist, but no estimates of the size of the economies have been obtained.

Large numbers of components such as integrated circuits are used in some units of capital equipment, e.g. computers. In other cases fewer components are used in each unit of capital equipment, and the component is special to the type of capital equipment. The O.E.C.D. report illustrates the economies for the production of such components with the following data for components used in radar installations.[1]

Total output	10	100	1,000	10,000
Component A (W.R. — 159 Sidewall Hybrid)				
			Cost $ per unit	
Fabricated	200	56	43	38
Investment casting	116	25	15	13
Die casting	–	109.5	19	9
Least cost	116	25	15	9
Component B (W.R. Waveguide Binds)				
Investment casting	65	11	5.75	4.80
Die casting	–	32	4.50	1.30
Least cost	65	11	4.50	1.30

(2) Capital equipment

An indication of the effects on manufacturing costs for runs was obtained from two firms.

For the first firm the typical length of run was 300 units. The general view was that manufacturing costs[2] fell by about half during the course of the run, owing to learning, and that for some complex items the ratio of manufacturing costs at the commencement and the end of the run may be as much as 3 : 1. However, most of the reduction in costs was reckoned to be achieved when 100 units were made. The manufacturer provided the following illustration of the relationship between output, initial and production costs.

(1) A recent production run for this type of component by a U.K. firm was 7,000 units.

(2) Costs included labour and overheads, but not materials. The rule of thumb the firm used for buying components was that the price of these should fall by 10% if purchases were doubled. The extent to which this reflected economies of scale for suppliers was not known.

Total output (units)	100	300
	£'000	£'000
Initial Costs [a](total)	400	400
Initial Costs (per unit)	4.0	1.3
Production Costs (per unit)	5.0	5.0
Total (per unit)	9.0	6.3

(a) Including the costs of learning. Costs for the first 100 units are above the norm, and the extra costs for these units are included in the initial costs.

The duration of production affects costs in two ways:

(a) it takes longer to recoup the initial costs and the interest charge on these costs is therefore higher;

(b) there are learning effects, (although these are hard to quantify).

The other firm which provided information made longer runs of a different type of equipment. They provided the following estimates of the effects of the length of run on labour requirements and the cost of materials.

	Product 1		Product 2			
Total output (units)	200	1,500	20	50	100	500
Average man hours per unit (index)	100	63	–	100	75	60
Cost of Materials per unit			£9.8		£8.1	£8.0

V. The division of output between factories

Most of the large firms operate more than one factory. Where production facilities are divided, the division can be vertical (i.e. different products in different plants) or horizontal (i.e. different stages of production in different plants). The way in which firms organize production varies, often depending to some extent on historical accident, since the industry has been subject to rapid growth and a number of mergers. However, in the case of the firms visited, our informants were firmly convinced that the major difficulty which arose from the plurality of plants was that of production control.

It was sometimes admitted that horizontal divisions were more rational, in that specialisation by stages of production might imply better use of the total resources available, while on the other hand vertical divisions often meant that many items of plant and types of labour had to be duplicated. It was, however, still felt that this duplication was preferable to the loss of control and the possibility of design faults, bottlenecks, rejection of batches of supplies and other problems that might emerge with horizontal division of output. It was significant that all our informants were of the opinion that the most efficient method of production would be in one very large plant. Although the advantages of unified production on this scale might not be quantifiable, they were felt to be very real. Generally speaking, informants made light of such difficulties as breakages, packaging, or transport costs: in all cases the problem of control was seen as the most important major difficulty created by the division of facilities.

VI. The size of firms

(1) *Research and development*

Since research is of enormous importance to the industry, large firms which control finance have a great advantage where the production of an item in quantity is concerned, or where items produced are complex or of very large size. R. and D. expenditure on these types of equipment is generally substantial, and it is in these areas that large firms do in fact predominate. However, as pointed out above, the scope for very specialised research is great, and the pace of advance of the industry is so rapid that there is ample scope for the highly specialised small firm to find a niche. Even large research teams tend in fact to consist of a large number of almost independent groups specialising in particular areas. This aspect of the industry has been responsible for the success, to a greater degree in the U.S.A., perhaps than in the U.K., of 'breakaway' groups of researchers. They leave a large laboratory en masse, and are able to obtain sufficient finance to go into at least pilot scale production. The life of such 'breakaway' firms may be short – indeed they may be set up mainly to attract a buyer in the shape of some other large firm – but their success, either as independent firms or in selling themselves to a large buyer, has often been spectacular.

(2) *Marketing*

The main advantage of scale in marketing comes from the ability of large firms either to modify equipment to suit customers or produce ancillary equipment. In the case of computers, for example, experience has been that when a new generation was introduced, a large number of new models appeared, and strong competition ensued among the large firms and also among smaller firms or importers hoping to stake a place in the growing market. The weaker of these competitors are those who are not able to supply adequate ancillary facilities, individual modifications, software design and other services: and these firms are, almost by definition, those with a small scale of production. The larger firms, who are able, partly owing to their experience and partly to the volume of work they have to support, to provide such services, tend thus to be in a very strong position during these crucial periods. For other capital goods too, similar conditions exist: thus it is well-known that the secret of success in the competitive mobile radio market is the existence of adequate and widespread servicing facilities, which could only exist as concomitants of a large scale of production. Similarly, equipment of this sort often requires modification for particular purposes – for example for military purposes. Here the large scale producer is often able to make modifications or undertake development more readily than his smaller rival.

(3) *Vertical integration*

No estimates of the economies, if any, for integrating component and final product manufacture were obtained. A good deal would depend here on the extent to which components were standardised for the industry as a whole, thus giving economies of scale to non-integrated manufacturers of components.

VII. Conclusions & summary

The conclusions which emerge are the familiar ones that there are very large economies of scale for the production of electronic capital goods. Replication of research by many firms, whether in one country or a number of countries is, given its high cost, uneconomic. The main problem is to decide how to obtain the economies of scale on an international scale while defending national economic interests and, if this is a consideration, prestige. I.C.L. was created as a result of government pressure, and yet further structural changes in the British industry, such as closer association between I.C.L. and a U.S. computer manufacturer, or between G.E.C.'s electronic interests and some European manufacturer, might well strengthen U.K. producers in their competition with such firms as I.B.M.

Table 22.3. *Summary of Minimum Efficient Scale for Electronic Capital Goods*

For many products the initial costs form a substantial proportion of total costs: a typical figure is probably as high as 12%. The following figures are for such a product. They show that the entire British market may be needed for the minimum efficient scale of about 1,000 units to be achieved.

Products	Production Run (units)	% of U.K. Market	% increase in total average costs for a run or scale of a half the size shown.	% increase in average value added for a run or scale of a half the size shown.
Representative	1,000	100	(about) 8	(about) 13

It is not possible to specify a minimum efficient scale for the manufacture of electronic capital goods, as relatively small firms can operate successfully if they specialize, but it is possible to estimate the minimum efficient scale for a firm attempting to compete with a comprehensive range of electronic data processing equipment.

| Firm producing a Range of E.D.P. equipment. | — | 100 | (about) 10 | (about) 16 |

23. Cotton Textiles

I. General introduction

(a) General

The industry now uses substantial quantities of man-made fibres, and the distinction between cotton and other textile industries is becoming increasingly blurred. This tendency has been accentuated by the moves in recent years by producers of man-made fibres to merge with textile firms.

During the 1960's Courtaulds and Viyella spearheaded a series of take-overs and mergers in the cotton industry – a traditionally fragmented industry – and I.C.I. supported this movement towards concentration by making funds available to several companies.[1] As a result of the movement towards concentration in the industry, the four main groups – Courtaulds, Viyella, Carrington and Dewhurst, and English Calico – now control more than a third of the industry's total capacity.[2] However, in terms of the number of establishments (i.e. mills), the cotton industry is still relatively fragmented. In 1968, there were more than 1,000 firms in the industry, and more than 400 weaving mills alone.

(b) The dimensions of scale

The two most important features of the industry for the purpose of a study of the economies of scale and of industrial structure are:

(1) *The increased efficiency of modern equipment.* The greatly increased labour productivity which can be achieved with modern machines was described in the Textile Council's Report on Cotton and Allied Textiles. The report indicated that direct labour productivity for equipment of 1968 vintage may be twice as much as that for 1950 vintage, and for certain equipment, three times.

(2) *The economies of long runs.* As the economies of scale for mills and firms per se are relatively small, the main consideration for deciding the optimum structure of the industry is to suggest the structure that is most appropriate for re-equipping the industry and achieving the long runs which

---

(1) The motives for, and the effects of, producers of man-made fibres controlling outlets for fibres are discussed in Chapter 6.

(2) In 1968 the proportion of capacity owned by these groups was 47% for spinning, 33% for weaving, 53% for fabric finishing (bleaching, dyeing and printing) and 28% for converting (commissioning the finishing of the cloth and acting as merchant.) Cotton and Allied Textiles, Vol. I, The Textile Council (Manchester, 1969). The proportions are based on numbers of employees.

Table 23.1 *Profile of the Cotton Textile Industry*

	Spinning and Doubling					Weaving				
	1963	% of all manufacturing industry	1968	% of all manufacturing industry	1968 as % of 1963	1963	% of all manufacturing industry	1968	% of all manufacturing industry	1968 as % of 1963
Number of Employees ('000)	104.3	1.3	84.8	1.0	81	89.1	1.1	68.6	0.8	77
Sales (£m.)	248.0	0.9	312.2	0.8	126	255.3	0.9	289.5	0.7	113
Net Output (£m.)	77.0	0.7	114.9	0.7	149	74.0	0.7	86.1	0.5	116
Capital Expenditure (£m.)	9.4	0.9	–	–	–	10.5	1.0	–	–	–

<u>Concentration</u>. Concentration ratio for the 5 largest firms in 1963.

Spinning and Doubling

Average for 4 product groups distinguished   51.9%
Sales for these groups.   £106.1m.

Weaving

Average for 3 product groups distinguished   30.5%
Sales for these groups   £46.6m.

227

Size of Establishments and Enterprises (1963)

Number of Employees	Establishments				Enterprises			
	Number		% Employees		Number		% Employees	
	Spinning and Doubling	Weaving	Spinning and Doubling	Weaving	Spinning and Doubling	Weaving	Spinning and Doubling	Weaving
Less than 100	276	447	10	18	202	339	7	11
100 – 999	288	330	80	74	126	217	41	59
1000 and over	7	5	10	7	17	15	52	38
	571	782	100	100	345	571	100	100

are related to this. At the present time, technical progress is the most important feature of the industry, and economies of scale are mainly of interest because of their interaction with it.

II. The structure of costs

The breakdown of costs in Table 23.2 indicates the relative importance of the various stages of production for two products. The costs are for work involving long runs and were provided by a 'vertical' group, i.e. a group which itself performs all the main stages of production.

Table 23.2 *A Costing for Two Types of Fabric*

	Sheeting	Dress Fabric
	% of total costs	% of total costs
Raw Materials	29.5	26.2
Spinning: Labour	8.6	8.3
Overheads [a]	7.7	6.8
Sub-total	45.8	41.3
Weaving: Labour	12.7	13.3
Overheads [a]	26.7	24.6
Sub-total	39.4	37.9
Bleaching [a]	11.2	9.0
Crease Resistant Finish		7.7
Administration, Selling and Transport	3.6	4.1
Total	100.0	100.0

(a) Including depreciation based on the historical costs of fixed assets.

III. The length of production runs

For spinning and weaving the main sources of economies for long runs are:
   (1) economies of scale for operations associated with spinning and weaving;
   (2) the spreading of the set-up costs of machinery;
   (3) reduced costs for buying and administration;
   (4) improved control of stocks and labour productivity.
Although the capacity of spinning machines is very limited, the capacity of supporting equipment i.e. speed frames, draw frames, cards and opening equipment is much greater. Table 23.3 shows the number of units of equipment required for a new mill with 18,000 spindles — about 0.5% of the capacity of the industry in terms of spindles. There is some scope for economies of scale for long runs on this equipment.

Table 23.3 *Plant for a New Spinning Mill with a Capacity of 18,000 Spindles*

Opening ranges [a]	1
Cards (tandem)	11
Draw frames	5
Speed frames	4
Ring frames	45
Automatic winders	6

(a) There is least duplication for opening ranges, but the cost of this equipment represents less than 6% of the total cost of machinery.

The Textile Council gave the following estimate for weaving of the effects of the length of run on operating costs.

Table 23.4 *Effects of the Length of Runs on Operating Costs*

Typical length of run: yds	3,800	7,700	15,500	31,000	62,000
			pence per yard		
Labour Costs	2.9	1.5	1.2	1.1	1.0
Other Operating Costs	1.0	0.8	0.8	0.8	0.75
Total Operating Costs	3.9	2.3	2.0	1.9	1.75

Total output for the industry was 1,500m. sq. yds. in 1968 and the average length of run about 8,000 yds. [1]

For finishing processes, many of which are process type operations and for which the length of run is usually smaller, the economies of long runs are substantial. Estimates of prices made by Robson[2] suggest that prices for dyeing rise sharply for runs of less than 1,800 yards. The price for runs of 240 yards is 50% above that for 1,800 yards. For printing, declining costs continue up to 50,000 yards. If the price for 50,000 yards is taken at 100, that for 1,000 yards is 125, and for 500 about 150. The Textile Council also gives estimates of the effect of runs on finishing costs. They estimate, for example, that dyeing costs are 0.8p per yard for runs of 3,000 yards, and that they level out at about 0.5p per yard for runs of 50,000 yards. [3]

The overall effects on costs of the length of production runs depend on how late in the production sequence variety is introduced, and the relative importance of finishing operations. If yarn counts are not standardized, and colour is introduced as early as the yarn stage, the diseconomies for short runs of products are considerable.

(1) When considering the average, some allowance should be made for the practice of firms to increase the length of runs when trade is brisk. At other times the savings attributable to increasing the length of run would be smaller. Such increases would increase the extent of surplus capacity, but there might be scope for some economies for labour costs.

(2) R. Robson, 'The Cotton Industry in Britain', London, 1957, p. 100.

(3) In absolute terms the saving is small, and some consumers might well prefer to pay this penalty if it enabled them to obtain greater variety.

IV. Specialization

Fabrics made with cotton and man-made fibres are sold in a wide range of
qualities and to a variety of markets, and firms and mills in the industry
can, and do, specialize not only on processes but also on a limited range
of products. Robson has analysed in some detail the effects of the degree
of specialization. For the earlier processes, spinning and weaving, his conclusion was that, as far as it was possible to measure the technical economies, the advantages of greater specialization in reducing the range of yarn
counts made, and in longer production runs than those allowed by the existing structure of the industry, were limited. [1] But this was a qualified conclusion, and he pointed out that the reduction of variety yields economies
in a large number of directions which in total can add up to a great deal.
This is particularly so where modern machinery, carrying relatively heavy
capital charges, is in use. Also the capacity of machinery, particularly for
the processes associated with spinning, has increased a good deal since
Robson prepared his study. The Textile Council in its report stressed the
importance of both variety reduction and longer runs for all processes.

V. Mills

(a) Spinning and weaving

As the capacity of spinning and weaving machinery is very small in relation
to the output of the industry, the technical economies of scale for large
mills are small. [2] The main sources of economies for large mills are:

(1) The spreading of overheads, particularly the costs of administration
and technical staff, over a larger output. This can be achieved either by increasing scale through greater output for one process or by increasing the
range of processes. (Some overheads can also be spread over separate
mills, especially if they are situated close together.)

(2) Economies for capital costs, apart from machinery. For a new
spinning mill, it was estimated that the capital cost of the factory and services represented about 40% of total capital costs. [3] (However, in this in-

(1) The initial costs of designing a new fabric or variety of fabric are small, and
    for many types of product, e.g. sheeting, changes in products are infrequent.

(2) Even for the processes associated with spinning, the maximum capacity is
    small in relation to the total output of the industry.

(3) We obtained some evidence from the Ministry of Technology which suggested
    that any relationship between the size of new factories and costs per square
    foot of factory space are not straightforward. Estimates of building costs for
    nearly 250 factories which are summarised in the table below suggest that
    there is a weak relationship between the size of new factories and their costs,
    but that the economies of scale are small.

Index of Building Costs for Department of Trade and Industry Factories

Size of Factory (th.sq.ft.)	less than 10	10–25	25–50	50–100	100–200
Number of Factories built 1964/5 to 1970/71	17	108	90	22	7
Index of average cost per sq. ft. [a]	118	101	100	87	91

(a) Building costs exclude the cost of land, but include the cost of site works.
    Costs were adjusted to allow for price changes during the period.

dustry, a firm intending to equip a small spinning or weaving mill can acquire an existing mill. Old buildings are not ideal, but they cost very much less than new buildings.)

It is generally agreed that the technical optimum size for individual spinning and weaving mills is small relative to the total output of the industry. Mr. Ormerod[1] in a discussion of the structure of the industry, has expressed the view that the optimum size of a modern textile plant is not large, and has quoted a report on the New England textile industry which places the optimum scale for a combined spinning and weaving operation at 60,000 spindles and 1,300 looms.[2] The Textile Council gives estimates of 30,000–40,000 spindles and 500 looms and at these levels of capacity all types of machinery and equipment, would have to be duplicated. The latter estimate represents about 1% of the current capacity of the U.K. cotton industry in terms of the number of spindles and looms, although a weaving shed equipped with 500 of the most up-to-date looms could produce about 2% of U.K. output if it were operated continuously. The view that the minimum technical optimum for individual mills in the industry is small has also been supported by an economist of a large company in the industry; he quoted, privately, much lower figures than those mentioned above.

(b) Finishing

The information obtained about the economies of scale for finishing plants was limited. In this section of the industry, process type operations are employed, and so we should expect the economies of scale to be greater than for spinning and weaving. An estimate obtained from one firm suggested that above an annual output of 8m. yards, it would not be possible to reduce costs for a bleaching plant, but this estimate seems low in relation to the maximum capacity of new plant. Another firm has estimated that finishing costs for shirting fall with increases in capacity of plants up to 50m. yards of fabric. An output of 50m. yards of fabric represents more than the total U.K. output of woven shirting in 1967 (40m. yards), but it represents only 5% of total U.K. output of cotton cloth and 3% of total woven cloth (including man-made fibres).

Finishing costs vary for different products, being much lower for some standard commercial products (e.g. tyre cord) than for fashion fabrics. Thus the extent to which there are economies of scale varies by product. The finishing section of the industry is more highly concentrated than spinning or weaving, and these operations can be bought-out by those not possessing their own facilities. During our discussions with a leading firm at the finishing end of the industry, the differences in costs for new and existing plants, and the economies for long runs were stressed. But small existing finishing plants which specialize, are competitive.

(1) A. Ormerod, 'Integration of the Textile Industry', Investment Analyst, May 1965 (Mr. Ormerod is a director of a textile company).

(2) The balance between spindle and loom capacity would depend on the type of cloth made. Relatively fewer looms are required for fine cloth.

VI. Vertical integration

The extent to which vertical integration of spinning, weaving etc., within a single mill or a single firm provides economies, is open to question. There would appear to be no single substantial source of technical or transport economies [1] open to a vertical firm, whether it operates vertical or specialised plants, as compared with a combination of horizontal groups. There are, however, a number of sources of individually small economies. One integrated group has suggested that the main advantage of such a group is that it is in a better position to control quality and also delivery dates. If a firm makes a specialist product, the overall control of production enables it to buy the best mix of raw materials and to modify equipment for its special requirements. There are also small potential economies for buying and selling costs to be achieved by vertical integration. [2]

Mr. Ormerod has emphasised the advantages to be achieved by vertically integrated firms by reference to the character of firms forced into liquidation during the early 1960's. He shows that the integrated firms had a higher rate of survival, although the integrated firms also tend to be the larger firms. To illustrate one source of advantage for vertically integrated firms, Ormerod quotes figures which show that changes in demand for the products of the earlier operations of the industry are much greater than for later operations and for retail sales. He attributes this imbalance to changes in the level of stocks. Vertical integration should reduce fluctuations in the level of stockholding because integrated firms can take account of the overall effect of their decisions, and do not need to guarantee supplies by excessive ordering during a boom. An independent converter would ignore the losses incurred by spinning and weaving firms caused by his reducing his stocks, but a vertically integrated firm would take these into account.

An important aspect of the structure of vertically integrated firms is the balance of their operations. The leading firms in the industry have more spinning than weaving capacity, but it is not clear that their weaving capacity is greater than their converting capacity, because a substantial proportion of cloth converted in the U.K. is imported. Also, the leading firms concentrate on different stages of production, with, for example, Courtaulds having more spinning capacity and Viyella more converting capacity. [3]

It has been suggested that the ideal structure for a textile firm is an inverted pyramid, or even a T-shaped structure with capacity concentrated on the final stages of production. The primary advantage of this structure is that a firm can fully employ its spinning and weaving capacity during a recession by reducing the proportion of those operations it buys out. This

(1) Robson has estimated the cost of transport of cotton from spinner to weaver in Lancashire as between ¼% and 1½% of the spinner's margin.

(2) Selling costs for spinners (excluding the cost of providing credit) and buying costs for weavers form a very small proportion of total costs, generally less than 1% of total costs in each case.

(3) The balance of these two firms' operations is partly an accident of their historical development.

may well be an ideal structure for an individual firm, but it inevitably means that other firms, taken together, tend to have the reverse type of structure, unless peak demand for the products of earlier processes is supplied by imports. The inverted pyramid type of structure does not therefore have corresponding advantages for the industry or the economy as a whole, though it may clearly have advantages for individual firms.

One company in the industry carried out an exercise to measure the effects of product specialization and vertical integration in one particular case, and gave us the results. The company was considering setting up a vertically integrated plant for spinning, weaving and converting a fabric for the manufacture of shirts, and some estimates of the possible savings in costs had been made. The figures were hypothetical, but were based on the experience of a number of textile manufacturing units operated by the company. The estimates indicated that, compared with having the operations performed by independent horizontal units, there would be savings for spinning. These were attributable to the elimination of transport between mills, economies in mill operating costs due to greater specialization, greater control of production, the holding of proportionately smaller stocks and longer production runs. These savings would be of the order of 10.5% of the spinner's margin in all — equivalent to 4.5% of the cost of the yarn. In addition, there were expected to be savings in distribution and administration, which increased the savings to 12% of the spinner's margin. For weaving, the estimated economies represented 15% of the weaver's margin. Overall, the economies, excluding any economies for finishing, represented 8 — 9% of the cost of having the product made by horizontal non-specialist groups. Other things remaining constant, this reduction in costs would increase profits, and the return on capital would be still further increased by the reduction in capital required. In the case described, the savings in capital achieved by longer runs etc., which increase output per machine and per unit of factory space, together with the reduction in stocks, were estimated to be 30% of the requirements for horizontal non-specialist groups.

Inevitably these estimates were tentative because they were for a hypothetical plant. But an executive of one small U.K. textile company, who has had experience of vertically integrated production in the U.S., expressed surprise that the economies were estimated to be so low. He stressed the advantages of having all the operations on one floor — preferably in a single storey building, although it is difficult to quantify the economies through better control in this type of operation.

A disadvantage of specialization which is difficult to measure, and is not allowed for in the above calculations, is the possibility of fashion changes, necessitating a change in the type of material used. This could result in an imbalance of production in the mill, which would not be in a strong position to obtain other work. The inability to shop around for quotations with which to test the effeciency of the mill might also be a disadvantage. These disadvantages would be smaller for a multi-mill firm and for a vertically integrated group in an industry predominantly organized on a horizontal basis, since such firms would be in a better position to obtain alternative work. Finally, there are qualifications to the estimated savings, because independent firms might reduce the scope for economies by close co-operation and limited specialization.

In addition to dealing with the benefits of vertical integration described above, the Textile Council has emphasized the importance of marketing advantages, the stimulus to product innovation and direct contact with final markets. The importance of these factors varies; for specialized fabrics for which long runs are not possible, product innovation is much more important than, for example, in the case of sheeting.

Perhaps the most important benefit of vertical integration is that it enables some firms to re-equip with the latest, most efficient, types of machinery, because they have greater control over future demand and they can ensure long runs. Protection from competition from low wage countries is also claimed to be an important requirement for long runs of 'bread and butter lines' produced on modern equipment. Long runs are difficult to achieve for special lines in which low wage countries do not compete.

VII. The size of firms

There are a number of possible sources of economies for large firms in the industry. These are discussed below.

(a) Management and technical expertise

One possible source of economies for large firms is the ability to employ management experts and provide greater technical expertise. However, smaller firms can buy advice from consultants who specialize in providing advice to the textile industry. Firms in the industry can also obtain technical assistance from the machinery manufacturers, and in some cases the manufacturers of man-made fibres.

The survival of many small firms in the industry not only supports the view that the technical economies of scale are small, but suggests that any advantages for management are also small. But the effects of the scale of the large firms which have been created in recent years, on the viability of smaller firms are not yet clear.

(b) Specialization

The scope for achieving economies by specialization has been outlined above, but the extent to which multi-plant horizontal groups have in the past achieved longer runs at their plants is not proven. Robson provides figures which tentatively indicate that during the early postwar period, the production of the spinning mills of the multi-unit firms was only slightly more specialized than that of independent units.[1] It was claimed by several firms that in the past the larger firms rarely took full advantage of the scope for standardising production in their mills. Also, many of the

(1) Op. cit., p.71

235

smaller independent firms and plants have a high degree of plant specialisation on processes and types of product.

(c) *Rationalisation and capacity utilization*

A recent case study [1] has shown the extent of the economies which can be
achieved by rationalisation. In this case, the economies achieved by concentrating production and closing some plants were substantial, but they
are not economies of scale in the sense that this term is usually used. For
estimating the 'static' long run average cost curve it is assumed that firms
have an ideal adjustment of their capital stock. However, with conditions
of demand continuously changing, a multi-plant firm may be better able to
continuously relate its capacity to demand. The case study showed the
effects of rationalisation for the Combined English Mills Limited, now a
member of the Viyella group. The results of rationalisation − of concentrating production on plants operated at a high level of capacity − are
summarized in table 23.5.

Table 23.5 *The Effects of Rationalisation*

	Position Before Re-organisation	Current Position
Number of spinning mills	14	7
Weight produced (m. lbs)	28	25
Spindles installed	404,000	221,000
Production per spindle year (th. lbs. p.a.)	70	113
Average running hrs. per week	59	111
Number employed	3,983	2,318
Production per person employed (th. lbs. p.a.)	7.0	10.0
Stock of Yarn £'000	754	196

The figures demonstrate the advantages of rationalisation in an industry
suffering from over capacity, especially as the competitive process may
take much longer to squeeze out independent small firms and achieve
similar results. However, the fact that C.E.M. was in a position to undertake such a drastic scheme of rationalisation, suggests that large firms may
be slow in taking advantage of the scope for rationalisation. It may also be
noted that some of the smaller firms maintain high levels of capacity utilisation, so that the effects of working at a high level of capacity cannot be
considered an automatic economy of multi-plant operation. [2]

(1) 'A Case Study in Rationalisation', Ernest Cummins. The Textile Weekly, July
29th and August 5th 1966.

(2) Other data obtained from the Cotton Board suggest that large firms may not
have a greater ability in spinning to achieve higher rates of capacity utilization.
But data comparing the utilization of capacity in the weaving section of the industry, which is more fragmented, show that the average number of loom-hours
worked, per loom in place, was higher for the larger firms. In 1964 the average
for nine firms, with over 2,000 looms each, was 293 hours per month, and for
199 firms with less than 200 looms each, was 180. Figures for October, 1966
showed similar relationships to those for October, 1964. The difference between
spinning and weaving is probably linked to the higher proportion of automatic
looms used by the larger firms, and possibly the greater fragmentation of
weaving operations among firms.

236

It may be noted that some vertically integrated firms have achieved consistently high levels of capacity utilization, but this may in part reflect the demand for the type of products that they make. Also there is considerable variation within size groups, and one firm with about 1% of the industry's capacity consistently works its looms 420 hours a month.

(d) Economies for buying

Companies making synthetic fibres give discounts for large purchases, and a large textile company giving its business to one or other of the producers of synthetic fibres obtains a significant discount. One estimate obtained during the first half of 1966 suggests that these discounts were about 5% for very large buyers, although they do not apply to all fibres. This could be an important feature of the switch to man-made fibres when considering the significance of the economies of scale in this industry, as there are very few reductions in costs to be achieved by buying large quantities of cotton. When buying man-made fibres, small firms are at a bigger disadvantage. It is doubtful whether the discounts for man-made fibres reflect any real economies for the producers, except that it may enable them to plan ahead with less risk if a system of discounts is used to tie markets.

The marketing advantages of the large groups are difficult to assess. As in many other industries, there is considerable advertising of brand names for final products, but horizontally organized spinning and weaving firms cannot brand their products. Small vertically integrated firms cannot launch a new brand with an advertising campaign on the scale of the large groups, but there are other ways of marketing final products — through wholesalers, multiple stores or direct to mail order firms. For intermediate products, which are sold to industrial firms, selling costs can be kept down to a small percentage of total costs.[1]

(f) Diversification

Some firms own a number of textile plants performing different processes, for example, cotton spinning and warp knitting. An advantage of a diversified group covering a number of textile trades is that it may be able to even out the flow of profits and concentrate its capital on profitable processes. This may have attractions for shareholders and thus for the raising of new capital.[2]

---

(1) It may be noted that in the cotton industry many brands have been built up by firms that were relatively small when they launched the brand name. It may well be difficult, however, for very small firms to establish new brands successfully in the future, especially for products for which brands have been established. Relatively small firms may also have difficulty in keeping abreast of fashion changes emanating from other countries.

(2) Some reduction in risk may be important if the capital of a company forms a substantial part of the shareholders' total wealth, as happens in the case of some family businesses. In such circumstances, firms may be deterred from taking risks which a large company could balance with other ventures.

237

(g) New investment in development areas

Another advantage of large groups in the textile industry has been illustrated by Courtaulds. It is building new mills in development areas in order to obtain investment grants on the investment. With additional grants of 20% (making 40% in all) for purchases of plant and machinery, and subsidies for for labour costs through the Regional Employment Premium, this provides an important advantage compared with a firm building and operating a new plant outside the development areas.[1]   Even if a small firm could provide the capital, including the cost of disruption, for a move to a development area, it might be reluctant to accept the risks involved. However, compared with firms with plants in traditional areas which have kept up with modern trends by replacing machinery, new plants in development areas will be relatively expensive in terms of capital costs despite the higher investment grants. It is possible that some large firms may invest even when the rate of return is quite low, say, 10%. They may be willing to do this because of profits made on fibre production, for which they are able to ensure guaranteed outlets of their own.

VIII. Conclusion

In general, this industry exhibits only small technical economies of scale. The situation regarding economies for firms is much more complex, and has been discussed above at some length. Perhaps the main advantage of the concentration of the industry which has occurred in recent years is that the large firms invest heavily in the industry. It is difficult to determine whether this higher rate of investment is attributable to the links of the large firms with the production of synthetic fibres or is also a function of their size, but for whatever reason Courtaulds and the other leading firms have invested relatively heavily in new plant in recent years.

Table 23.6 *Summary of Minimum Efficient Scale for Cotton*[a]

Products

Economies continue to large outputs of individual products, i.e. there are significant economies for long runs.

Mills	Size of Mill	% of Industry Output	Increase in Costs at 50% of the 'm.e.s.'
Spinning standard products (number of spindles)	< 60,000	< 2%	Estimates of the increases in costs
Weaving standard products (numbers of looms)	< 1,000	< 2%	were not obtained

Firms

Providing a small firm adopts a policy of specialization, and makes an appropriate selection of processes and products, it can operate efficiently. There are, however, potential economies of larger firms in certain cases.

(a) The estimates of economies of scale for finishing costs which we obtained were limited, but it is clear that economies of scale are more important for these processes.

(1) Another possible source of advantage for building in development areas is that it is easier to arrange for three shift working in these areas.

238

24. Hosiery

Table 24.1. *Profile of the Hosiery and Other Knitted Goods Industry*

	1963	% of all manufacturing industry	1968	% of all manufacturing industry	1968 as % of 1963
Number of Employees ('000)	124.5	1.6	136.0	1.7	109
Sales (£m.)	283.5	1.0	457.0	1.2	161
Net Output (£m.)	117.6	1.1	195.1	1.2	166
Capital Expenditure (£m.)	10.9	1.1	—	—	—

Concentration

Average concentration ratio for 5 largest firms in four markets in 1963 — 28.9%.

Size of Establishments and Enterprises (1963)

	Establishments		Enterprises	
Number of Employees	Number	% of Employees	Number	% of Employees
Under 100	899	24	709	18
100 – 999	331	67	190	42
1,000 and over	7	8	25	40
	1237	100	924	100

I. General introduction

Much of the information about the economies of scale for the production of hosiery which we have obtained, relates to the section of the industry engaged in warp knitting.[1] We discuss the economies of scale for the hosiery industry as a whole first and then deal with the warp knitting section of the industry in more detail.

(1) Structure of the industry

The hosiery industry produces a wide range of products, including knitted fabrics, stockings, underwear and knitted outerwear, and has a very fragmented structure. Even when allowance is made for the fact that many firms specialise, there are at least thirty firms producing each of the main types of hose, and for some product groups, such as women's outerwear, there are more than a hundred manufacturers.

---

(1) The data on economies of scale for warp knitting were provided by Mr. B. Chiplin who made a study of the warp knitting industry whilst Viyella Research Fellow at the University of Nottingham in 1966 and 1967.

(2) *Processes*

The characteristic process of the hosiery industry is knitting. Various types of machines are used for this e.g. warp and circular knitting machines. There are a number of other important processes — finishing, making-up garments, etc.

(3) *The dimensions of scale*

The dimension of scale which is generally of most importance for hosiery is the length of production runs. Economies also relate to the output capacity of factories and firms.

II. The structure of costs

Apart from the costs of materials, the main costs of production are for labour. The operations and costs of making hosiery vary for different types of product, but for the industry as a whole about 20 per cent of the labour force is employed on knitting operations, and the remaining 80 per cent, mainly women, are employed on operations such as sewing, welting, mending, folding and packing products.

For firms who do not carry out finishing operations, the most expensive items of plant are knitting machines. These may cost as little as a few hundred pounds, but some models cost more than £10,000. Some of the more expensive types of knitting machines are used for the production of women's hosiery. Other features of the production of women's hosiery are rapid technical innovation and fashion changes. Twice since 1960 firms have had to re-equip with knitting machines, first to make seamless stockings (about 1962) and from 1968 to make tights. The need to replace machinery has increased the relative importance of capital charges.

Finishing operations are process type operations which are relatively capital intensive, and for which economies of scale extend to higher levels of output than for knitting operations. The type of finishing process varies, underwear is generally knitted with grey fibres and is then bleached, cheap fashion outerwear is usually dyed after knitting, while some high quality outerwear is knitted with fibres which have been dyed. For some products finishing costs are relatively important, but the possibility of buying-out finishing operations enables firms which manufacture these products to produce on a relatively small scale. For stockings and tights which are dyed in vats the finishing operations are relatively simple. One crude estimate was that the capital cost of plant for this operation for a plant with 300 knitting machines, would be about £50,000, compared with the cost of the knitting machines of £1.5m. (Stenters are not required for women's hosiery).

III. Production runs

(a) *Women's hosiery*

The range of sizes of stockings and tights made with synthetic fibres, does not affect the knitting operation as the size is determined when the stockings are 'moulded'[1] after knitting. For products made with traditional fibres these processes cannot be used, but the knitting machines can be quickly adjusted to make different sizes. The costs of introducing new products e.g. women's tights, depend on whether new machinery is required. If it is required, then the costs are very substantial.

(b) *Other products*

In a survey of the Irish Hosiery and Knitwear Industry, the Committee on Industrial Organisation obtained information from eighteen firms about the effects of increasing production runs for products.[2] Firms were asked to what extent they would have to increase their runs to reduce their costs to the minimum practical level or to the level of competition elsewhere. Among the firms making outerwear, the order of increase needed was from one and a half to twenty times their existing runs, with increases of from four to six times being frequently mentioned. The longest runs of garments of the same size, colour and style achieved already by these firms varied, but for most of them it was from ten to twenty dozen of a garment only. Seven firms mentioned reductions in costs of from 10 to 15% if the necessary increases in production runs could be achieved, and for all the firms providing estimates the average was 10%. The sources of economies for long runs mentioned were the minimization of machine down-time, the learning effect, the introduction of flow production and increased mechanization, improved quality, and management economies. Some economies of scale from these sources continue to much higher levels of output.

IV. Factories

The scope for achieving *technical* economies of scale for large hosiery factories is small because of the limited capacity of machinery. A factory making special products which employs fifty people, could fully employ machinery, other than finishing plant. Even for the production of standard products such as stockings and tights, the technical disadvantages for factories with, say, a hundred employees would be small.

V. Firms

(a) *Technical economies*

In a study[3] made during the early 1950's Professor Pool and Mr. G. Llewellyn summarised the position regarding economies of scale for hosiery firms by saying 'that large hosiery firms differ from small, primarily in

---

(1) Recently there has been a trend towards selling tights without moulding them. They acquire their shape in use. For this type of hose a range of three sizes is used for all fittings. (One firm sells a single size for all fittings.)

(2) Committee on Industrial Organisation, 'Survey Team's Report on the Knitwear Industry'. Dublin, 1964.

(3) A.G. Pool and G. Llewellyn, 'The British Hosiery Industry. A study in competition.' University College, Leicester, 1953.

having more machines and workers of the same kind, not in carrying further the specialisation of men and machines; hence the technical economies of scale are comparatively slight and do not prevent the smaller firms from holding their own in competition with larger'. They also found that the firms entering the industry during the early post-war period were aided by their ability to buy second-hand knitting machines which could be bought more cheaply than new machines.

In many cases the larger firms in the industry operate a number of factories and tend to produce a wider range of products than small firms. The main advantages of the multi-factory firms relate to the spreading of risks, such as the chance that demand for one type of product may fall and the spreading of costs of administration.

(b) Design and marketing

The larger firms may also have advantages in design and marketing. A large firm can employ specialist designers. The manager of a small firm may, however, be able to produce competent designs, or he may make products designed by retailers or buy out designs. Again, with selling, a small firm can sell through chain stores, mail order houses or wholesalers and thus avoid the cost of selling to independent retailers. The advantage of a large firm for marketing is that it is more likely to be able to bear the cost of advertising a brand, and this may enable it to charge a higher price for its product. Advertising gives it a method of marketing which is uneconomic for a small firm, except perhaps when it is selling a specialised product. Another scale advantage is that Marks and Spencer, an important customer for hosiery, buys from firms which make *products* on a large scale. For example they are only willing to buy women's tights from firms which can supply 50,000 pairs a week. If M. & S. were to buy small quantities of each type of product from many firms, this would increase its buying costs and increase the problems of quality control which is very important.

(c) Comparisons of costs

The hosiery industry has developed arrangements for the comparison of firms' costs to a degree probably greater than any other U.K. industry, and provides an example of co-operation between small firms which enables them to achieve some advantages of multi-plant firms. Comparisons (unpublished) are made by the National Hosiery Manufacturers' Federation. It has not been possible to make use of these comparisons in detail, but the implication of the comparisons, which cover more than one hundred firms, is that any relationship between scale and costs is swamped by other factors. Nor is it a case of small firms making a different type of product, as comparisons are made for each product group. In many cases there is no substantial difference in the type of product produced by the large and small firms, although there may be differences of quality.

The unpublished comparisons of costs made by the N.H.M.F. suggest that for each operation (and there are more than twenty operations involved in the manufacture of some types of hose) the ratio of the labour productivity

242

of the most efficient firms, compared with the least efficient, is of the order of two and a half times in many cases. There are similar differences if comparisons are made in terms of cost. Substantial differences also occur in the ratio of net profit to sales. For 1964, the ratios for about twenty firms making one type of product varied from -25.6% to $+17.7\%$, and the range for this particular type of product was not exceptional.

Another important variable thrown up by the comparisons was the proportion of imperfect products. For some firms these represented more than ten per cent of output. Again the proportion varied considerably. The price obtained for imperfect products averages about fifty per cent of that for perfect products, and a rejection rate of ten per cent of output therefore represents a substantial cost.

One conclusion which the N.H.M.F. obtained from the comparisons was that there were some economies of scale for administration. For example, the number of directors of larger firms did not increase proportionately. This did not appear to be simply a matter of the titles used to describe jobs. Also large firms may employ only one accountant where three smaller firms with the same total output would employ three accountants. The small firms may, however, obtain some advantages from employing a higher ratio of staff to other employees, such as obtaining more detailed and up to-date accounting data. They are also likely to pay their staff lower salaries.

VI. Warp knitting

(1) Structure of the trade

Employment in the warp knitting section of the hosiery industry was of the order of 10,000 in 1967. Of the hundred or so firms in the industry, two groups, Courtaulds and Viyella, accounted for more than 60% of production, and the twenty biggest for more than 75%. The leading firms in the industry concentrate on the production of fabrics made in large quantities, such as fabric for lingerie and shirting, while many of the smaller firms make special products including fabrics for furnishings, shawls, laces etc. One possible explanation for the high degree of concentration for standardised products in the warp knitting industry is that man made fibres predominate and that there are quantity discounts for man-made fibres used in warp knitting.[1] [2] For special products, fibres form a smaller percentage of total costs. Also the warp knitting trade has expanded very rapidly and the present structure is less dependent on its historical development than the structure of the cotton and woollen industries. The rapid growth of the business is in part attributable to the increasing capacity and general improvement in efficiency of knitting machines. Firms, such as Courtaulds, have encouraged the development of new machines because they have wanted to expand the

(1) The cost of fibres represents about 50% of total factory costs for work involving long runs, and dyes account for up to 20% of costs.

(2) I.C.I. has officially abandoned its discount scheme, and the size of discounts allowed at present is not clear.

market for their yarns in this industry.

(2) *Processes and costs*

The main warp knitting operations are winding or 'warping' the fibre on to a beam, knitting and finishing. The finishing operations include heat setting and dyeing, but these operations can be sub-contracted. The relative import-ance of costs varies for different products. Yarn and other materials gen-erally account for 60 – 70% of total costs. Knitting and finishing costs, which are the most expensive operations, each account for about 7 – 10% of total production costs including material costs. The costs of dyeing are particularly variable, as they depend on the colour. Deep shades and blacks generally have substantially higher costs than whites and pastels. The cost of warping, the other principal operation, is less than half that of knitting or finishing operations.

(3) *Economies for long runs*

Stenters, the equipment used for heat setting, have to be reset for changes of fibres, but not for changes in width and colour of fabric. As changes of fibre are very infrequent, the length of production runs is relatively unim-portant for this process. The length of run does have a limited effect on the earlier processes, and where changes of dyes are required, there are significant economies for long runs. As in the case of cotton textiles, the effect of short runs on costs depends upon where variations are introduced.

(4) *Economies of scale for factories*

The most important processes contributing economies of scale for factories are the finishing processes. The cheapest stenter costs about £20,000 as compared with knitting machines which generally cost from £2,000 to £4,000.[1] These small stenters have a capacity equivalent to the output of at least 50 knitting machines, about 1.5% of the warp knitting machines installed in the U.K. Equipment for dyeing fabrics is also expensive and there are advantages to be obtained by integrating the dyeing process at the knitting factory, rather than sub-contracting to another firm. A firm with an integrated factory has greater control over the timing of the operation, the cost of packing and unpacking the fabric is avoided, and there are no intermediate transport or selling costs. However, most of these costs are relatively small providing close co-operation can be established with a local dyer.[2]

The effect of the scale of factories on costs is limited as in the cotton and wool industries. But as the total output of the industry is much smaller, the optimum size of factories represents a higher proportion of total output in the case of warp knitted fabrics. There would be economies of scale for

(1) There are advantages to be achieved by using large knitting machines; for ex-ample the cost of an 84" machine is about £2,500 while the cost of an equiv-alent 168" model is £3,300. The latter are the largest machines built.

(2) The advantages of integration increase with the size of knitting factory as there are economies of scale for dyeing operations.

a factory at which standard products are made and finishing operations carried out, up to at least 100 knitting machines — 3% of the industry total: this probably represents the minimum optimum scale for this type of production. The main sources of economies would be for finishing operations and the spreading of management costs. For factories at which the finishing processes are bought-out, and/or special products are made, the minimum efficient scale would be lower.

(5) *Firms*

The main source of economies for large firms, apart from the operation of large factories, is the discounts obtained on fibre prices. An interesting difference between the large and small firms found by Mr. Chiplin was the comparatively high level of capacity utilization achieved by the large firms. The small firms had lower levels of capacity utilization because of short runs and also a shortage of demand, but it was not clear whether it was the vertical integration of the large firms or their size as knitters which enabled them to achieve high rates of capacity utilization.

Table 24.2. *Summary of Minimum Efficient Scale for Hosiery*

	Capacity of factory	% of U.K. capacity	Costs for factories with a smaller capacity than that shown
Warp knitting of standard products (e.g. shirting)	< 100 knitting machines	< 3%	The increase in costs for smaller units would depend on whether finishing operations were bought out. If they were not, average costs might be of the order of 2 − 3% higher, and value added perhaps 5% higher at 50% of the scale shown. If they were bought out, the difference would be small.

Hosiery. For both factories and firms the minimum efficient scale is very small. Nevertheless there are sources of economies for large firms which are important for some products.

25. Footwear - An Addendum

Table 25.1. *Profile of the Footwear Industry*

	1963	% of all manufacturing industry	1968	% of all manufacturing industry	1968 as % of 1963
Number of Employees ('000)	106.6	1.3	101.4	1.3	95
Sales (£m)	215.9	0.8	280.0	0.7	130
Net Output (£m)	101.9	0.9	140.6	0.9	138
Capital Expenditure (£m)	2.9	0.3	—	—	—

Concentration

Concentration ratio for the 5 largest firms in 1963:

Men's shoes	—	30.3%
Women's shoes	—	28.9%

Size of Establishments and Enterprises (1963)

	Establishments		Enterprises	
Number of Employees	Number	% of Employees	Number	% of Employees
Under 100	642	21	494	15
100 – 499	269	56	168	36
500 – 999	22	15	17	11
1,000 and over	5	8	17	38
	938	100	696	100

I. General introduction[1]

The economies of scale for footwear production were described in the interim report. Since the publication of that study we have obtained a report of a detailed study of the effects on the costs of production of the length of production runs from a firm which makes women's shoes.

II. Production runs

The length of production runs is the most important dimension of scale for achieving economies of scale for firms with an output of more than 1,200 pairs a day.[2] In the interim report it was suggested that there are few economies for runs of more than 1,000 pairs, but the new evidence suggests that

(1) A detailed description of the structure of the footwear industry, the processes of production, and the costs of production are given in Chapter 3 of the interim report.

(2) This represents 0.2% of the industry's output.

246

economies in direct labour and other costs continue above this level. The following estimates of labour productivity were based on data for six production runs.[1]

Length of run	Labour productivity running at a rate exceeding productivity on the first day by:
From 5 to 9 days	10%
From 10 to 14 days	15%
From 15 to 19 days	18%

In addition the firm found that there were similar increases in labour productivity for making and finishing, but there was no evidence of increases in productivity for clicking. There was also evidence of other economies — for example, it was found that the quality of work, as measured by repairs to shoes, improved. By the twentieth day these repairs had been reduced by about a half, but most of the savings occurred during the first five days, and the savings were small in relation to total costs.

III. Output of a style

Other economies for large outputs of a style are for lasts, knives, operative training and for wholesaling. For this firm the cost of a set of lasts for a style was estimated to be £250, of knives £150, of operative training for a new style £400, and for wholesaling each style £690. However a change of style may not require new lasts, the cost of knives and training depend on the degree of differences of styles, and if a small output of a style were expected, it is possible to reduce initial costs.[2]

It is also necessary to consider which styles are eliminated to assess the effects of a reduction in the number of styles. If the number of existing styles is reduced there will be few savings for lasts, knives and operative training, and the savings for wholesaling would be limited. If the number of radically new styles were reduced, the savings for these items would be very much greater.

There are reasons for expecting greater economies of scale and increases in productivity for long runs of styles of women's shoes than for men's shoes. For women's shoes changes of colours, which necessitate changing the twine in sewing machines, are more frequent, and there is a quicker turnover of styles so a greater learning effect would be expected. Finally materials, for which there are few economies, account for a higher proportion of the cost of men's shoes and this damps down the economies of

---

(1) Between 300 and 400 pairs were produced each day depending on the style.

(2) It is possible to reduce initial costs for styles by substituting hand clicking for press clicking, by reducing the number of sizes or fittings, or by making short runs or speeding up production to economize on the number of lasts required. However a firm with a good deal of experience of short runs suggested similar figures for the cost of new sets of knives and lasts.

scale, but not the increases in labour productivity.

It may be noted that increases in productivity of the size indicated are small compared with the gains in productivity which can be achieved in process and engineering industries by increasing scale. Nevertheless the economies of long runs are important. Some firms are still making some styles in very short runs — in the case of one firm visited (in terms of total output one of the largest firms in the industry) runs of a dozen shoes were often made, particularly at the end of the season.

Table 25.2. *Summary of Minimum Efficient Scale for Footwear* [a]

| | Output per year (pairs) | % of U.K. output | Increase in Costs at 50% of the Minimum Efficient Scale | |
			Total Costs per unit	Value Added per unit
Factories	300,000[c]	0.2%	2.0[b]	5[b]
Firms	Quantitative estimates for the economies of scale for large firms were not obtained, but the m.e.s. for firms which specialize is small in relation to the output of the industry.			

(a) This summary is based on the data given in Chapter 3 of the interim report and the information described in this chapter.

(b) In practice the extent of the economies would depend on the range of products manufactured, and the processes used. For certain processes the economies of scale are larger than those shown, and significant economies extend beyond an output of 300,000 pairs a year. Also if the length of runs increased with scale the economies would be larger.

(c) If we had adhered to the definition of the m.e.s. given in Book 1, it would have been lower than 300,000.

26. Newspapers

Table 26.1. *Profile of the Newspaper Trade*[a]

	1963 (Census)	% of all manufac- turing industry	1968 (estimates)	% of all manufac- turing industry	1968 as % of 1963
Number of Employees ('000)	85.3	1.1	96.3	1.2	113
Sales (£m)	250.7	0.9	350.4	0.9	140
Net Output (£m)	153.0	1.4	241.8	1.5	158
Capital Expenditure	9.9	1.0	—	—	—

(a) Based on data for firms employing 25 or more people.

I. General introduction

(1) Structure of the industry

The economics of printing and publishing newspapers have been explored by the Royal Commission on the Press,[1] and by the Prices and Incomes Board.[2] The newspaper market can be divided into the following classes according to national and local readership and degree of sophistication.

Morning Dailies	National quality
	National popular
	Provincial
Sundays	National quality
	National popular
Evenings	London
	Provincial
Weekly	Provincial

At present there are eight daily and seven Sunday national newspapers with a circulation of more than 200,000 copies, approximately 75 local morning or evening newspapers, and a large number of local weekly papers.

(2) Dimensions of scale

The main dimensions of scale which affect costs are the sales of individual newspapers (which is of great importance because of proportion of costs which are initial or first copy costs) and the number of papers produced by

(1) Report of the Royal Commission on the Press, 1961–1962. H.M.S.O. 1962.

(2) N.B.P.I. Reports 43 and 141.

one firm, either at one place, e.g. a national daily, a London evening and a Sunday paper, or at a number of places, as with a chain of local papers.

II. Structure of costs

New data on costs were not collected from firms in the industry. The main feature of the costs of producing newspapers is the high level of first copy costs — the costs of writing and editing the paper, and setting up type. These costs are incurred each time a paper is published: for other industries initial costs of products can be spread over production for a much longer period of time. The Prices and Incomes Board in its second report on the industry[1] estimated that in 1969 first copy costs for eight national daily, and seven Sunday newspapers, ranged from 54% to 79% of total costs.

It might be expected that first copy costs as a proportion of total costs would decline with increases in circulation i.e. that first copy costs are relatively fixed and would be a higher proportion of costs for newspapers in a small county, say, Sweden, than in the U.K. In practice, however, total first copy costs may rise as the circulation of a class of newspapers increases, as managements use their ability to spread first copy costs over a larger output to improve the quality of their coverage by widening the range of news etc., or by deepening its coverage, or by collecting news etc. more rapidly.

III. Newspapers

The main source of economies of scale for a newspaper with a large circulation, relative to other newspapers within its class, is the ability to spread first copy costs. There would also be some relatively small economies for other costs. In addition to these advantages, a paper with the largest circulation in its class has an advantage for attracting advertising revenue, because advertizers tend to go for the largest readership first. (For 'quality' daily papers advertising revenue provides as much as 72% of total revenue and for 'popular' dailies 38%[2]).

The position within a class of papers, once one paper has a larger readership than the others, is illustrated by the estimates shown in table 26.2.

The difference between the two low circulation papers A and B is that A attempts to emulate the high circulation paper in size and quality of news coverage etc., while B attempts to cut its costs in an attempt to remain competitive. It is difficult to maintain the first course because of the losses the paper incurs and the latter strategy is likely to lead to a smaller circulation, unless a paper can make a distinctive appeal — in effect be a different class of newspaper. The inevitable tendency is towards monopoly within each class and this has occurred to most of the regional press.

(1) N.B.P.I. Report No. 141, op cit, p.8.

(2) N.B.P.I. Report No. 141, op cit, p.4.

Table 26.2. *Illustrative Figures for Different Types of Popular Sunday newspapers in 1960*

	High Circulation Paper	Low Circulation Papers	
		A	B
1. Circulation (million)	5	1.5	1.5
Revenue and costs per copy in pence		pence	
2. Price	4.0	4.0	4.0
3. Sales revenue received by the publisher	2.7	2.7	2.7
4. Advertising revenue	2.4	2.2	2.2
5. First-copy costs	1.1	2.8	1.8
6. Variable costs	3.7	4.0	3.1
7. Profit or loss	(profit) 0.3	(loss) 1.9	—

Source: W.B. Reddaway,'The Economics of Newspapers', Econ, Jnl., July. 1963.

There is a tendency towards monopoly within each class,[1] but there are opportunities for product differentiation to meet the variations in the tastes and special interests of the public by expressing different opinions (this is a source of competitiveness for the Guardian competing with the Times, which has been heavily subsidised by the Thompson Group, and for the Financial Times), or by providing different coverage of events. An example of the second type of policy is that followed by 'free newspapers' which provide limited news coverage and features, and obtain all their revenue by scale of advertising space. Product differentiation affects not only costs and the price of a paper, as readers may be willing to pay a higher price for a different product, e.g. the Financial Times, but also advertising rates. If the effectiveness of advertisements is increased by the selectiveness of the readership, advertisers are willing to pay a higher milli-inch rate. Quality and specialist newspapers are clearly a case of product differentiation which is of real value for consumers.

IV. The number of papers published by a firm

It is not possible to generalise about the economies for the production of a number of newspapers by one firm. Where the production of a number of papers by one firm results in the use of fewer presses and operatives, as could be the case where two, or more, local papers are printed on the same presses, there *could be* substantial economies.[2] But in many cases the scope for economies is limited. If, for example, a morning and evening paper are printed on the same presses the printing staff has to be duplicated,

(1) The tendency towards monopoly in the national press would have been carried further, but for the fact that the proprietors of some newspapers have been willing to produce papers in spite of achieving a low rate of return on the capital employed.

(2) It should be noted that the use of common printing facilities does not necessarily require common ownership of the papers.

and in other cases employees demand higher wages — (the latter reduces the financial but not the real economies.)[1] Also editorial, reporting, advertising and publicity staff are usually duplicated even where there is common owner-ship because it is found that this is a more efficient arrangement.

Where a firm publishes a number of papers from separate offices, e.g. a chain of provincial papers, the economies again appear to be small and relate mainly to the joint provision of services such as Parliamentary corre-spondents and a London news service, and even this type of advantage can be offset if independent papers co-operate to provide services, or make use of news agencies. Again most papers which are jointly owned have separate editorial staff and advertising representatives. Some economies arise from bulk purchasing, but any economies for newsprint are small and overall economies for purchasing materials appear to be marginal. Another source of advantage claimed for a company publishing a number of papers is its ability to compare the performance of its papers and find areas in which economies can be achieved. It may also be able to transfer men and new ideas between its papers, but an independent management is able to obtain experienced staff and follow the development of other papers.

Table 26.3. *Summary of Minimum Efficient Scale for Newspapers*

	m.e.s. (% of market)	% Increase in costs at 50% of m.e.s.	% Increase in value added at 50% of m.e.s.
A newspaper	100% for class of newspaper	> 20%	> 40% [a]
Size of firms	Generally only small economies for multi-newspaper firms but there are important exceptions.		

(a) Based on costs for popular daily and Sunday newspapers.

(1) The vintage of presses used is of some importance in determining these econ-omies. Capital charges for new presses are substantial and the economies for spreading these charges are appreciable.

27. Books - An Addendum

I. General introduction[1]

Book printing was one of the trades included in the interim study. In this chapter we summarise the estimates of the economies of scale given in the interim report and add some additional information which was received in response to the earlier publication.

With the exception of repeat printing orders and new editions of old titles, publishers and printers make a succession of new products. In practice a publisher usually has a monopoly for each title he publishes and he generally places one order for the initial printing of each title. The size, shape, type of print, number and type of illustrations, and formulae, vary from book to book and because of this variation, and the varying number of copies of each title printed, firms specialise. In addition many firms which do other types of printing, produce some books, and some firms specialise in setting up type and preparing and binding covers.

II. Titles

There are substantial economies to be achieved by spreading the first copy costs of composition and the cost of setting up type. These economies are illustrated by the estimates of printing costs for orders of varying size for a standard title, shown below. Most book printing orders placed in this country fall within the range shown, but many titles have higher first copy costs per page than the novel used for this example, because they contain tables, diagrams etc.

The economies to be achieved for subsequent orders for a title are less marked than for extending the initial run because there would be additional composition and set up costs.[2]

III. Firms

Printers print a range of titles and, though there are economies to be achieved by the use of large capacity presses and by standardising the

(1) For a detailed description of the structure of the industry and the costs of production see Chaper 2 of the interim report. Data for all firms which print books are not shown separately in the Census. Many firms print books and publish books or print books and other products. Of the order of 40,000 people are engaged in printing books.

(2) The additional composition and set up costs for a second run of a standard title in hardback form would amount to about £100, depending on the state of the type.

Table 27.1. *Printing Costs for an Initial Printing Order for a 256 Page Title*

Number of copies printed	Cost per copy, including the cost of paper and binding	
Thousands	Hardback-Index of costs	Paperback-Index of costs
1	100	
5	34	100
10	25	80
20	21	59
50	18	41
100		34
200		30

range of sizes of titles printed, a firm with $300-400$ employees can employ the most efficient presses and, if it specialises, can be technically competitive.[1] Where small firms produce a wide range of work they are under some disadvantages because they cannot fully utilise the most efficient types of equipment, but it was not possible to measure the overall effect of these disadvantages.

The relationship between managerial and marketing costs and scale are as always difficult to assess. One set of data on management costs was obtained from a specialist printing house which had increased its total staff from 100 to 232 between 1948 and 1965. The managing director of this company when commenting on our interim report said he considered the economies in management and selling costs to be major sources of economies of scale and produced the data shown in table 27.2 illustrate this. Not only had the number of office staff, which included sales staff, not risen as rapidly as factory staff, but the average quality of the staff had declined i.e. there had been a trend towards employing less skilled and younger staff. The total saving in salaries represented a reduction in average unit costs of 10%. However comparisons of this sort over time are subject to a number of qualifications, such as the introduction of new accounting techniques, the effect of learning by experience, whether staffing was at the lowest level compatible with the level of output in the base period, and the extent to which staff 'help out' with factory work.

Vertical integration

From the 1963 Census it appears that about 15% of the books printed in the U.K. are printed by firms which also publish the books.[2] Firms mentioned two main points about the advantages and disadvantages of vertical intergration — firstly the advantages of control over deliveries, and secondly

(1) Many small firms in the industry specialise either on certain types and sizes of books, or on operations such as composing and binding, but others accept a wide variety of work. One reason suggested for failing to specialise mentioned by some printers was that if they refused orders outside their chosen field publishers would not provide them with other more suitable work.

(2) These estimates were based on data given in the Census of Production 1963.

254

Table 27.2. *Managerial and Sales Staff and Scale*

	1948	1964	% Change
Factory staff — number	80	190	138
Office staff — number	20	42	110
Total — number	100	232	132
Sales at actual prices £th	97.5	420	331
Sales at 1964 prices £th	169	420	149
Sales per factory employee 1964 prices £	2,113	2,211	5
Sales per office employee 1964 prices £	8,452	10,000	18
Office staff salaries, 1964 rates £th	34	49.2	45

the disadvantage of not being able to shop around for the lowest tender.

Diversification

Apart from fifty, or so, firms which specialise in book printing, there are more than a hundred general printers, and printers who specialise on other types of work, who also print books.[1] One advantage of book printing work for some of these firms is that it enables them to use capacity usually employed for other purposes, such as printing company accounts, for which there is a seasonal demand. However apart from special cases it is doubtful whether there are significant advantages to be achieved by diversification.

Table 27.3. *Summary of Minimum Efficient Scale for Books*

	Output	% of U.K. Market	Percentage increase at 50% of m.e.s.	
			average total cost	value added
A title:				
Hardback	(say) 10,000	more than 100% for most titles	36	50
Paperback	(say) 100,000	more than 100% for most titles	20	30

There are economies for firms to be achieved through specialization, and for increasing the output of a standardized range of titles (books of the same size and type, etc.), but a firm with a small percentage, say, 2 per cent of the industry's output can achieve most of the technical economies of scale if it specializes.

(1) These estimates were based on data given in the Census of Production 1963.

28. Plastic Products[1]

Table 28.1 *Profile of the Plastic Moulding and Fabricating Trade*[a]

	1963	% of all manufacturing industry	1968	% of all manufacturing industry	1968 as % of 1963
Number of Employees ('000)	71.0	0.9	96.6	1.2	136
Sales	170.4	0.6	345.1	0.9	203
Net output (£m.)	84.3	0.8	172.8	1.1	205
Capital Expenditure (£m.)	11	1.1	–	–	–

Concentration

Average for 4 types of product in 1963 — 29%[b]

Size of Establishments and Enterprises (1963)

Number of Employees	Establishments		Enterprises	
	Number	% of Employees	Number	% of Employees
Less than 100	1240	36	1120	30
100 – 749	180	56	148	48
750 and over	6	8	11	21
	1426	100	1279	100

(a) This table reproduces the information given for the Census trade, but the Census trade does not cover the whole of plastic conversion. For example plastic belting and hose, plastic floorcovering, games and toys made of plastic, plastic outerwear and plastic footwear are all included in other trades.

(b) Total sales of these four groups of products was £26m. in 1963 — 15% of total sales of the Census trade.

(1) Simply defined, plastics are organic materials which can be shaped as required by heat and pressure, and will then retain that shape on cooling. Plastics derive this and other properties from their polymeric structure. There are two main groups of plastics. Thermoplastics are materials which can be softened repeatedly by heat, and have a long-chain molecular structure. Thermosetting materials undergo a chemical change when originally shaped, and cannot be shaped thereafter. There are several hundred distinct plastics with widely differing properties.

I. General introduction

1. The structure of the industry [1]

The plastics industry can be divided into two sections — chemical processing and the moulding and fabrication of plastic products. The production of plastic polymers is generally similar to the production of polymers for synthetic fibres, described in Chapter 6. The second stage of production is the processing of polymers, usually as powders or granules or sheet, into plastic products which include components for building cars etc., consumer goods such as toys, plastic housewares, and a wide variety of packaging products e.g. film, crates, bottles. A feature of the industry is its rapid growth; since 1948 world consumption of plastics has increased from 1m. tons to more than 20m. tons a year and there is an immense and growing diversity of products made by the industry.

The production of plastic polymers is dominated by the large chemical and oil companies, most of which operate on an international scale, but some of the older plastics and specialities are made by smaller chemical companies. In contrast, polymers are processed by more than 1,000 firms in the U.K. Many of the polymer manufacturers have integrated forward and some users of plastic products, including car manufacturers, have integrated backwards to make plastic components. In addition there are many independent firms processing plastics.

2. Production processes

(a) The production of polymers involves the use of process type operations of the sort dealt with in Chapters 4 and 5.

(b) There is a range of processes used for the conversion of polymers, including various types of moulding, extrusion, sheet forming and callendering. We obtained information for two processes, moulding and extrusion. A number of other processes are employed at plastic processing factories — assembling plastic and other components, packaging etc.

---

(1) A report 'Shell in the Plastics Industry' has been used in the preparation of this section.

3. Dimensions of scale

We should expect large economies for the production of plastic polymers, and we obtained data supporting this view, but in this chapter we have concentrated on the economies of scale for the conversion of polymers. [1] There are a number of dimensions of scale for the conversion of polymers, including the output of products, the output of a range of products using the same plastic, the size of firm, etc.

II. Economies of scale for products made by injection moulding

1. Costs

Table 28.2 shows a breakdown of costs for the production of a plastic product. Although there are differences in costs for different products, depending upon their size, shape and quality, [2] materials generally represent 50 per cent, or more, of the costs for products made in long runs.

Table 28.2 *Cost Breakdown for a Plastic Bucket*

	New Pence	%
Materials	11	63
Direct Labour	0.5	3
Overheads (incl. depreciation)	2.5	14
Manufacturer's Profit	3.5	20
Manufacturer's Price	17.5	100

Initial costs for new products include the costs of initiating a new idea, designing the product, making tools and testing the product. A firm's expenditure on initial costs is affected by a number of factors;

(1) The data we obtained were for the production of a group of plastic polymers. A chemical company provided the following index of costs.

Output (thousand tons a year)	25	50	100	150
Material costs %	47.5	42.5	41	40
Operating costs %	52.5	30.0	24	20
Index of Average costs %	100	72.5	65	60
Index of Marginal costs %		45	57.5	50

The index of costs was based on the changes in costs achieved by the firm as it increased production over time. Officials of the firm guessed that about half the decline in average costs was attributable to technical progress and half to economies of scale. The estimates in the E.C.N. Supplements on Large Plants also support the view that there are substantial economies for the production of plastic polymers.

(2) Material costs can vary by up to 100 per cent according to the plastic used for products, the type of plastic used is an important determinant of quality. Different types of plastic can not necessarily be used in a tool because of differences in shrinkage.

258

(a) whether it specializes in making industrial products or household products. (The former generally have a longer life).

(b) whether it makes high quality products. (design and tool costs tend to be higher for quality products, but these products tend to have a longer life than cheap products).

(c) whether it is expanding. (If a firm is to expand, new products have to be introduced, and the faster a firm's expansion, the more it will tend to spend on initial costs).

The costs of inventing and designing new products are variable. Some U.S. firms have spent very large sums designing plastic houses; at the other extreme a firm may design a plastic bucket at negligible cost. Of the order of 2% of employees in the industry are engaged in designing products. The costs of making tools for products which we discuss below are a much more important item of costs.

2. Techniques

There is basically one operation involved in injection moulding — heated plastic is injected under pressure into a mould. Variations in the cycle time for moulding units are determined primarily by the time it takes to cool the plastic in the mould and this depends on the size of the product and other technical factors. The time varies from less than one minute for small components to ten minutes for a large product such as a bin.

The cost of injection moulding machines depends mainly on their size, measured in terms of ounces of plastic injected per shot, and varies from £2,000 to more than £100,000. An indication of the relationship between the cost of machines and capacity is provided by the following estimates;

Capacity of Machine per shot ozs	Cost £thou.	Index of cost per oz.
8	9	100
80	35	39
400	110	24

The speed of operations of machines declines with size. The obsolesence of machines due to technical progress is quite rapid and firms usually write them off over a period of five to seven years. (The performance of machines is improved by increasing the rate at which they operate, [1] increasing the size and complexity of mouldings which can be made, and improving the quality of products, through more precise control of temperature. Firms use their older equipment for work involving relatively short runs, smaller and less complex mouldings.) In addition to the machines, moulds (tools) are required and these are an important item of costs. Tools also vary in cost, from less than £1,000 to more than £10,000 according to the size and complexity of the products. Some savings in costs can be achieved for tools, if

(1) The substitution of plunger injection machines by screw machines during the early 1960's increased capacity by about 20%.

a short run is expected, by using cheaper metal alloys, but these savings are small because the cost of steel for tools represents only, about 10% of their cost. Also the use of cheaper materials may result in a decline in the quality of products. [1] The life of a small mould is from 3m. to 5m. but the life of large tools is much shorter, and the use of certain plastics results in shorter life. Costs of repairing tools represents 15 per cent or more of the original cost of the tool, per million units. One firm suggested as much as 50 per cent. Cheaper alloys have a shorter life.

For small products another variable for tools is the number of cavities. An example of the differences in costs attributable to the number of cavities is that the cost of a single cavity tool is £2,000 — £3,000 compared to £10,000 for an eight cavity tool for the same component.[2] This indicates a source of economies for large outputs of products where precision is not very important, as is the case with toys. If precision is important, there are difficulties in maintaining quality with a number of cavities. Tool costs are particularly important if a range of sizes or fittings has to be made or for work involving short runs. An indication of the importance of tool costs was provided by a firm which specialized in making injection mouldings. About 10 per cent of its employees were engaged in making tools, and these employees accounted for about 15 per cent of the total wage and salary bill. In addition this firm bought out about 40 per cent of the tools used.

The change-over time for tools in an injection unit again varies according to the size and complexity of the tool. In the case of a small tool it may take from one to two hours, but for a large complicated unit it may take a day and a half to set up the mould and make it function properly. Changes of colour also take time depending on the colour change. A change from red to black can be achieved in half an hour, but a change from black to yellow takes several hours and as in other industries, firms arrange the sequence of colour changes to minimise the time required for change overs.

The moulding machine operator can 'finish' some mouldings by cutting or scraping away surplus plastic. But for some products there are additional finishing, assembly and packaging operations, though these are generally of minor importance in relation to total cost — in terms of labour cost alone they are more significant. There are usually few economies of scale for these operations, and they have not been allowed for when making the following estimates of costs.

3. Output of a product

Table 28.3 shows the relationship between output and cost for a five gallon container made by injection moulding. It is assumed that the containers are

(1) Alternatively it may be possible to use a cheaper mould with a different process — see Table 28.4.

(2) The source of the economies for multi-cavity moulds is that the costs of setting up machine tools to make the cavities can be spread over the number of cavities and there is a learning effect. A factor tending to reduce the number of cavities is the problem of reliability of a multi-cavity mould.

made in one production run and that there are no economies for operating
expenses or machine depreciation. Where the output of a narrow range of
products is increased, there are in some cases substantial economies for
operating costs to be achieved by using more expensive and faster operating
injection moulding machinery. However the economies of scale shown in
Table 28.3 may be reduced by using different operations for an output of
less than about 50,000 units. Table 28.4 illustrates the difference in costs
for alternative processes. The economies of scale for the other processes
are smaller because the tools are much less expensive, but the use of the
alternative techniques is only economic for certain products.[1] The economies of scale shown in table 28.4 could also be reduced by using a less
expensive tool for the short runs.

Table 28.3 *Unit Production Cost for a Container*

Production (thousands)	1	10	100	1,000
		New Pence		
Raw materials[a]	16½	16½	16½	16½
Operating Expenses	2½	2½	2½	2½
Machine Depreciation	1½	1½	1½	1½
Mould Depreciation	300	30	3	½
Total	320½	50½	23½	21
Index	1526	240	112	100

(a) The relationship between scale and material costs are
discussed in section V. In practice there would be some
small in process economies for materials, associated with
the start of producing different batches.

Source: 'Plastics', October, 1965.

Table 28.4 *Unit Production Cost for a Container if Made by Different Processes*

Production (thousands)	1	10	100	1,000
		New Pence		
Injection Moulding	320½	50½	23½	21
Blow Moulding	105½	33½	26½	25½
Rotational Moulding	36½	34½	32	31½
Minimum cost	36½	33½	23½	21
Index	174	160	112	100

Source: 'Plastics', October 1965

To illustrate the effects of colour changes and production runs of varying
length, it is assumed that the average time for a colour change is two hours.
The effects of producing 100,000 units in a variety of colours and of runs is
illustrated by the following figures. Comparing extreme cases, the extra

(1) The appropriate technique to use for a product depends on its shape and complexity as well as the quantity produced.

costs of producing in runs of 200 of each colour, increases costs by 10% compared to producing one run of 100,000 units of the same colour. These economies are achieved by spreading the cost of setting up the machine over a greater output. In addition to the economies for long runs which are shown, there would be some economies for material costs. The material lost during the running in stage depends on the size and complexity of the product. For a large product made in small quantities, the loss of material may amount to as much as 10% of the total materials used, but the loss is usually a much smaller percentage. For colour changes the loss of material is generally quite a small item of costs.

Number of runs	1	10	100
Number of colours		New Pence	
1	24	24	24½
2	24	24	25
5	24	24	26

III. Economies of scale for extruded products

Table 28.5 shows a cost breakdown for a range of five types of extruded plastic products.

Table 28.5 *Cost Breakdown for Extruded Products*

	Range of Costs
	%
Raw Materials	41 – 64
Labour	9 – 25
Depreciation	4 – 11
Overheads, incl. selling expenses	23 – 32
Total	100

Techniques

As for moulding there are a few distinct processes used in the production of extruded products. Polymer is fed in at one end of the machines and shaped products are extruded. One of the most important types of extruded product is film for packaging and many other uses. Table 28.6 shows a comparison of costs of production for a small and a large extrusion machine used in the production of film. The comparison shows substantial economies of scale for depreciation, labour, and other works costs.

Table 28.6 *Costs for Extruders*

	Small	Large	Ratio
Extruder Capacity (lbs. per hr.)	135	1230	9.1
Costs per lb.	(p)	(p)	
Depreciation of Machines and Tools	0.59	0.13	0.2
Direct Labour	0.42	0.22	0.5
Other Works Costs	0.96	0.57	0.6
Total operating costs	1.96	0.92	0.5
Materials	5.75	5.71	1.0
Costs of Production	7.71	6.63	0.9

The capacity of the largest film extrusion machines now in use is about 7,000 tons a year, and, where a firm has sufficient production to employ a small range of these machines, it can achieve all the main technical economies of scale. The main sources for further economies are reductions in stocks in relation to sales. In the case of a firm which had greatly increased its output of several ranges of products there had been a large reduction in the ratio of stocks to sales — for one group of products, raw material stocks as a percentage of sales fell by more than two-thirds.

IV. Factories

Estimates of the effects on costs of the overall output of factories were not obtained. A firm setting up a new factory would expect substantial economies of scale for overhead costs, but small firms operating small factories can keep down costs as described in the following section.

V. The size of firms

(a) Economies for buying

The existence of many small firms in this industry suggests there is no overwhelming source of economies of scale for firms or substantial barriers to entry. Perhaps the main source of advantage for the large firms, apart from technical economies attributable to producing products in greater quantities, is for buying. There are substantial quantity discounts for buying large amounts. Industry sources suggested the following approximate relationships. [1]

Quantity purchases per year (tons)	Small lots	500/1,000	10,000
Index of prices	115	100	85

In practice a firm's total purchases of polymers, as well as its purchases of individual polymers, may affect the size of the discounts it receives.

---

(1) This data referred to the mid 1960's.

(b) Other sources of advantage for large firms

The large firms have advantages for spreading the cost of employing experts and for developing certain new plastic products. (For developing products with complex structures and/or very long life considerable financial and technical resources are required). Also the larger firms can spread the costs of marketing over a greater output.

(c) Sources of competitiveness for the smaller firms

The small firms have several sources of advantage. They may well be able to pay lower wages and salaries, not provide such comprehensive welfare facilities and can keep down overheads (many firms are aptly described as back yard operators by their larger competitors). Also manufacturers of raw materials and machinery manufacturers are often willing to 'nurse' small firms, especially those developing new lines, by extending credit and providing advice and technical service facilities. There is a market in second hand machines and tools which may help small firms to get established, and small firms can sell to wholesalers, or locally, to avoid heavy marketing costs. Finally the small firms can simply avoid design costs by producing simple products or products developed by other firms, or they may concentrate on such new lines as may have low development costs.

Summary of minimum efficient scale

Products

There are economies of scale for producing individual products in large quantities. For many products (particularly where complex shapes or a range of sizes are required) technical economies of scale extend to a substantial proportion of U.K. output.

Firms

In this industry small firms with, say, 20 employees, which specialise on appropriate products can be competitive. Their main handicap is that they pay higher prices for materials.

Book 3. Conclusions

29. Coverage of the Industry Studies

Table 29.1. lists the trades covered by the industry studies. The information obtained for trades did not always coincide with the Census trade definitions, but very approximately we covered one third of manufacturing industry in terms of employment, and nearly a half in terms of capital expenditure in 1963. However, three trades, chemicals, steel and motors, accounted for one third of our coverage in terms of employees, and more than a half in terms of capital expenditure.

Every industry has distinctive characteristics, but it is possible to classify many industries to three broad groups, based on the type of operations employed. The three groups are process, engineering, and textiles and clothing.[1] Many trades do not fit into these groups either because processes of more than one type are used, and are important,[2] as with synthetic fibres, or because the operations do not fit into our three groups, as is the case for printing. Table 29.2 summarises Census data according to this very crude classification, and indicates our coverage for each group of trades.

Our coverage of trades enables us to make some tentative generalisations about the technical economies of scale in the first three groups of trades, but not in the fourth, 'rag bag', group.[3] Another point crudely illustrated in table 29.2, is the relative capital intensity of the process trades — they account for a much higher proportion of capital expenditure in 1963 than of the number of employees.

(1) The main process operations are the mixing, heating, cooling, distillation, compression and expansion of materials and gasses which are performed in pressure vessels, kilns, furnaces, rolling mills and other types of mill. The principal operations used in the engineering industries are pressing and machining components, welding and assembly of products. The main operations employed in the textile and clothing industries are spinning, weaving, knitting and sewing.

(2) For the purposes of classification, a trade is included in a group if the main operations used in the trade are of a type associated with the group. In a number of trades subsidiary processes of other types are used.

(3) In terms of the S.I.C. Orders, the main orders for which our sample is not representative are food, drink and tobacco (2 out of 15 trades included) miscellaneous metal goods, timber, furniture, etc., and 'other' manufacturing industries.

Table 29.1. *The Coverage of the Industry Studies*

Industry	Type of Industry[a]	EMPLOYEES[b]				CAPITAL EXPENDITURE[b]	
		1963		1968		1963	
		Number (thousands)	% of all manufacturing industry	Number (thousands)	% of all manufacturing industry	£m	% of all manufacturing industry
1. Oil Refining	P	20.5	0.3	17.7	0.2	11.9	1.2
2. Chemicals	P	233.0	2.9	232.4	2.9	99.5	9.7
3. Synthetic Fibres	O	37.3	0.5	42.5	0.5	11.7	1.1
4. Soap and Detergents	P	21.8	0.3	16.8	0.2	4.1	0.4
5. Bread	P	160.2	2.0	155.0	1.9	17.8	1.7
6. Brewing	P	86.6	1.1	86.9	1.1	32.2	3.1
7. Cement	P	14.2	0.2	14.0	0.2	11.2	1.1
8. Bricks	P	35.9	0.5	38.0	0.4	4.4	0.4
9. Steel	P	269.5	3.4	262.0	3.2	101.6	9.9
10. Iron Castings	O	113.2	1.4	102.6	1.3	12.1	1.2
11. Motor Vehicles	E	444.9	5.6	466.2	5.8	88.0	8.6
12. Aircraft	E	254.6	3.2	229.1	2.8	11.4	1.1
13. Bicycles	E	17.5	0.2	14.3	0.2	0.0	0.0
14. Machine Tools	E	74.4	0.9	77.1	1.0	7.1	0.7
15. Diesel Engines	E	54.9	0.6	44.9	0.5	3.3	0.3
16. Design of Chemical Plants	E	n.a.	n.a.	(15.0)	–	n.a.	n.a.
17. Turbo Generators and Electric Motors	E	41.0	0.5	35.0	0.4	2.2	0.2
18. Domestic Electrical Appliances	E	72.3	0.9	71.7	0.9	5.5	0.5
19. Electronic Capital Goods	E	85.6	1.1	93.3	1.1	5.6	0.5
20. Cotton Textiles	T	193.4	2.4	153.4	1.8	19.9	1.9
21. Hosiery	T	124.5	1.6	136.0	1.7	10.9	1.1
22. Footwear	T	106.6	1.3	101.4	1.3	2.9	0.3
23. Newspapers	O	85.3	1.1	96.3	1.2	9.9	1.0
24. Books	O	40.0	0.5	41.0	0.5	4.3	0.4
25. Plastics	O	71.0	0.9	96.6	1.2	11.0	1.1
		2658.2	33.4	2624.2	32.3	488.5	47.5
All Manufacturing Industry		7951.7	100.0	8077.3	100.0	1026.0	100.0

(a) Types of industry: P - process, E - engineering, T - textiles and clothing, O - other trades.
(b) Employment and capital expenditure data for the design of chemical plants, turbo generators, electric motors, and books are not distinguished in the Census. The figures given for these trades are estimates.

Table 29.2. Groups of Industries

	Total						Our Sample		
Type of Industry	Number of Census Trades 1968	Number of employees in 1968 th.	%	Capital Expenditure[a] 1963 £m.	%	Net output per head £	Number of Trades	Number of employees in 1968 (thousands)	Employees in trades covered as % of total Employees
Process	32	1,376	17	373	36	2,655	12 [b]	823	60
Engineering	35	2,938	36	282	27	1,925	8 [c]	1,032	35
Textiles	25	1,163	14	73	7	1,287	4 [d]	391	34
Other	49	2,601	32	298	29	2,002	5	379	15
	141	8,078	100	1,026	100	1,982	29	2,624	32

(a) Capital expenditure data for 1968 is not available.
(b) Includes five chemical trades for 'chemicals'.
(c) Excludes the Design of Chemical Plants.
(d) Includes two trades for cotton textiles – spinning and weaving.

30. Conclusions on the Technical Economies of Scale

I. Summary of the technical economies of scale

The diversity between industries, and the qualifications which relate to any estimate of the economies of scale, make it difficult to summarize the studies we have reported in Book 2. Nevertheless, some broad conclusions about economies of scale for production costs – technical economies – did emerge.

In the conclusions to the interim study, economies for single product plants were discussed first, but in a subsequent article based on this study, the author described the economies for a 'narrow range of products.'[1] This term is useful as very few plants indeed produce a single product. The term 'narrow range of products' is used to mean a group of products made on the same machinery e.g. a range of chemicals made in a plant, steel sheet of similar, but not necessarily constant, dimensions, a car model and its derivatives, footwear of a single style or a number of styles involving small variations.

Our broad conclusions are that there are large technical economies of scale for such ranges of products in many industries. For 'process' industries the main sources of these economies are the less than proportional increase in the external dimensions of plant as scale is increased, which reduces capital costs per unit of capacity, economies for operating costs for large units, and in the case of some new products, for spreading initial costs. For many engineering industries there are substantial economies for spreading initial costs of developing new products, through learning and the use of more efficient techniques for longer runs and higher rates of output. For the products of the textile and clothing industries, the scope for technical economies of scale are generally limited, but there are some economies for long runs in these industries, attributable to reducing the proportion of time used for setting up machines and to learning. Also there are important economies in all industries for organising and controlling long sustained production of a narrow range of products, though these are difficult to measure.

Table 30.1. summarizes the main estimates which we prepared of the minimum efficient scale of production (m.e.s.) and of the economies of scale below these levels of output. The cost data to which these estimates relate exclude the costs of marketing and distribution. The definition of

(1) C.F. Pratten, 'The Merger Boom in Manufacturing Industry' Lloyd's Bank Review, October 1968.

Table 30.1 Summary of the Estimates of the Minimum Efficient Scale (M.E.S.) and the Economies of Scale[1]

Industry and Type of Plant etc.	Type of Industry[3]	Vintage of Plant	M.E.S. in absolute terms[4]	M.E.S. as percentage of U.K. output in 1969.	M.E.S. as percentage of regional market for which transport costs are important, and sub-markets for trades making a range of products[2]	Percentage increase in costs at 50 per cent of M.E.S. compared with the M.E.S. level.	
						Total costs per unit	Value added per unit.
1. Oil A general purpose refinery	P	New	A capacity of 10 m.t.p.a.	10%	40% of a regional market equivalent to 25% of the U.K. market	5	27
2. Chemicals Size of ethylene plants	P	New	A capacity to produce 300,000 t.p.a. of ethylene	25%	100% of a regional market equivalent to 25% of the U.K. market	9	30
Sulphuric acid plants		New	1 m.t.p.a.	30%	100% of a regional market equivalent to 25% of the U.K. market	1	19
Dyes: a new dye made in a new plant		New	The output of dyes varies but the M.E.S. generally exceeds the U.K. output of individual dyes. (The estimates of economies of scale are for dyes produced in large quantities).	100%		22	44
Chemical Works			The M.E.S. is small in relation to U.K. output of all chemicals because of the scope for specialization.				

269

Table 30.1 *Summary of the Estimates of the Minimum Efficient Scale (M.E.S.) and the Economies of Scale (cont)*

Industry and Type of Plant etc.	Type of Industry	Vintage of Plant	M.E.S. in absolute terms	M.E.S. as percentage of U.K. output in 1969	M.E.S. as percentage of regional market for trades for which transport costs are important, and sub-markets for trades making a range of products	Percentage increase in costs at 50 per cent of M.E.S. level compared with the M.E.S. level	
						Total costs per unit.	Value added per unit.
3. Synthetic Fibres Plant for the manufacture of polymer	P	New	80,000 t.p.a. of polymer	33% of U.K. output of synthetic fibres	66% of U.K. output of nylon	5	23
Plant for the extrusion of of filament yarn	T	New	40,000 t.p.a. of yarn	16% of U.K. output of synthetic fibres	33% of U.K. output of nylon	7	11
4. Beer A brewery	P	New	At least 1m barrels p.a.	3%	6% of a market equivalent to 50% of the U.K. market	9	55
5. Bread A plant bakery	P	New	A throughput of 30 sacks of flour per hour.	1%	33% of a market for a city with a population of 1m.	15	30
6. Soap & Detergents A plant to make detergent powders	P	New	70,000 t.p.a.	20% of U.K. output of synthetic detergent powders		2.5	20
7. Cement A portland cement works	P	New	2 m.t.p.a.	10%	40% of a regional market equivalent to 25% of the U.K. market	9	17
8. Bricks Size of works making non-Fletton bricks	P	New	> 25m. bricks p.a.	0.5%	5% of regional market equivalent to 10% of the U.K. market	25	30

		M.E.S.	% of U.K. output		5–10	12–17
9. Steel P						
Production of steel via blast & L.D. furnaces	New	9 m.t.p.a.	33%			
Steelworks making a range of rolled products including wide strip	New	4 m.t.p.a.	80%		8	13
Steelworks making rods & bars from billets	New	<0.5 m.t.p.a.	<10%			
Types of special steel	New	The output of types of special steel varies, but for many types the M.E.S. exceeds U.K. output				
Steelworks	New	The M.E.S. is small in relation to U.K. output because of the scope for specialisation, and the production of steel from scrap.				
10. Iron Castings Products O						
	New	No estimate, but economies continue up to the level of U.K. output of many castings				
Foundry making cylinder blocks	New	50,000 t.p.a.	1% of U.K. output of all castings	30% of U.K. output of cylinder blocks for cars	10%	15%
Foundry making small engineering castings	New	10,000 t.p.a.	0.2% of U.K. output of all castings		5%	10%
11. Motor Cars E						
A firm making one model and its variants	Plant built up over a period of time	500,000 cars per year	25% of the U.K. output of cars.	50% of U.K. output of cars of about 1,200 c.c.'s.	6%	10%

Table 30.1 Summary of the Estimates of the Minimum Efficient Scale (M.E.S.) and the Economies of Scale (cont)

Industry and Type of Plant etc.	Type of Industry	Vintage of Plant	M.E.S. in absolute terms	M.E.S. as percentage of U.K. output in 1969	M.E.S. as percentage of regional market for trades for which transport costs are important, and sub-markets for trades making a range of products	Percentage increase in costs at 50 per cent of M.E.S. level compared with the M.E.S. level	
						Total costs per unit	Value added per unit
A range of of models made by a firm			1m. cars per year	50% of the U.K. output of cars		6%	13%
Size of Works				No estimate because of the scope for separating the production of components.			
12. Aircraft A type of aircraft	E	As for motor cars	> 50 aircraft	There have been wide variations in the output of U.K. aircraft, but 50 aircraft of one type are more than internal U.K. demand for large aircraft.		> 20%	>25%
Firm producing advanced passenger aircraft			No estimate made, but the M.E.S. would be large in relation to the capacity of the U.K. airframe industry.				
Works			No estimate was made because of the scope for separating the production of parts and components.				

No.	Item							
13.	**Bicycles** A firm making a range of models	E	As for motor cars	< 100,000 bicycles a year	4% of U.K. output			A small increase
14.	**Machine Tools** Models	E	As for motor cars	The output of motor cars models varies but the M.E.S. generally exceeds the output of similar models in the U.K.	> 100% of U.K. output of similar models		5%	10%
	Factories which manufacture tools		300 employees		0.5% of employment in U.K. machine tool industry		Depends on the range of models manufactured at a factory	
15.	**Diesel Engines** Models of diesels in the range 1–100 h.p.	E	New	100,000 units p.a.	10% of U.K. output of all diesels in the range 1–100 h.p.	100% or more of U.K. output of most sizes of diesels in the range 1–100h.p.	4%	10%
	Factories at which large marine diesels are made		As for motor cars	An annual output of at least 100 000 h.p.	10% of U.K. output	At U.K. factories output is divided between different sizes of diesels and the production of a range of products increases costs	8%	15%
16.	**Design of Chemical Plants** A type of plant made by a firm	E	Not applicable	> 2 plants a year	100% of U.K. output for many types of plant		5%	10%
	Firms		The M.E.S. is small because of the scope for specialization		A small percentage			
17. (A)	**Turbo Generators** Designs	E	As for motor cars	An output of 4 a year	100% of the current output of designs for the C.E.G.B.		≃ 5%	≃10%

Table 30.1 Summary of the Estimates of the Minimum Efficient Scale (M.E.S.) and the Economies of Scale (cont)

Industry and Type of Plant etc.	Type of Industry	Vintage of Plant	M.E.S. in absolute terms	M.E.S. as percentage of U.K. output in 1969	M.E.S. as percentage of regional market for trades for which transport costs are important, and sub-markets for trades making a range of products	Percentage increase in costs at 50 per cent of M.E.S. level compared with the M.E.S. level	
						Total costs per unit.	Value added per unit.
A firm making a range of turbo generators		As for motor cars	An output of at least 6,000 M.W. p.a.	50% of U.K. output			50%
(B) Electric Motors (1–100 h.p.) A range of models made by a firm		As for motor cars	Output of £10m. (1969 prices)	60% of U.K. output		15%	20%
18. Domestic Electrical Appliances A firm making a range of 10 appliances	E	As for motor cars	At least 0.5m. appliances a year	20% of U.K. output of all appliances	50% of U.K. output of refrigerators or washing machines	8%	12%
19. Electronic Capital Goods A product	E	As for motor cars	1,000 units	100% of U.K. output of the product		8%	13%

(This product is representative of computer and radar equipment, but the industry makes a wide range products some of which are relatively unsophisticated and for which the economies of scale are smaller.)

| A firm which manufacturers a range of E.D.P. equipment | | As for motor cars | An output of at least £200m. a year | 100% of U.K. output | | 10% | 16% |

20. Cotton Textiles	T	The vintage of plants is not important for the conclusions about the m.e.s. summarised in this table	Economies of scale continue to large outputs of individual products i.e. there are significant economies for long runs		
Products					
Spinning mills making standard products			<60,000 spindles	<2% of U.K. spinning capacity The M.E.S. forms a much higher proportion of the output of each group of products on which mills specialize.	Small increases in costs only
Weaving mills making standard products			<1,000 looms	<2% of U.K. weaving capacity	
21. Knitting	T	As for cotton textiles	Similar to the position for cotton textiles		
Products					
Warp knitting mills making standard products			A mill with less than 100 knitting machines	<3% of warp knitting machines installed in the U.K. The M.E.S. forms a much higher proportion of the output of each group of products on which mills specialize.	Small increases in costs only
22. Footwear	T	As for cotton textiles	Economies extend to production runs of 20,000 pairs of a distinct style, but the M.E.S. is smaller than this.		
Products					
Factories			<300,000 pairs a year	0.2% of total U.K. output ≃2% oU.K. output The M.E.S. forms a much higher proportion of the output of each group of products on which factories specialize.	≃5%

Table 30.1 Summary of the Estimates of the Minimum Efficient Scale (M.E.S.) and the Economies of Scale (cont)

Industry and Type of Plant etc.	Type of Industry	Vintage of Plant	M.E.S. in absolute terms	M.E.S. as percentage of U.K. output in 1969.	M.E.S. as percentage of regional market for trades for which transport costs are important, and sub-markets for trades making a range of products	Percentage increase in costs at 50 per cent of M.E.S. level.	
						Total costs per unit.	Value added per unit.
23. Newspapers A Newspaper	O	As for cotton textiles	Even for classes of newspaper with the largest circulation i.e. popular Sunday Papers, the M.E.S. is equivalent to the output of the class of newspaper.	About 30% of all popular Daily or Sunday Newspapers	100% of any class of newspaper	> 20%	> 40%
The size of Firms			Generally small economies only for firms which produce a number of newspapers, but there are important exceptions.				
24. Books A book title – hardback	O	As for cotton textiles	10,000 copies	100% or more of the output of most hardback titles		36%	50%
Book printing firms			Output equivalent to a small percentage of U.K. capacity	About 2% of U.K. output		Small increase in costs only	
25. Plastic Products Individual products	O	As for cotton textiles	Substantial economies continue to large outputs of many products.	100% of U.K. output for many products		Substantial economies.	

Firms making a range of products	Capacity equivalent to small percentage of the industry's capacity.	< 1%	Small increase in costs only.

(1) Many qualifications relate to our estimates of economies of scale, but these qualifications are not repeated here, in order to save space and avoid duplication with the chapters describing the industry studies. For the purpose of making the estimates of economies of scale given in this table, it is assumed that the extent of vertical integration is not affected by scale.

(2) For industries for which transport costs are a substantial proportion of the delivered price, we have related the m.e.s. to a regional market. The size of regional markets varies because of variations in transport costs as a percentage of total costs, and because, in the case of bread, the commodity is perishable and for this reason is best made near to the market. The sizes of regional markets have been selected to indicate the size of the largest U.K. regional markets as determined by transport costs.

(3) The 'types of industry' were defined in chapter 29.

(4) m.t.p.a. is an abbreviation for million tons per annum.

the m.e.s. given in Book 1 was: 'Within the range of scale for which we have estimates, the m.e.s. is the minimum scale above which *any* possible subsequent doubling in scale would reduce *total* average unit costs by less than 5%, and above which any possible subsequent doubling in scale would reduce average value added per unit (total cost less the cost of bought out materials, components and services) by less than 10%.'

For some industries where the m.e.s. represents a small proportion of the output of the industry, we have not adhered to this definition, partly because our estimates of economies of scale for these industries do not enable us to specify the m.e.s. accurately.

The vintage of plants

The estimates in table 30.1 can be divided into three sections. The first ten industries for which most of the estimates of technical economies of scale which we obtained related to *new* plants, the engineering industries for which the estimates generally relate to plants built up over a period of time, and the textile and other trades for which our estimates were based on new and existing plants, but for which the vintage of plant is not generally very important for determining the m.e.s.

Firms in all trades operate plants which are built up over a period of time. But in the long run firms, if their output is sufficient, may be able to take full advantage of the economies of scale for new plants by replacing and rebuilding plants. Although this may only occur in the *very* long run in some industries, the experience of the cement and steel industries illustrates the relevance of the economies of scale for large plants. A.P.C.M. and the British Steel Corporation are building or planning very large works to replace many smaller ones.

For the engineering industries the estimates relate to plants built up over a period of time, but they are based on costs for firms which have expanded their capacity and followed an active replacement policy, i.e. when weighting different components of costs — materials, wages and salaries and capital charges, the breakdown of costs for these firms has been used. However even firms which expand and replace existing plant tend to retain those parts of plant e.g. press shop plant in the case of motor vehicles, which are most capital intensive and for which the economies of scale tend to be largest. Thus economies of scale for existing plants tend to be smaller than for new plants. But the economies of scale for initial, material and component costs, which are not greatly affected by the vintage of plants are more important in the engineering trades than in the process trades.

A reason for treating the engineering industries differently from the process industries is that it is usually possible to replace machine tools in an engineering shop and build up capacity to make products; in the process trades substantial increases in capacity to make ethylene, steel, etc. are usually achieved by building new plants. For the engineering industries, such as cars, machine tools, and small diesels, in which firms have built new factories in recent years, we obtained data for these plants, but U.K.

278

firms which build electricity generating plant, slow speed marine diesels, bicycles, aircraft and domestic appliances have not built and equipped new factories since 1960.

For the textile trades, printing, and fabricating plastic products, the vintage of plant is not generally important for conclusions about the economies of scale. In the textile trades the capacity of most items of new machinery for spinning, weaving and knitting is small, and for printing the spreading of first copy costs is the dominant source of economies of scale.

If for the process or other industries we had attempted to estimate the minimum economic scale for *existing* plants of any vintage, the estimates would have been much lower than for new plants,[1] and would have depended on the vintage of the smaller plants. In industries where the small plants are of a recent vintage, it may be economic to continue to use them, but costs for new large plants may be lower than for old small plants in spite of their low (historic) capital costs.

Economies of scale for narrow ranges of products

The data in table 30.1 show that for many individual products and ranges of products the m.e.s. forms a substantial proportion of U.K. output. For industries for which exports exceed imports, and this applies to the engineering trades particularly, the m.e.s. forms a higher proportion of the U.K. market, than of U.K. output, as shown in the table. (For some industries the proportion of the U.K. market could be as much as double the proportion of U.K. output.) For the products of process industries for which transport costs are significant, the m.e.s. often represents a very large proportion, or multiple, of regional markets — the appropriate basis for comparison when considering the significance of the m.e.s. for competition in these trades. For many products the increase in costs at half the m.e.s. is also noteworthy, especially in relation to the value added to products of the process, engineering and 'other' industries included in our sample, and in many industries the increase in costs becomes progressively larger with each successive halving of scale. (We have not shown the increase in costs at less than 50% of the m.e.s. in table 30.1., but they are given in many of the industry studies.)

In addition to the economies shown in table 30.1. a firm producing a narrow range of products in relatively large quantities, compared to a firm with a diversified output, can achieve a higher level of technical efficiency, because it can concentrate the efforts of management. This source of economies for a large output of a limited range of products is difficult to measure, but is very important.

Although there are large economies of scale for the production of many products, the relationships are not uniform. For the brick, bicycle, textile and clothing industries, the economies for large scale production are limited. It is possible to list the main forces determining cost/scale

(1) The answer would probably be the minimum size of plant in existence. (If they were not economic they would have been closed.)

relationships and which account for the differences between trades.

(a) the type of process which is used: in general process operations allow the greatest technical economies of scale and textile operations much smaller economies.

(b) the magnitude of first copy or initial costs (where these costs are substantial, the m.e.s. tends to represent a large proportion of the output of a trade).

Economies of scale for plants

When we move from the output of individual products or specific ranges of products to the relationship between the m.e.s. and the output of multi-product industries, the position is more complex. In most, if not all, industries there is scope for specialization by producing products for which the market is small (shoes with special fittings, lorries with unusual dimensions, etc) and for which there are few, if any, economies for production with other products. Thus the m.e.s. for plants and firms is usually very small, both absolutely and in relation to the output of an industry. Nevertheless in many industries there are considerable economies of scale for plants and firms where changes in these dimensions of scale reflect increases in the scale of production of products.

As between trades the following points are noteworthy. In the textile and clothing industries the m.e.s. for mills and factories is small in relation to the output of these industries. For the production of castings, plastic mouldings, and books, which some firms produce on a 'jobbing' basis, the m.e.s. of plants is again small in relation to the output of each of these industries. (Many firms in these trades compete for temporary monopolies for the production of products). Similarly in industries which manufacture a wide range of products which have to be made in batches or in separate plants, e.g. machine tools, some chemicals and electronic capital equipment, the m.e.s. for a plant or factory is small in relation to the size of the industry, but this in part reflects the definition of industries (the diversity of products included within a single trade). However, in a number of multi-product industries a firm has to have a large share of the output of the industry to achieve the main economies of scale for the manufacture of certain products e.g. popular cars, advanced jet aircraft, computers, new synthetic fibres.

Economies of scale for multi-plant firms

No attempt has been made in the table to quantify the economies of multi-plant operation. Where firms operate a number of similar plants at different sites, as in the cement and brewing industries, the main advantages of multi-plant firms for achieving *technical economies* are that they are better able to organise and finance the construction of large plants and larger capacity production lines. It is important to note that, if firms are to build plants which take full advantage of the economies of scale, then in the

280

process type trades they probably require an output of at least three times that of the plant to finance its construction and incur the risks associated with building a new plant. The output of a firm does not have to be in the same trade, or in the U.K., to provide the advantages of scale for risk taking and raising finance, but, if a firm's output of the products to be made at a new plant is large, this facilitates full utilization of a new plant because the firm can transfer demand from other plants. (Although absence of a secure market for a new plant may spur a firm to expand its market by, for example, exporting, it may simply not build the plant). In the other groups of trades there is more scope for building up a plant over a period of time without sacrificing the economies of scale, and so a firm does not need such a multiple of the m.e.s. scale of output to take advantage of the economies of scale in the long run.

Another source of advantage for a multi-plant firm compared with a firm operating a single plant and serving a market of equal size is distribution costs. This source of economies has been discussed in the industry studies for process industries.

Vertical Integration

We have not assembled estimates of the effects of vertical integration, but these were discussed in some detail for textiles. An important source of advantage for vertical integration which we were told exists in many industries was increased control over the supply of materials, components etc., but it was not possible to quantify the effects of improved control.

A feature of a number of engineering and other industries is that the extent of vertical intergration is affected by scale. Firms with a relatively small output tend to buy out more components and processes. Usually the firms which supply the components and processes supply a number of firms, and so achieve economies of scale, which their customers would not achieve if they did not buy out. This is not a very important qualification to the estimates of economies of scale given in table 30.1. Differences in the proportion of the bought out content would not be very significant over the range of scale of from half the m.e.s. to the m.e.s., but, if estimates of economies of scale over the range from 10 per cent of the m.e.s. to the m.e.s. were given, the effects of varying the proportion of output bought out would have to be taken into account.

II. Growth and the technical economies of scale

Many of our estimates of economies of scale are based on comparisons of estimated costs for new plants, where adaptation to scale is possible. In practice many new plants are primarily built to meet increased demand. There is therefore a case for relating the m.e.s. for process plants — refineries, chemical plants etc. — to the average growth of demand over a period of, say, two years. Other things being equal, the greater the economies of scale for plants, the greater the incentive to anticipate demand by building larger units which will not be fully utilized until demand builds up. One way in which firms building plants in a country where demand is increasing relatively slowly can offset this, is by building large plants which are underutilized for a time, but firms in countries where demand is increasing more rapidly can adopt the same practice with even larger plants.

If the m.e.s. for process plants are related to the growth of demand over periods of two, or four years, they form a much higher percentage or multiple of the growth of demand than of output. The position is similar for production lines to produce engineering products such as cars and diesel engines.

III. Labour productivity and scale

A feature of our estimates of the technical economies of scale is the relationship between labour costs and scale. Economies of scale for labour costs were found to be much greater than for total unit costs of production for the following reasons.

1. In most industries materials and services bought out form the largest component of costs, and economies for these costs are generally small compared to those for other costs including labour.

2. In the process industries we have shown that the labour required to man plants increases very slowly as the scale of plants is increased.

3. In the engineering industries it is possible to substitute different techniques as scale is increased and reduce the labour input. The total initial capital costs for the plant required for the optimum techniques increases with scale, but labour (and often capital) costs *per unit* of capacity, are lower.

4. In all industries increases in the length of production runs result in lower labour costs, because of a reduction in 'set up' times. Also the cost of overhead labour for organizing and supervising production is reduced.

5. An important source of economies in many industries is the spreading of initial costs for designing and planning the introduction of new products and for new tools and jigs. A high proportion of these costs are labour costs.

A possible offsetting source of increased labour *costs* for larger scale production is that higher wages may have to be paid even where the skill required of employees is not increased by a change of scale. However this does not reduce the effect of scale economies on labour *productivity*.

IV. A note on learning effects

We have not summarised estimates according to the source of economies of scale, but we summarise here our conclusions about learning effects, as there has been much discussion of these effects in the literature.

When firms start producing new products, such as aircraft, machine tools, turbo generators, marine diesels, etc., there are learning effects which enable the firms to reduce the time required and the cost of making successive units. For complex aircraft the estimates given in chapter 15 show that this learning process continues for the production of many units, but for most products these effects diminish relatively quickly - for example, after producing four or five turbo-generators, firms find that any further learning effects are small. In the case of mass produced products such as cars and television sets, firms spend more heavily on production planning to avoid learning by experience — for example, the motor manufacturers ensure as far as possible that components will fit, before starting production. (Although these firms aim to reduce the learning period by production planning they are not always successful.) The reason why aircraft manufacturers, machine tool manufacturers etc., do not reduce the learning period for new products is that the costs of cutting the learning period would, on balance, increase costs.

It is well known that when new machinery is introduced the performance obtained from the machinery improves with experience — we described this effect for chemical plants and it applies in many industries. There are also learning effects related to the level of investment which are a function of size and the rate of growth of capacity because:

(i) the manufacturers of machinery enjoy learning effects for each generation of plant and may introudce new generations of plant more rapidly.

(ii) the firms installing new plant and machinery learn by experience which are the best type of plant to install, and the costs of finding out about new plant can be spread over the total new plant installed.

We have not directly illustrated or discussed these learning effects. But it is noteworthy that international trade in machinery, the existence of engineering consultants who operate on an international basis, and international companies, result in some transmission of these learning effects between countries — between advanced and other countries, and between countries whose economies are expanding rapidly and others.

In addition to the types of learning listed above, progress, apart from technical progress attributable to expenditure on R. & D., may relate to cumulative experience. Some effects of this type, if they exist, may relate to cumulative output rather than time, i.e., firms with a larger output of a range of products may achieve more learning effects of this sort. However, the continued existence of firms with very different levels of output in some trades, and the high levels of productivity achieved in industries in some countries which in terms of cumulative output have a relatively small output, suggest that such learning effects may not be very important. In any event, we have not obtained any measures of these effects.

31. Marketing[1]

I. Introduction

Economies of scale for marketing were discussed at some length for the soap and detergents and motor industries, but were dealt with briefly in the other industry studies. We found difficulty in analysing marketing within the context of economies of scale — reductions in costs attributable to differences in scale where complete adaptation to each scale of operation has occurred — for a number of reasons which we now summarise.

1. In practice a part, and sometimes a substantial part, of a firm's marketing expenditure is aimed at expanding the firm's sales, rather than maintaining its existing volume of sales.

2. Many firms spend large amounts on marketing new products, and in most trades firms have to introduce new products from time to time in order to maintain sales, let alone increase them. (If this were the only problem, initial marketing costs could be treated in the same way as other initial costs — spread over production of the products to which they relate).

3. Marketing costs actually incurred by firms are not closely related to scale or changes in scale because:

(a) There are a number of channels of distribution — direct sales by manufacturers to independent retailers, sales to multiple stores or mail-order houses, sales to wholesalers or through agents, and marketing costs vary for different channels.[2]

(b) Firms may adopt different strategies e.g. concentrate on promoting their products by advertising rather than low prices, or vice versa, or rely on the quality or distinctiveness of their product.

(c) The effects of expenditure on marketing are often difficult to determine at all accurately, and so the allocation of finance to marketing by

(1) We include the costs of advertising, sales promotion, and sales representation in marketing costs.

(2) For goods sold to mail order or multiple stores groups, such as Marks and Spencer, selling costs may be negligible, and it may not be necessary to advertise the product. However firms may obtain lower net prices for sales to multiple groups and mail order houses than for sales to independent stores. Multiple groups (firms with more than 10 branches) accounted for more than 35% of all retail trade in 1966, and the proportion was much greater in some trades. (Census of Distribution 1966. Report on the Census in the Board of Trade Journal, 23rd Feb. 1968). In addition buyers' cooperatives have been formed to supply some 'independent' stores, and selling to some of these cooperatives is similar to selling to multiples.

284

firms is to some extent arbitrary.

(d) The optimum expenditure by a firm on marketing may depend on the expenditure of other firms. For example if one firm in a trade spends heavily on marketing, others may have to do the same in order to maintain a large share of the market because retailers[1] or consumers respond to advertising. But it may be in the interests of a firm which faces competition from a firm or firms which spend heavily on advertising, to spend very little on this type of promotion, and concentrate on cutting its price, or providing a good service to customers. (Similarly if one firm in a trade sells direct to retailers or users, a competitor or a new entrant may have an inducement to sell exclusively through wholesalers or agents, if an alternative channel of distribution of this type exists.)

(e) There are imperfections in markets which affect marketing costs. For example some manufacturers own or control retail outlets, or enjoy the goodwill of customers which gives them tied markets and reduces selling costs; such goodwill may reflect the support of small firms for other small firms, partly because this is the only way they expect to obtain adequate priority. Also the quality of the goods and the services provided by a company in the past and its advertising, affect its current reputation and goodwill.

The classification of industries

The classification of trades which we used for summarising technical economies is not appropriate for marketing costs. A possible distinction for marketing is between consumer goods and intermediate and capital goods. In general marketing costs are more important for consumer goods, because final consummers are more likely to be influenced by advertising than commercial customers, and there are more final customers to influence. However there are exceptions to this general rule. For example the manufacturers of some intermediate products, including synthetic fibres, promote their products to final consumers. Also the marketing function may be very important to the success of a firm in spite of marketing costs forming a small percentage of total costs.

II. Advertising

Although, there are problems in measuring the economies of scale for marketing costs, these are important particularly in many consumer trades. We deal first with advertising.

The 1963 Census of Production showed total expenditure on advertising by manufacturing firms as £325m — 3 per cent of net output,[2] and 1.2 per

---

(1) The reaction of retailers is important because for many products, retailers only handle a limited range of brands. In these circumstances the decisions of retailers can be decisive in determining the choice available to consumers.

(2) Net output is the value added to materials by the process of production. Net output is obtained by deducting from the gross output the cost of purchases adjusted for stock changes, payments for work given out to other firms, and payments to other organisations for transport. The census figure for expenditure on advertising excludes the cost of the employees of firms engaged on advertising. This is probably a small part of total expenditure on advertising.

cent of sales. But there are wide variations between industries, and for the soap and detergents industry advertising expenditure represented as much as 35 per cent of net output. The only other trades included in the industry studies for which advertising expenditure as a percentage of net output was more than 2.5 per cent were: domestic appliances 10.3, oil refining 8.1, beer 4.2, bread (including biscuits) 2.9, and synthetic fibres 2.8. The proportion also varies for firms within each trade. Information to illustrate the extent of this variation is not available, but data collected for the 1963 Census suggest that the larger firms in each industry generally account for a disproportionately large share of expenditure on advertising.

Firms whose brands have a large share of their market, or who can spread their advertising over a large total output of different brands, have important advantages. If firms which have different shares of the market spend in proportion to their market shares, the advertising of a firm with a large share may be proportionately more effective in influencing retailers and/or consumers. A loose relationship of this type may exist for a number of reasons. For example retailers may stock, say, two or three brands, and select brands according to expected future advertising, among other factors. Limited advertising of a brand with a small share of the market may have no effect on retailers' selection, if two or three firms spend much greater amounts. Also repeated advertisements may be proportionately more effective for influencing consumers than comparatively isolated advertisements.[1]

In practice many of the smaller firms and some large firms in manufacturing industry spend very little on advertising, and have lower advertising costs per unit of output. Their lower advertising costs may be offset by higher costs of representation partly because they do not advertise. Also they may lose their share of a market because they do not advertise. One reason why they may lose their share of markets is that the leading firms introduce new products and *quickly* build up large markets for these products by advertising. It is then difficult or impossible for other firms to win back a share of the market without advertising. But it is not inevitable for firms which do not advertise to lose their share of markets. (See Chapter 9). Some retailers advertise the products of certain manufacturers, and advertising may not convince all customers that there are real or imagined differences between advertised and other competing products. In all the industries in our sample, except synthetic fibres for which advertising costs represented more than 2.5% of sales, there were firms in each trade which sold products without advertising.

It is possible to consider expenditure on advertising in a different way. If firms with a large share of markets have to advertise to maintain their share of markets against firms which do not advertise, then advertising is

---

(1) Instead of spending less on advertising, firms with a small share of the market may compete by advertising and spend as much as their competitors with a larger share of the market, but if they adopt this strategy, they will have higher advertising costs per unit of output.

a source of diseconomies of scale. Some advertising can be regarded as the cost of persuading customers to start buying and, for many products, to repeatedly buy a standardised product — thus permitting the achievement of economies of scale. However, in trades such as soap and detergents where firms advertise heavily, although much of each firm's expenditure on advertising is intended to maintain its share, the main threat to its share is from other firms which manufacture on a large scale and which advertise. In practice it is not possible to separate expenditure on advertising which is designed to win a larger share of a market, to protect a firm's share of a market against other firms which advertise, or to prevent other firms entering the market or firms which do not advertise from winning a larger share of the market.

It is worth noting that, as for technical economies of scale, economies and diseconomies for advertising primarily relate to products, rather than the production of a range of products: firms usually advertise brands, often without indicating the name of the manufacturer. But the practice of advertisers varies and some of the effects of advertising may 'rub off' onto products sold by a firm which advertises, even if it does not use a common name or theme when advertising.[1]

III. Other marketing costs

There are economies of scale for other marketing costs besides advertising. Some important examples are listed.

(a) Sales representation can be spread over sales of a brand with a large share of a market or a range of products. (The costs of sales representation for the smaller manufacturing firms which sell to independent retailers often represent several percent of sales.)

(b) There are economies associated with selling in bulk to individual customers[2] and for large volume of sales to an area.

(c) Where one firm operates in more markets than other firms, either within one country or internationally, it can spread some marketing costs such as acquiring marketing knowhow and experience.

---

(1) A firm which advertises a number of products can pool its expenditure for purposes of obtaining discounts on prices for advertising space, and this is another source of economies.

(2) The following illustrative calculations for a manufacturer of grocery products indicate the economies, including the economies for delivery costs, which can be achieved by selling in bulk.

Value of Consignment	£10	£40	£100	£400
Selling Costs per £1 of Sales (p.)				
Sales and invoicing costs	6.7	2.2	1.1	0.5
Transport costs	2.0	1.5	1.2	0.6
Depot costs	2.5	2.0	1.8	0.6
Supervision	0.7	0.2	0.1	0.0
Total	11.9	5.9	4.2	1.8

(d) There are economies for providing servicing facilities (see the industry studies for motor vehicles and domestic electrical appliances). As for advertising it may be possible for firms simply not to provide these services, they may leave the maintenance of products to retailers.

(e) A firm whose brand has a large share of a market may be able to adopt a multiple marketing approach. It may be able simultaneously to spend relatively large amounts on advertising and to cut its prices, or make special offers.

(f) A large firm can afford to spend heavily on marketing to rectify mistakes. For example if a large firm is late, compared to its competitors in developing a new type of product, it can spend heavily on marketing to win a share of the market once it has developed the product. Inevitably most firms make mistakes of this sort from time to time.

A source of advantage for certain firms, with a small share of the markets in which they operate, is that some retailers like to market distinctive products for which they charge higher prices. Although some manufacturers with a large share of their markets make distinctive products for such retailers, it is often left to separate firms to make products of this type. Also some industrial customers like to maintain alternative sources of supply, in case of a breakdown in supplies from a single source and to ensure that there is competitive pressure on prices. In order to maintain alternative sources of supply, industrial buyers are sometimes willing to pay higher prices to their subsidiary suppliers.

IV. Conclusion on economies of scale for marketing

Our conclusion is that there are economies of scale for marketing particularly in some consumer industries, and that there is no reason to suppose that the inclusion of marketing costs generally damps down the large technical economies of scale which we have shown to exist in many industries. However in many of the industries studied marketing costs were a small proportion of total costs,[1] and any economies of scale for marketing costs were not of great importance in these trades. Also there is a distinction between technical and marketing economies: because of market imperfections, the diversity of channels of distribution, and the possibility of concentrating sales in one area, some firms with a small share of markets can avoid scale disadvantages for marketing.

V. Market limitations on scale

An important feature of marketing in the context of economies of scale, is that marketing may limit the extent to which firms can take advantage of the economies of scale for production. Heavy advertising or other costs,

(1) Apart from advertising expenditure, selling costs, excluding delivery costs, are usually 5% or less of total costs. But, where goods are sold by an agent his commission is often at a higher rate than this.

or low prices, may be required to increase a firm's share of a market. For most of the industries we studied, competition between U.K. firms was very limited in terms of the number of firms producing directly competing products, and it was difficult for firms to rapidly increase their share of the home market. These market limitations to increasing scale apply to the capital goods industries as well as the consumer trades. Firms are reluctant to buy machine tools or aircraft from a new supplier, unless there are significant advantages: the new entrant starts with a handicap.

VI. Marketing advantages of scale

Apart from the economies of scale for marketing which have been described, there are important marketing advantages associated with scale. A large firm can carry losses incurred when it enters or builds up a market, and it can absorb losses on part of its operations while independent producers may be forced to close or merge with other firms. Such advantages certainly exist and are exercised, but they are not always used wisely. In the past certain large diversified companies have allowed some of their subsidiaries to operate while producing low returns on capital, and with no clear prospect of these returns increasing.

32. Risk Taking, Research, Innovation and Finance

I. Risk taking

A large firm has a greater ability to take risks, to try new products and models, and to absorb changes in the tastes of consumers or government policy, and the effects of mistaken decisions. These advantages are particularly important in rapidly evolving industries. But small firms also have advantages. For example, by price cutting they may be able to maintain their output during a recession, whereas a producer with a large share of a market is generally unable to offset the trend of market demand. Also the ability to take risks, and the willingness to do so, have to be distinguished. The management of some large companies probably do not search out risky, though possibly profitable ventures, because they are satisfied with the status quo.

An important distinction between the scale advantages for risk taking and the technical and marketing economies should be noted. The scale advantage for risk taking relates to the total output of a firm, rather than the output of particular products.

II. Research and development

Total current and capital expenditure on R & D by U.K. firms and public corporations within the manufacturing sector in 1967/8 was £564m., equivalent to 3.5% of the net output of the sector in 1968.[1] Expenditure on basic or fundamental research represented only 3% of all R and D expenditure, and applied research 'undertaken with either a general or a particular application in mind' accounted for a further 21%. The remaining 76% was for development expenditure directed to the introduction or improvement of specific products or applications, up to and including the prototype or pilot plant stage. We have included development expenditure in initial costs. There is no particular virtue in separating development costs from other initial costs, such as market research, the purchase of special jigs and tools for a model, planning the production of new models, and the costs of disruption caused by introducing a new model into production.[2] We have shown

(1) Data given in 'Statistics of Science and Technology', 1970. Department of Education and Science — Min. of Tech. H.M.S.O. 1970. Expenditure on R & D by Research Associations represented 0.1% of the net output of the manufacturing sector.

(2) It could be misleading to distinguish different initial costs because there is some trade off between them. For example large scale manufacturers tend to spend relatively more on development in order to minimize the costs of disruption when a product is first manufactured.

that the spreading of initial costs, including development costs, is a vitally important source of economies of scale in many industries, particularly chemicals, synthetic fibres, motor vehicles, aircraft, machine tools, turbo generators, electronic capital goods, newspapers, books and plastics, and that initial costs are a significant item of costs in a number of other industries.

This is a convenient point to draw attention to the importance of research and initial costs. Total R & D expenditure financed by U.K. manufacturing industry in 1967/8 was about £350m.,[1] and initial costs excluded from this figure — special jigs and tools, disruption costs, etc. — may amount to a further £300m. or more a year. Together research and initial costs represent more than 30% of the profits of manufacturing industry before charging these items of expenditure and before tax. This comparison is important because most research, development and initial expenditure is charged against current profits. Also successful development of new products is an important source of advantage in home and export markets, and it may be a source of profits for financing further developments — success may breed success.

When we look at expenditure on R & D alone, by trades, there are wide differences in expenditure in absolute terms, and relative to net output and sales. Of the industries included in the industry studies, R & D expenditure (including R & D financed by the Government) represented more than 2.5% of net output for the following trades in 1968.

	Per cent of net output
Aerospace	33
Electronics	17
Oil refining[2]	8
Diesel engines	6
Chemicals & allied trades (incl. soap & detergents)	5
Man-made fibres	5
Electric motors & generators	5
Motor vehicles	4
Machine tools	4

Expenditure on R & D as a percentage of output has substantially increased during the post-war period, and the range of industries for which R & D is important has also increased. For example, since 1950 R & D has become more important for the soap and detergents and textile industries because of the use of synthetic materials; in the machine tool industry, the introduction

(1) This figure excludes R & D financed by the Government.

(2) The oil companies concentrate a substantial proportion of their research in the U.K., and the net output figure to which R & D is related may be artificially low because of the methods used to value oil taken from associate companies. Oil companies allocate profits to the different stages of the production of oil products in the most appropriate way for tax purposes.

of electronics has made R & D much more important, and the toy industry is an example of an industry which has recently been affected by firms following a more aggressive policy of development.

Research & development expenditure and the size of firms

A number of studies[1] have shown that expenditure on R & D is positively related to the scale of firms, both for all firms and for firms within industries. Also the proportion of employees engaged on R & D, and R & D expenditure as a percentage of sales, tends to increase with scale for all firms and for firms within industries. But these relationships are very loose. The scope for spending on R & D varies in different trades, because of differences in the return on R & D expenditure and, for reasons described below, firms within trades can adopt different strategies.

It is best to start the description of the relationship between research and scale by stressing the advantages of a firm with a large output of a product or range of products to which research relates. Such a firm can and often does spend more heavily than its competitors on research, and spread the cost over a larger output, or it can spend the same amount and have lower research costs per unit of output. The advantages conferred by the former strategy depends on the type of research performed and the progress made, by higher expenditure on research. Where the research is aimed at improving methods of production, a firm with a relatively large output and/or rate of growth of output of a product or products made with a similar processes, clearly has an advantage for spreading R & D costs, but where the research is aimed at creating new uses for products or new products, a firm with a large output may need to create more new products etc., to maintain its share of markets. (A qualification to this argument is that a firm which already has a large share of a market may gain a similar share for new products and variants of existing products because of its marketing position). Each of these types of research accounts for of the order of 35% of expenditure on research.[2] For both types of research there may be economies of scale: for example, the costs of expensive research equipment can be spread over more applications by a firm which has a large research programme, and a number of research programmes may result in duplication of research.

Relationships between scale and R & D are complicated by the fact that firms can adopt different strategies. Some firms may rely on buying out research, or copy the results of other firms' expenditure on research.[3] Also the distinction between an aggressive policy on R & D aimed to give a firm

(1) The studies have been summarized by C. Freeman in an unpublished paper 'Size of Firm, R & D and Innovation'. (Mr. Freeman is Director of the Unit for the Study of Science Policy, University of Sussex, Brighton.)

(2) Federation of British Industries, 'Industrial Research in Manufacturing Industry 1959-60.' LONDON, 1961. Of the remainder of expenditure on research, 10% was estimated to be for basic research and 20% for technical and other services.

(3) The scope for buying out research results may diminish as international trade increases in response to reductions in tariffs, and as firms invest in production plants in many countries.

292

a lead with new developments and a defensive 'me too' R & D policy aimed to enable a firm to develop new products after these have been launched by other firms, has an important bearing on R & D expenditure. Expenditure required for a defensive strategy is often much less than for an aggressive one.

The practice in some trades for firms supplying raw materials and/or machinery, and for research associations, to carry out research for the trade, should also be mentioned, this reduces the need for firms, including the smaller firms, to carry out research. Among the industries we studied, the R & D work carried out by suppliers and research associations was particularly important for castings, textiles, footwear and plastics. Many firms in these trades carried out no research, but they were kept informed about developments.

Another feature of the scale/research relationships is that the advantage conferred on firms which carry out research varies with the success of the research, and the degree of success may vary through time. A small or medium size firm may 'get away' with spending very little on research for a time, but at some stage developments achieved by other companies may jeopardise its position.

Finally the scope for spreading research and some initial costs over production in a number of countries should be noted. This is an important source of economies of scale for international manufacturing companies in certain industries. Increasing scale by international expansion is particularly appropriate for achieving economies of scale for R & D, and for spreading the costs of acquiring know-how, if the expansion results in the production of the same or similar products in a number of countries.

III. Innovation

Innovation is not simply a function of expenditure on R & D. Firms may innovate in many ways; for example, by using different channels of distribution, advertising their products more heavily, wrapping them differently, etc.

The advantages of large firms for innovation are that they can spend more heavily on looking for new ideas. They can spread the risks of looking for innovations, and they have the finance to develop products such as synthetic fibres and aircraft for which development costs are very great. However, in most trades many individual innovations do not require heavy expenditure on R & D: it is the ideas which are important. Perhaps a higher proportion of the staff of smaller firms are looking for innovations and small firms may be more responsive to market changes and new ideas. In some cases, the smaller firms may have less to lose by making changes. For example, a firm which has a large share of a market and distributes to a wide range of retailers, may lose more custom than it gains by supplying branded products to discount stores. A firm with a smaller share of the market may be able to switch all its production through a new channel of distribution. Also, on average, large firms may be more reluctant to branch out into producing new lines. It is possible that it is difficult for large firms to initiate production of a new type of product on a small scale, and when demand has built up, entry may be difficult because the existing producers may have lower costs than the new entrant. Also it may be difficult to delegate the management of the production and marketing of new lines not closely related to the main products of a company.

A number of attemps have been made in the U.S.A. to measure the relationship between size of firms and innovation. The conclusions of these investigations are listed below, but little, if any, weight can be placed on the results because of the measures of inventiveness used, the limited coverage, and other qualifications described in the studies.

(1) Inventive output, as measured by the number of patents obtained, increases with the size of firms, but generally at less than a proportionate rate i.e. small firms obtain more patents in relation to their size than large firms. This might be taken as an indication that there are diseconomies of scale for research expenditures as large firms spend proportionately more on research than other firms. However the number of patents is *not* a reliable guide to the results of research.[1]

(2) When the number of important innovations was used as a measure of inventiveness, it was found that in one of the two manufacturing industries studied, the largest firms accounted for a disproportionately large share of inventions.[2][3]

(3) There is some evidence that the relative inventiveness of the smallest firms has declined since the inter war period.[2] This may result from the easier inventions having been made, and the increase in planned R & D by the larger firms.

In the long run innovation is vital to the success of most firms, but it is difficult to judge how changes in the structure of industries would affect innovation. We discussed the position for chemicals in Chapter 5. It may be that for innovation, it is best to have firms of varying size following different strategies in some industries. The large firm(s) can then develop

(1) F.M. Scherer. 'Firm Size, Market Structure, Opportunity and the Output of Patented Innovations'. Am. Econ. Rev 1965 pp. 1097—1125.

(2) E. Mansfield, 'Industrial Research and Development Expenditure'. Jnl. of Pol. Econ. Aug. 1964; and 'Industrial Research and Technological Innovation. An Econometric Analysis', London, 1969.

(3) An example of the problems encountered in studies of the type made by Mansfield is that the steel industry is treated as one industry. Although some important innovations for the production of crude steel have been made, innovations in the steel industry tend to be concentrated on special steels for which the largest companies have a relatively small share of the market. Also the period to which the data used for the study related, ended in 1958, and may not reflect the current position.

products requiring heavy R. & D. expenditure, while the existence of smaller firms may ensure that less expensive new developments are not missed or ignored, and that developments in other countries are followed. However the benefits of spreading R. & D. expenditure over a larger output in trades where R. & D. is important leads to a strong presumption in favour of concentration in these trades, but not necessarily in favour of concentration of the output of products to which separate R. & D. programmes relate, e.g., dyes and pharmaceuticals.

We shall argue in chapter 35 that a factor contributing to the relatively slow growth of the U.K. economy has been relatively slow innovation in certain industries, including parts of the chemical industry and machine tools. It is doubtful whether the structure of these trades in the U.K. was a major factor causing slow innovation. In the case of the U.S. economy there is more incentive to innovate to reduce labour costs because labour costs are higher. Also American firms can spread the costs of development over a larger output. In the case of W. Germany the reasons for higher expenditure on R. & D. and development in certain industries is more difficult to specify. The greater division of output between German chemical companies might contribute to the differences in the chemical industry (see Chapter 5). But German chemical and mechanical engineering companies have a tradition of development which is supported by their education system, and fewer R. & D. resources have been devoted to aircraft development and defence work.

IV. Finance

The ease with which a firm can raise finance, and the costs of finance are determined by a firm's status — whether it is a public or private company, etc. — its profitability and riskiness. Where large scale increases profitability, the acquisition of finance provides an example of the principle of 'to him that hath shall be given'. A profitable large firm has more profits to invest (retained profits are the largest source of new capital for companies), and its high profitability should enable it to attract funds. Large firms may be regarded as, and probably are, less risky investments, and, though investors can spread risks, we should expect the valuation of large companies to be somewhat higher, other things being equal, for this reason. Also the economies of scale for large issues through spreading costs of prospectuses etc., and the money markets, such as foreign money markets, open to large companies but probably not to smaller ones, deserve mention. It is also possible, and this would be important, that at times of financial stringency the imperfections of the money market bear more heavily on smaller firms.

It is worth noting that some subsidiaries of large companies which we visited claimed that the main advantage of their being part of a large group was that the head office could provide large amounts of finance. In general, large firms will only be able to produce proportionately more finance over the whole range of their operations if they are more profitable or can raise proportionately more new capital. They may of course provide large amounts of finance to some sections of their business.

V. Conclusion

With the possible important exception of innovation, we should expect large organisations to have advantages for risk taking, research, innovation and the acquisition of finance. These advantages augment technical and marketing economies of scale where these exist.

33. Management[1]

I. Introduction

In Chapter 2 we outlined some of the possible relationships between scale and the effectiveness and cost of management. We now expand this description, and summarize the results of the industry studies which provided a number of insights to the relationships between management and scale. First we discuss the general relationships.

1. The motivation of managers may change with scale. Managers of large corporations may be willing to sacrifice profitability for growth, or aim to satisfy a number of objectives such as growth, high profitability, good relations with staff and employees, and their own prestige and salaries, and the other aims may interfere with their determination to maximise profits. However, the managers of smaller firms may also have conflicting aims. For example, the selection of managers from within families may impede efficiency. The managers of smaller firms are often just as keen on growth at the expense of a high rate of profitability on capital, and, if their firms are not public companies, they may have greater freedom to exercise this preference. [2]

2. The quality of the information available for staff taking decisions may fall as the number of tiers of management increases with scale because the accuracy and amount of information may decline as it is passed to higher tiers of management. [3] This problem may be avoided by delegation, but the senior management of firms may be unwilling to delegate. On the other hand large firms have some advantages for obtaining information. They can employ specialist staff to collect information and spread this 'first copy' cost over their larger output, and among their employees there may be a wider range of expertise. The value of this advantage varies for different industries.

(1) There are two main functions of management, planning operations and innovations, and controlling the operation of a firm. The relative importance of these two functions varies a great deal for different firms, because circumstances differ.

(2) Public companies may have to aim for a high rate of profitability and pay substantial dividends to maintain their independence.

(3) A model of the control of firms based on the decline in the quality of information as it passes through the tiers of a management hierarchy has been described by O. E. Williamson, 'Hierarchical Control and the Optimum Firm Size', Jnl. of Pol. Econ., April 1967.

3. There may be a relationship between scale and the quality of managers. Large firms may, or may not, be able to recruit a higher proportion, in relation to their size, of the talent available, and smaller firms may, or may not, have an advantage in providing all round management experience and responsibility at an earlier age.

4. The scope for controlling managers may decline with scale because of the difficulties of assessing performance, particularly when increased scale involves an increase in the diversity of production. In practice the organisation of companies with a wide spread of interests — diversified companies — varies from a 'family of companies', with the head office providing little more than advice on policy to its subsidiaries, to organisations in which the head office controls the policy of its subsidiaries in detail. Many diversified companies operate a loose type of control. Large schemes of capital expenditure are vetted centrally and senior appointments are made by the head office, but provided an adequate profit record is maintained, the head office does not interfere in day to day management. This type of head office control through checking on profitability may well become weaker as diversity increases, and the ability of head office staff to pinpoint areas of weakness is reduced. Also control through profitability is negative in the sense that it will show up loss making areas, but will not show how these activities can be made profitable or bring to light new activities which would be very profitable. Current profits and losses reflect decisions taken several years previously in many industries, and so they may be an out of date guide to the quality of management. Nevertheless control by a head office may be more effective than control by independent shareholders which is the probable alternative.

5. The ability of operatives and staff to organise restrictive practices and resist attempts of management to achieve higher profitability may increase with the number of employees, because it is easier for agitators to organise a large number of employees, and because the 'family spirit' may be lost in a large firm.

One common feature of all the relationships between scale and management which we have listed is that, although there may be some tendency for there to be such relationships, we should not expect the relationships to be at all close. Also they may change as greater experience of operating large firms is acquired and techniques of management are improved.

II. The industry studies

We now turn to consider the evidence provided by the industry studies. Before discussing the evidence for types of industry, some features of the relationships between management and scale which are common to a number of industries are described. The first feature is the existence of 'step relationships'. We described an example of one of these relationships when dealing with the design of chemical plants. In effect firms have to change the structure of their management and the number of tiers of management at certain scales. There may be management diseconomies for a larger scale

298

of output when a firm reaches one of the steps, but economies of scale once it has reorganised its management and got above a step.

Another general feature of management is that many small firms, with less than, say, 200 employees, and some larger firms, operate with low overheads. They do not carry personnel, training, purchasing, market research, planning departments, etc., or have commissionaires, chauffeurs, board rooms, etc. For many small firms access to specialist departments would provide only limited benefits and not offset the costs. The managers of such firms can plan for the future, train staff on the job, etc. Whether there are net advantages to be obtained from access to specialist departments depends on the complexity of the products manufactured by a firm, the processes of production, and the strategy of a firm — whether it competes by operating on the frontier of technical expertise, etc.

A third feature of management costs is that many of the costs which are commonly included as management costs relate to the planning and design of new products and marketing. We have already dealt with the economies of scale for these functions.

Conclusions for groups of trades

(a) Process industries

In all the process industries which were studied the organisation of production was considered to be a source of economies for large plants, and this was not surprising. Increases in output are achieved by building larger units or the duplication of units, the number of operating staff rises slowly in relation to output, and the number of decisions to be taken is unlikely to rise very rapidly. Also the number of specialist staff such as brewers, chemists, etc. usually rises very slowly as scale increases.

There are sources of economies for the management of a number of plants at one site. The supervision of individual plants has to be delegated, but there are economies for providing specialist services such as quality control and laboratory testing and, if plants perform a vertical chain of processes, there are economies for dealing with the problems of co-ordination if the plants are on one site. For firms operating a number of similar process plants at a number of sites there are economies for managing production by providing some services centrally. But again economies from these sources are generally very small in relation to total costs, and the smaller firms may be able to buy out or copy the work of special service departments.

It is much more difficult to be sure about the effectiveness of *control*. For individual process plants it seems unlikely that increased scale per se would involve greater problems of control, but where the number of plants operated by a firm increases, whether at one complex or at a number of sites, the extent of delegation must increase, and the quality of control could decline. However, where the plants are similar, e.g. cement plants, control may be improved because performance can be compared.

299

(b) Engineering industries

(i) *The output of products.* In Book 2 the substantial technical economies for increasing the output of individual engineering products and narrow ranges of products were described. These can be achieved by increasing the rate of production or the period during which production continues. The problems of coordinating and organising production must increase with the rate of production as this will usually involve a greater division of operations and specialisation. But where the range of products does not increase with the rate of output, the cost of organising production should not increase as fast as output i.e. economies for organising production should be achieved.[1] Economies for organising production should also be achieved if the life of a product is extended, for example the original costs of planning production can can be spread over a larger output.

(ii) *Increasing the range of products.* The problems of managing production of a range of engineering products at one factory were discussed for the machine tool industry in Chapter 17. A factory at which narrow range of products is made has important advantages for the effectiveness of its management compared to a factory with the same output and a wider range. When a large firm or factory making a diverse range of products is compared to a smaller more specialised unit, it is not possible to generalise about the comparative effectiveness of management.

The problems of controlling employees are a greater potential source of diseconomies for large scale production in engineering industries because the ratio of employees to capital is higher, and economies for direct labour costs are smaller than for many process industries.

(c) Textile, clothing and 'other' industries

The problems of organising production in these industries are similar to those for engineering, but there is more duplication of machinery, and this simplifies the problems of organising and controlling production.

A general conclusion which emerged from the industry studies was that there are often sources of management economies for larger scale if this is achieved by changing the output of a constant range of products. (See particularly the industry studies for bricks, marine diesel engines and books.) Where increasing scale involves diversification, it is not possible to generalise about the the effects of increased scale on the costs or effectiveness of management.

III. The management of expansion

Finally the management of expansion — of moving to a larger scale of operation — is considered. It has been suggested that the management of expansion may place a limit on the rate of expansion and, thus in the short

---

(1) It is assumed that adaptation to each rate of output has been achieved i.e. that firms are accustomed to producing at their rate of output. There may be substantial costs involved in changing the rate of output.

run, on the size of firms.[1]

The very rapid rates of expansion achieved by some specialist firms suggests that where expansion of a narrow range of products is involved, very rapid rates of expansion can be achieved without major problems.[2] By definition many firms grow at a much slower rate than the high flyers, but the explanation for their slow growth is not the problems raised by management of expansion of their existing, or very similar lines. Usually market forces limit the increase in output of existing lines, or output is limited by a shortage of skilled personnel, or the capital cost of additional capacity would be much higher than the 'book' capital costs of existing capacity (see Chapter 34). One alternative is to take over firms making similar products, and very rapid rates of growth, over 20% per year, have been sustained by companies which have done this.

Another avenue for expansion is to increase the number of products made either by the development of new products or by take overs. Clearly, the introduction of new products without take overs involves problems of obtaining expert knowledge and this may require a change of structure. For example a firm which specialises in making injection moulded plastic products may expand by making plastic products by other processes, but, if so, it will have to acquire knowledge of these processes. Also if a firm expands by diversification, senior managers may have to delegate more decision taking. Existing personnel may find it very difficult to make such a tranition, and may not be well equipped to perform different functions.

Another difficulty for introducing new products *without take overs* is inventing, or finding, profitable lines. In the case of a firm expanding rapidly by introducing new products, it is essential that profitability is achieved quickly, otherwise the flow of new capital will be reduced. Initial technical and selling costs are substantial for some products and, unless these can be offset by high prices, it may be difficult to achieve accounting profits quickly. Also the effort required to find new products is likely to increase with the number required i.e. with the rate of growth.

---

(1) Robin Marris, 'The Economic Theory of Managerial Capitalism', New York 1964 (p. 114 et seq.) and Edith Penrose, 'The Theory of the Growth of the Firm', Oxford, 1959.

(2) The rates of expansion considered here are of the order of 20% per annum. At some rate of expansion the problems of transmitting experience and expertise must become increasingly difficult, and this rate may be lower for large companies than small ones. But this is not the factor which limits growth for most companies.

34. A View of the Conclusions

I. Introduction

In this chapter we summarise our conclusions about the economies of scale, differences in labour productivity for different vintages of plant, and the data describing the structure of industries in advanced manufacturing countries, which we collected. In the following chapter we discuss the implications of the conclusions.

II. The shape of scale curves

There has been a theme underlying some of the past work dealing with the economies of scale, that there is a general, or typical, shape for the long run average cost curve, or, as we have called it, the scale curve. Throughout this paper we have emphasised the diversity of the firms operating within industries, and the differences between industries. The effects of scale vary for each type of plant over different ranges of scale, for plants and firms in different industries, and for firms following different strategies within an industry. Nevertheless our estimates show that there are substantial technical economies of scale for the production of many products. Also, where two firms have different sales of a similar range of products, the firm with the larger sales can achieve economies by spreading certain marketing and management costs, and in some cases by spreading expenditure on research. Although there must be qualifications to any conclusions, we would emphasise the sources of economies of scale which generally apply to producing a constant range of products on a larger scale. For reasons we describe in Appendices C and D data obtained from company accounts and the Census of Production do not conflict with this conclusion.

Where differences in scale are attributable to differences in the range of products made, there are no simple rules such as 'the bigger the better.' In some cases there are substantial benefits, in others we should not expect significant scale of economies to emerge.

III. Changes in the economies of scale

A number of writers have implied that the economies of scale do not change over time.[1] Our studies suggest that the range of output to which they apply and the magnitude of the economies of scale are increasing. There are a number of forces contributing to larger economies of scale.

1. The rapid growth of output of manufactured products in many countries involves heavy investment and makes it economic to meet the first copy costs of developing new sizes of plant. The experience of building larger scale plants, acquired both in the U.K. and abroad, has increased the range of output to which economies apply in many industries.

2. Many new technical processes are increasing the economies of scale and increasing their range, and though some new techniques such as continuous casting, and numerically controlled machine tools, reduce the economies of scale, the impression obtained from the industry studies was that these are exceptional cases. Also many new techniques make it possible to substitute capital for labour, and this reduces the management limitations on efficient scale.

3. Improvements to the efficiency of products like turbo-generators, and increases in the size of such equipment as ethylene plants mean that the number of units of equipment or plant required to meet a given demand for the final product (electricity or ethylene) is reduced, and the capacity of factories and firms to produce the equipment is increased, where the capacity to produce equipment is measured in terms of the capacity of the equipment manufactured.

4. The substitution of synthetic for natural materials increases the economies of scale in some industries because of the greater uniformity of quality of synthetic materials and because they can be manipulated by different processes. Also there is less scope for small firms to succeed by 'playing the market' for their raw materials, because synthetics are usually cheaper, and their prices are relatively stable.

5. Transport facilities and communications are constantly being improved, reducing the relative importance of transport costs and the inconveniences of buying from, and relying on, more distant suppliers who operate on a relatively large scale.

6. The techniques, equipment, and personnel available for managing larger units are being improved by learning by experience and increased general and management education.

7. The relative importance of research and development has greatly

---

(1) O. E. Williamson, 'Economies as an Antitrust Defence: The Welfare Trade Offs', A. E. R., March, 1968, p 25 'although a merger may have positive effects immediately (cost savings exceed dead-weight loss), when allowance is made for the possibility of internal expansion these effects can become negative eventually (the cost savings persist, but these could be realised anyway and the dead-weight loss could be avoided by prohibiting the merger)'. No mention is made of the possibility of economies of scale and hence cost savings increasing through time.

increased in many industries. The life of new models of machine tools, etc., is shorter, and the latest models often involve much heavier costs at the development stage. The spreading of initial costs is an important source of economies of scale, and these costs are increasing.

These factors have increased the potential economies of scale in many industries. In addition, the fact that some firms have taken advantage of the economies of scale has put pressure on other firms. A clear example of such pressure has occurred in the newspaper industry. As the share of the market held by the most popular paper in each class has increased, the other papers have been under increasing pressure to keep their costs down while maintaining their falling share of the market, and many have been forced to close. A more general example is the effect of the increased scale of companies to cover operations in a number of countries. Such firms are able to relate their overall research and development expenditure, and their expenditure on products, to their total sales in the countries in which they operate, and this is a source of significant advantage in some manufacturing industries. [1]

Indications of the increases in the range of plant scale to which economies of scale apply were given for two of the industries we included in the interim report — oil refining and steel. In both these industries economies of scale now extend to higher scales of output (see Chs. 4 and 12).

A comparison of our estimates of the minimum efficient scale of production and the estimates of economies of scale made by Professor J.S. Bain [2] might be expected to illustrate the same trends, as his estimates were made before 1956. However, comparison of our results with Bain's is not straightforward because he included a different range of industries — comparisons can be made for six industries only — and we placed more emphasis on measuring the economies of scale for products. Numerical estimates of the effects of scale on value added were not shown in Bain's study, and our definition of the m.e.s. does not correspond to his definition of the minimum optimum scale — 'the most efficient size of plant'. (In many industries some economies of scale would be expected for plants larger than those we have defined as the m.e.s. [3]

For steel and cement, two of the six industries which are common to both studies, our study gives the m.e.s. as more than three times the scale given by Bain. For oil our figure is also higher than that given by Bain. For shoes, soap and detergents, and motor vehicles, comparisons are difficult because of differences in the dimensions of scale to which the estimates relate, but the figures are compatible. The comparisons therefore do not conflict with the view that the range of scale to which economies of scale apply has increased in many industries.

(1) W.B. Reddaway, 'Effects of U.K. Direct Investment Overseas. Final Report', Cambridge University Press, 1968 p. 317 et seq.

(2) J.S. Bain, 'Barriers to New Competition', Cambridge, Mass. 1956.

(3) For a definition of the m.e.s. see p. 26.

304

IV. New vintage of plant

In order to estimate the economies of scale as traditionally defined, it is unnecessary to estimate differences in efficiency for different vintages of plant, but these are an important source of economies for labour requirements for rapid growth where, as is usually the case, this involves the introduction of additional capacity which incorporates plant which is more efficient than earlier vintages of plant. In a number of studies including brewing, bricks, machine tools, diesel engines and textiles, we have noted the very large differences in labour productivity for new equipment compared to older plant. In some cases output per man for new plant is 100% or more above that for some plant in use. Put another way if the plant at present used in some factories was replaced with current vintages of plant to produce the same output, the labour force could be reduced by 50 per cent or more.

An important source of higher productivity for new vintages of plant is that they are physically larger, as in the case of many types of process plant, or have a larger capacity because they operate more rapidly, as with steel furnaces and some machine tools. It is often very difficult to distinguish accurately, the part of increases in productivity for new vintages of plant which are attributable to increases in scale and those which are attributable to other causes, partly because technical progress often takes the form of eliminating the obstacles to building larger plants.

The connection between the introduction of new techniques and investment, that much technical innovation cannot be introduced into practice without new plant, has been stressed in the literature. This also applies to taking advantage of many of the economies of scale. Firms have to build large process plants to take advantage of the economies for large plants, and engineering and textile firms usually need to obtain some new equipment to take full advantage of longer runs.

Given that large differences in labour productivity for new and old plants exist, an important question is whether large firms introduce new generations of equipment and replace old equipment more rapidly than smaller firms. The effects of the scale of firms on investment depend on many complex relationships, including the effects of scale on the ease with which firms can raise finance, on their profit record, on the motivation of managers, and on the relative cost of operating new and existing plants. But it is noteworthy that investment per employee is generally higher for large enterprises than for smaller enterprises (see Appendix C). However, Census data do not show whether larger firms tend to invest more heavily than smaller firms for the production of similar products, or whether this relationship continues indefinitely with increases in scale.

V. A note on Salter's model[1]

The relationships between labour productivity for plants of different vintages which we described in the previous section were a central theme of Salter's

(1) W. E. G. Salter, 'Productivity and Technical Change', Cambridge 1960.

description of the relationships between the growth of labour productivity and technical change. Salter's model stressed the importance of investment for bringing into use new techniques and new sizes of plants, and hence for achieving higher productivity.

Figure 34.1 'Economic' Costs for Plants (Costs per Unit of Output).

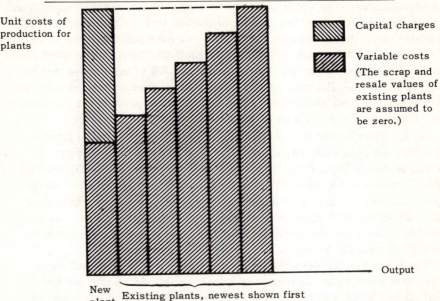

Salter's analysis was based on the 'economic' costs of production. Capital charges based on the original costs of new plants were included in the costs for these plants, but for existing plants capital charges were based on resale or scrap values. Salter could then assume that costs for existing plants (the variable costs plus a capital charge based on resale or scrap values) increased with the age of existing plants – while the newer vintages of existing plants had lower costs.

For many purposes, such as calculating costs for the purpose of setting prices and for preparing their annual accounts, firms make calculations of costs in terms of historical accounting costs. If the profiles of costs for plants of different vintage are compared on an 'historical' cost basis, the pattern is rather different to that for costs calculated on an 'economic' basis, (see diagrams 34.1 and 34.2).

The relationship between historical capital costs per unit of capacity, and the vintage of plants, depends on a number of conflicting forces. Technical progress and increases in scale are forces which tend to reduce capital charges for successive vintages of plant, but capital charges tend, on balance to be inversely related to the vintage of plants in many industries, for the following reasons.

(a) Price inflation increases the capital cost and charges for the latest plants to be built. (The inflation effect increases with the rate of inflation.)

306

Figure 34.2 'Accounting' Costs for Plants (Costs per Unit of Output).

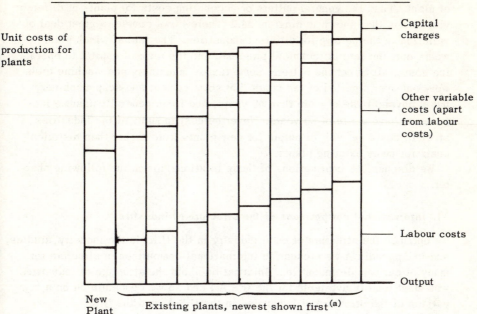

(a) It is assumed that all plants are of the same size.

Accountants sometimes make crude adjustments to allow for the effects of inflation, but this alone would not change the pattern.

(b) In some cases the depreciation charge is excessive during the early years of operation of a new plant i.e. firms simply take too pessimistic a view of the life of their new plants.

(c) The interest charges for the newest plants are relatively high because the accumulated depreciation to set against the initial capital cost is small during the early years in the life of an asset. When firms make a charge for interest they base it on the written down capital employed; they do not attempt to spread interest charges in proportion to the expected profits from the use of assets. In practice many firms do not include a charge for interest on capital in their costings, but the large amount of capital employed in new plants reduces the ratio of profits to capital.

(d) It takes some time to get new plant up to rated capacity, and so profitability is reduced during this period.

(e) New plants incorporate equipment required to meet controls aimed to minimize pollution, to ensure good working conditions, etc. These controls are not usually enforced as rigorously on existing plants. This is a significant factor in certain industries, such as the production of iron castings.

In a number of industries we studied, including chemicals, bread, soap and detergents, machine tools and diesel engines, capital costs for the latest vintages of plant are highest and they diminish as the vintage of plants increases, but variable costs have a reverse pattern because there are no forces offsetting the tendency for technical progress and increases in

307

scale to reduce operating costs per unit of output for successive vintages of plant. Thus the general pattern of accounting costs for plants of different vintages is that shown in diagram 34.2 There is, of course, a great deal of variation in the pattern for different industries. The rate at which plant wears out, the rate of technical progress, and the ratio of capital to operating costs, all affect the pattern: some textile machinery and machine tools wear out over a period of ten years, but some cement and soap machinery has a physical life of more than 40 years, and firms generally assume factories to have a life of 50 years. Nevertheless, in many of the industries studied, costs per unit of output for new plants were higher than historical costs for many existing plants.

We discuss the implications of these relationships in the following chapter.

VI. International comparisons of the structure of industries

We outlined the structure of each industry in the U.K. in the industry studies, and in Appendix A we present an international comparison of structure for many of our sample industries. Information about the structure of industries was most readily available for the U.S.A., and so we concentrated on a comparison of the structure of industries in the U.S.A. and the U.K.

In general the comparisons show that firms' outputs of products are greater in the U.S.A. than in the U.K., and that American plants and firms are larger than their U.K. equivalents. However these are very broad conclusions and the comparisons do not indicate uniform relationships between the structure of industries in the two countries.

The industry studies emphasised the importance of the output of individual products for spreading initial costs of research and development, design etc., and there are marketing and management costs which relate to products. Our comparisons of the output of products are tentative because comprehensive data describing the output of firms are not available, but the comparisons do suggest that many American firms have a much greater output of products than their U.K. equivalents. Estimates for industries for which initial costs are important and for which we have data are summarized in Table 34.1.

	Output		U.S.A. as a multiple of the U.K.
	U.S.A.	U.K.	
Chemicals			
Average ratio of the output of each chemical per firm	3	1	3
Synthetic Fibres			
fibres per firm [a] (th. tons)	50	50	1
Motor Cars			
Average output per model (th.)	400	100	4
Machine Tools			
Average ratio of the output of models	2.2	1	2.2
Newspapers			
Average circulation of daily newspapers (thousands)	35	232	(0.15) [b]
Books			
Ratio of average number of copies of each title printed	5	1	5
Average ratio			(about) 3.5 [a]

(a) For calculating the average, newspapers were excluded. This trade is thought to be exceptional, and its inclusion would give a misleading result.

For turbo generators, electric motors, domestic appliances, aircraft and computers, we have been unable to make comparisons because information about firms' product ranges is not available. But the differences in output per firm which are shown in Appendix A, and estimates of differences in product ranges, suggest that the average ratio of firms' outputs of products in these industries is more than three to one.

Comparisons of the size of plants indicate smaller differences between the average size of plants in the two countries, than might be expected. For the thirteen industries for which comparisons could be made, the output of U.K. plants was on average about 64% of that of U.S. plants, i.e. American plants were 50% larger than their U.K. equivalents. In this context we have used the term 'plant' as synonymous with location or site. In practice there may be important differences in the size units of plant operating at each site. Also, when considering these relationships, the greater geographic concentration of output in the U.K. should be borne in mind — the scope for concentration on large plants is greater in the U.K. because of lower transport costs.

We also compared the average output for all establishments in manufacturing industry in the two countries. Output was measured in terms of the value of output, and U.S. output was converted to U.K. prices by using the official rate of exchange, 2.4 $ to the £. On this basis the average output of all U.K. establishments was 44% of that of U.S. establishments, and for establishments with more than 50 employees, 29%. As U.S. prices are higher than U.K. prices, this measure exaggerates the differences between U.S. and U.K. output. If we assume U.S. prices of manufacturers are on average 33% above those for the U.K., the percentages would be 59% and 39%. However these comparisons are very crude. There may be differences in the practice of Census authorities; for example, their insistence on separate returns for the establishments of multi-plant companies may differ. Also the comparisons are affected by differences in the relative importance of industries — for example, a higher proportion of U.S. output may be obtained from industries in which relatively large plants are common.

The disparity in volume of output of the three largest firms in the two countries is, as we should expect, greater than for the average size of plants. On average the output of U.K. firms is about half that for U.S. firms. (This average is based on information for thirteen industries). The differences for some of the engineering industries are particularly marked. (In these industries the average size of plants is less important because of the scope for specialization, and for concentrating production of parts for which there are large economies of scale.)

For the comparisons with other advanced manufacturing nations, apart from the U.S.A., we first compared rates of growth. Although the growth of U.K. industries is generally slower than that of equivalent industries in many of the countries with which the comparisons were made, the differences in rates of growth vary for different industries. For example the growth of output of synthetic fibres, cement and domestic electrical appliances was similar in the U.K. and W. Germany between 1957 and 1967, but the growth of output of dyes, beer, machine tools and detergents was much faster in W. Germany than in the U.K. We have not reproduced the data we assembled because they are readily available in official sources.

Apart from comparisons between the U.S.A. and the U.K., the main comparisons we made were between the U.K. and W. Germany. Table 34.2 gives our estimates of the ratio of outputs of products for three important industries.

Table 34.2 *Estimates of the Ratio of the Annual Outputs of Products for Selected Industries — U.K. and W. Germany*

	Approximate Ratio of Outputs in 1970	
	U.K.	W. Germany
Chemicals		
Average ratio of the output of each chemical per firm	1	1.5
Motor Cars		
Average output per model	1	3
Machine Tools (other than standard tools)		
Average output of models	1	2.5

When comparisons were made of the size of plants the results varied. For brewing and cement production the average size of plants in W. Germany was significantly less than in the U.K. (In Germany there are a great many very small breweries). The average size of oil refineries and synthetic fibre plants was also somewhat smaller in W. Germany, but steel plants, chemical complexes, and motor car assembly works were significantly larger in W. Germany than in the U.K. The two main factors responsible for the greater concentration of *these* three important industries in W. Germany are that the industries were already more concentrated when production restarted after the war, and new investment has not been fragmented by so active a regional policy as in the U.K.

Another factor we tried to compare was the size of new units of plant and new plants in the U.K. and other countries, to see whether countries with faster growth rates built larger new plants or simply more new plants. If the construction of new plants and the expansion of existing plants in the U.K. at each point in time were more concentrated than in other countries, this would offset slower growth for achieving economies of scale for new plants. The extent to which expansion is concentrated depends in part on the initial structure of an industry in terms of the number of firms operating in the industry, and the rate of growth. The comparisons which we were able to make suggest that on average manufacturing industry in the U.K. is not generally more concentrated in terms of the number of firms operating in each industry, than in other advanced manufacturing countries, and, although we should expect expansion to be more concentrated in the U.K. because of the slow rate of growth, we would expect this to only partially offset the effect of the slow rate of growth on the size of new plants.

For certain industries, including chemicals, synthetic fibres, cement and steel, it is possible to make some comparisons of the number and size of new plants built in European countries from reports in trade papers. There are wide differences in the size of plants *reported* to have been built, but the clues available suggest that in these industries plants built in the U.K. do not generally differ from those built in countries whose industries expand faster.[1] The differences in the growth of capacity appear to be attributable to the number of plants built, rather than the size of plants. However, in terms of the proportion of output controlled by the largest firms, these industries are highly concentrated in the U.K., and are probably not representative. Also differences in the size of plants may apply to small plants built to make special chemicals, etc. Which are not reported.

Some similar comparisons between the U.K. and Japan suggest that there is a tendency for larger chemical and steel plants to be built in Japan. But again differences in the growth of capacity are attributable to the number of new plants built as well as the size of new plants. Indeed in the steel industry the average capacity of the 42 L.D. furnaces built in Japan between 1965 and 1970 was 170 tons, and for the 9 furnaces built in the U.K., 190 tons. Comparison of the size of new blast furnaces is not possible because none have been built in the U.K. since 1965.

An important point to note is that even if the size of new plants is the same in the U.K. as in countries with faster growing economies, the size of new plants is generally larger than existing plants, and so construction of more new plants in other advanced industrial countries tends to increase the *average* size of plants in other countries relative to the U.K. An example of these effects can be obtained by comparing the U.K. and Japanese Steel Industries. The average capacity of blast furnaces and steelworks is now substantially greater in Japan than in the U.K.

Table 34.3 *The Steel Industries of the U.K. and Japan*

	U.K.	Japan
Output of Crude Steel in 1958 (m. tons)	20	12
Output of Crude Steel in 1969 (m. tons)	27	80
Number of Works in 1969 producing steel via blast and steel furnaces	23	19
Average output per Works (m. tons)	1.2	4
Average output of three largest works	2	8
Number of blast furnaces in operation at the end of 1969	71	61
Average output per blast furnace (m. tons)	0.4	1.0
L—D Converters — number	18	73
Average output per converter (m. tons)	0.4	0.8
Number of hot strip rolling mills (mid 1969)	5	19
Average output per mill (m. tons)	2.5	2
Number of tandem cold strip mills	9	15
Average output per mill (m. tons)	0.5	1
Output of hot rolled stainless steel in 1969 (th. tons)	200	1,000

Also, even where the size of individual new ethylene plants, rolling mills, etc. is the same, if more new plants are built at *complexes* in other countries, companies there will obtain economies by being able to spread some administration costs, etc. over more plants.

(1) Some cement kilns with a capacity of 1m. tons a year are being constructed on the continent. The maximum size in the U.K. is 600,000 tons.

35. The Implications of the Conclusions

I. Introduction

The evidence we have described, suggests that there are important economies of scale in many industries. This has many implications for Government policy and we discuss some of these implications in this chapter. First we discuss the implications of our results for merger policy, and the other strategies for taking advantage of the economies of scale. We then consider the contribution of economies of scale to high levels of labour productivity and growth, and suggest some reasons for the relatively slow growth of the U.K. economy.

II. Merger policy

The significance of our results for merger policy, or for State inspired schemes to rationalise the structure of industries, depends on the value put on the benefits of competition for stimulating the efficient use of resources by firms, and for the allocation of resources between industries. This is because the achievement of the maximum economies of scale is not, on our evidence, compatible with the existence of competition of many firms for a large number of products within the U.K.

If an economy were being built up from scratch and the benefits of competition were ignored, our estimates of economies of scale suggest that there should be a very high degree of concentration of production of many products, and that very few plants should be built to produce products such as crude steel, cement, detergents, etc. In practice however, one is not starting with a clean slate. Old works exist which may be able to earn a profit for some time to come. Also many people place great emphasis on the virtues of competition, and would presumably choose to keep firms and plants in existence simply to increase the extent of competition, even where this was done at the cost of losing some of the benefits of economies of scale.[1] [It is worth noting that even if it were only existing plants (rather than new plants) which retained their independence in order to provide competition, this would result in some loss of economies of scale, because scope for specialization and long production runs which, as we have seen result in substantial economies for some products, would be lost.] However our view is that a high degree of concentration is compatible with efficient operation, and that the importance of economies of scale should be emphasized.

(1) Neither logic nor appeal to any 'facts' at present available makes possible the estimation of the benefits of competition relative to the economies of scale.

This view is difficult to support with data, but is based on the apparent efficiency of the many industries in the U.K. and the U.S.A. which are dominated by two or three firms.

Our broad conclusion is that many of the 'horizontal' mergers between companies in the manufacturing sector which have occurred during the 1960's, including the GEC - AEI - English Electric merger, and less certainly the BMC - Leyland merger,[1] were justified by the scope for achieving economies of scale *in the long run*. But it is important to note that by the term horizontal merger we mean mergers of firms making products which can be made efficiently, at least in part, on the same machinery or for which there are substantial common initial costs. The definition used by the Board of Trade and followed by a number of writers is very much wider. Mergers between firms classified to the same industry group are included as horizontal mergers within their definition, and so a merger between a soap manufacturer and a manufacturer of fireworks would be regarded as a horizontal merger. Many other bizarre examples of mergers which would count as horizontal could be given.

There is still scope for more mergers in order that advantage may be taken of the economies of scale. Table 35.1 indicates the scope available for increasing efficiency in the long run by concentrating output on larger plants. Evidence of reorganisation and concentration of output at large plants described in the industry studies dealing with beer, cement, turbogenerators, and domestic appliances show that in the long run, many firms do take advantage of increases in scale achieved by mergers to rationalize production, and reap the economies of scale.

The results of this research suggest that there is a widespread and sharp conflict between the achievement of economies of scale and the maintenance of competition between a number of suppliers of products to the U.K. market, but, if a market the size of EEC and EFTA combined is considered, the conflict is less sharp. This market is very approximately five times the size of the U.K. market, and for most products, for which transport costs are not large, it provides scope for some competition and for achieving the economies of scale. But, if full advantage is to be taken of the scope for achieving economies of scale within an enlarged E.E.C., much greater concentration of output will be required, and mergers between companies in different countries could play an important part in achieving this concentration.

III. The achievement of the economies of scale

There are a number of widely publicised strategies for achieving economies of scale. The classical route is through the expansion of markets and trade as, for example, by the U.K. joining the EEC. Another possibility which

---

(1) Many of the potential economies of scale for this merger could have been achieved by the two companies specialising and by cooperation in some overseas markets.

314

	M.E.S. (output per annum)	Average Annual Output of Existing Plants
Oil refineries	10m. tons	4m. tons
Breweries	1m. barrels	0.1m. barrels
Cement plants	2m. tons	0.3m. tons
Steel works[b]	9m. tons	1m. tons

(a) Our estimates of the m.e.s. were based on costs of production, but our review of other sources of economies of scale did not suggest that these estimates would be materially changed if marketing, management and R & D costs were included. Also the estimates of the m.e.s. for plants make no allowance for transport costs. The inclusion of these costs may justify the building of a number of plants of less than the m.e.s., but this would not affect the conclusions in relation to competition.

(b) Much of the steel industry's capacity is, of course, controlled by the B.S.C., but it is included in this table because the concentration of the industry has not yet substantially changed the average size of works, and the fragmentation of the industry is typical of other industries.

has been suggested is to increase the share of the manufacturing sector within the U.K. economy by increasing the level of taxes on services relative to manufactures. Policies to encourage conglomerate mergers may lead to the achievement of economies of scale.[1] An alternative strategy is to put more pressure on inefficient firms, including firms which are relatively inefficient because of the scale of their operations. Raising taxes on costs, rather than profits by substituting a value added tax for corporation tax, is one means of applying this pressure.

Our enquiries provide useful evidence to support these policies, but they do not provide conclusive evidence, because we have not examined many of the issues involved with their introduction, and although, in general, the results support policies aimed to increase scale, care has to be used in the interpretation of the results. For example, if the U.K. joins the E.E.C. this would be expected to result in an increase in scale, but our comparisons of structure suggest that in many of the chemical and engineering industries, W. German firms now have important scale advantages. Productivity in the chemical and engineering industries is relatively high, and this provides an advantage for countries which specialise in producing chemicals and engineering products. Many W. German firms in these industries may have an advantage like that of a newspaper with the largest share of the circulation of its class. If however wages are lower in the U.K., this may offset the advantage W. German firms obtain from larger scale and other factors.

Before completing this brief discussion of methods of taking advantage of the economies of scale three points are worth emphasising. In order to reap the economies of scale, firms often need to apply an aggressive pricing

(1) A conglomerate can organise horizontal mergers and can finance expansion by some of its subsidiaries to take advantage of the economies of scale.

policy, particularly in export markets.[1] It may be that managers of U.K. firms have been more reluctant to use aggressive pricing policies for fear of spoiling their market, than their competitors. It is possible that they are more averse to taking risks and are less keen to expand. Another explanation which contributes to differing performance is that overseas firms have built more new plants and that capital costs, but also economies of scale, are greater for these plants. The relatively low variable costs for new plants encourage overseas firms to export.

The position of a number of U.K. firms which have fallen behind in terms of scale also deserves mention. For example G.E.C., British Leyland and the British Steel Corporation have more fragmented facilities than many of their competitors. Similarly, a number of machine tool companies have fallen behind in the rate at which they are introducing innovations. Many of these companies are taking steps to improve their position, but there is a case for the Government to provide temporary help, perhaps in the form of low interest loans, for these firms to modernise, although this type of aid is at present unfashionable.

Another important point to emerge from the study is the significance of the efficiency with which new plant is operated. New plant and equipment are the vehicle for introducing new techniques and in many cases for changing scale. If new plant is not operated efficiently this slows down the introduction of new techniques and increases in scale. The capital costs for many existing plants are very low, and even if inefficiently operated they are often able to compete in home and overseas markets.

We presented some estimates of international differences in the efficiency of operating new steel plants in Book 2. Output and labour and capital productivity are perhaps 50 per cent higher in new Japanese steel works compared to U.K. works. This is not an isolated case. Costs for operating new plants may be relatively high in the U.K. for a number of reasons.

(a) Simply because of less efficient management and operatives. In the past this applied to parts of the motor vechicle and steel industries..

(b) Less experience of operating new plants — failure may breed failure in this respect.

(c) Powerful trade union bargaining, which increases wage rates and earnings for staff operating new plants and/or results in over manning or under-utilization of new plants. In the past this applied to parts of the cement, newspaper and diesel engine industries.

(d) Reluctance to operate three shifts as in parts of the textile industry.[2]

(e) The erratic growth of demand which results in the under-utilization of new plants.

---

(1) Even if prices do not have to be cut, extra selling and servicing costs may have to be incurred to increase exports.

(2) Three or four shift working not only reduces capital costs per unit of output, but speeds up the rate at which new machines have to be replaced because they wear out more quickly.

(f) Regulations which affect the siting of new plants, pollution control and working conditions at new plants more than at existing plants.

Also in some industries (parts of the chemical industry and machine tools) the development of new products and other innovations has been slower in the U.K., and so fewer new plants and expansions of capacity have had the protection of making new products. In industries where we have spent more on R & D than continental countries or Japan, aircraft and computers, we have faced severe competition from the U.S.A., where R & D expenditure on these products has been many times the U.K. level. We have been the second producer in these markets and this position has not paid off, because of the advantage achieved by American firms from much higher R & D expenditure. (For the U.S.A., exports of aircraft and computers represented 13 per cent of all exports of manufacturers in 1969.) All these forces have retarded the switch to new plants within industries and between industries in the U.K., and so limited the growth of the size of plants.

IV. The contribution of economies of scale to achieving high levels of labour productivity and growth

In chapter 30 we drew attention to the magnitude of the economies of scale for labour costs, and hence the contribution of scale to high levels of labour productivity. An argument which may be used to reduce the significance of our estimates of economies of scale for labour costs, is that they are most reliable when dealing with direct labour costs for process plants, for labour employed on assembly lines, etc., but that direct labour costs form only a small proportion of the total labour costs of a firm, and that for indirect labour, scale effects are smaller. We reject this line of criticism for the following reasons.

(a) In a number of industries including motors, steel, castings, direct labour costs are a substantial proportion of all labour costs.

(b) Our estimates suggest that there are substantial economies for initial, maintenance, buying, management, and research costs in many industries, where differences in scale are attributable to differences in the output of a constant range of products.[1] As labour costs are an important element of all these groups of costs there are substantial economies for indirect labour.

When considering the contribution of economies of scale to high levels of labour productivity, there are two relationships which have to be distinguished.

(a) The effects of different rates of growth of output on the size of new plants built, and hence for the possibilities of achieving economies of scale.

---

(1) Also some employees of many firms are engaged in planning investments and in some cases constructing new plants, and economies of scale apply to the building of large new plants.

(b) The costs for new plants compared with those for existing plants, i.e. the relationship between the additional labour and capital required for increase in output compared to the existing labour force and capital stock.

We now illustrate these relationships in terms of very crude orders of magnitude.

The relationship between rates of growth and the size of plants

We make the following initial (unrealistic) assumptions.

(a) There is no change in the product mix as scale is increased.

(b) All industries expand capacity at the same rate.

(c) All the increased capacity comes from new plants, and the number of new plants is not affected by the rate of growth.

(d) All economies of scale relate to the size of plants.

For manufacturing industries the effects of expansion will differ between industries, but for two industries, oil refining (typical of the process industries) and footwear (typical of the textile and clothing industries) the effects of different rates of growth on labour and capital requirements are illustrated in table 35.2.

So far it has been assumed that the rate of growth does not affect the number of new plants built and, therefore, that the size of new plants increases in line with the rate of growth. In practice the rate of growth and the number of plants built are inter-related, and we should expect fewer plants to be built in an industry which expands relatively slowly. If we 'heroically' assume that the average for oil refining, an industry subject to large economies of scale, and footwear, for which scale economies are small, are representative for manufacturing, and that half the differences in rates of growth are accounted for by differences in the number of new plants built, and half to the size of new plants, we can suggest some orders of magnitude for the labour-grid capital requirements for growth of the output of manufacturing industry.

Output capacity of new plants as percentage of the economy's existing capacity	1	2	4	8
Index of additional labour required per unit of extra output	100	92	87	83
Index of additional capital required per unit of extra output	100	89	82	76

So far no allowance has been made for any relationship between rates of growth and the trades which expand. Relatively fast growth may be accompanied by greater concentration on industries which are capital intensive

Table 35.2. *The Resources Required for Growth*

Oil Refining

Output capacity of new plant as percentage of the industry's existing capacity	1	2	4	8
Index of additional labour required	100	120	145	175
Index of additional capital required	100	150	230	350

Footwear

Output capacity of new plant as percentage of the industry's existing capacity	1	2	4	8
Index of additional labour required	100	190	370	730
Index of additional capital required	100	190	370	730

Average for the two industires [a]

Output capacity of new plants as percentage of the industries existing capacity	1	2	4	8
Index of additional labour required	100	167	295	545
Index of additional capital required	100	157	253	413
Index of labour required per unit of extra output	100	84	74	68
Index of capital required per unit of extra output	100	78	63	52

(a) It is assumed that labour requirements for 1% growth for footwear are twice those for for oil refining, and that capital requirements for oil refining are five times those for footwear.

and/or subject to greater than average economies of scale. In a footnote[1] we illustrate the changing pattern of output in the U.K., W. Germany and Japan. The faster decline in the proportion of output accounted for by the textile industries in W. Germany and Japan, and the greater increase in the proportion of output derived from chemicals in W. Germany, and the engineering industries in Japan, is noteworthy. The average value of output per head in the chemical industries is much greater than in engineering or textile industries, and is higher for engineering than textiles.[2]

Labour requirements for growth

The second relationship to consider is that between the additional resources required for growth and the existing labour force and capital stock. We have

(1) The following estimates illustrate differences in the changing distribution of resources between groups of industries in the U.K., W. Germany, and Japan:

Percentage Breakdown of the Output of Manufacturing Industries

	U.K.		W.G.		Japan	
	1963	1969	1963	1969	1963	1969
Basic Metals	8.0	7.3	9.2	9.3	9.2	10.2
Chemical Industries	9.5	11.1	12.1	15.9	13.1	13.5
Engineering	41.8	42.1	37.1	36.1	35.6	46.0
Textiles	11.0	11.1	9.3	8.0	10.1	6.3
Other Trades	29.7	28.4	32.3	30.7	32.0	24.0
	100.0	100.0	100.0	100.0	100.0	100.0

(2) Average value added per head is higher in chemicals primarily because production is more capital intensive. The scope for more R. & D., concentration of output in the hands of relatively few firms, and relatively high wages and salaries paid by firms in the chemical industry, also contribute to the differences. Similar, but smaller, differences apply between the engineering and textile industries.

319

concentrated on labour requirements. The labour requirements for a 1% growth of output from new plants would be less than 1% of the existing labour force because new plants incorporate new and more efficient techniques, new plants are often larger than existing plants, and because expansion tends to be concentrated on trades with relatively high labour productivity.

We cannot pretend that we have measured these relationships, but the clues we have obtained suggest that labour productivity for new vintages of plant in manufacturing industry may average 50% or more above those for the average for existing plants producing the same products, because of the use of more efficient techniques and larger scale plant (for some types of plant it is more than 100%). Thus an increase of 1% in the labour force may be sufficient to provide a 1.5% increase in output.[1] If within trades and between trades the increase in output is concentrated on the production of products for which labour productivity is relatively high, the ratio may be 1:2 or 1:2.5, rather than 1:1.5. If it is further assumed that a 2% rate of growth is required to obtain the scale effects referred to in this paragraph, then labour requirements for faster growth, based on the estimates given above would be:

Annual rate of growth (%)	2	4	8
Additional labour required as percentage of existing labour force.	0.8 - 1.0	1.4 - 1.8	2.7 - 3.4
Percentage increase in labour productivity	1.0 - 1.2	2.2 - 2.6	4.5 - 5.2

These very crude calculations are intended to illustrate the potential contribution of economies of scale and new vintages of plant to the growth of output and labour productivity. However, the shift to trades with high labour productivity implies a shift to trades which are capital intensive. Capital requirements for rapid growth would be correspondingly high.

V. Some reasons for the slow growth of the British economy

Finally we look at some implications of our study for the growth of the British economy.

Differences in the relative efficiency with which new plants are operated, and the extent to which new plants are protected by innovations, are fundamental reasons for the slow growth of productivity in the U.K. which have received insufficient emphasis. There are forces which reinforce progress brought about by innovation. Innovation facilitates investment, new plants enjoy proportionately greater economies of scale, and this reinforces the incentive to export which is aided by innovation. If a country innovates

---

(1) The increase depends on the trades in which the increase in output is concentrated. For the estimate given it is assumed that it is spread in proportion to the existing output.

and builds new plants, it can increase wages relative to those in other countries, and this increases the pressure on plants with low labour productivity in the country which innovates because imports are sucked in. It is a virtuous circle, but the entry to the circle is via improved efficiency, innovation by creating new products, etc., not by lowering wage costs relative to the wage costs of competitors. Lowering wage costs by devaluation is likely to improve the competitiveness of all plants, including those with relatively low labour productivity, and not change the relative efficiency with which new plants are operated compared to older plants, or much affect the rate of innovation. [It is, of course, better to maintain the utilization of capacity by devaluing to reduce labour costs, rather than to create surplus capacity by deflation in order to avoid devaluation.]

Another explanation of the slow growth of the U.K. economy — 'premature maturity' [1] — is also supported by our calculations. If the labour force available for employment in manufacturing industry increases through time, this facilitates growth of output and labour productivity. The high proportion of the labour force already in manufacturing industry was a factor slowing the growth of output and productivity in U.K. manufacturing industries. But, if more firms in U.K. manufacturing industry had innovated, and had been in a position to build new plants with high labour productivity, they would have been able to attract labour both from other firms in manufacturing industry with much lower labour productivity, and the non manufacturing sectors of the economy. There are rigidities in the labour market, but firms which achieve relatively high labour productivity can pay relatively high wages and thus attract labour. Indeed, other things being equal, a shortage of labour is a spur to increasing labour productivity by substituting capital for labour, and by using labour more efficiently. Also, if labour is *transferred* from operating plant which involves low labour productivity to new plant with higher than average productivity, this increases average labour productivity by more than simply increasing the labour force to operate the new plants, while retaining low productivity plants.

It might be argued that if an economy is expanding rapidly firms have more incentive to replace existing plant at the same time as they expand their capacity, and so take advantage of the higher productivity associated with new vintages of plant, but it is doubtful whether this is, in practice, an important source of the differences in the rate at which firms and countries replace assets. A good deal of investment has taken place in U.K. manufacturing industry, and so most firms have had opportunities for incorporating replacements in extensions to capacity, although these opportunities do not occur as often in the U.K. as in faster expanding economies. An indirect way in which fast growth may speed up the replacement of existing plant is that the relatively rapid increase in real wages associated with it, will tend to make older vintages of plant which are labour intensive less competitive, but it is difficult to assess the importance of this effect.

(1) See N. Kaldor 'Causes of the Slow Rate of Economic Growth of the United Kingdom', Cambridge University Press, 1966.

The argument that fast growth facilitates the replacement of equipment can be reversed. If a firm is expanding slowly it may scrap existing plant so that it can fully utilize new plant or machinery, or it may take over another firm in order to fully utilize an existing or new plant or machine.

If our analysis is correct, some of the reasons for the slow growth of the British economy are deep seated. Indeed, the position of the British economy in the late 1950's, relative to European competitors and Japan, can be compared to that of the Cooperative Societies relative to the multiple traders, such as Marks and Spencer and Tesco. The author provided some assistance for a study of productivity and capital expenditure in retailing during the early 1960's.[1] The conclusion reached by that study was that the increase in productivity achieved by the Cooperative Societies was wholly attributable to the increase in capital per head, while a substantial part of the increase in productivity achieved by the other traders was attributable to technical and organisational knowledge. It seemed to the present writer that to say the Cooperative Societies had made no progress except that attributable to the employment of more capital, was an incomplete explanation. In terms of changes of technique employed, such as the introduction of self-service, etc., which are only in part connected with new capital expenditure, the progress of the Cooperative Societies was more impressive than that of other firms, many of which were simply expanding their business along well established lines. However, although the Cooperatives were introducing new methods, generally they had difficulty in operating them as efficiently as their competitors who had more experience of the methods.

The explanation of the apparent paradox between the estimated contribution of technical progress etc., and the observed improvements in the techniques employed, was that the position was not in equilibrium at the beginning of the period studied (1961). If the Cooperative Societies had not changed their methods of business their productivity would have declined. The progress of other retailers along already established lines meant that the Cooperative Societies would have faced declining labour productivity had they not changed their methods, because they would have lost more business to other traders.

The position of the British economy has been similar, although not as serious. The continuing progress of our competitors, notably W. Germany, Japan, France and Italy, has meant that some of our export markets have been lost, and these have had to be made up before any net increase of exports could be achieved. By the early 1960's, other countries had established a lead in many industries; Japan in steel, Germany in many types of chemicals and machine tools, Italy in domestic appliances. They were then protected by economies of scale, large plants, and established market links which were difficult to break down without new innovations, or significantly

(1) 'Productivity and Capital Expenditure in Retailing' by K.D. George in collaboration with P.V. Hills, Cambridge, 1968.

lower wage costs, and hence prices.

Two other implications of the analysis are that the success of a government's policy for increasing growth cannot be assessed by comparing crude growth rates for two short periods of, say, five years — the negative growth factors — such as the effects of the increased competitiveness of other countries — may change between two periods. Also policies to increase growth rates by increasing the rate of innovation are likely to take a number of years to become effective. The type of policies required are policies to improve the supply of qualified and trained personnel to firms, to encourage the development of new products and market research in overseas markets, and to reduce the cost of capital for new plants.

Appendix A: International Comparisons of the Structure of Manufacturing Industries

Table A. 1 *A Comparison of the Structure of Manufacturing Industry in the U.S.A. and the U.K.*

(The figures are for 1968 unless another year is indicated)

		U.S.A.	U.K.	U.K. as percentage of U.S.A.
POPULATION	(million)	201	55	27
AREA[a]	(th. sq. miles)	3,022	95	3

(a) The figure for the U.S.A. excludes Alaska and Hawaii.

(A) MANUFACTURING INDUSTRY

		U.S.A.	U.K.	U.K. %
Contribution to G.N.P. (£ th.m.)		102.67	12.63	12.3
Employees	(million)	19.8	8.1	40.9
Investment in New Plant and Machinery (£m.)		11.8	1.2	9.9
Number of Establishments 1963 th.		307	84	28
Output per Establishment[a] (Output in 1968 divided by establishments in 1963)	(£th.)	336	147	44
Number of Establishments with more than 50 employees 1963 (th.)		52	23	44
Output per Establishment[a] (for establishments with more than 50 employees.) (Output in 1968 divided by establishments in 1963)	(£m.)	1.7	0.5	29

(a) The comparison is based on values of output. This comparison exaggerates differences in real output because U.S. prices are on average higher than U.K. prices of manufactured products.

(B) OIL REFINING

		U.S.A.	U.K.	%
Total Throughput of Oil	(m. tons)	501.2	81.8	16
Number of Refineries		262	22	8
Average Throughput per Refinery (m. tons)		1.9	3.7	195
Average Capacity of Refineries which accounted for 80% of Capacity (m. tons)		5	8	160
Average Capacity of each of the 3 largest firms	(m. tons)	45	24	54

(These estimates are very approximate[a])	U.S.A.	U.K.	U.K. as % of USA
Ratio of Industry Sales (Output) [b]	6	1	17
Average ratio of firms manufacturing each type of chemicals. [c]	2	1	50
Average ratio of output of each chemical per firm	3	1	33
Average ratio of the number of plants operated by each firm to produce each type of chemical	2	1	50
Average ratio of output of each chemical per plant	1.5	1	67

(a) The estimates have been weighted by number of chemicals, not the value of sales of each type of chemical.

(b) It is assumed that on average prices of chemicals in the U.S. and the U.K. are the same, so that differences in sales indicate differences in output. It is also assumed that the range of chemicals made in the two countries is similar.

(c) This estimate is based on a comparison of entries in industry directories.

Ethylene (1967)			
Total output (m.tons)	5.4	1.2	22
Number of locations at which ethylene was made	35	7	20
Average output per location (th.tons)	154	170	110
Average capacity at the three sites with the largest output (th.tons)	n.a.	320	—
Average capacity of three largest units (th.tons)	459	180	39
Average capacity of the three firms with the largest capacity (th.tons)	867	340	39

Sulphuric Acid			
Total output (m.tons)	25.5	3.28	13
Number of locations at which sulphuric acid was made	220	43	20
Average output per site (m.tons)	0.12	0.08	67
Average capacity at three largest sites (th.tons)	1,100	400	36
Average capacity of three leading sulphuric acid manufacturers (m.tons)	2.5	0.5	20

Synthetic Fibres			
Total output of synthetic fibres (th.tons)	1,450	270	20
Number of sites at which synthetic fibres were made	129	38	30
Average output per site	11.0	7.0	63
Average output at three largest sites (th.tons)	70	25	36
Average output of three leading firms (th.tons)	300	85	28

Nylon			
Total output (th.tons)	595	120	20
Number of sites at which nylon was made	35	8	23
Average output per site (th.tons)	17	15	88
Output at largest site (th.tons)	100	50	50
Output of leading firm (th.tons)	240	80	33
World output of leading firm (th.tons)	320	120	38

	U.S.A.	U.K.	U.K. as % of U.S.A.
Total output (m. barrels)	87.7	31.4	36
Number of breweries	149	243	163
Average output per brewery (th. barr.)	589	129	22
Average output of three largest breweries (m. barr)	6.5	1.5	23
Average output of three largest firms (m. barr)	8.5	3.6	42

(E) BREAD

Total output (m. tons)	6.1	2.8	46
Number of bakeries (thousands)	5.0	6.0	120
Average output per bakery (tons)	1,220	470	39
Average output of three largest firms	290	560	193

(F) DETERGENT POWDERS

Total output, 1966. (th. tons)	2,973	416	14
Size of detergent plants operated by the leading firms	Plants are of a similar size		

(G) CEMENT

Total output (th. tons)	56,420	14,720	26
Number of cement works	175	51	29
Average output per works (th. tons)	320	290	91
Average capacity of three largest plants (m. tons)	1.9	0.8	42
Average capacity of three largest firms (m. tons)	5.9	5.5	93

(H) BRICKS (incl. Flettons)

Total output (m. bricks)	7,557	7,464	99
Total number of brickworks	400	500	125
Average output per brickworks (m. bricks)	19	15	79

(I) STEEL

Total output of crude steel (m. tons)	117.4	25.9	22
Number of sites at which crude steel made	100	34	34
Average output per site (m. tons)	1.2	0.8	67
Number of integrated crude steel works (with blast furnaces)	46	23	50
Average output of the three plants with the largest output (m. tons)	7	2	29
Average output of three leading firms (m. tons)	20	24[a]	—

(a) Output of the B.S.C.

Iron Castings

Total output (th. tons)	15,254	3,756	25
Number of foundries	2,133	920	43
Average output per foundry (th. tons)	7.15	4.08	57

(J) MOTOR VEHICLES

	U.S.A.	U.K.	U.K. as % of U.S.A.
Total output (thousand)	8,820	1,816	21
Number of assembly plants [a]	40	12	30
Average output per assembly plant (th.)	221	151	68
Average output of three leading companies (th.)	2,800	500	18
Average output of each model made by the three leading companies [b]	400	100	25

(a) Excluding assembly plants at which less than 5,000 cars were built in 1968.

(b) Excluding sports cars.

(K) AIRCRAFT

	U.S.A.	U.K.	U.K. as % of U.S.A.
Value of output of Aerospace Industry (£m.)	9,000	900	10
Average sales of three largest companies (£m.)	1,000	300	30

(L) MACHINE TOOLS

(These estimates are very approximate)

	U.S.A.	U.K.	U.K. as % of U.S.A.
Total output (£m.)	1,150	250	22
Ratio of manufacturers of each type of machine [a]	2	1	50
Ratio of average output of each type of machine per firm [b]	2.2	1	45
	350	300	86
Numerically Controlled Machine Tools			
Total output (number)	2,917	558	19
Value (£m.)	147.5	11.8	8

(a) The ratio is based on a comparison of entries in trade directories.

(b) No allowance is made for differences in the range of products made. The American machine tool industry may produce a wider range of types and models than the U.K. industries.

(M) MARINE DIESELS

U.S. output of slow marine diesels is negligible.

(N) TURBO GENERATORS

	U.S.A.	U.K.	U.K. as % of U.S.A.
Output of steam-turbo-alternators (M.K.W.)	25,460	7,031	28
Number of manufacturers	2	2	100
Output per manufacturer (M.K.W.)	12,730	3,515	28

(O) ELECTRIC MOTORS 1—100 h.p.

	U.S.A.	U.K.	U.K. as % of U.S.A.
Output (Approximate ratio of output)	4	1	25
Share of the national output of the leading manufacturer	60%	45%	
Output of leading manufacturer (Approximate ratio of output)	5	1	20

	U.S.A.	U.K.	U.K. as percentage of U.S.A.
Refrigerators			
Output of Refrigerators (th.)	5.150	1,085	21
Output of Refrigerators and freezers (th.)	6,275	1,200	19
Number of manufacturers of refrigerators and freezers	14[a]	7[a]	50
Average output per manufacturer (th.)	368	155	42
Washing Machines			
Output of Washing Machines (th.)	4,482	884	20
Output of Washing Machines and Dryers (th.)	7,344	1,427	19
Number of manufacturers of home laundry equipment	12	14	117
Average output per manufacturer (th.)	612	102	17

(a) Refrigerators only.

	U.S.A.	U.K.	U.K. as percentage of U.S.A.
Value of output (£m.)	1,300[a]	130[a]	10
Output of leading manufacturer (£m.)	1,100	60	5
World sales of largest manufacturer (£m.)	2,500	92	4

(a) Excluding peripheral equipment.

	U.S.A.	U.K.	U.K. as percentage of U.S.A.
Spinning			
Output of yarn excluding wool yarn (th.m.lbs.)	9.5	0.75	8
Number of mills (U.S. 1967, U.K. 1968)	354	131	37
Average output per mill (m.lbs)	27	6	22
Number of firms (U.S. 1963, U.K. 1968)	234	63	27
Average output per firm (m.lbs)	41	12	29
Average output of the three largest firms (m. lbs.)	700	90	13
Weaving			
Output of fabrics excluding wool fabrics (th.m.yds)	12.7	1.29	10
Number of weaving mills (U.S. 1967, U.K. 1968)	837	398	48
Average output per mill (m.yds)	15	3	21
Number of firms (U.S. 1967, U.K. 1968)	500	279	56
Average output per firm (m.yds)	25	5	20
Percentage of industry owned by three largest firms	25	15	60
Average output of three largest firms (th.m.yds.)	1.1	0.1	6
Percentage of industry owned by spinner weavers			
Spindles	75	59	79
Looms	85	36	42

	U.S.A.	U.K.	U.K. as percentage of U.S.A.
Output of shoes (mill pairs)	642	281	44
Number of factories	750	500	67
Average output per factory (th.pairs)	856	562	66
Average output of each of the four leading firms (m. pairs)	29	25	86

(T) NEWSPAPERS AND BOOKS

(These estimates are very approximate)

Newspapers

Average daily sales of newspapers (m.)	62	25	41
Number of daily newspapers	1761	109	6
Average circulation per newspaper (th.)	35	232	660

Books

Number of titles published including reprints (th)	30	31	103
Titles printed (th)	26	25	96
Book Printers' turnover (£m.)	800	110	14
Ratio of book prices	2	1	50
Ratio of the average number of copies of each title printed	5	1	20

Table A. 2 *A Comparison of the Structure of Manufacturing Industry in Japan and the U.K. in 1968*

	U.K.	Japan	U.K. as % of Japan
Population (Millions)	55	101	55
Area (th. sq. miles)	95	143	66
Oil Refining			
Total throughput of oil (m. tons)	81.8	114.6	71.4
Number of Refineries	22	54	40.7
Average throughput per Refinery (m. tons)	3.72	2.12	175.5
Chemicals			
Ethylene			
Total output (m. tons)	1.2	1.3	92.3
Number of locations at which ethylene was made	7	11	63.6
Average output per location (th. tons)	171	118	144.9
Sulphuric Acid			
Total output (m. tons)	3.28	4.44	73.9
Number of locations at which sulphuric acid was made	43	65	66.2
Average output per site (m. tons)	.08	.07	114.3

	U.K.	Japan	U.K. as % of Japan
Nylon			
Total output (th. tons)	120	214	56.1
Number of sites at which nylon is made	8	11	72.7
Average output per site (th. tons)	15	19.5	76.9
Beer			
Total output (m. barrels)	31.4	15.8	198.7
Number of breweries	243	25	972.0
Average output per brewery (th. barrels)	129	632	20.4
Cement			
Total output (th. tons)	14,720	44,230	33.3
Number of cement works	51	59	86.4
Average output per works (th. tons)	289	750	38.5
Bricks (incl. Flettons)			
Total output (m. bricks)	7,464	233	3,203
Total number of brickworks	500	247	202.4
Average output per brickworks (m. bricks)	15	.94	1,596
Steel [1]			
Cars			
Total output (th.)	1,816	2,011	90.3
Number of assembly plants	12	18	66.7
Average output per assembly plant (th.)	151	112	134.8
Domestic Appliances			
Refrigerators			
Output of Refrigerators (th.)	1,085	3,199	33.9
Number of Manufacturers	7	13	53.8
Average output per Manufacturer (th.)	155	246	63.0
Washing Machines			
Output of washing machines (th.)	884	3,328	26.6
Number of manufacturers of Home Laundry Equipment	14	9	155.6
Average output per Manufacturer (th.)	63	370	17.0
Textiles			
Spinning			
Output of yarn excluding wool yarn (th. m. lbs.)	.75	1.04	72.1
Number of mills	131	219	59.8
Average output per mill (m. lbs.)	5.7	4.7	121.3

(1) Data for the steel industry is given on page 312.

Appendix B: The Sensitivity of Estimates of economies of Scale to Changes in the Basis of Calculating Capital Charges

There are a number of reasons why the estimates of capital charges could be misleading.

(1) The rate of obsolescence may be under, or over, estimated. On average accountants are probably too cautious in estimating the effects of obsolescence, and hence the rate at which they write off plant.

(2) A rate of interest of about 10% was often used in the industry studies for estimating capital charges. It could be argued that in present conditions the rate should be higher because firms aim for higher rates of profit. But there is a qualification to this argument. High rates of interest reflect, in part, rapid price inflation. If money is borrowed at a high, but fixed, rate of interest and inflation occurs, this reduces the effective rate of interest. Given that the rate of interest on debentures is now about 10-11 per cent, there is a case for using a substantially lower rate for test calculations, if revenues and costs are estimated at current prices.

(3) Estimates of depreciation and interest on capital per unit of output are based on assumptions about capacity utilization. Certainly in recent years some businessmen have been over-optimistic about the levels of capacity utilization they would achieve when making ex-ante estimates of costs and when fixing prices. (Under utilization of capacity has been caused by the slow growth of demand and to a lesser extent by strikes.)

(4) The costs of planning and commissioning new plants are usually omitted from capital costs. If they were included as capital costs, this would increase the capital charges.

The first two factors have tended to result in an over estimation of capital charges and the last two have tended to result in an under estimation. It is not possible to estimate whether on balance our estimates of capital charges are biassed, but we can assess the sensitivity of our estimates of economies of scale to changes in the capital charges.

The first estimate of economies of scale for which we provided a breakdown of costs in Book 2 was for Ethylene plants. Table B.1 reproduces the data in table 5.2 in a more convenient form for considering the effects of varying assumptions about capital charges.

For ethylene plants changing the basis for charging depreciation and interest on capital would not change the picture of proportionately large economies of scale for value added by new plants, because there are substantial economies of scale for both capital and operating costs of plants. But, if capital charges were changed relative to material costs, then the

Table B.1. *Ethylene Plants — Costs and Scale*

Output of ethylene (th. tons)		100		200		300
		(operating costs per ton of ethylene)				
Materials:						
Feedstock, chemicals, & utilities		41.2		41.2		41.2
Labour:						
Operating labour, supervision, maintenance & works overheads		3.5		2.7		2.1
Capital:						
Depreciation (10% of cost per year)	8.4		6.8		5.5	
Interest at 10% on:						
Average fixed capital	6.3		5.1		4.2	
Working capital	0.4	15.1	0.4	12.3	0.4	10.1
Total		59.8		56.2		53.4

economies of scale would be damped down or increased, depending on whether capital charges were reduced or increased. However, it is worth noting that the materials (naphtha, chemicals and fuel) are produced in capital intensive plants, and costs for these plants would be affected in a similar way to those for ethylene. If the costs of materials were broken down into capital, labour and imported materials, the effect of increasing capital charges relative to labour costs would be closer to the effects of such a change on value added alone.

Conclusion

For ethylene plants any plausible change in the basis for calculating capital charges would be unlikely to change the pattern of economies of scale for *new* plants. In our view this conclusion applies to new plants in other industries for which large economies of scale have been shown to exist.

New and existing plants

For dyes and a number of other products we illustrated costs for new and existing plants. Capital charges are generally much higher for new plants, and any change in the basis for calculating capital charges which resulted in a general increase in these charges *without* a corresponding increase in other costs, would increase relative costs for new plants, and tend to perpetuate the life of existing (usually small) plants.

One source of higher capital charges is higher interest rates. If interest rates change, without other variables changing, then fewer existing plants will be replaced by new plants. But if a rise in interest rates reflects an acceleration of inflation, and the relationship between interest rates and inflation is taken account of by industrialists in their pricing policy and investment planning, then the effect of higher interest rates on the replacement of existing plants would be offset by the effect of faster inflation. However, this is a partial analysis; there are a number of other factors which are important in practice.

(a) Inflation may result in uncertainty and inhibit investment in new plants.

(b) Businessmen may not allow for the effects of inflation increasing net revenue during the life of assets, when they plan investments.

(c) If existing plants are operated by different firms to those which operate new plants, inflation may help to perpetuate the life of the existing plants. Profits on stocks attributable to inflation may enable firms operating old plants to continue in operation. Without these profits the equity capital of such firms might be exhausted more rapidly.

Other effects of monetary policy on the scale of production

Changes in capital brought about by changes in interest rates should not be considered in isolation from other implied changes in the financial climate. Higher interest rates are related to tighter credit, and the latter may in practice affect the scale of plants. If firms cannot obtain finance for new plants this may perpetuate the life of existing (small) plants, particularly if credit restrictions hit hardest at expanding firms.[1] Also many firms face a choice between building large plants and not using the full capacity of the plants at first, and building smaller plants more often to meet the growth of demand. Shortage of credit presses firms towards the second option.

However there are factors going the other way. Tightness of credit may make firms search for ways of economising on the use of capital. One source of economies for, say, an international oil company is to build fewer and larger plants. Also shortage of credit tends to result in firms expanding on existing sites to avoid the initial costs of building up production facilities at a new location. (Regional subsidies may have an opposite effect in a period of tight credit).

(1) Expanding firms would be expected to require more new finance.

Appendix C: The Census of Production - Productivity

I. Introduction

The estimates of the economies of scale described in the industry studies were based on the experience and judgement of people with expert knowledge of the industries concerned. This is the most satisfactory way of making estimates of the economies of scale, and the only method by which reliable estimates for individual industries can be prepared, but it is inevitably a slow procedure, dependent on the goodwill of individuals in the industries concerned. The Census of Production and the accounts of public companies provide data for all manufacturing industries, and it was decided to see if a general guide to the existence of the economies of scale could be obtained from these sources.

A comparison of actual costs has some advantages over estimates of costs for hypothetical plants and firms. If large firms are comparatively inefficient because of an absence of competition or because they can shelter behind substantial technical economies of scale, this may only be apparent from a comparison of actual costs.

The most comprehensive existing attempt to use Census data in connection with estimating economies of scale was a study by Johnston.[1] His analysis was based on the U.S. Census of Manufactures for 1939 and showed that for most broad industry groups there was a positive relationship between output per head and size, over the range of scale of existing establishments. The comparisons described in this chapter are based on the 1958 U.K. Census of Production in which data are analysed according to the size of *enterprise*.[2] [3] This study also differs from Johnston's work in that data for individual census trades are analysed, different statistical tests are employed, and an attempt is made to measure the effect of scale as well as to establish the type of relationship i.e. whether cost and scale are positively or negatively related.

(1) J. Johnston, 'Statistical Cost Analysis', McGraw Hill, New York, 1960.

(2) For the Census the term enterprise is defined as one or more firms under common ownership or control as defined in the Companies Act 1948. An enterprise normally consists either of a single firm, or of a holding company together with its subsidiaries. However establishments are classified to individual trades and all the establishments owned by an enterprise in each trade are consolidated. Thus if a firm has establishments in two trades it will appear as two enterprises.

(3) The Census also provides some data analysed according to the size of establishments, but the net output of establishments was not given according to this classification and, as net output per employee is the most satisfactory guide to productivity, the enterprise classification was used.

II. Difficulties involved in using the census to estimate the economies of scale

Attention has already been drawn to the many dimensions of scale to which economies may relate. Census data can be used to compare the performance of existing enterprises of varying size and to obtain an indication of the effect of this dimension of scale on costs. The effect of the size of enterprise on costs may to some extent incorporate the impact of differences in other dimensions of scale. Large enterprises may organise production in large plants and achieve comparatively long production runs and large outputs of individual products, and they may also perform stages of production, operations or processes which small enterprises buy out. If it could be shown that, as between enterprises making the same products, there are no savings in costs for large enterprises, this would indicate that given existing markets there are few, if any economies to be obtained by increasing the size of plants, the length of production runs and the output of particular products, or by integrating the stages of production or manufacturing operations, because large firms should be in a stronger position to take advantage of any potential economies of this type and would be expected to do so, if such economies exist.

The Census data on enterprises are analysed according to size measured by the number of employees and so this is the only indicator of scale that can be used for analysing data about enterprises for individual trades. The bias in this classification has been discussed by Johnston. If two enterprises are considered, each with the same output measured in terms of products, then the enterprise with the highest labour productivity will tend to be in a smaller size group. The classification according to numbers employed tends to understate any economies of scale, indeed it might erroneously indicate that there are diseconomies of scale. Also numbers employed are only a partial measure of scale as no account is taken of the capital input or the quality of labour employed.

The Census gives details of net output[1] and most of our comparisons are in terms of net output per employee.[2] The implication is that if output per head, measured in this way, increases with size, then economies of scale exist, but this does not necessarily follow. For example large units may employ more highly qualified staff or use more capital. The qualifications to any conclusions about the economies of scale obtained from comparisons of net output per employee are discussed in more detail in section five.

---

(1) The net output of a firm is its sales plus any increase in stocks during the year, less purchases of materials and fuel, and payments for transport. Net output as defined in the Census differs from value added, in that the former includes payments to other firms in connection with selling, advertising and other services such as postage and accountancy.

(2) Data for gross output per employee are available, but this was not used because comparisons would be affected by any systematic differences in the proportion of operations bought out.

III. The method used

For each Census trade, the 1958 Census of Production provides the following information for enterprises grouped according to size as measured by the number of employees.

1. The number of establishments
2. Total sales
3. Net output
4. The number of employees, distinguishing between operatives and others
5. Wages and salaries
6. Capital expenditure in 1958
7. Net output per person employed

The size distribution for enterprises in each Census trade is heavily skewed. There are many more small enterprises than large ones and there are often several classes for small enterprises each representing a very small proportion of a trade's labour force. In many trades the largest category has few enterprises but they employ a substantial proportion of the employees in the trade. If regressions for average net output per employee for the categories available were calculated a heavy weight would be given to the classes for small enterprises because there would be more observations, or, if observations were weighted according to the number of employees in each group, a few groups would dominate the regressions. Also there tended to be considerable fluctuations in net output per head between one size group and another, apart from any trend, and this makes it impossible to estimate regression coefficients with a satisfactory level of significance. In addition Johnston has described why the trend of value added per head for the first few classes may be misleading because of the bias already referred to. [It was not possible to make use of the tests which Johnston employed to indicate the bias because the U.K. Census only classifies enterprises in each trade by size according to the number of employees and does not give a classification according to total sales.]

In the event it was decided to use a very simple test — net output per employee for large and small enterprises was compared. As far as possible enterprises employing 25 per cent of a trade's labour force were included in each group but the numbers in the largest and smallest groups did not add to exactly 25 per cent because sufficient data were not given in the Census. This applied particularly to the largest size group and in a number of cases substantially more than 25 per cent of a trade's labour force were included in this group. However, where more than 60 per cent of a trade's labour force was in one class, the trade was excluded from the comparisons. For the purpose of these calculations enterprises with less than 25 employees were also excluded because estimates of net output were not available for these enterprises. In addition the residual census trades were excluded, as the problems of firms operating in different sub-trades would make comparisons particularly unreliable for these trades, but this problem applies to many other census trades in less acute form. It should be noted that the comparisons are for the largest and smallest enterprises in each trade, whether or not the large enterprises are large relative to enterprises in other industries.

In addition the net output for firms in the range between the small and large enterprises was calculated and was compared to the other two groups.

A measure of the difference in size was obtained by comparing the average size of enterprises in the largest size group with the average for the smallest size group in each trade. The median for the 86 trades was 25 i.e., for the median trade the enterprises in the largest size group were 25 times the size of those in the smallest size group. The arithmetic average was 35. The large enterprises on average operate more establishments than small enterprises and the (arithmetic) average difference in size for establishments was approximately 7.8 times.

IV. The results

Table C.1. shows the results of the comparisons. Comparing the largest and smallest groups, the largest enterprises in 58 trades, and the smallest enterprises in 28 trades had a higher level of net output per employee. Similarly if medium size and small enterprises are compared the medium size enterprises in 59 trades had a higher level of net output per employee and in 27 trades the reverse applied. Comparisons of the largest and medium size firms show smaller differences. The median percentage differences between the groups for the 86 trades were also calculated and are shown at the foot of table C.1. For the median trade, output per employee was 11% higher for the largest group of enterprises compared to the smallest, and so on.

Table C.1. *Comparison of Net Output per Employee*

Per Cent	Large Firms compared to Small Firms (1)		Medium Size Firms compared to Small Firms (2)		Large Firms compared to Medium Size Firms (3)	
	(Number of Trades)					
130 and over	14		7		10	
120 - 130	13		5		6	
110 - 120	19		22		12	
100 - 110	12	58	25	59	20	48
90 - 100	16		21		19	
80 - 90	10		6		12	
Less than 80	2	28	0	27	7	38
		86		86		86
Medians	111		106		104	

The Census data is divided into volumes corresponding to industrial orders and this results in similar trades being grouped together. The data shown in columns 1 and 2 of Table C.1. was analysed according to volumes of the Census and this breakdown is shown in Table C.2. Any conclusion based on this analysis must of course be very tentative, but the comparisons suggest that there is a positive relationship between output per head and scale over the existing size range of firms for many of the trades in the following groups of industries: food and drink; chemicals; metals; engineering; metal goods; bricks, pottery and cement; and timber, paper and other. The comparisons also suggest that there is a negative relationship for only one group, leather goods and clothing. For the remaining groups, shipbuilding, electrical goods and textiles, the analysis tends to indicate a positive relationship.

Table C.2. *Average Net Output per Employee for the Large and Medium Size Enterprises Compared to the Small Enterprises*

Industrial Orders	Per Cent							Total
	130 & over	120 - 130	110 - 120	100 - 110	90 - 100	80 - 90	Less than 80	
	(Number of Trades)							
1. Food and drink	5	—	6	4	4	1	—	20
2. Chemicals	5	4	2	2	4	1	—	18
3. Metals	—	2	1	1	1	—	1	6
4. Engineering	2	2	6	7	2	1	—	20
5. Electrical goods	—	1	4	—	1	2	—	8
6. Shipbuilding and Vehicles	1	—	3	1	2	1	—	8
7. Metal goods	1	3	2	1	3	—	—	10
8. Textiles	1	2	4	9	5	2	1	24
9. Leather and clothing	—	—	5	3	9	7	—	24
10. Bricks, pottery and glass	2	3	2	1	—	—	—	8
11. Timber, paper and other	4	1	6	8	6	1	—	26
	21	18	41	37	37	16	2	172

An analysis of changes in the concentration of British industry during the period 1935–58 based on census data was published by Armstrong and Silberston[1] in 1965. Although their analysis was based on the size of establishments not enterprises, the only two industry groups shown in table C.2. for which the largest *establishments* failed to expand their share of total employment between 1935 and 1958 were textiles and leather and clothing. These were also industry groups for which our industry studies suggested the economies of scale are generally small in relation to the output of the industry. It is also worth noting that the general trend towards larger plants as measured by output and employment, shown by the study of concentration, is consistent with the view that over the range of existing plant sizes there are some net economies of scale.

The data shown in table C.2. was reclassified to the broad industry groups described in chapter 29. This classification is shown in table C.3.

(1) A.G. Armstrong and Aubrey Silberston — 'Size of plants, size of enterprise, and concentration in British manufacturing industry' 1935–58, J.R.S.S., September, 1965.

In so far as differences in net output per employee indicate differences in economies of scale over the existing range of sizes of enterprises, the data suggest economies of scale in the process industries, smaller economies in the engineering industries, an absence of economies of scale for the textile and clothing industries, and substantial economies of scale for the other industries. The results for the first three groups are consistent with the findings of the industry studies.

Table C.3. *Average Net Output per Employee for the Large and Medium Size Enterprises Compared to the Small Enterprises by Type of Trade*

Industry Group	Total	130 & over	120 - 130	110 - 120	100 - 110	90 - 100	80 - 90	Less than 80
Process	50	12	7	9	9	10	2	1
Engineering	44	4	6	14	9	7	4	–
Textile & Clothing	48	1	2	9	12	14	9	1
Other	30	4	3	9	7	6	1	–
	172	21	18	41	37	37	16	2

V. The qualifications

One reason why the results described in the previous section may under-estimate or overestimate any economies of scale is that the enterprises included in a single trade often make different products. For example brewers and maltsters are grouped in a single trade and so are the manufacturers of flat glass and other glass products such as bottles. Assuming the maltsters are predominantly relatively small scale firms and the brewers large scale firms, there could be economies of scale for both brewing and malting without there being any great difference in the average output per head for both groups. In such circumstances the Census may not show any difference in output per head between large and small enterprises, though there may be economies of scale in both trades, and concentration of both industries might bring substantial economies. Until a finer breakdown of Census data is available there is no way of assessing the increases in output per head and the economies of scale related to the scale of output of narrow ranges of products.

Another reason why the results described may underestimate any economies of scale is that firms may charge different prices for the same or similar products. Firms may be able to consistently charge different prices for the same or very similar products because of imperfect knowledge, product differentiation, control over some buyers, or because they only have to obtain a small share of a market. There is evidence that in certain industries some small firms do charge higher prices for similar products – examples are bread and clothes – but there is usually some difficulty in assessing the value of differences in the quality of products and the service provided in such cases. Also firms – often, but not always – the larger firms, which export may accept lower prices for exports than for products sold on the home market. On the other hand large scale manufacturers in some industries obtain higher prices for their products particularly for products which they advertise. In at least three industries, rubber, footwear and soap it is thought that this position applies for certain products. Any tendency for large firms to obtain lower prices may be offset, or partially offset, by their monopoly power when buying raw materials and services.

Another reason why the estimates may understate the economies of scale is the arithmetic bias referred to above. Only for manufacturing industry as a whole is an alternative classification by sales of enterprises instead of number of employees provided. The classification by sales indicated net output per employee of the largest enterprises 54.5% higher than for the smallest. (In each case approximately 25% of the employees were included in each group.) The equivalent figure for the classification by number of employees was 28%.[1] If it is assumed that the arithmetic mean of the two figures gives the best estimate of the relationship between scale and net output, this would indicate a figure approximately 50% higher than that obtained from the classification by number of employees. [It cannot be assumed that the same relationship holds for trades.]

On the other hand there are reasons for thinking that the comparisons exaggerate any economies of scale. The comparisons of net output per head may reflect differences in the quality of labour employed rather than efficiency. To test whether there was any difference in the quality of labour employed by large and small firms the ratio of other employees[2] to operatives and average wages per head, were calculated for the groups of large and small firms. For 60 of the 86 trades the large firms employed a higher proportion of other employees and a smaller proportion of operatives. The average proportion of other employees was 31% for the large enterprises and 27% in the case of the small enterprises.

The difference in the ratio of other employees to operatives may be taken as a guide to the extent to which large firms have to employ more staff to coordinate activities. But there are other possible explanations, such as that large firms perform for themselves services which small firms buy out, or that the higher proportion may reflect the higher productivity of the operatives of large firms. On the other hand the smaller enterprises in many trades make products in short runs and these could require proportionately more managerial time for organising production. If large firms were to make products in short runs they might have a higher proportion of other employees to operatives than they already have.

For 65 of the 86 trades the average wage per operative paid by the large firms was greater than that paid by the small firms. On average the difference was 10% for the 86 trades. In some trades e.g., rubber, these differences may simply reflect the fact that the large enterprises on average employ proportionately more men (as opposed to women) than small enterprises

(1) The average difference for the 86 trades was 17%.

(2) Other employees include technical and clerical employees. The wages and salaries per head of the other employees are on average substantially higher than the wages of operatives.

340

because of differences in the type of work involved.[1] Also firms with higher output per head may voluntarily pay higher wages for similar work. However the comparisons of 'status' and the wages of operatives suggest that large firms do employ labour of a higher average quality. Insofar as the quality of labour employed by large firms was higher than for small firms, the estimates of net output per employee overestimate any economies of scale.

There is also some evidence that the capital employed per head by large enterprises is greater than for small enterprises. For 58 of the 86 trades capital expenditure per head in 1958 by the large enterprises was greater than for small firms. Thus, assuming (heroically) that the difference in capital expenditure for one year indicates differences in total capital input, the estimates of net output overestimate economies of scale. However, even if capital expenditure provides an indication of fixed capital per employee, it does not provide any indication of working capital per employee.

The difference in capital expenditure per head was substantial. For the 86 trades expenditure by the large enterprises was on average 36% higher than for the small enterprises. The equivalent median was 18%.

Regression analysis was used to see if differences in capital intensity, as measured by capital expenditure in one year, were related to the differences in net output per employee. The relationship tested was $Y_t = a_0 + a_l X_t$, where Y_t was net output per head for large enterprises in each trade as a percentage of that of the small enterprises, and X_t was the capital expenditure per head of the large enterprises as a percentage of that for the small enterprises. For the process trades R^2 was 0.40 and for the engineering trades R^2 was 0.15. Capital expenditure could also explain the differences between the industry groups. In the process and engineering industries it may be possible to increase capital intensity (capital per employee) indefinitely with increases in scale. In the textile and clothing industries this is not usually possible.

The differential rate of investment per employee could be important. If concentration leads to a greater propensity to invest this itself might increase the rate of growth of the economy. Unfortunately it is not possible to conclude from these figures alone that there is a real difference in the propensity to invest of large and small enterprises carrying out the same operations, as the smaller enterprises may on average tend to concentrate on labour intensive operations such as assembly. Also in some trades the smaller firms make products for which labour intensive methods of production are relatively more efficient because the level of demand necessitates short runs etc. [It has been shown that as between industries, there is a relationship between capital intensive production and the size of plants[2] – 'industries with large plants prevailing are on the whole

(1) It is not possible to say how important differences in the type of labour are because details of the labour force are not available in the Census.

(2) P. Sargeant Florence. 'The Logic of British and American Industry.' London 1961, p. 68.

industries with a high degree of mechanization' — and the same tendency would be expected within industries because there are often substantial economies of scale for large units of capital equipment.] It may be noted that the arithmetic bias referred to earlier also applies to capital expenditure. A similar comparison to that described above for net output per employee showed that for manufacturing industry as a whole, expenditure per head was 3½ times higher for the large, compared to the small, enterprises, according to the sales classification, and 2½ times according to the employment classification.

Net output includes payments for advertising, and in some industries the expenditure of the larger enterprises on advertising is proportionately higher than for the smaller enterprises. Thus a comparison of net output in these industries gives an exaggerated indication of any economies of scale for total costs. On the other hand small enterprises may buy out more of other services.

Another qualification to the results described above is that employment in head offices, laboratories etc. is sometimes included in the total employment of an enterprise and sometimes excluded. Whether it is included depends upon whether the head office and research facilities are separated from an enterprise's other establishments. This leads to an understatement of the number of employees of large enterprises which more often have a separate head office, and this will tend to exaggerate the difference in net output per head for large and small firms. However, the number of employees at the head office is usually relatively small, of the order of 1% of total employment.

There are other possible qualifications to the results such as that the results might be affected by factors not directly related to scale such as the incidence of strikes and the level of capacity utilization. Although these factors may distort the results for individual trades it is thought that they do not invalidate the comparisons for industry groups.

In view of the qualifications no firm conclusions can be drawn from the comparison of Census data. The data is compatible with the existence of economies of scale in a majority of trades. In addition the comparisons of Census data give a qualified indication of the industry groups in which there are economies of scale. They also suggest that large enterprises on average use more capital intensive methods of production, though not necessarily when making the same products as small enterprises.

VI. The U.S. Census (1963)

The U.S. Census data are analysed by size of establishments for more narrowly defined trades than the U.K. data. Table C.4. presents the relationship between the size of establishments, measured in terms of employees, and value added per employee for census trades corresponding to our sample of industries. The figures must be left to speak for themselves apart from the following brief comments.

(a) Many of the points mentioned above as affecting the relationship between the size of enterprise and value added per head, the bias caused by using employees to measure size, the inclusion of sub-trades, etc., again apply.

(b) The range of value added per head which varies from less than $6,000 to more than $40,000 for different trades is the most striking feature of the table.

(c) For many trades the relationship between value added and size of establishment does not conflict with the conclusions of the industry studies.

Table C.4. *Value Added per Employee by Size of Establishment* [a]

(U.S.A. 1963)

A. Size of Establishments (Number of Employees)
B. Number of Establishments
C. Number of Employees (thousands)
D. Value Added per Employee ($th.)

Oil Refining						Industry
A	20-99	100-249	250-999	1000-2499	2500 and over	
B	103	83	85	16	10	427
C	5.0	13.9	40.3	23.2	36.0	119.3
D	20.7	27.3	26.9	36.4	19.6	26.3

Chemicals (Industrial Inorganic and Organic Chemicals.)						
B						1905
C						236.6
D						26.1

Synthetic Fibres				
A	10-249	500-999	1,000 and over	
B	6	7	12	25
C	0.6	4.6	36.2	41.4
D	4.3	19.1	23.0	22.3

Beer						
A	20-99	100-249	250-499	500-999	1,000 and over	
B	61	52	33	23	11	222
C	3.1	8.6	11.4	15.6	23.6	62.6
D	12.6	19.1	21.5	20.7	21.7	20.5

Bread (Wholesale Bakeries only)							
A	5-20	20-49	50-99	100-249	250-499	500 and over	
B	1324	624	366	413	121	20	4287
C	13.3	19.7	26.3	64.4	39.6	14.3	180.4
D	6.5	7.3	10.1	11.3	11.8	11.3	10.4

Soap and Other Detergents							
A	20-49	50-99	100-249	250-499	500-999	1000 and over	
B	86	29	28	15	9	5	704
C	2.7	2.0	4.0	5.8	6.4	7.4	30.8
D	21.2	29.4	25.2	48.7	47.2	40.8	36.9

(a) Details for size groups are not given for trades making a particularly wide range of products e.g., chemicals, motor vehicles *and* parts.

Cement
Industry

	20-99	100-250	250-499	500 and over	Industry
A	20-99	100-250	250-499	500 and over	
B	30	112	31	6	188
C	2.1	18.9	9.9	3.8	34.9
D	26.8	23.1	21.2	20.8	22.5

Bricks and Structural Tiles

	10-49	50-99	100-249	250 and over	
A	10-49	50-99	100-249	250 and over	
B	222	163	50	8	512
C	6.8	11.2	7.4	2.9	28.6
D	7.3	7.6	7.9	7.1	7.6

Steel (Blast Furnaces and Steel Mills)

A	
B	288
C	500.6
D	15.4

Iron Castings (Gray Iron Foundries)

	10-19	20-49	50-99	100-249	250-499	500-999	1000 & over	
A	10-19	20-49	50-99	100-249	250-499	500-999	& over	
B	138	279	219	176	56	23	14	1139
C	2.0	9.2	15.3	26.8	19.8	15.7	30.9	120.5
D	6.7	7.6	8.0	8.9	10.9	9.7	11.3	9.7

Motor Vehicles and Parts

A	
B	1958
C	649.9
D	19.0

Aircraft and Parts

A	
B	1346
C	679.4
D	11.6

Bicycles (Motor cycles, Bicycles and Parts)

A	
B	88
C	9.7
D	8.5

Machine Tools (Metal-cutting Machine Tools)

	20-49	50-99	100-249	250-499	500-999	1000-2499	2500 & over	
A	20-49	50-99	100-249	250-499	500-999	1000-2499	& over	
B	118	56	44	22	15	11	3	801
C	3.6	3.7	6.9	7.7	10.7	15.5	9.7	61.1
D	11.4	11.6	12.6	12.2	12.8	10.5	10.6	11.5

Diesel Engines

B	143
C	55.7
D	13.2

Turbo Generators (Steam Engines and Turbines)

	Industry
B	22
C	30.9
D	12.3

Electric Motors (Motors and Generators)

	100-249	250-499	500-999	1000-2499	2500 and over	Industry
A						
B	68	39	34	17	4	384
C	11.2	13.6	23.8	24.9	16.0	94.2
D	9.3	8.7	10.7	10.7	12.8	10.5

Domestic Appliances
Household Refrigerators

	1000-2499	2500 and over	Industry
A			
B	6	5	34
C	8.1	31.3	43.1
D	11.2	16.3	14.7

Household Laundry Equipment

	250-499	500-999	1000 and over	Industry
A				
B	4	3	7	39
C	1.2	2.5	13.3	18.3
D	6.8	21.2	20.7	19.3

Electronic Capital Equipment
Computing and Related Machines

	100-249	250-499	500-999	1000-2499	2500 and over	Industry
A						
B	25	24	10	11	10	248
C	4.0	8.8	7.6	17.0	55.6	96.4
D	10.8	10.2	16.2	14.5	10.1	11.4

Telephone and Telegraph Apparatus

	Industry
A	
B	90
C	89.5
D	11.3

Cotton Textiles
Yarn Mills, Except Wool

	50-99	100-249	250-499	500 and over	Industry
A					
B	45	134	57	22	317
C	3.4	22.2	19.1	15.7	61.6
D	6.4	6.0	5.4	6.2	5.9

Weaving Mills (Cotton)

	100-249	250-499	500-999	1000-2499	2500 and over	Industry
A						
B	59	109	87	49	3	407
C	10.5	40.4	60.9	69.0	25.6	209.0
D	6.0	5.6	6.1	6.2	5.8	6.0

Hosiery
Women's Hosiery

	20-49	50-99	100-249	250-999	1000 and over	Industry
A						
B	80	53	50	46	6	355
C	2.6	3.8	7.3	19.8	11.7	46.6
D	5.8	5.2	5.6	5.9	6.2	5.9

Knit Fabric Mills Inc. Warp Knitting

	20-49	50-99	100-499	500 and over	Industry
A					
B	66	41	46	4	291
C	2.1	3.0	10.1	2.5	18.7
D	11.5	12.3	9.5	8.9	10.3

Footwear (Shoes except rubber)

	20-49	50-99	100-249	250-499	500-999	1000 and over	Industry
A							
B	110	104	247	288	62	4	1040
C	3.5	8.0	.41.7	101.7	38.5	7.1	201.7
D	5.0	5.5	5.4	6.3	6.0	7.6	6.0

Newspapers (daily)

	20-49	50-99	100-249	250-499	500-999	1000-2499	2500 & over	Industry
A								
B	534	310	278	106	55	41	8	1560
C	17.4	21.4	42.7	37.5	39.8	60.7	30.0	252.5
D	7.9	9.5	10.4	11.5	12.3	11.8	12.3	11.2

Books

	20-49	50-99	100-249	250-499	500-999	1000 and over	Industry
A							
B	161	49	37	13	9	6	683
C	4.9	3.5	6.0	4.9	6.1	7.9	36.1
D	10.5	12.0	9.9	9.0	8.8	9.8	9.9

Plastic Products

	10-19	20-49	50-99	100-249	250-499	500-999	1000 & over	Industry
A								
B	677	854	423	294	78	20	5	4334
C	9.5	27.0	29.7	45.5	27.6	13.2	7.0	166.3
D	9.4	9.1	9.8	10.0	10.1	11.4	12.8	10.0

Appendix D: Company Profitability

I. Introduction

Before the 1967 Companies Act, public companies were not required by law to publish any measure of their turnover or the number of their employees, and, in the past, many large companies and most of the smaller ones took advantage of the law and simply did not publish this information.[1] Consequently the only published indicator of scale available for comparing the performance of large and small U.K. companies is capital employed.

An indicator of performance which can be related to scale when measured in terms of capital is pre-tax profit per unit of capital.[2] If there are economies of scale not related to particular trades — greater choice of industries in which to invest because of the substantial minimum capital requirements for entry into some industries, for the acquisition of management expertise, for buying, etc. — a positive relationship between scale and profitability would be expected. Also, if there were substantial differences in the size of companies producing similar products and performing similar operations, and, if economies of scale operate over this range, a positive relationship would be expected to exist between capital employed and return on capital for these companies.[3]

II. Profitability and scale

A number of studies of the relationship between profitability and scale for U.K. companies have been published.

(1) Data for the years since 1967 is not yet readily available from official sources.

(2) An alternative or additional indicator of performance which could have been used was the rate of growth of companies. It has been suggested that this can be used to indicate the optimum size of firm. For example Singh and Whittington (A. Singh and G. Whittington in collaboration with H.T. Burley, 'Growth Profitability and Valuation.' Cambridge 1968, p. 73.) have suggested that, if the law of proportionate effect applies, then there is no optimum size of firm. However, for this study profitability has been selected as a more direct indicator of performance. One reason for preferring this measure to rates of growth, was that the latter may be affected by motivation (willingness and desire) to expand to a greater extent than profitability, though the two measures are inter-related.

(3) It may be noted that the estimates of economies of scale summarized in Table 30.1 indicate large economies in relation to companies profits. Inland Revenue data show that pre tax profits were about 6.5% of turnover for manufacturing companies (circa 1960,)

September, 1967, C. F. Pratten, 'Does Bigness Breed Profits?' Management
Today.
May, 1968, J.M. Samuels and D. J. Smyth, 'Profits, Variability of Profits and
Firms Size,' Economica.
1968, A. Singh and G. Whittington, 'Growth, Profitability and Valuation.'
Cambridge University Press. Since the completion of this publication,
one of the authors has extended the study from four to twenty or so
groups of industries.

The conclusion of these studies was that there was no evidence of a
positive relationship between profitability and scale for populations of all
public companies, or companies in most broad industry groups, and we have
to consider whether this conclusion conflicts with our results showing that
large economies of scale exist in many industries. The simple answer to
this question is that comparisons based on all public or quoted companies,
are for multi-product firms making different ranges of products, and therefore
provide no indication of technical economies of scale. When attempts are
made to compare profitability for companies making a narrow range of products, then for industries in which there are large economies of scale, there
are generally very few firms indeed. One industry for which it is possible to
make some comparisons is cement. The profitability of six firms which
specialise in the production of cement can be compared, but it was shown in
Chapter 10 that it is not possible to draw any conclusions about the economies of scale from such comparisons because there are so many factors
which affect the relationship between profitability and scale.

It is perhaps worth listing the factors apart from economies of scale which
affect the relationship between profitability and scale.

(1) Profitability is affected by the degree of monopoly power enjoyed by
firms, if large firms tend to have greater monopoly power, then they may be
expected to have higher profits.

(2) The incentive to maximise profits as a percentage of capital may be
affected by scale. If this results in large firms limiting their prices or
'overpaying' their employees, this reduces profitability, but is not a source
of diseconomies of scale.

(3) Differences in the general efficiency, or X efficiency, of firms affect
the comparisons. If large differences in general efficiency are distributed
among companies in a random manner, this makes it difficult to establish
other relationships, but, if large companies tend to be operated less efficiently than smaller companies, this would be a source of diseconomies of
scale.

(4) The choice of definition of capital — equity, equity and loan capital,
etc. — affects profitability. (Some tests we made suggested that the choice
of definition of capital does not affect the conclusion that there is not a
positive relationship between profitability and capital.)

(5) Although there is no evidence of a positive relationship between
profitability and scale, it has not been possible to establish any significant
relationships i.e., if it were possible to have a larger population of companies, the average profitability of the largest companies might be higher

than the average for all companies, but the estimates of the relationship between profitability and scale which are given in the studies to which reference has been made are the best estimate available.

(6) The valuation of assets may affect profitability. Large firms may revalue their assets to a greater extent. [1] (A study of the revaluations made by 174 companies suggested that large companies revalue more often, but that their revaluations generally represent a smaller proportion of their assets, and that these two factors approximately cancel out.)

(7) Companies which grow rapidly may tend to have lower profitability because of the effects of inflation on the valuation of assets and capital. However there is no evidence that there is a positive relationship between growth and size of companies.

(8) The comparisons of profitability for public or quoted companies may be misleading if it is a biased sample of all companies. For example some relatively profitable large companies which are subsidiaries of overseas companies are usually omitted. (Profitable small companies are also excluded for the same reason.) At the bottom end of the company size range, public and quoted companies represent a much smaller proportion of all companies, and may include a higher than average proportion of the most profitable small firms. High profitability reduces the assets required to obtain a stock exchange quotation, and a quotation provides a way to capitalize the 'goodwill' or the expertise of the management of a highly profitable business. Similarly some small companies which manufacture special products are very profitable and these firms may allow themselves to be taken over when their markets are threatened.

(9) Some of the trades to which the largest companies are committed have relatively low returns on capital. For the period before nationalisation this applied to steel, and it has applied to aircraft production and heavy electrical engineering over an extended period. Companies committed to these trades cannot withdraw their assets quickly, and it may not pay them to do so anyway, because of the price at which they could sell the assets.

(10) In Appendix C it was suggested that the larger enterprises (companies) tend to operate in the capital intensive sectors of industry, i.e. their fixed capital costs are relatively high compared to their labour costs. There could be a tendency for capital intensive industries to make a lower return on capital employed. This could occur in part because accountants have in the past concentrated attention on the ratio of profit to turnover, or because capital intensive plants etc. are less flexible if there are changes in the level and/or character of demand. If capital intensive firms tend to have a lower return on capital, then large companies would tend to have a lower return than small companies.

(1) If a company increases the value of its assets by revaluation this reduces its profitability, because the assets to which profits are related are increased. Also the depreciation charge may be increased by a revaluation and this again reduces profitability.

(11) Large firms on average undertake more R. & D. than smaller firms, R. & D. is usually written off against profits as and when incurred. This deflates profits, and though each year's profits may be increased by benefits from past R. & D., on balance the accounting treatment used deflates the profits of large companies more than those of smaller companies, during a period when expenditure on R. & D. is increasing.

Comparisons of profitability do not show a significant relationship with size, and it is clearly of interest to relate the points we have listed to the relationship between profitability and size.

Factors significantly reducing the profitability of large companies relative to smaller companies:—

(1) On average, payments to labour for equivalent work are probably positively related to scale.

(2) The charging of R. & D. and other initial costs against profits when the costs are incurred, tends to reduce the profits of large companies more than smaller firms.

(3) The sample of companies included may exaggerate the profits of small companies.

On the other side, large companies may enjoy greater benefits from market concentration.

On balance there may be some tendency for the comparisons to understate the relative profitability of large companies.

III. U.S. data

The most comprehensive study of the relationship between size and return on capital for U.S. Corporations was made by Steckler.[1] His study which was based on data for the period 1947—57, showed that during the period 1955—57 pre-tax profitability as a percentage of *total assets* increased with the size of corporations up to the asset class size $ m 10 − 25.[2] For the larger size groups profitability was lower than for this class. A qualification to these comparisons was that the largest size category was assets of $ 200m. and over. At the end of 1966, 60% of the assets employed in manufacturing industry in the U.S.A. were owned by corporations of this

(1) H.O. Steckler, 'Profitability and Size of Firm' Berkeley, 1963. Steckler surveyed earlier studies of the relationship between size and profitability. Many of these related to the 1930's when the relationship may have been different than now exists.

(2) It may be noted that these comparisons were for quoted and unquoted corporations. In this population the problem of births and deaths may be smaller than for the quoted U.K. companies. Also comparisons were based on profitability as a ratio of total assets, and where profitability was related to equity the increase in profitability over the initial size classes was smaller.

size and there could be important differences in profitability within this group. [1]

A study of the relationship between profitability and size for the largest U.S. corporations during the period 1956–1962 was made by Hall and Weiss. [2] Their study showed a positive and significant relationship between scale and profitability. This result could be explained by the varying profitability of the industries in which the large corporations are concentrated, rather than general advantages of large companies. Nevertheless the comparisons suggest that the relatively low profitability of the largest U.K. companies is not an inevitable consequence of size.

IV. Stability of profits and growth

The Singh and Whittington study showed that the variability of rates of profitability and growth decline with size. It has been suggested that the greater variability of the growth of small companies indicates that some are expanding rapidly to take advantage of economies of scale while others are declining, or expanding slowly, because they have not been able to reap the economies of scale. [3] This argument is weak if the profitability of small companies is on average no lower than for larger companies. [4] It has also been argued that because the profitability of large companies is more stable than that of small companies, but not as much more stable as would be expected if the large companies were made up of a number of small companies with the same variation of profits as existing small companies, this indicates the existence of economies of scale. It is suggested that large companies would have diversified more to achieve greater stability of profits if it were not for economies of scale. However, this tendency could also be explained by inertia on the part of businessmen, a lack of interest in marginal increases in stability of profits, or diseconomies for diversification. Also many large companies must have above average profits and, if this were attributable to the industry in which they operate, they would have less incentive to diversify. Relatively unprofitable companies have more incentive to diversify but greater difficulties in doing so. Finally the profitability of increases in investment in a company's existing activities may well be higher than the average return, and induce firms to continue to

(1) Steckler and other writers who have studied the relationship between size and profitability have often made a careful distinction between profitable and unprofitable firms. This distinction has not been used in this study because the division between profitable and unprofitable is arbitrary.

(2) Marshall Hall and Leonard Weiss, 'Firm Size and Profitability'. The Review of Economic Statistics, August, 1967.

(3) P. Pashigan and S. Hymer, 'Reply to H.A. Simon', in Jnl. of Pol. Econ. 1964.

(4) H.A. Simon has suggested other arguments for discounting those given by P. Pashigan and S. Hymer. 'Comment on Firm Size and Rate of Growth'. Jnl. of Pol. Econ. 1964.

concentrate on their existing activities.

Stability of growth rates and profitability is a source of advantage for employees and shareholders [1] of large companies. This should result in economies for large companies as they should be able to raise capital at lower interest rates and pay lower salaries [2] other things being equal. These relationships with scale are discussed in book 3.

V. Conclusions

The initial comparisons of returns on capital for U.K. quoted companies suggest that there is not a positive relationship between profitability and size. There are, however, a number of qualifications to these comparisons.

The comparisons do not provide any information about the existence of economies of scale for the output of narrow ranges of products, nor do they provide firm conclusions about whether there are on balance general economies or diseconomies of scale for firms. But taken with the Census data the comparisons do suggest that some caution is required when considering the significance of economies of scale for large firms.

(1) A more important indicator of stability for employees may be employment itself.

(2) A qualification to this argument is that, if greater stability is attributable to diversification, security for many individual employees may not be greater because they are not moved from declining to expanding sections of the business.

Economies of Scale in Manufacturing Industry

C. F. PRATTEN

Research Officer, Department of Applied Economics
University of Cambridge

This paper is the final report of the Department's study of
economies of scale in manufacturing industry. An interim report
was published in 1965 entitled *The Economies of Large Scale*
Production in British Industry : an Introductory Study, by
C. F. Pratten, R. M. Dean and A. Silberston (Occasional Paper
No. 3). This final report describes the economies of scale in
twenty-five industries, including chemicals, synthetic fibres,
motor vehicles, machine tools and cotton textiles. The industries
were selected in order to include all the important types of
industry from a technical point of view.

The studies will be of interest to industrialists and their
advisers, as much of the information about the relationships
between scale and costs has not previously been published. The
results are of interest to governments in both advanced and
developing countries, because evidence of substantial economies
of scale in many industries has important implications for
economic policy. The industry studies will also be of particular
value for students of economics and business studies, as they
provide a guide to the structure and cost relationships of a wide
range of U.K. industries. Finally, the book will be useful for all
who are interested in finding the causes of the relatively slow
growth of the U.K. economy, compared to that of a number of
advanced industrial countries, during the postwar period.

CAMBRIDGE UNIVERSITY PRESS
Bentley House, 200 Euston Road, London NW1 2DB
American Branch: 32 East 57th Street, New York, N.Y.10022

0 521 09669 3